Social Theory and Philosophy for Information Systems

Social Theory and Philosophy for Information Systems

Edited by

John Mingers

Canterbury Business School
University of Kent

Leslie Willcocks

Warwick Business School
The University of Warwick

John Wiley & Sons, Ltd

Other Wiley Editorial Offices

John Wiley & Sons Inc., 111 River Street, Hoboken, NJ 07030, USA

Jossey-Bass, 989 Market Street, San Francisco, CA 94103-1741, USA

Wiley-VCH Verlag GmbH, Boschstr. 12, D-69469 Weinheim, Germany

John Wiley & Sons Australia Ltd, 33 Park Road, Milton, Queensland 4064, Australia

John Wiley & Sons (Asia) Pte Ltd, 2 Clementi Loop #02-01, Jin Xing Distripark, Singapore 129809

John Wiley & Sons Canada Ltd, 22 Worcester Road, Etobicoke, Ontario, Canada M9W 1L1

Wiley also publishes its books in a variety of electronic formats. Some content that appears
in print may not be available in electronic books.

Library of Congress Cataloging-in-Publication Data

Social theory and philosophy for information systems / edited by John Mingers, Leslie
Willcocks.
         p. cm.—(John Wiley series in information systems)
     Includes bibliographical references and index.
     ISBN 0-470-85117-1 (cloth : alk. paper)
   1.   Information technology—Social aspects.   2.   Information
technology—Philosophy.   3.   Information science—Social aspects.   4.
Information science—Philosophy.   I. Mingers, John.   II. Willcocks, Leslie.
III. Series.
     HM851.S653   2004
     303.48'33—dc22

                                                                    2004003684

British Library Cataloguing in Publication Data

A catalogue record for this book is available from the British Library

ISBN 0-470-85117-1

Typeset in 11/12.5pt Palatino by Laserwords Private Limited, Chennai, India
Printed and bound in Great Britain by TJ International, Padstow, Cornwall
This book is printed on acid-free paper responsibly manufactured from sustainable forestry
in which at least two trees are planted for each one used for paper production.

Wiley Series in Information Systems

CURRENT VOLUMES IN THE SERIES

Wiley Series in Information Systems

Editors

RICHARD BOLAND   Department of Management Information and Decision Systems, Weatherhead School of Management, Case Western Reserve University, 10900 Euclid Avenue, Cleveland, Ohio 44106-7235, USA

RUDY HIRSCHHEIM   Department of Information Systems and Decision Sciences, Ourso College of Business Administration, Louisiana State University, Baton Rouge, LA 70803, USA

Contents

List of Contributors

Debra Howcroft is a Senior Lecturer in Information Systems at the Manchester School of Accounting and Finance, University of Manchester. Her research interests lie in the area of the social and organizational aspects of IS. Debra.a.howcroft@man.ac.uk.

Minh Q. Huynh earned his PhD in Management Information Systems from Binghamton. Currently he is an Assistant Professor at Southeastern Louisiana University. Previously he taught at Washington State University for three years. His research interests include the application of Critical Social Theory in IS research, e-learning and outsourcing. His publications appear in such journals as the *Communications of ACM*, *Journal of AIS*, *Communications of AIS* and *European Journal of IS*. Minh.Huynh@selu.edu.

Fernando M. Ilharco is Assistant Professor at the Catholic University of Portugal, Lisbon. His PhD is from the London School of Economics and Political Science (2002). Co-founder of the Phenomenology, Organisation and Technology international working group, Ilharco's research interests are the philosophical, cultural, social and organizational dimensions of contemporary technologies of information and communication.

Lucas D. Introna is a Reader in Technology, Organisation and Ethics at Lancaster University. Previously he lectured in Information Systems at the London School of Economics and Political Science. His research interest is a critical orientation to the political and ethical aspects of information technology in organizations and society from a phenomenological perspective. He is co-editor of *Ethics and Information Technology* and a founding member of the International Society for Ethics and Information Technology (INSEIT). l.introna@lancaster.ac.uk.

Matthew Jones is a University Lecturer in Information Management at the Judge Institute of Management and Department of Engineering at the University of Cambridge. His research interests are concerned with the relationship between information systems and social and organizational change, and theoretical and methodological issues in information systems research. mrj10@cam.ac.uk.

Heinz K. Klein holds a PhD from the University of Munich and an honorary doctorate from the University of Oulu, Finland and has held visiting professorial positions at major universities on four continents. Since 2001 he has served as the Doctoral Program Director for the MIS Department of Temple University. Well-known for his contributions to the paradigm foundations of research methods, he has also published on many other topics in the area of alternative approaches to information systems development (ISD). His articles have appeared in the best journals of the field such as the *CACM*, *MISQ*, *Information Systems Research*, the *Journal of MIS* and *Information and Organization*. He has authored or edited several research monographs in IS and serves on several editorial boards. hkklein@temple.edu.

Allen S. Lee is Professor and Associate Dean in the School of Business at Virginia Commonwealth University. He has been Editor-in-Chief of *MIS Quarterly*, Senior Editor of *MIS Quarterly Executive*, a visiting professor at the London School of Economics and Queen's University Belfast, and a visiting scholar at Indiana University. AllenSLee@alum.mit.edu.

M. Lynne Markus is Trustee Professor, Department of Management, Bentley College. Professor Markus's research interests include the management of IT-enabled change, electronic business, enterprise systems integration and knowledge management. She holds a BS in Industrial Engineering from the University of Pittsburgh and a PhD in Organizational Behavior from Case Western Reserve University. mlmarkus@bentley.edu.

Yasmin Merali is Director of the Information Systems Research Unit at Warwick Business School. Her publications focus on organizational transformation in dynamic contexts. Current research interests include complexity, networks and competition in cyberspace, information and public-sector change dynamics, and post-acquisition integration. Her consultancy experience spans a range of UK-based and multinational organizations. She contributes to MBA and executive programmes internationally. Yasmin.Merali@warwick.ac.uk.

John Mingers is Professor of OR and Information Systems and Director of Research at Kent Business School, University of Kent. His research interests include the use of systems methodologies in problem situations, particularly the mixing of different methodologies within an intervention (multimethodology); the development of critical realism as a philosophy for information systems; the development of theory concerning the nature of information and meaning; and autopoiesis and its applications. He has published several books, including *Self-Producing Systems: Implications and Applications of Autopoiesis* and *Information Systems: An Emerging Discipline?* (with Professor Frank Stowell). j.mingers@kent.ac.uk.

Nathalie Mitev is at the London School of Economics, following positions at Salford University and City University. She has French postgraduate degrees, an MBA and a PhD in IS from Salford University. Her research career initially concentrated on information retrieval and HCI and has moved to IS and organizations. She has published on implementation issues in small businesses, the health, travel and construction industries. Her theoretical inclinations are towards the social construction and history of technology and she has applied actor-network theory to analysing IS failures. n.n.mitev@lse.ac.uk.

Kamal Munir is University Lecturer at the Judge Institute of Management, University of Cambridge. He earned his PhD from McGill University, Canada in 2001. Kamal's research is concerned with the evolutionary, organizational and competitive dynamics surrounding technological discontinuities. He is a member of the editorial board of *Organization Studies*. km288@hermes.cam.ac.uk.

Michael D. Myers is Professor of Information Systems and Associate Dean (Postgraduate and Research) at the University of Auckland Business School, New Zealand. He currently serves as Senior Editor of *MISQ Discovery*, Associate Editor of *Information Systems Research* and Editor of *University of Auckland Business Review*. m.myers@auckland.ac.nz.

Wanda Orlikowski is Professor of Information Technologies and Organization Studies at the Sloan School of Management, and holds the Eaton-Peabody Chair of Communication Sciences at the Massachusetts Institute of Technology. She received a PhD from the Stern School of Business at New York University. Her primary research interests focus on the recursive relationship between organizations and information technology, with particular emphasis on organizing structures, cultural norms, and work practices. wanda@mit.edu.

Stephen K. Probert is Senior Lecturer in Systems in the Department of Information Systems at Cranfield University, Swindon. His research interests are in the theoretical foundations of information systems. He has published a number of papers and book chapters in this area. He has also acted as a consultant to many industrial companies in the UK. s.k.probert@rmcs.cranfield.ac.uk.

Leslie P. Willcocks is Professor of Information Management at Warwick Business School. He received a doctorate from the University of Cambridge, is visiting professor at Erasmus and Melbourne Universities, and joint Editor-in-Chief of the *Journal of Information Technology*. He is co-author of 23 books and has published over 140 papers in journals ranging from *Harvard Business Review* to *MIS Quarterly*, *MISQ Executive* and *Journal of Management Studies*. His research interests include organizational issues, politics, outsourcing, implementation, e-business and evaluation. Willcockslp@aol.com.

Melanie Wilson is a Lecturer in Management Information Systems and Technology Management at the Manchester School of Management, UMIST. Her research interests focus on gender, evaluation and IS success/failure.

Series Preface

The information systems community has grown considerably in the twenty years that we have been publishing the Wiley Series in Information Systems. We are pleased to be a part of the growth of the field, and believe that this series has played, and continues to play, an important role in the intellectual development of the discipline. The primary objective of the series is to publish scholarly works which reflect the best of the research in the information systems community. These works should help guide the IS practitioner community regarding what strategies it ought to adopt to be successful in the future. Books in the Series should also help advanced students—particularly those at the graduate level—understand the myriad issues surrounding the broad area of management of IS.

To this end, the current volume—*Social Theory and Philosophy for Information Systems*, edited by John Mingers and Leslie Willcocks—provides a welcome addition. This book is geared for the IS research community and covers an area that many in the field have been struggling to come to grips with, viz. how philosophy and social theory can be effectively applied to IS. The editors have done an excellent job securing top academics in the field to write focused articles on key philosophers and social theorists such as Habermas, Adorno, Foucault and Giddens. Important philosophical approaches such as phenomenology, functionalism, hermeneutics and critical realism are similarly explored in this volume. Overall, this is an impressive collection of philosophical areas, and their application or possible application in information systems advances the state of the field markedly. This volume should be on the bookshelf of every serious IS academic. We are delighted to have it as part of our Wiley Series in Information Systems.

Rudy Hirschheim

Preface

John Mingers and Leslie P. Willcocks

Some years ago, at a European IS conference, the editors were bemoaning the state of IS research. In particular we were concerned about its very narrow focus. As many surveys of the literature have shown, the great proportion of IS research stems from a positivist or functionalist paradigm, with the occasional foray into the murky waters of critical theory or hermeneutics. We were both very interested in philosophy and social theory and knew that there were many important and insightful theoretical avenues that would be of great relevance for IS and yet were never explored.

One of the main reasons for this is the costs involved in coming to understand some of these ideas. Many of the important philosophers are highly abstract and very difficult to grasp—one thinks of Foucault, Heidegger or Adorno—and would require a significant amount of time with no certainty of a useful outcome at the end. This led us to see that what was needed was an accessible but scholarly introduction to a range of important ideas written specifically for the IS community; and thus this book was born.

This was around 1999. Our original idea was to provide a comprehensive review, but as we played with the names, schools, theories and philosophical issues, a group of ideas and thinkers slowly came to the fore. We gradually leaned towards not being too classificatory and going for selective, focused coverage. Our purpose became to provide sufficient critical coverage in one book on some major social theory and philosophy that has either been already utilized over several years in IS—for example Giddens, functionalism or Habermas—or that has been rarely or not at all used—for example Adorno, Foucault or Bhaskar.

Important questions we asked ourselves were: Who has been influential and what more can be said about them? Who or what has been undeservedly neglected? We also wanted to redress the tendency for IS—perhaps out of its own "disciplinary anxiety"—to import thinkers, ideas and easy-to-grasp frameworks somewhat uncritically from other reference disciplines. In practice, of course, every social theory and philosophy you will find in this book has behind it a storm of controversy and debate. Moreover, we wanted the theories and philosophies contextualized and understood from the inside, in their own terms, as much as possible.

Now that the book has been completed we both feel that it has far exceeded our expectations in terms of the range, balance, quality and freshness of coverage and we would like to thank all our splendid contributors for the enormous effort they have put in. On a personal note, having some of our favourite IS writers writing just for us has been an undiluted pleasure.

In developing the book the readers we had in mind are experienced IS academics and researchers who know little about the subject matter of a particular chapter. The aim is that they should be able to acquire sufficient knowledge to judge whether the approach will be useful to them, and then be able to go into the literature to discover more. We have tried to keep to several principles:

- That all of the authors are involved in information systems as well as being experts in the theory that they are writing about. We could have got sociologists or philosophers to contribute, but we felt that they would not be able to contextualize the material, properly.
- That each chapter should have a fairly narrow focus on just one or two thinkers or a well-defined area so that it could treat the subject in some depth and really get to the heart of the issues.
- That each chapter should be not merely exposition but should also explore criticisms and limitations and contrasts with other positions.
- That each chapter should be seen as a resource giving as much guidance to the relevant literature as possible.

One of the hardest decisions at the beginning was which areas to cover or, more accurately, which to leave out, as there were many that we felt were potentially interesting. In the event, this partly came down to the importance of the theory, partly the availability of excellent authors, partly limitations of space. Many interesting perspectives on our original list had to be omitted, for example Merleau-Ponty, Maturana, Luhmann, Lefebvre and Bourdieu; contemporary approaches like those of Virilio, Baudrillard, Haraway or Hayles; and whole areas of the philosophy of technology that remain to be addressed, as for example those by Borgmann and Ihde. Clearly, we need to turn our thoughts to a second volume!

1

Thinking about Social Theory and Philosophy for Information Systems

Allen S. Lee

The phrase 'social theory and philosophy for information systems' invites an examination of following terms: social, theory, philosophy, information, systems, information systems, philosophy for information systems, and social theory for information systems. I shall refrain (no doubt to the relief of the reader) from providing the definition and scholarly treatment that each and every one of these terms deserves. Instead, I will pursue just a few issues where my intention is to suggest an imagination that is helpful to thinking about philosophy, social theory and information systems. Much as C. Wright Mills (1959) sought to instill in his readers a sense of what he called 'the sociological imagination', I will attempt to suggest to the reader a means of thinking about philosophy, social theory and information systems that, in a way, is more important than whatever the content of such thinking might be. The content of such thinking can and should change from philosophy to philosophy, from social theory to social theory and from information system to information system. However, once a person captures a particular imagination for raising and addressing questions about philosophy, social theory and information systems, the content of such thinking becomes nothing more than an ephemeral instantiation of a longer-lasting and more significant form of knowledge. It is this form of knowledge that motivates this chapter. I will draw on my own experiences in becoming a scholar to help evoke such an imagination and also to help explain what the terms 'philosophy', 'social theory' and 'information systems' have come to mean for me. I will also relate some actions that I have attempted in order to share these meanings with other information systems researchers.

PHILOSOPHY

In my roles as author, reviewer, editor and colleague, I have often observed the situation in which information systems scholars appear unwilling to acknowledge and accept philosophy as seriously as they do their own information systems research literature. The attitude has sometimes appeared to be one of outright resistance. Such an attitude is ironic in two ways. One would suppose that people who hold the degree of doctor of philosophy would be familiar with philosophy and receptive to its perspectives. Second, if the acceptance of philosophy can be compared to the acceptance of a technology of knowledge, one would then also suppose that scholars who bemoan resistance to technological innovations should themselves not be guilty of the same.

The outcome of taking a philosophical attitude is not so much an accretion to one's knowledge as it is a change in meaning, to oneself, of one's own knowledge and even knowledge in general. In my development as a scholar, it was unfortunately only after I completed all of my formal course work that I encountered three insights from philosophy that compelled me to learn more from it. The insights were Hume's problem of induction (see the appendix to this chapter), Gödel's proof, and the discrediting of logical positivism by the very school of thought that had advanced it in the first place. Though better classified under social theory than philosophy, a provocative first-person account of a social scientist as an expert witness (Wolfgang, 1974) also provided me with an insight no less philosophical than the first three. Altogether, the four insights awakened me from my slumber as a researcher of the empirical world. On awakening, I apprehended another empirical world—one consisting of my own research institutions, my colleagues and myself—which was just as demanding of research and explanation. I have come to believe that unless I am able to understand and explain the latter world, I cannot properly understand and explain the former world.

Hume demonstrated that induction, as a method of justification, is invalid.[1] My encounter with Hume's problem of induction moved me to suspend, if only momentarily, my scientific thinking about the empirical world and to inquire into scientific thinking itself. At the time of the encounter, I believed that science was inductive. My inquiry led me to see how the logic of justification in the empirical sciences—positivist as well as interpretive—must be deductive. This, in turn, enabled me to grasp what it means for a theory to be described by these synonymous terms: falsifiable, disconfirmable, disprovable and testable. I prefer the term 'empirically testable'. These terms all refer to why a theory can be disproved but never proved. A colleague and I recently wrote a paper (Lee and Baskerville, 2003) that, among other things, employs Hume's problem of induction in a critique of how information systems researchers have misapplied the valid notion of statistical generalizability in criticisms of case studies and how it may be properly applied instead. Interestingly, a reviewer of the paper doubted the validity of Hume's problem of induction. I found this astonishing, because doubting Hume's problem of induction is no more sensible than doubting the Central Limit Theorem. The reviewer accepted Hume's problem of induction only when my co-author and I laid out a step-by-step proof of it in the third and final version of our paper.[2]

I learned about Gödel's proof from a colleague who remarked that it can serve to explode logical positivism. Gödel's proof demonstrates that 'within any rigidly logical mathematical system there are propositions (or questions) that cannot be proved or disproved on the basis of the axioms within that system and that, therefore, it is uncertain that the basic axioms of arithmetic will not give rise to contradictions' where, furthermore, this proof 'ended nearly a century of attempts to establish axioms that would provide a rigorous basis for all mathematics.'[3] This had the effect of demolishing all pronouncements about logical positivism as the route to objective knowledge. Like Hume's problem of induction, Gödel's proof directed me to examine my own manner of scientific reasoning. Eventually I still concluded that scientific theory can be objective; however, I came to regard an objective theory not as one that exists independently of human beings and their contaminating influences, but as a social object that forms over a period of time from a process of social construction in which many generations or cohorts of researchers participate and whose properties and behaviours can be observed and explained through such empirical disciplines as the history and sociology of science.[4]

From Schön's classic, *The Reflective Practitioner*, I learned that positivism had 'fallen into disrepute in its original home, the philosophy of science' (1983, p. 48). How then, I wondered, could it be that social scientists, including many information systems researchers, still espouse and practice positivism as their approach to science? Schön quotes Bernstein (1976, p. 207):

> There is not a single major thesis advanced by either nineteenth-century Positivists or the Vienna Circle that has not been devastatingly criticized when measured by the Positivists' own standards for philosophical argument. The original formulations of the analytic-synthetic dichotomy and the verifiability criterion of meaning have been abandoned. It has been effectively shown that the Positivists' understanding of the natural sciences and the formal disciplines is grossly oversimplified. Whatever one's final judgment about the current disputes in the post-empiricist philosophy and history of science... there is rational agreement about the inadequacy of the original Positivist understanding of science, knowledge and meaning.

Given this development in philosophy—and in the technology of knowledge in particular—one may view the persistence of social scientists in adhering to traditional positivism to be an extreme case of resistance to technological innovations.

Effective, devastating accounts of positivism are nothing new or novel, despite the fact that the majority of information systems researchers have not learned about them. Popper (1965), who rejected logical positivism and explicitly described his own position as anti-positivist, brought Hume's problem of induction to bear on and demolish logical positivism's verifiability criterion of meaning. It was in reaction to this deficiency that Popper formulated his demarcation criterion for distinguishing science from non-science, where the criterion pertains to what Popper called falsifiability.

Wolfgang's first-hand account as a social scientist who gave expert witness testimony in court (1974) caused me to pause and reflect as much as did my encounters with Hume's problem of induction, Gödel's proof and the discrediting of logical positivism. Testifying in an American court regarding the death penalty, Wolfgang offered statistical evidence that black men receive the death penalty more often than white men, all other factors being equal (such as the severity of the crime committed). In the cross-examination, he was asked if the random sample of counties in his statistical analysis included the county where the crime was committed. When Wolfgang replied in the negative, the judge ruled his testimony irrelevant.

An insight that I derived from Wolfgang was that, even though this result was absurd from a scientific viewpoint, it was entirely rational from a legal viewpoint. This insight led me to the philosophy of law. Then, with the philosophy of law providing a vantage point that placed science and the philosophy of science in relief, I came to see science as just one form of knowledge and expertise that was not necessarily any better or worse than, but simply different from, other forms of knowledge and expertise. In this way of observing science, I could find no justification that scientific thinking, as just one form of knowing, must be regarded as the ideal after which all other forms of knowledge and expertise must necessarily model themselves. Regarding Wolfgang's experience as an expert witness, I now explain to my students that the logic of scientific reasoning is neither right nor wrong and the logic of the legal rules of evidence is neither right nor wrong; the two logics are simply different, just as the languages and cultures of two ethnic groups are neither right nor wrong, but simply different from each other (Lee, 1982).

Hume's problem of induction, Gödel's proof, the discrediting of logical positivism and Wolfgang's insight all eventually taught me that, in order to become a scholar, I needed to shift the focus of my study, if only occasionally, away from the objects typically examined by the natural and social sciences and instead towards scholarly knowledge itself as the object of inquiry. I have come to regard philosophy as being this kind of study.

Any discussion of philosophy that stands beside a discussion of social theory also needs to consider these terms: *ontology*, *epistemology*, *methodology* and *method*. These terms have usually confused me despite whatever dictionary or textbook definitions I have consulted. Part of the problem is that the '-ology' suffix of the first three indicates that they refer to fields of study, whereas common usage of the terms indicates that they refer to the subject matters of study. It is in the same way, it has been said, that the term 'history' can refer to both a subject matter (the past) as well as the scholarly field that studies it (the academic discipline of history). Learning from history, I have chosen to ignore the -ology suffix of the three terms and regard them instead as referring to subject matters.

A scholarly school of thought's *ontology* comprises its members' foundational beliefs about the empirical or 'real' world that they are researching. Some information systems researchers who subscribe to logical positivism proceed from the belief that the physical and natural world studied by the natural sciences constitutes the only true reality, with the important exception of quantifiably measurable constructs (such as IQ) harboured in human individuals. In contrast, some information systems researchers who subscribe to social constructionism believe that certain entities—such as the shared beliefs held by a long-established group of people, their social structure and their culture—also form part of the real world, even though these entities are invisible, intangible and, in a real sense, subjective. Furthermore, social constructionists believe that these human-made (30 years ago, the adjective would have been 'man-made') entities are social objects and, in being objects, are as real for human beings as any aspects of the physical and natural world. One's beliefs about what comprises the real world have an effect on what one seeks to observe, what one subsequently observes, how one explains what one observes, and the reasoning process by which one performs each of these. Researchers usually accept their school of thought's ontology as 'given', do not question it and need not even be aware of it. In fact, to the extent that researchers are not aware of their ontology or even this term's definition, we might better refer to it as their ontology-in-use.

Epistemology is sometimes defined as the theory or science of knowledge. I find this definition unsatisfactory because it begs the question of what a theory is. This question, in turn, is complicated by the fact that what a theory is depends on, among other things, an epistemology.[5] I now conceptualize an epistemology as a broad and high-level outline of the reasoning process by which a school of thought performs its empirical and logical work. For example, unlike hardcore positivist researchers, social constructionists believe that scientific investigations of socially constructed realities, such as the culture of a given organization, call for reasoning processes different from those used in scientific investigations of rocks, circuit boards and animals. Also worth noting is that the same ontology can lead to more than one epistemology. A positivist ontology, for example, can lead to the highly mathematical reasoning process seen in economics as well as to the qualitative reasoning process that framed Darwin's development of his theory of evolution. And for the same reason that we might prefer the term ontology-in-use to ontology, we might prefer the term epistemology-in-use to epistemology.

Less high level than epistemology is *methodology*. It refers to a more specific manner in which to do empirical and logical work. The same epistemology can have several methodologies. A social constructionist epistemology, for example, would recognize Van Maanen's ethnography (1979) and the grounded theory of Strauss and Corbin (1998) to be methodologies.[6] Furthermore, the device of differentiating first-order concepts and second-order concepts and the device of uncovering facts through informants' lies are *methods* that fall under Van Maanen's ethnographic methodology. Likewise, we may regard the procedures of open, selective and axial coding to be methods in Strauss and Corbin's grounded-theory methodology.

Some information systems researchers regard published writings about ontology, epistemology, methodology and methods as if they constituted a body of law to be looked up, learned, applied and obeyed, where any researchers who disobey are to be treated as deviants. I hold a different view. I regard explicit descriptions of ontology, epistemology, methodology and methods to be human-made entities that, as Kaplan would say (1964), are *post hoc* logical reconstructions of actual logics-in-use. It is always possible for a reconstruction to be wrong (and, to the extent that a map is never a territory, all reconstructions are necessarily imperfect). Hence the pronouncement of any ontology, epistemology, methodology and method need not be received as sacrosanct but can be judged, disputed, rejected and replaced. For example, even though most scholars would share the opinion that positivist and interpretive ontologies are contrary and conflicting, an instance of actual research that integrates the two should not be summarily dismissed for having broken 'the law', but can be usefully regarded as the instance that refutes and overthrows the shared opinion. After all, based on the philosophical imagination that can emerge from Hume's problem of induction, Gödel's proof, the discrediting of logical positivism and Wolfgang's account as an expert witness, one can and must regard all scholarly knowledge itself as a social construction. It is not immutable but under our power as a community of scholars to question, amend, correct and improve.

SOCIAL THEORY

'Theory' is difficult to define explicitly, but seasoned information systems researchers seem to recognize theory readily when they see it and are quick to voice criticism when they do not see it. (For example, referees of papers submitted to journals and audience members at research seminars are often quick to sniff: 'This paper has no theory!') My understanding of what constitutes a theory follows less from any explicit definition and more from examples and tacit knowledge that I carry from situation to situation.

The clearest and most basic example of theory arguably comes from the natural sciences and those sciences that emulate them.

In the natural sciences, a theory is typically operationalized as a collection of independent and dependent variables that are related to one another by the rules of mathematics or formal logic and that, furthermore, are related to an empirical referent by the rules of experimental design. Popper (1965) has commented that the propositions making up a scientific theory need to satisfy four conditions: they must exhibit internal logical consistency, they must be empirically testable, they must survive attempts at empirical testing, and they must be at least as explanatory or predictive as any rival theory. This operationalization can readily suit those social sciences that model themselves on the natural sciences, but is at best an incomplete operationalization for researchers who focus on the social dimension in social science.

Schutz (1962b) provides an ingenious device—involving the distinction between first-level constructs and second-level constructs—to account for the social dimension of social theory. According to Schutz, a social science theory and a natural science theory are no different in their logical form. Of course, there remain major differences between them, one of which pertains to some empirical work that a social scientist, but not a natural scientist, needs to perform prior to formulating a theory. In the given organizational or other social setting that a social scientist is observing, the social scientist's empirical work consists of interpreting the meanings that the observed human individuals create and share, and that they attach to one another, to their organizational setting and to their history. Being part and parcel of the real world that the social scientist encounters, these subjective meanings are objective reality. As such, they require data collection or observation by the social scientist no less than does any other aspect of objective reality that he or she encounters. Schutz conceptualizes these subjective meanings as first-level constructs—meanings constructed by the human subjects in the social setting that the social scientist seeks to explain. It is only on the basis of these first-level constructs that the observing social scientist may properly found the constructs (hence, second-level constructs) comprising his or her scientific theory.[7] Because subjective meanings or first-level constructs exist in the empirical subject matter of social science but not natural science, it is appropriate to describe the subsequent second-level constructs or theory as being *social* theory.

An interesting consequence that follows from Schutz's view of social theory is that natural science methodology can be seen as a limiting case or subset of social science methodology. In the

language of mathematics, we can say that natural science methodology represents the limiting case of social science methodology
where the first-level constructs (the meanings that the subject matter has of itself, its setting and its history) 'go to zero'. Equivalently
stated, a social science theory (second-level constructs) not only
must satisfy all the same logical and empirical requirements that a
natural science theory satisfies (e.g. Popper's four conditions), but
must also account for the world of subjective meaning (first-level
constructs). In the sense that natural science deals only with the
former but social science must deal with both the former and the
latter, natural science methodology may be regarded as a subset of
social science methodology.

A social theory, whether positivist or interpretive, need not
be stated in terms of independent and dependent variables. It
may be stated in the form of propositions not mentioning any
variables, as long as the propositions are logically consistent, are
empirically testable, survive attempts at empirical testing, and are
at least as explanatory or predictive as the propositions comprising
any rival theory. Process theory is a genre of theory fitting this
description, whereas variance theory is the genre that makes use of
variables (Mohr, 1982; Markus and Robey, 1988).

The term 'social' in social theory requires additional comment.
For some researchers, any theory about human individuals is social
theory. For other researchers, social theory is not so much about
human individuals as it is about shared, socially constructed institutions that endure even when the individuals who are momentarily
present are replaced by new ones. Consider the conceptualization of
an organization as a collection of people. Such a conceptualization
would mean that when all the people in the organization change,
the result would be a new organization—but this need not be the
outcome at all. This suggests an alternative conceptualization: the
organization is that which stays the same even when all the people
change. The things that stay the same, or at least change at a much
slower pace than the turnover of people, would be social objects that
include the organization's culture, its social structure, its standard
operating procedures, many of its business processes, its folklore
and its norms for behaviour. In this alternative conceptualization,
the unit of analysis in social theory would not be individuals por-
trayed as decision makers, but would be the social objects that
enable, constrain and otherwise shape the behaviours and thinking of all the different generations of individuals who enter, pass
through and leave the organization. Just as the data populating

a database can be seen as a fleeting instantiation of the enduring database schema, the individuals populating an organization can be seen as a fleeting instantiation of the organization's enduring culture and social structure. In this analogy, social theory would more properly be about extra-individual entities such as culture and social structure than directly about individuals themselves.

In any case, what social theory is about therefore depends on the ontology of the school of thought that is doing the theorizing. The ontology positing that individuals are agents of social structures, where the social structures shape what the individuals think and how they act, would result in a genre of social theory quite different from the ontology positing that individuals determine their own fates through the decisions they make and the actions they take. To recognize further the significance of the term 'social' that this discussion suggests, one may argue that the former ontology would be better suited to developing a social theory while the latter ontology would be better suited to developing a theory of the individual.

INFORMATION SYSTEMS

The terms 'information', 'systems' and 'information systems' have fallen into such careless use that they seemingly no longer denote anything different from one another. In the same way, 'information' has come to be used interchangeably with 'data' and 'knowledge', while 'systems' has almost always come to denote computer systems. And 'information systems' can mean the same as 'information technology', where both terms sometimes simply designate 'the computer'. Such usage trivializes and obscures the rich ideas that these terms originally signified.[8]

Systems theory is a well-developed body of knowledge and offers ideas that can advance current information systems research and practice. Some of its basic concepts are that systems are composed of subsystems, that the subsystems interact with and transform one another, and that the properties of the system as a whole result not only from the properties of its respective subsystems, but also from the interactions across them. Emery and Trist (1960) offer an explanation that still rings true today. Elsewhere (Lee, 2003) I have fashioned an application of their explanation to organizations and information technology, the gist of which follows.

A conventional (and incomplete) view of information systems focuses on information requirements—which describe the information that an organization requires from an information technology so that it can function and achieve its goals—as well as how to design, implement, install or otherwise procure information technology so that it can deliver the information required. This view dominates the assorted waterfall models of systems design and, one can argue, still permeates some of the recent and sophisticated notions of information systems development. This view is incomplete because it is blind to systems other than the technical system as well as to the mutually transformational interactions that unfold between technical systems and other systems.

In addition to the information technology comprising the technical system, there is also the organization comprising the social system. Just as there are information requirements that the social system poses to the technical system, there are organization requirements that the technical system poses to the social system. The hardware and software of an ERP system, for example, can pose the requirement that the organization must reengineer its manufacturing processes to fit the processes that the ERP software was programmed to manage.

Once the technical system is designed and implemented so as to provide the information required by the social system, the technical system itself would be changed, where the change would then trigger new and different organization requirements for the social system to satisfy. Then, once the social system is designed and implemented so as to deliver the organization required by the technical system, the social system itself would be changed, where the change would then trigger new and different information requirements for the technical system to satisfy. These mutually and iteratively transformational interactions can be expected to continue without end. Hence whatever results from them is not determinate but emergent.

An information system can be defined as this emergent result. An information system is not the information technology alone, but the system that emerges from the mutually transformational interactions between the information technology and the organization. In an early sociotechnical study in the information systems discipline, Bostrom and Heinen (1977, p. 18) express, at least in my paraphrasing of them, that an information system is that which results from the intervention of an information technology into an already existing social system, as much as an information system is that which results from of an intervention of a social system into an already existing information technology. In my reformulation of this, I emphasize that an information system is the result of an information technology enabling an organization, as much as an information system is the result of an organization enabling an information technology (Lee, 2003).

In sociotechnical systems in general, the social system does not have to be an organization. It can be an ethnic group, a virtual team, a neighbourhood and so on. Likewise, the technical system does not have to be a collection of hardware, software, networks and data structures, but can be technology in other forms, such as the division of labour across different work roles that would help in processing a firm's raw materials into the products or services that it sells. Both systems theory in general and sociotechnical systems in particular predate the computer era and have accumulated a large body of insights that can be mined for application to information systems.

This discussion of information systems presumes a scenario in which the information technology is indeed designed and implemented for the purpose of satisfying the organization's requirements and the organization is indeed designed and implemented for the purpose of satisfying the information technology's requirements. Not all situations, of course, fit this ideal. In the situation where an information technology (the technical system) is scrupulously designed, implemented, installed or otherwise procured, but no accompanying preparations are made in the organization (the social system), the information technology's requirements of the organization will nonetheless manifest themselves by evoking undesigned and therefore, most likely, undesirable changes in the organization. Such results can include human resistance to the information technology (Markus, 1983; Orlikowski, 1989) and even the failure of the information technology and hence the information system overall. The point is that changes in either the social system or the technical system will be accompanied by changes, whether designed or not, in the other system. The emergent result is more likely to achieve the intended goals if, first, the continually evolving requirements of both the social system and the technical system are regularly monitored and taken into account and, second, the required changes materialize by design before undesirable changes materialize by default.

The immediately preceding discussion presumes that an information system is simply an instance of a sociotechnical system in general. In other words, does the established body of sociotechnical systems theory necessarily apply in the case of an information system? The answer depends, in part, on what the term 'information' means. The *Oxford English Dictionary* offers these and other definitions:[9]

> The action of informing...; communication of the knowledge or 'news' of some fact or occurrence; the action of telling or fact of being told of something.
> Knowledge communicated concerning some particular fact, subject, or event; that of which one is apprised or told; intelligence, news. spec. contrasted with data.
> As a mathematically defined quantity...; now esp. one which represents the degree of choice exercised in the selection or formation of one particular symbol, sequence, message, etc., out of a number of possible ones, and which is defined logarithmically in terms of the statistical probabilities of occurrence of the symbol or the elements of the message. The latter sense (introduced by Shannon..., though foreshadowed earlier) is that used in information theory, where information is usually regarded as synonymous with entropy.

Because the second definition of information mentions 'data', its definition would also be helpful. An *OED* definition of datum is:[10]

> pl. The quantities, characters, or symbols on which operations are performed by computers and other automatic equipment, and which may be stored or transmitted in the form of electrical signals, records on magnetic tape or punched cards, etc.
> **1970** A. Chandor *et al. Dict. Computers*... Data is sometimes contrasted with information, which is said to result from the processing of data.

These definitions indicate that information itself is a rich phenomenon that deserves its own separate focus no less than either information technology or organizations. These definitions also suggest that information cannot be neatly categorized under either the 'social system' heading or the 'technology system' heading. Perhaps a third type of system, the 'knowledge system', needs to take an equal place next to the social system and the technical system (where this would raise the non-trivial issue of how to define 'knowledge') [see Chapters 6 and 7 for some contrasting views—Eds]. In this suggested framework, an information system would be the emergent result of the mutually and iteratively transformational interactions among the social system, the technical system and the knowledge system. As for the design, behaviour and properties of a knowledge system and how it interacts with a social system and a technical system, one could take advantage of numerous existing bodies of knowledge, which include information theory, hermeneutics, phenomenology and the sociology of knowledge, and the history, sociology and philosophy of science, where science is regarded as being about only one form of knowledge. Information systems scholars whose investigations implicitly examine the interactions among the three systems include Liebenau and Backhouse (1990), Mingers (1995), Lee (1994a, 1994b) and Ngwenyama and Lee (1997).

One might suppose that people who call themselves information systems researchers are already well familiar with the systems approach and that it distinguishes their research from those of other scholars also interested in information technology. Unfortunately this is not the case. A large segment of information systems research consists of behavioural studies of how people and organizations do and do not use, adopt or diffuse information technology, where the studies do not account for the mutually and iteratively transformational interactions between the social system and the technological system. Indeed, in most of these studies the term 'system' or 'information system' appears to be interchangeable with 'information technology'. Arguably, many of these studies are not information systems research at all, but organizational research. Similarly, there are studies that focus on information technology, see the system only as the technology and do not account for interactive effects between the technological and the social. Information systems researchers include some who are systems theorists, such as Checkland and Holwell (1998), but the information systems research community overall has not come to realize the significance of this body of work.

ILLUSTRATIONS

No ideas on ontology, epistemology, methodology and methods are sacrosanct and immutable. They can and should always be further developed. I have applied my conceptions of 'philosophy', 'social theory' and 'information systems' in attempts to move the information systems field forward. I am pleased with some outcomes but not others.

Believing that logical positivism's flawed, inductive theory of knowledge could be replaced, I offered my own account of positivism in which its theory of knowledge is not inductive but deductive, involving hypothetico-deductive logic (Lee, 1989). This account was the result of my ruminations about philosophy and social theory and formed the core of my demonstration that even the study of a single case, such as the field study of an information system in a single organizational setting, can satisfy all the same criteria of rigour that are satisfied in natural science research. To my knowledge, this substitution of a deductive theory of knowledge for an inductive one went unnoticed by the community of information systems researchers, positivist and otherwise, even though this particular article has been highly cited.

Accepting Schutz's ideas about both the distinction and the relationship between first-level constructs (which as we have seen refer to the understandings that observed human subjects have of themselves, their setting and their history) and second-level constructs (which refer to the theory that researchers develop in order to explain what they are observing and that they craft to satisfy their criteria of rigour), I rendered Schutz's idea into an account (Lee, 1991) of how interpretive research and positivist research are not opposed and mutually exclusive, but compatible and mutually supportive. I designed this framework to move forward not only traditional positivism and traditional interpretivism, but also the state of social relations within the community of scholars, often suffering from a warring-camps mentality among positivist and interpretive researchers. Scholars already well entrenched in a positivist or interpretive research tradition have reacted, if not with polite silence, then with animated protestations that I am going against time-honoured definitions of the ontological, epistemological and methodological dimensions of positivism and interpretivism. Of course, given my belief that ideas on ontology, epistemology and methodology are always in need of further development, I only saw progress in liberating myself (and hopefully others) of the older ideas. Interestingly, some younger (i.e. not yet entrenched) scholars have seen no problem in my effort to integrate positivist and interpretive approaches to organizational research and have even wondered what my 1991 article says that is new or different!

DISCUSSION

Two puzzles facing the community of information systems researchers are the persistence of traditional, inductive positivism (positivism that is unaware of Hume's problem of induction and the accompanying difference between inductive and deductive theories of knowledge) and the lack of a systems approach among information systems researchers. To examine the puzzles, we can take an approach informed by philosophy, social theory and information systems. The resolution of these puzzles would exceed the scope of this chapter and is likely to require a multi-year, multi-site research programme.

We may frame the two puzzles as requiring us to develop scholarly knowledge about scholarly knowledge itself. As mentioned earlier, philosophy can be regarded as being this kind of study. For a long-term research programme, this suggests that lessons from earlier investigations in the philosophy of science would be relevant. And because it can be difficult to separate the philosophy of science from the history of science and the sociology of science, a research programme for resolving the two puzzles might similarly consider the perspectives of philosophy, history and sociology as reinforcing one another.

A social theory perspective, which can be historical and sociological, can provide the key to resolving the two puzzles. Rosabeth Moss Kanter (1977, p. 291) offers a method that is useful in interpretive social theory. When a researcher observes what appears to be someone engaging in irrational behaviour, then either (1) that person is actually behaving in a way that they themselves would consider irrational or (2) the researcher has not yet grasped the bigger picture in which the person's behaviour is rational. The method is to begin with the assumption that no person behaves in a way that they themselves would consider irrational and then to seek additional facts and to build or refine a theory that would allow the researcher to see how the behaviour is rational. Of course, it is still possible that the person *is* behaving in an irrational way; however, this would be accepted not as an opening observation, but only as a conclusion carefully drawn from a thorough empirically and theoretically based investigation.

This method can be helpful to a resolution of the two puzzles. First, there is what initially appears to be irrational behaviour in the majority of information systems researchers who abide by positivism. Abiding by traditional, inductive positivism would initially appear to be irrational because it has 'fallen into disrepute in its original home, the philosophy of science' (Schön, 1983, quoted above). Second, there is what initially appears to be irrational behaviour in the majority of information systems researchers who apparently do not take a systems approach. Therefore, either the majority of information systems researchers are behaving irrationally or there is a bigger picture in which the rationale of their behaviour would become evident.

For a possible example of such a bigger picture, consider the speculation in which positivist information systems researchers not only lack knowledge of the discrediting of logical positivism in the philosophy of science, but also face sanctions against acquiring and using such knowledge. There are some information systems doctoral students who have not read *The Structure of Scientific Revolutions* by Thomas Kuhn (1996) or *The Sciences of the Artificial* by Herbert Simon (1981). Some have read little or none of the philosophy that explains the foundations of different traditions of scientific research, including their own. Furthermore, some mention that their professors advise them against pursuing research that departs from any positivist/quantitative approach; doctoral students, who exist in dependency relationships with their professors, are in no position to disagree. Continuing the socialization are faculty recruitment committees, editorial boards of journals, programme committees of conferences, and tenure and promotion committees—where, in the United States and Canada, the pro-positivist members of these decision-making bodies largely outnumber those who are familiar with, much less accept the validity of, research approaches beyond positivism.

In light of this bigger picture, an information systems researcher's embrace of positivism clearly emerges as rational behaviour. Such a picture, however, is only illustrative of what the situation might be. To determine what the bigger picture actually is, a long-term research programme would be required and might include an ethnography of information systems researchers. Furthermore, whereas this discussion has only focused on how one might possibly explain the apparently irrational behaviour of information systems researchers who persist in abiding by logical positivism, one could similarly explain the apparently irrational behaviour of information systems researchers who do not take a systems approach.

A systems approach could also help in resolving the two puzzles. Taking a systems approach, a long-term research programme that investigates information systems researchers themselves could examine their technical system (the system of processes by which they transform research inputs, including existing theory and research methods, into research outputs, such as published articles), their social system (the system of roles, rules and other elements that help form the information systems research community), their knowledge system (the system of espoused theories about how to do research, theories-in-use about how to do research, shared beliefs and historical knowledge that, in interacting together, form what information systems researchers know), as well as how the three systems interact, transform one another and support the emergence of an information system among information systems researchers. The analysis of such a system could identify how the interactions among its three subsystems allow the emergence of a situation where key information does not materialize, is not accepted or is suppressed. In particular, this key information refers to information about the discrediting of positivism by the philosophy of science and information about the systems approach.

CONCLUSION

Taking an approach informed by philosophy, social theory and information systems to the study of information systems research and information systems researchers can lead to findings that would help the information systems research community do better information systems research. Such an approach would require a philosophical imagination, a social theory imagination and a systems imagination. Better information systems research will emerge if information systems researchers capture the three imaginations.

A GUIDE TO THE LITERATURE

Regarding philosophy and social theory for information systems, a good starting point to the literature is the work of Thomas S. Kuhn. His monograph *The Structure of Scientific Revolutions* (1996) is seminal, but also readily and widely misunderstood, as indicated in the anthology *Criticism and the Growth of Knowledge* (Lakatos and Musgrave, 1970). Kuhn's own anthology *The Essential Tension* (1997) is helpful for underscoring the strongly historical and sociological dimension to his philosophy of science. If one comes to understand or describe Kuhn's concept of 'paradigm' without any reference to the sociological or without any acknowledgement that Kuhn is presenting a social theory of science, then one has missed the significance of the role that the scientific *community* plays in Kuhn's depiction of what science is and what scientists do.

Regarding social theory specifically, a good point for motivating many of its methodological and philosophical issues is the debate between Alfred Schutz and Ernest Nagel in the anthology *Philosophy of the Social Sciences* (Natanson, 1963), along with Nagel's *The*

Structure of Science (1961) and the three volumes of Schutz's *Collected Papers* (1962a, 1964, 1966). Two books by Richard J. Bernstein, *The Restructuring of Social and Political Theory* (1976) and *Beyond Objectivism and Relativism: Science, Hermeneutics, and Praxis* (1983), helped to bring coherence to much of my own thinking on philosophy and social theory.

Regarding the matter of what constitutes an information system, I consider two articles—one by Bostrom and Heinen (1977), 'MIS problems and failures: A socio-technical perspective, Part 1: The causes' and the other by Emery and Trist (1960), 'Socio-technical systems'—to be my favourites for capturing and conveying the spirit of what an information system is. There is, of course, a large body of systems theory that originated long before the emergence of electronic information technology and that information systems researchers have appropriated and further developed; however, as intellectually impressive and forceful as this body of literature has been, its availability seems to have had no impact on the emergence and permanence of the idea that an information system is, basically, 'the computer' or that the terms 'information systems' and 'information technology' can usually be used interchangeably.

Similarly, regarding the matter of what information is, I consider a paper by Boland (1991), 'Information systems use as a hermeneutic process', to be excellent and unique in its demonstration, in very human terms, of what information is. However, most of the information systems literature has always seemed to treat the terms 'data', 'information' and even 'knowledge' interchangeably, despite the literature's espoused definitions otherwise.

APPENDIX: HUME'S CONTRIBUTION TO THE UNDERSTANDING OF INDUCTION[11]

Induction refers to a process of reasoning and can be a synonym for generalizing. It refers to a reasoning process that begins with statements of particulars and ends in a general statement. Reasoning from data points in a sample to an estimate of a population characteristic is an instance of induction. Campbell and Stanley call attention to 'some painful problems in the science of induction' (1963, p. 17, original emphasis retained):

> The problems are painful because of a recurrent reluctance to accept Hume's truism that *induction or generalization is never fully justified logically*. Whereas the problems of *internal* validity are solvable

within the limits of the logic of probability of statistics, the problems of external validity are not logically solvable in any neat, conclusive way. Generalization always turns out to involve extrapolation into a realm not represented in one's sample. Such extrapolation is made by *assuming* one knows the relevant laws. Thus, if one has an internally valid Design 4,[12] one has demonstrated the effect only for those specific conditions which the experimental and control group have in common, i.e., only for pretested groups of a specific age, intelligence, socioeconomic status, geographic region, historical moment, orientation of the stars, orientation of the magnetic field, barometric pressure, gamma radiation, etc. *Logically*, we cannot generalize beyond these limits; i.e., we cannot generalize at all. But we do attempt generalization by guessing at laws and checking out some of these generalizations in other equally specific but different conditions. In the course of the history of a science we learn about the 'justification' of generalizing by the cumulation of our experience in generalizing, but this is not a logical generalization deducible from the details of the original experiment. Faced by this, we do, in generalizing, make guesses as to yet unproven laws, including some not yet explored. . .

Hume, an eighteenth-century Scottish philosopher, 'is almost universally credited with discovering the problem of induction' (Rosenberg, 1993, p. 75). Wood (2000) offers a detailed explanation of Hume's problem of induction. The problem of induction is about how to establish induction itself as a valid method for empirical inquiry.

Induction can be expressed in the form of Argument 1.1 in Figure 1.1. The status of induction as a valid method of empirical inquiry is open to question, because the second statement does not logically follow from the first. Wood refers to this as Problem 1. Wood continues: 'To make Argument [1.1] valid, we need an additional premise, such as [the] Uniformity of Nature assumption or: "The future will be like the past"', where the result is Argument 1.2.

Argument 1.2 employs a form of the uniformity of nature assumption as the first statement in an argument that takes the form of a syllogism, which consists of a major premise, minor premise and conclusion. The major premise is the first statement in the syllogism. The second statement, 'In past experience, all *F*s have been *G*s', plays the role of the minor premise. Applying the major premise to the minor premise leads deductively to the conclusion, 'Therefore, the next *F* will be a *G* or all future *F*s will be *G*s.' Note that the conclusion in Argument 1.2 is the same as the second statement in Argument 1.1. Therefore, if Argument 1.2 were

Argument 1.1

- In past experience, all Fs have been Gs.

- Therefore, the next F will be a G or all future Fs will be Gs.

Argument 1.2

- If in past experience, all Fs have been Gs, then the next F will be a G or all future Fs will be Gs.

- In past experience, all Fs have been Gs.

- Therefore, the next F will be a G or all future Fs will be Gs.

Figure 1.1   *First attempt to justify induction. Source: Based on Wood (2000)*

valid, it would provide a proper way of establishing the validity of induction.

Whereas Argument 1.2 performs its deductive reasoning correctly, the conclusion in any syllogism can be valid only if its major premise is valid. Wood refers to the following as Problem 2: In Argument 1.2, how would we know that the major premise—the uniformity of nature proposition—itself is valid? We would therefore need to take a step back in order to establish the validity of the uniformity of nature premise.

Wood explains that there are two ways by which we could attempt to establish the validity of the uniformity of nature proposition, which is denoted as Theory 1 in Figure 1.2. One way is by recourse to Argument 2.1, but its mode of reasoning is induction exactly as Argument 1.1's mode of reasoning was induction; therefore, the same Problem 1 that arose for Argument 1.1 would also arise for Argument 2.1. To remedy this instance of Problem 1, we would again need an additional premise, where the result is Argument 2.2.

Argument 2.1

- In past experience, all tests
  have confirmed Theory 1.

- Therefore, the next test will
  confirm Theory 1 or all future
  tests will confirm Theory 1.

Argument 2.2

- If in past experience all tests
  have confirmed Theory 1, then
  the next test will confirm
  Theory 1 or all future tests will
  confirm Theory 1.

- In past experience, all tests
  have confirmed Theory 1.

- Therefore, the next test will
  confirm Theory 1 or all future
  tests will confirm Theory 1.

Figure 1.2   *Second attempt to justify induction. Source: Based on Wood (2000)*

As it turns out, Argument 2.2 employs the uniformity of nature proposition as its major premise, just as Argument 1.2 did. Because Argument 2.2 takes the form of a syllogism, its conclusion can be valid only if its major premise is valid. The result is that Problem 2 would recur: How would we know that the major premise in Argument 2.2 is valid? We would need to take a step back in order to establish the validity of the major premise in Argument 2.2, just as we previously took a step back in order to establish the validity of the major premise in Argument 1.2. The result is that we would find ourselves in an infinite regress taking the form of what would then be Figures 1.3, 1.4, 1.5, and so on, where the stream of reasoning would have no conclusion. Rosenberg offers a succinct description of Hume's truism (1993, p. 75):

> Hume recognized that inductive conclusions could only be derived deductively from premises (such as the uniformity of nature) that themselves required inductive warrant, or from arguments that were inductive in the first place. The deductive arguments [e.g. Arguments 1.2 and 2.2] are no more convincing than their most

controversial premises and so generate a regress, while the inductive ones [e.g. Arguments 1.1 and 2.1] beg the question. Accordingly, claims that transcend available data, in particular predictions and general laws, remain unwarranted.

The enormous significance of Hume's truism leads Campbell and Stanley (1963) to take the positions that '*induction or generalization is never fully justified logically*' and that '*we cannot generalize at all*' (emphasis in the original, cited above).

ENDNOTES

[1] David Hume's own work and an extensive secondary literature on his work are readily available, including coverage in encyclopaedias and textbooks. Rosenberg (1993) provides a good example.

[2] The proof is reproduced in the appendix to this chapter.

[3] 'Gödel, Kurt', *Encyclopædia Britannica* retrieved April 14, 2003, from Encyclopædia Britannica Online, http://80-search.eb.com.proxy.library.vcu.edu/eb/article?eu=37902.

[4] In particular, I am referring to Berger and Luckmann's classic, *The Social Construction of Reality* (1967), and the corpus of Thomas Kuhn's work. The sociological influence in Kuhn's history of science is evident in the following (1970, pp. 237–8): 'Some of the principles deployed in my explanation of science are irreducibly sociological, at least at this time. In particular, confronted with the problem of theory-choice, the structure of my response runs roughly as follows: take a group of the ablest available people with the most appropriate motivation; train them in some science and in the specialties relevant to the choice at hand; imbue them with the value system, the ideology, current in their discipline (and to a great extent in other scientific fields as well); and finally, let them make the choice. If that technique does not account for scientific development as we know it, then no other will.'

[5] Hermeneutically speaking, one can argue that the terms ontology, epistemology, methodology and method can only be understood in one another's context and that, therefore, their unrelated dictionary definitions are necessarily incomplete.

[6] Mingers (2001) offers helpful distinctions within methodology itself.

[7] Giddens' idea of the 'double hermeneutic' (1984) embodies the distinction and relationship between first-level constructs and second-level constructs. The double hermeneutic is the idea that a social theory contains interpretations of everyday life, which itself can then form its own interpretations of the social theory and thereby be changed by it, which in turn would call for the social theory to render interpretations of the changed everyday life. In other words, second-level constructs contain interpretations of first-level constructs, which themselves can then form their own interpretations of the second-level constructs and thereby be changed by them, which in turn would call for the second-level constructs to be based on interpretations of the changed first-level constructs. The idea of first-level constructs and second-level constructs can also

be found in the work of Van Maanen (1979), where they appear as 'first-order concepts' and 'second-order concepts'.

[8]Mingers (1995) also laments the lack of clear definitions within the information systems field and suggests a model of the relations between information, meaning and data.

[9]Accessed on April 20, 2003 at http://80-etext.lib.virginia.edu.proxy.library.vcu.edu/etcbin/oedbin/oed2www?specfile=/web/data/oed/oed.o2w&act=text&offset=203839170&textreg=0&query=information.

[10]Accessed on April 20, 2003 at http://80-etext.lib.virginia.edu.proxy.library.vcu.edu/etcbin/oedbin/oed.link?query=datum.

[11]Reprinted by permission from Allen S. Lee and Richard L. Baskerville, 'Generalizing generalizability in information systems research', *Information Systems Research*, 14(3): 223–4. Copyright 2003, the Institute for Operations Research and the Management Sciences, 901 Elkridge Landing Road, Suite 400, Linthicum, MD 21090 USA.

[12]Campbell and Stanley describe 'Design 4' as follows (1963, p. 13)

```
R  O1  X  O2
R  O3     O4
```

REFERENCES

Berger, P. L. and Luckmann, T. (1967) *The Social Construction of Reality: A Treatise in the Sociology of Knowledge*, Garden City, NY: Anchor Books.

Bernstein, R. J. (1976) *The Restructuring of Social and Political Theory*, New York, NY: Harcourt Brace Jovanovich.

Bernstein, R. J. (1983) *Beyond Objectivism and Relativism: Science, Hermeneutics, and Praxis*, Philadelphia, PA: University of Pennsylvania Press.

Boland, R. J. (1991) 'Information systems use as a hermeneutic process', in W. -E. Nissen, H. K. Klein and R. Hirschheim, *Information Systems Research: Contemporary Approaches and Emergent Traditions*, New York, NY: North-Holland, pp. 439–58.

Bostrom, R. P. and Heinen, J. S. (1977) 'MIS problems and failures: A socio-technical perspective', *MIS Quarterly*, 1(3): 17–32.

Campbell, D. and Stanley, J. (1963) *Experimental and Quasi-Experimental Designs for Research*, Boston, MA: Houghton Mifflin.

Checkland, P. and Holwell, S. (1998) *Information, Systems, and Information Systems: Making Sense of the Field*, Chichester/New York, NY: Wiley.

Emery, F. E. and Trist, E. L. (1960) 'Socio-technical systems', in C. W. Churchman and M. Verhulst (eds), *Management Sciences, Models and Techniques*, New York, NY: Pergamon Press.

Giddens, A. (1984) *The Constitution of Society*, Berkeley/Los Angeles, CA: University of California Press.

Kanter, R. Moss (1977) *Men and Women of the Corporation*, New York, NY: Basic Books.

Kaplan, A. (1964) *The Conduct of Inquiry: Methodology for Behavioral Science*, Scranton, PA: Chandler Publishing.

Kuhn, T. S. (1970) 'Reflections on my critics', in I. Lakatos and A. Musgrave (eds), *Criticism and the Growth of Knowledge*, New York, NY/London: Cambridge University Press, pp. 231–78.

Kuhn, T. S. (1996) *The Structure of Scientific Revolutions*, Chicago, IL: University of Chicago Press, 3rd edn.

Kuhn, T. S. (1997) *The Essential Tension*, Chicago, IL: University of Chicago Press.

Lakatos, I. and Musgrave, A. (1970) *Criticism and the Growth of Knowledge*, New York, NY: Cambridge University Press.

Lee, A. S. (1982) '*Cross cultural communication between scientists and lawyers in judicial policy making*', doctoral dissertation, School of Architecture and Planning, Massachusetts Institute of Technology, Cambridge, MA.

Lee, A. S. (1989) 'A scientific methodology for MIS case studies', *MIS Quarterly*, 13(1): 33–50.

Lee, A. S. (1991) 'Integrating positivist and interpretive approaches to organizational research', *Organization Science*, 2(4): 342–65.

Lee, A. S. (1994a) 'Electronic mail as a medium for rich communication: An empirical investigation using hermeneutic interpretation', *MIS Quarterly*, 18(2): 143–57.

Lee, A. S. (1994b) 'The hermeneutic circle as a source of emergent richness in the managerial use of electronic mail', *Proceedings of the International Conference on Information Systems*, Vancouver, BC, pp. 129–40.

Lee, A. S. (2003) 'Re-introducing the systems approach to information systems', keynote address at *ISOneWorld* Las Vegas, NV.

Lee, A. S. and Baskerville, R. L. (2003) 'Generalizing generalizability in information systems research', *Information Systems Research*, 14(3): 221–43.

Liebenau, J. and Backhouse, J. (1990) *Understanding Information*, London: Macmillan.

Markus, M. L. (1983) 'Power, politics, and MIS implementation', *Communications of the ACM*, 26(6): 430–44.

Markus, M. L. and Robey, D. (1988) 'Information technology and organizational change: Causal structure in theory and research', *Management Science*, 34(5): 583–98.

Mills, C. Wright (1959) *The Sociological Imagination*, New York, NY: Oxford University Press.

Mingers, J. (1995) 'Information and meaning: Foundations for an intersubjective account', *Information Systems Journal*, 5: 285–306.

Mingers, J. (2001) 'Combining IS research methods: Towards a pluralist methodology', *Information Systems Research*, 12(3): 240–59.

Mohr, L. B. (1982) 'Approaches to explanation: Variance theory and process theory', *Explaining Organizational Behavior*, San Francisco, CA: Jossey-Bass, pp. 35–70.

Nagel, E. (1961) *The Structure of Science: Problems in the Logic of Scientific Explanation*, New York, NY: Harcourt, Brace & World.

Natanson, M. (1963) *Philosophy of the Social Sciences: A Reader*, New York, NY: Random House.

Ngwenyama, O. K. and Lee, A. S. (1997) 'Communication richness in electronic mail: Critical social theory and the contextuality of meaning', *MIS Quarterly*, 21(2): 145–67.

Orlikowski, W. J. (1989) 'Division among the ranks: The social implications of CASE tools for system developers', *Proceedings of the Tenth International Conference on Information Systems*, Boston, MA, pp. 199–210.

Popper, K. (1965) *The Logic of Scientific Discovery*, New York, NY: Harper Torchbooks.

Rosenberg, A. (1993) 'Hume and the philosophy of science', in D. Fate Norton (ed.), *The Cambridge Companion to Hume*, New York, NY: Cambridge University Press, pp. 64–89.

Schön, D. A. (1983) *The Reflective Practitioner: How Professionals Think in Action*, New York, NY: Basic Books.

Schutz, A. (1962a) *Collected Papers: The Problem of Social Reality*, The Hague: M. Nijhoff.

Schutz, A. (1962b) 'Concept and theory formation in the social sciences', in A. Schutz, *Collected Papers: The Problem of Social Reality*, The Hague: M. Nijhoff, pp. 48–66.

Schutz, A. (1964) *Collected Papers: Studies in Social Theory*, The Hague: M. Nijhoff.

Schutz, A. (1966) *Collected Papers: Studies in Phenomenological Philosophy*, The Hague: M. Nijhoff.

Simon, H. (1981) *The Sciences of the Artificial*, Cambridge, MA/London: MIT Press, 2nd ed.

Strauss, A. L. and Corbin, J. (1998) *Basics of Qualitative Research: Techniques and Procedures for Developing Grounded Theory*, Thousand Oaks, CA: Sage.

Van Maanen, J. (1979) 'The fact of fiction in organizational ethnography', *Administrative Science Quarterly*, 24:4 539–50.

Wolfgang, M. E. (1974) 'The social scientist in court', *Journal of Criminal Law and Criminology*, 65: 230–47.

Wood, A. (2000) 'Hume: The problem of induction', Stanford, CA: Stanford University. Retrieved August 31, 2002 from http://www.stanford.edu/~allenw/Phil102/Hume%20-%20Induction.doc.

2
Fit for Function: Functionalism, Neofunctionalism and Information Systems

M. Lynne Markus

Functionalism was the first, and the dominant, theoretical orientation in sociology through the 1960s (Maryanski and Turner, 2000). Primarily associated with the work of Talcott Parsons (Abrahamson, 2001), functionalism emphasizes the distinctness of, and the linkages among, individuals, culture and society.

By 1970, functionalism had been largely discredited by attacks from many quarters. In the resulting theoretical 'crisis', new perspectives emerged that emphasized either individual action or culture and society but ignored the links between them. After about 1980 the streams began to converge, and various theorists attempted new unified conceptions of sociology (Abrahamson, 2001; Alexander, 1998). One example of this rapprochement is the work of Anthony Giddens (Alexander, 1998), discussed in detail by Jones, Orlikowski and Munir (this volume, Chapter 8). Another is neofunctionalism (Alexander, 1998), a broad school of thought built on Parsons' work but stripped of the more contentious aspects of Parsonian functionalism (Alexander, 1998). Although some scholars find the neofunctionalist revival 'interesting' (Marshall, 1998), others are sceptical of its contributions and prospects (Abrahamson, 2001).

Functionalism and neofunctionalism are known as 'grand' (or general) social theories; that is, 'theorizing without reference to particular empirical problems or distinctive domains' (Alexander, 1998, p. 164). Grand social theories are posited by their creators to apply across many (or even all) social processes. They stand in contrast to middle-range and micro-level theories. Middle-range theories, which have a definite substantive focus (e.g. theories of revolution, state formation or status attainment), are claimed to generalize to all specific instances of their class of phenomena (e.g. all revolutions, state formations etc.). By contrast, micro-level theories apply only to a particular instance of a class of phenomena (e.g. the French revolution, the Russian revolution, or the US revolution).

Applying functionalism and neofunctionalism directly to IS phenomena is challenging, because IS and IT are only tiny elements within the scope of these grand social theories. However, functionalist *explanation*, a style of reasoning commonly employed in the functionalist tradition, has clear relevance in IS research contexts. As I argue below, functionalist explanation has great potential utility in focused empirical investigations of IS phenomena.

THE GRAND THEORIES OF FUNCTIONALISM AND NEOFUNCTIONALISM

Although the grand theory of functionalism is most often associated with the work of sociologist Talcott Parsons, it has a long intellectual history. Some scholars see the origins of functionalism in the work of the 'Scottish Moralists' (circa 1860–80), including David Hume and Adam Smith (Abrahamson, 2001). Functionalism is characterized by three philosophical tenets held by the Scottish Moralists, but contested today in several streams of sociological thought. First, functionalism takes an 'etic' or outsider's view of phenomena, rather than seeking explanations in the meanings that those phenomena have for participants. (Many social theorists now argue strongly for taking an 'emic' or participants' point of view.) Second, functionalist theory distinguishes between individuals and collectives (groups or societies); concepts such as 'culture' are seen as structures that stand apart from the actions and intentions of individuals and thus as capable of influencing individual behaviour. (By contrast, many modern sociologists deny the existence of 'structures' that are distinct from the actions of individuals and that can impinge on individuals' freedom of action.) Third, functionalism holds that the parts of collectives are generally well integrated with each other, fulfilling the needs of the collectives (if not of all individual members) and tending towards stability once equilibrium has been established (Abrahamson, 2001). (Consequently, functionalism has been criticized for its social conservatism and for ignoring social conflict—an area that other sociological traditions explicitly address.)

Other scholars locate the origins of functionalism in the work of Emile Durkheim (circa 1895),[1] who, employing analogies from biology, viewed society as an 'organic' whole of which the parts work together to maintain each other homeostatically (Abrahamson, 2001; Marshall, 1998). According to Durkheim, functionalist explanations explain phenomena in terms of their consequences and should be distinguished from the equally important historical (or historicist) explanations, such as institutionalism, which explain phenomena in terms of self-replication. Durkheim explained crime and punishment in functionalist terms. Crime is a normal feature of everyday life, he argued, because it serves the function of defining the boundaries of socially acceptable behaviour; the act of punishing crimes serves to reinforce those same social norms (Abrahamson, 2001; Marshall, 1998).

Parsonian Functionalism

After Durkheim, sociologists' interest in functionalism diminished in favour of historicist explanations. In anthropology, however, functionalism flourished as a strategy for explaining aspects of culture such as the practice of witchcraft and belief in evil conspiracies. A major factor in the popularity of functionalism in anthropology was the inaccessibility of the histories of traditional societies, which prevented the use of historicist approaches.

In the 1930s, sociological functionalism was resurrected by a group of Harvard scholars led by Robert Merton, then a graduate student. In contrast to early functionalists, who viewed functions as 'manifest' (that is, as intended by members who are aware of the functions) and as beneficial, Merton and his colleagues emphasized that functions can be 'latent' (unintended and out of awareness) and possibly not beneficial in all respects or for all participants (Marshall, 1998).

Merton may have revived sociological functionalism, but 'it was Talcott Parsons, a young Harvard instructor during Merton's tenure as a graduate student, who [became] the archfunctionalist of modern times' (Maryanski and Turner, 2000, p. 1031). Through the 1960s, Parsons' influence was so powerful that 'even [his] sharpest critics. . . conceded that they had to define their own intellectual positions in relation to his' (Abrahamson, 2001, p. 141).

Parsons was concerned with the problem of non-rational social action and the 'functional prerequisites' (necessary conditions) of society (Abrahamson, 2001). Primary among these were social control mechanisms, needed to ensure that individuals were socialized into societal norms.

Functionalism attracted many criticisms during Parsons' ascendance. Parsons' focus on social control led him to view social change 'apprehensively' (Abrahamson, 2001), as an evolutionary response to changes in the environment (Mann, 1984). Critics decried functionalism's conservatism and lack of appreciation for the role of human agency. Other scholars challenged functionalism's tendency to downplay the importance of social conflict (Abrahamson, 2001).[2]

An undeniable source of criticism was the poor quality of many early functionalist explanations, especially in anthropology:

> Looking back on Merton's original essay and subsequent commentaries, it is amazing to see what a lot of bad functionalist argument was going around. (Douglas, 1986, p. 33)

Of specific concern was the failure of many functionalist explanations to describe causal mechanisms or processes (Marshall, 1998), such as *how* functions reinforce the social structures posited to produce them (Elster, 1983). Apparently, early functionalists often assumed that 'social institutions were adequately explained in terms of their putative effects' (Marshall, 1998, p. 242). This type of argument, which attributes 'purpose' or goal-seeking behaviour to non-human structures, is known as 'teleological'[3] (Mann, 1984)—a frequently challenged mode of thought. Consequently, some scholars have concluded that functionalism has no place in sociology (Elster, 1983), or that it could be replaced by rational choice theorizing (Elster, 1983) or by causal and historicist explanations (Marshall, 1998). As a result of these many criticisms, functionalism developed a bad reputation that continues to plague the theory to this day (Alexander, 1998; Douglas, 1986).

Neofunctionalism

When Parsonian functionalism broke down in the 1970s under the weight of sustained criticism, it was displaced by competing theoretical traditions that emphasized one or the other pole of the micro–macro theoretical continuum (Alexander, 1998). For example, on the micro side, George Homans developed exchange theory to elaborate the psychological underpinnings of social structure, and ethnomethodologist Harold Garfinkle reacted against functionalism's lack of attention to individual freedom of action. On the macro side, the traditional and conservative views of functionalism stimulated the development of feminist gender studies (Abrahamson, 2001), which emphasized the constraints that society places on individuals' behaviour.

As proponents of these new paradigms developed their arguments, they initially ignored the work of those at the opposite end of the continuum. Eventually, however, the need for integration became apparent. Resurgence of interest in Parsons' writings in the 1980s led to attempts to integrate functionalism with newer sociological paradigms that had stronger foundations in individual behaviour and critical social thought (Abrahamson, 2001). The new movement became known as neofunctionalism.

Central to understanding the neofunctional 'convergence' is the axiom that every social theory must take some position on two fundamental issues: action and order (Alexander, 1998). First, is human action to be understood as rational, instrumental and strategic or as idealistic, emotional and responsive to unconscious desires? The former implies responsiveness to external forces such as environmental pressure; the latter implies internal motivations. Second, is social order understood primarily as a product of history, existing outside of individual acts, or it is viewed as originating from negotiations among individuals? The former is a collectivist or cultural perspective; the contrasting individualistic position is attractive because it maintains a central role for individual freedom (Alexander, 1998). Parsonian functionalism is a natural starting point for the attempt to integrate the behavioural and macro-social streams of modern sociology, because it combines individual action and collective order (culture) in a unified theoretical framework (Alexander, 1998).

Neofunctionalism is better viewed as a broad school of thought with many variations than as a discrete theory (Alexander, 1998). Among those to whom the neofunctionalist label has been applied are Niklas Luhman in Germany, G. A. Cohen in the UK and Jeffrey Alexander in the US.[4] In Alexander's view, neofunctionalism should not be thought of as providing explanations, but rather as a description of the 'symbiotic relationships between social institutions and their environment, taking equilibrium (stability) as a reference point for analysis, *rather than as something*

which necessarily exists in reality, and treating structural differentiation as a major form of social change' (Marshall, 1998, p. 242,
emphasis added). Cohen similarly argued that certain features of
the social environment encourage the continuation of institutions,
without necessarily having caused them to come into being (Marshall,
1998). By these developments, neofunctionalists soften the concept
of 'function'. Whereas functionalists viewed functions as *causing*
social structures; neofunctionalists view them as 'social selection
mechanisms' (Maryanski and Turner, 2000).

The biological and systems theory origins of functionalism can
still be seen in neofunctionalist positions. However, neofunction-
ists' avoidance of explanation averts the charges of determinism
that plague functionalism. Nevertheless, positioning neofunctionalism as a descriptive framework rather than a type of explanation does not eliminate the concern formerly raised against
Parsonian functionalism—that it is merely a theoretical 'category
system'. Furthermore, this repositioning raises new concerns about
whether and how neofunctionalism relates to empirical sociological
research (Abrahamson, 2001).

In short, neofunctionalism integrates micro and macro sociology (Alexander, 1998) by preserving Parsonian distinctions among
individuals, culture and society, while eliminating the 'baggage of
functional requisites' (Maryanski and Turner, 2000, p. 1031) that
comprises the 'determinism of systems theory' (Marshall, 1998,
p. 242). But critics of neofunctionalism (similarly to Giddens' critics, see Jones, Orlikowski and Munir, this volume) contend that its
relationship with empirical research is far from clear (Abrahamson,
2001). In the paradigm's defence, neofunctionalist Jeffrey Alexander asserts that theoretical synthesis is of value in and of itself,
regardless of empirical fidelity or generativity of hypotheses for
empirical research.

Recap

As a grand social theory, functionalism was an explicit force in
sociology and an implicit thread in deterministic Marxist theory
throughout the twentieth century (Marshall, 1998). With its concerns for homeostasis and feedback loops, functionalism draws
analogies from the biological sciences. It is probably best understood as a form of general systems theory (Bertalanffy, 1969;
Miller, 1978) applied to the sociotechnical realm, although neofunctionalism strips away systems theory's more deterministic

aspects (Marshall, 1998). Because of its systems theory roots, the attraction of functionalism for the IS community should be strong.

Despite its prominence (or perhaps because of it), functionalism has been held in low repute in some sociological quarters for nearly 50 years (Douglas, 1986). Nevertheless, 'vibrant modes of functional analysis [persist] in many disciplines, both within and outside of the social sciences' (Maryanski and Turner, 2000, p. 1031). And some leading sociological thinkers (Alexander, 1998; Douglas, 1986; Stinchcombe, 1968) maintain that versions of functionalism (or at least functionalist explanations) retain certain advantages for the understanding of social behaviour. The next section identifies the core elements of functionalist explanation.

THE FUNCTIONALIST APPROACH TO EXPLANATION

Whatever one makes of functionalism and neofunctionalism as grand or general social theories, functionalist *explanations* deserve separate analysis. This section outlines the elements of functionalist explanation and presents an illustration in the IS context.

Essential Elements

Functionalist explanation 'starts by identifying a problematic activity—one which seen in isolation appears to make no sense' (Mann, 1984, p. 128). That which functionalist argument attempts to explain can be a *behaviour pattern* such as the Hopi rain dance or the practice of magic among Pacific islanders; it can be a *social structure* such as the rules governing inheritance (Stinchcombe, 1968); it can be a *belief system* such as belief in an evil conspiracy (Douglas, 1986); or it can be a *'thought world'* such as the idea systems of science, art or religion (Douglas, 1986). In short, functionalist explanation tackles what sociology and anthropology refer to as culture, structures and action; in the IS domain, functionalist explanation could be employed for the understanding of 'technological frames' (Orlikowski, 1993), IT 'appropriations' (DeSanctis and Poole, 1994), IS governance and/or control mechanisms (Kirsch, 1997), technologies-in-practice (Orlikowski, 2000) and so on.

The next step in functionalist explanation is to identify the function that explains the problematic activity. Once a problematic 'activity' has been identified, functionalist explanation places 'this activity. . . in a wider social context [where it is] shown to be meeting some social need(s) [that is, the function of the activity]. Identifying the function constitutes the explanation of the activity' (Mann, 1984, p. 128).

As noted above, controversy surrounds the latter aspect of functionalist methodology. Many critics have argued that functionalist explanations are incomplete unless they show precisely how the function 'causes' or maintains the behaviour or thought pattern of which the function is a consequence. Thus, complete functionalist explanations have these main elements (Stinchcombe, 1968):

1. The consequence (or function or 'homeostatic variable'), which empirically tends to be stable despite forces that tend to change it.
2. A 'structure' (or pattern of behaviour or belief system) that is to be explained; the causal connection between the structure and the consequence is what maintains the consequence.
3. Forces (or tensions or difficulties) that tend to destabilize the function, because, if the function would happen anyway, there would be no need for a structure to maintain it (or for a functionalist explanation).
4. A feedback loop from the consequence to the structure, such that the structure is maintained or reinforced.

Stinchcombe (1968) pictures functionalist explanations as shown in Figure 2.1.

Highly critical of functionalist explanations in the social sciences, Elster (1983) carefully articulated the conditions that good functionalist explanations have to satisfy (and claimed to find very few social science examples that meet these conditions). According to Elster (1983, p. 57), an institution (i.e. a structure) or behaviour

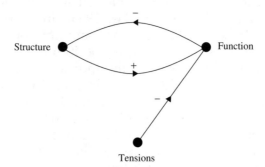

Figure 2.1 *Complete functionalist explanation, after Stinchcombe (1968)*

pattern can be persuasively explained by its function for a social group 'if and only if':

1. The function is actually a *consequence* of the structure.
2. The function is *beneficial* for the social group.
3. The function is *unintended* by the social group—in other words, the function is not a goal that people are attempting to bring about by their behaviour; instead, the function is a by-product of people's attempts to achieve some *other* goal.
4. The function (or at least the causal feedback loop between the structure and the function) is *not recognized* by the people (otherwise, it would be difficult to rule out an explanation in terms of rational choice or intentional goal-seeking behaviour).
5. The function maintains itself by a causal feedback loop that 'passes through' the people in the social group—in other words, whereas the function can be said to be a property of the group, it must be shown to be a by-product of *individual* actions.

Conditions 1 and 2 are true by the very definition of function. Conditions 3 and 4 are particularly important to ensure that functionalist explanations do not degenerate into deliberate goal-seeking behaviour by group members; that is, rational action (an explanation that Elster finds far more appropriate for the social sciences than functionalism). Condition 5 is essential not only to explain the persistence of the structure but also to ensure that the explanation does not degenerate into a teleological (deterministic) search for final causes. Without condition 5, functionalist explanations would exhibit the logical fallacy of explaining individual actions in terms of higher-level abstractions such as 'organizational efficiency tendencies' or 'market forces'.

Elster's chief objection to functionalist explanations in the social sciences was that he could find no social science analogue to the feedback loop of natural selection that is so important in the functionalist explanations of biology. He also complained that the function 'does not stay the same' in social science explanations but varies from explanation to explanation, unlike the function of reproductive advantage, which is invariant in biological functionalist explanations.

Despite Elster's contention that there are no social science selection mechanisms, Stinchcombe (1968) identified several:

- The behaviour may be selected by the differential survival of social groups who perform that behaviour (e.g. they perform better).

- The behaviour may be selected by people who plan to get beneficial consequences of that behaviour other than the function itself (i.e. people engage in the behaviour in order to get benefits other than the function; the function is a by-product).
- The behaviour may be maintained by people because they find its consequences (other than the function) satisfying, even though they did not plan to achieve these consequences (i.e. there are unintended positive consequences of the behaviour other than the function).
- The behaviour may have pleasant consequences for other people who reward those who engage in it (i.e. other people reward the group members because the unintended consequences of group members' behaviour are positive for those other people).
- The behaviour may benefit people who can control the conditions of the behaviour (i.e. group members' behaviour may benefit others who provide conditions that favour the group members' behaviour, e.g. education improves productivity, so employers mobilize support for the educational system).

Stinchcombe provided no ammunition for a response to Elster's complaint that the function in social science explanations does not stay the same from one context to another. He did, however, note that *behavioural* variety is an indicator that a functionalist explanation might be useful. When people who want something are foiled in their efforts to get it, they usually try another approach. Thus, uniformity in the *consequences* of action in the presence of a great variety of behaviours producing those consequences (a condition that systems theorists refer to as 'equifinality') strongly implies that people are motivated to achieve the function in the face of forces tending to disrupt it. Therefore, in his list of criteria of good functionalist explanations, Stinchcombe included one that is absent on Elster's list: tensions that threaten to disturb the function and may stimulate varied manifestations of the structure.

Stinchcombe's emphasis on motivated behaviour in the face of difficulties apparently supports Elster's contention that functionalist explanations are really rational choice explanations at base.[5] However, anthropologist Mary Douglas (1986) resolved the superficial contradiction. She agreed with Elster that the functions vary from one sociological functionalist explanation to the next, but she argued that the *reason* the function is beneficial often *does not* vary: the benefits of a thought or behaviour pattern for a social group often derive from the fact that the function contributes to the preservation of the group. Douglas also pointed out that, whereas people may like or desire the *benefit* of the function (e.g. group survival), they may not like or desire the function itself (in the case of Douglas's theory, belief in an evil conspiracy). Therefore, in many functionalist explanations, people cannot be argued to intend the function (thereby avoiding the degeneration of a functionalist explanation into a rational choice argument) and they may remain unconscious of the function and its links to their behaviour (thereby addressing one of Elster's key conditions). In this way, Douglas showed how behaviour intended to achieve one goal may achieve that goal but also have undesirable consequences that people are powerless to change. Thus, good functionalist explanations are potentially very useful for explaining the unintended consequences of intentional behaviours.

Douglas (1986) further elucidated the nature of functionalist explanations by pointing out that functions need not be behaviour patterns or activities, but can also be beliefs and 'thought worlds'. She disputed Elster's contention that there are few examples of good functionalist explanations in the social sciences. Although she agreed with Elster that the literature holds many bad or incomplete functionalist explanations, by using the criteria that Elster 'most helpfully' provided she identified several good ones and detailed one of her own. In so doing, she closed an important gap in economic theories of cooperation (collective action) and conflict.

Douglas's problem was that of how latent groups survive without collapsing or becoming formal groups. Latent groups are collections of people with common interests who have not coalesced into self-acknowledged social groups capable of taking collective action. According to Douglas, the consequences in modern society of the failure of latent groups to coalesce are major. (Think of life without parent–teacher associations, trade unions, political parties etc.) She first demonstrated that collective action is conceptually as problematic in small-scale and traditional societies as it is in large and modern ones. Then she explained how cooperation and solidarity coexist with rejection and mistrust in small-scale traditional societies.

Her explanation consisted of three related functionalist arguments. She first restated economic arguments about collective action as two functionalist arguments, as follows. By definition, the members of a latent group do not have strong interests in remaining in the group. Should members threaten to leave the group, their threat is always credible. The unintended and deplored consequence of a credible threat of withdrawal is weak leadership, which benefits members by enabling them to resist 'unwelcome demands' from a strong leader. Weak leadership in turn maintains the threat of withdrawal by preventing 'the development of coercive regulations' that would replace weak leadership with strong leadership.

Second, according to economic theory, achieving collective action in latent groups requires mechanisms to prevent free riding. Insisting on equality and 100 per cent participation creates, unintendedly and out of awareness, a well-defined boundary around the group, which benefits the group by consolidating membership. The boundary, in turn, maintains the equality rule by making free riding costly—the punishment for failure to participate equally is expulsion from the group.

Having restated economic theory as two functionalist cycles, Douglas's question was what pattern of beliefs could justify their simultaneous emergence. She found the answer in a third functionalist explanation based on anthropological evidence: accusations that members are betraying the founding principles of society create the unintended and unperceived effect of a shared belief in an evil conspiracy. This belief is beneficial for the society in checking exploitative behaviour. It maintains the pattern of mutual accusations because no other, more direct form of political action is possible in the face of weak leadership.

Putting all three cycles together into a single functionalist explanation, Douglas concluded that weak leadership and strong group boundaries produce conspiracy beliefs (the function). Conspiracy beliefs benefit the community by keeping the community together. They maintain the pattern that caused them (the feedback loop), in this case weak leadership and strong boundaries, in two ways. First, when community members suspect treachery (such as a would-be leader's attempt to impose unwanted regulations on the others), they expel the traitors, reinforcing the boundaries around those who remain. Second, the history of prior expulsions tends to curb the ambitions of would-be strong leaders, thus maintaining weak leadership. These effects (the feedback loop) are not perceived, nor is the function of conspiracy beliefs intended, because it is insulting to charge fellow members with duplicity. Thus, Douglas's useful explanation of how latent groups can survive as latent groups satisfies all of Elster's criteria for a good functionalist explanation.

The next section provides an IS illustration to clarify the elements of functionalist explanation and demonstrate its potential utility in IS domains.

Illustration in an IS Context

In a study of email use at HCP Inc, Markus (1994a, 1994b) reported both efficiency benefits and negative social consequences. Functionalist explanation sheds light on the emergence and persistence of these contradictory outcomes.

Email use at HCP Inc began in 1983 when the chairman of the company learned that a primitive email system, called 'Mail', had been bundled with the systems software on the company's minicomputer system. After a demonstration, he was convinced that email use would substantially improve efficiency and insisted that all managers in the company use it. When I studied the company in 1987, virtually all managers in the company were using email, many quite heavily, and they overwhelmingly attributed efficiency improvements to their use of Mail (Markus, 1994a).

At the same time, in interviews and in questionnaires, they reported numerous negative social consequences of email use, such as feelings of depersonalization, use of email as an excuse to avoid 'personal interactions' in emotional situations, use of email to publicly penalize people for various infractions and so forth. Recognizing that email use could have negative social effects, people at HCP Inc took steps to prevent or ameliorate negative outcomes, but the negative consequences occurred in spite of, and perhaps even *because of*, their preventive and corrective measures (Markus, 1994b).

This case is particularly appropriate for functionalist explanation because, at the time the data for the case study were collected, email use was not the commonplace feature of everyday organizational life it is today. In the late 1980s, email use was well entrenched mainly in a few high-tech companies and educational institutions, but HCP Inc was a health insurance company. The intensive usage of email observed at HCP Inc was quite uncommon in similar companies, and home email use was rare in society as a whole. People at HCP Inc had little access to outside sources of knowledge about how they were 'supposed' to use email, about how people in other companies used email, or about how technology vendors would eventually enhance email software to mirror users' emerging needs and work practices. HCP Inc's managers had to learn about email use by doing it, and what they learned is a microcosm of societal learning about electronic communication.

To reiterate, the methodology of functionalist explanation is to find the function served by a problematic activity and to show how the function reinforces the activity so that it persists. The emergence and persistence of negative social consequences of email use at HCP Inc are the 'problematic activity' to be explained. In a nutshell, the functionalist explanation attributes the negative social consequences to the shared belief at HCP Inc that Mail was the primary medium of work-related communication.

The chairman of HCP Inc insisted that people use Mail to gain efficiency benefits, but he did not (and could not) tell them *how* to do so. When people began experimenting with Mail, they quickly discovered its challenges as an organizational communication medium. There were several, such as the filtering out of cues about message senders and receivers, but worst perhaps was the problem of non-response. In an era before email use became an ingrained, unthinking habit, people did not check their messages regularly. Because notification of email messages waiting is *only available to people who check their email*, the chances were great that some people would not respond to the messages sent to them. For senders to follow up unanswered messages with telephone calls rewards non-response, and the collapse of email use is a likely result.

Collapse of email use was undesirable at HCP Inc, because email use was expected to produce efficiency benefits. Therefore, managers at HCP Inc required solutions to the problem of non-response and other technology-related challenges. (Table 2.1 lists tensions that threatened to destabilize email use and how they were overcome at HCP Inc.) Put differently, getting the efficiency benefits of email required that HCP Inc's employees develop email use patterns such as the regular checking for, and answering of, Mail messages.

How did this happen at HCP Inc? A shared understanding emerged of email as 'the primary medium of work-related communication at HCP Inc', first among the officers and later throughout the organization. This shared belief is the 'function' that explains the problematic activity (persistent negative social consequences). The function was beneficial to the people at HCP Inc by ensuring the achievement of a desired outcome (efficiency benefits). The function reinforced the problematic activity as follows (the feedback loop): belief that Mail was the primary medium of organizational communication promoted certain behaviours that overcame the challenges of email (the 'tensions' threatening to destabilize email use). For example, HCP managers answered phone messages with email messages, used email to schedule telephone calls, rarely held face-to-face meetings and disciplined people who did not use Mail

Table 2.1 *Tensions threatening organizational use of email and how they were overcome at HCP Inc*

Type of tension	How tension hindered use of Mail	How the tension was overcome at HCP Inc
Email filters out cues important for communication		
Cues about message originators and recipients are limited.	• The Mail system permitted 12-character user IDs that did not adequately identify the senders and intended receivers of email messages. • The Mail system lacked a 'c.c.' feature, requiring all recipients to be listed on the 'to' line, making it difficult to know who was expected to respond or take action.	• Users originally chose mnemonic email IDs that signified their organizational position; however, they were reluctant to change email IDs when they changed organizational roles, which led to great confusion over the identity of email senders; users adapted by nearly always using redundant salutations and signatures. • Using redundant salutations to name particular recipients when there were multiple individuals on the 'to' line made it clearer who was expected to take action and for whom the message was an 'FYI' (i.e. people on the 'to' line but not in the salutation).
Cues about the nature of the communication event and the meanings of message content are limited.	• The Mail system had only one communication mode (the 'message') that had to serve for various events such as formal meeting notices, informal conversations, etc. • Other than regular keyboard characters, the Mail system offered no features (e.g. no voice annotations, pictures, video clips) that could help clarify the meaning of a message.	• Users varied the degree of visual formatting and other stylistic elements to create at least three distinct communication 'genres' with varying degrees of formality: Memorandums, Reports and Messages; 'Messages' were differentiated by deliberately uncorrected typos and other errors that conveyed an informal tone. • Users distinguished urgent messages by using typographic energy, emotional appeals and personalization; however, they used these devices rarely so as not to dilute their usefulness.

(*continued overleaf*)

Table 2.1 (*continued*)

Type of tension	How tension hindered use of Mail	How the tension was overcome at HCP Inc
Email is an asynchronous communication medium		
Asynchronous email communication can inhibit the information exchange among group members that is necessary if email is to serve as a primary medium of organizational communication.	• Someone using the Mail system's REPLY feature would only reach the sender of the original message, no matter how many other recipients had been listed on the original message's 'to' line; when this happened, it broke the chain of group communication. • Because of time delays and multiple parallel communication streams, recipients of REPLYs could not always remember to which 'conversation' a particular message applied.	• Users routinely used the FORWARD feature in lieu of the REPLY feature, even though this involved more work (reentering the ID of the sender), because the message would go to all email IDs listed on the original message's 'to' line. • Using the FORWARD feature (although it required more work) had the added advantage of appending the original message, thus avoiding the problem of forgetting; by successively invoking the FORWARD feature, users created 'mosaic messages' by which they documented a discussion; mosaic messages could be used to bring a new person quickly up to speed about a topic.
Asynchronous communication raises the possibility of delays in message receipt and provides no clues about the reasons for non-response.	• Non-response to messages challenged continued use of email, because the likely reaction in the case of non-response is a follow-up telephone call, which is costly for the sender and fails to discipline the recipient for not responding to the message.	• Users sent important information only through email, thereby penalizing those who had not logged on; they subordinated the telephone to email by delaying responses to telephone messages, by requiring email scheduling of telephone calls and so forth, thus ensuring that recipients continued to use Mail; senders sometimes used 'shotgun messages' to get a response quickly without going through channels; this created enough havoc that people were motivated to check email regularly, so they would have a chance to contain the damage.

- Notification that there were messages waiting could only be received by people who were already logged into the Mail system; therefore it was possible that people would not respond to messages promptly.
- The Mail system offered no indication of why a recipient had not responded to a message, i.e. had the recipient not received it or was the recipient just ignoring it?

- People generally stayed logged on to Mail whenever they were at their desks, which gave them audible notification when messages arrived; they generally responded to messages as soon as they came in, simulating near-synchronous communication.
- Users developed norms about acceptable response times and formal procedures about how non-response to Mail messages should be handled via Mail rather than by phone, i.e. by putting 'Second (or third) request' in the 'SUBJECT' line, and keeping copies that could be, and were, used later when necessary to document 'lack of accountability' (unresponsiveness); eventually, the second or third response procedure was generalized to all failures of accountability, not just non-response to email; this use of 'forwarded documentation' contributed to an organizational culture characterized by low-level feelings of alienation and paranoia.

'appropriately'. People on the receiving end of these behaviours not only learned the behaviours through observation and imitation, they acquired the belief that Mail was the primary medium of work-related communication at HCP. Through their Mail use behaviour people at HCP Inc achieved the intended efficiency benefits, but they also (and unavoidably) experienced negative social outcomes such as stress, feelings of depersonalization, accountability game playing and so on.

HCP Inc's managers observed that their subordinates suffered in the absence of personal contact, and they tried to manage subordinates' stress with regular phone calls 'whether we need it or not for business purposes'. Nevertheless, preventive measures like these had limited success. Procedures put in place to prevent non-response to email spread to other situations: email was increasingly used to document and publicly chastise people for any failure of accountability. People throughout the organization came to experience Mail as a source of overload, stress, depersonalization and distancing from other people and the organization.

Table 2.2 shows how this *functionalist* explanation satisfies the criteria provided by Stinchcombe, Elster and Douglas. It is *not* a *rational choice* explanation. People at HCP Inc did intend to get the efficiency benefits of email, but they did not intend the negative social consequences. In fact, they deplored the negative outcomes and tried to prevent or ameliorate them. They also did not recognize that the negative consequences stemmed from the same source as the efficiency benefits they sought.

This explanation is also *not* a *historicist* explanation, such as one derived from institutionalism. A behaviour pattern with negative social consequences persisted (for a while[6]) at HCP Inc, not because it existed elsewhere and spread, nor because it had existed at HCP Inc for a long time in the past. It persisted because of an emergent local belief system of fairly recent origin, and it collapsed when the new leadership of the company did not buy into those beliefs.

Finally, this explanation it is *not* a *causal* explanation that might, for example, attribute the behaviour pattern solely to the directive of the chairman or to the features of email. Although the chairman's directive initiated Mail use and although features of the Mail system shaped the email use patterns observed at HCP Inc, the precise form of email use at HCP Inc owes much to emergent 'culture'—the belief in, and use of, email as the primary medium of work-related communication at HCP Inc.

Table 2.2   *A functionalist explanation of negative consequences of email use*

Essential elements	Illustration
Structure to be explained	Patterns of email use at HCP Inc (e.g. not scheduling meetings, use of FORWARD in lieu of REPLY, aggressive uses of email to establish accountability failures) that result in persistent, unintended negative social consequences, such as feelings of depersonalization, deterioration in organizational culture etc.
Function	Shared belief in email as 'the primary medium of communication at HCP Inc' (e.g. in lieu of frequent face-to-meetings and telephone calls).
Destabilizing tensions	Email filters out social cues that communicators need to interpret certain communications, and it is an asynchronous communication medium with high potential for non-response. Considerable ingenuity is needed to overcome these limitations so that email can be used successfully as a primary organizational communication medium.
Causal loop passing through the social group by which the function maintains the structure	Belief that email was the primary medium of organizational communication at HCP Inc reinforced behaviour patterns such as not scheduling meetings, answering phone calls by email etc.
Warrants that the function is a consequence of the structure	Email use behaviours such as answering phone messages by email, requiring phone conversations to be scheduled, infrequent face-to-face meetings, communicating important information only via email etc. taught recipients that email was the primary medium of organizational communication at HCP Inc.
Warrants that the function is beneficial for the social group	Using email in ways that maintain a group history of the communication provide efficiency benefits relative to paper memos, telephone calls and face-to-face meetings.
Warrants that the function is unintended by the social group	People at HCP Inc did not set out to make email their primary medium of organizational communication nor to achieve negative social consequences: their goal was to achieve efficiency benefits; the function and negative social consequences were unintended consequences of the way they achieved their efficiency goals.
Warrants that the function (or at least the feedback loop between function and structure) is not recognized by group members	People at HCP Inc *were* aware of their shared belief that email was their primary medium of organizational communication. They were *not* aware that this function reinforced email use patterns that produced the negative social impacts that they deplored. They were unable to explain convincingly why they used Mail's features in certain ways (e.g. FORWARD in lieu of REPLY) with functional consequences.

Recap

Although functionalism as a grand social theory has largely been discredited, 'functionalism... still has a place in sociology—albeit a more restricted place than when the Parsonian version was dominant' (Marshall, 1998, p. 243). That more restricted place is functionalist explanation.

> Sociology can so little afford to do without functionalist arguments that one starts to look suspiciously at the anti-functionalist platform... Without a functionalist form of argument, we cannot begin to explain how a thought world constructs the thought style that controls its existence. (Douglas, 1986, pp. 42–3)

Functionalist explanation not only addresses the *construction* of beliefs and behaviour patterns, it also explains their persistence; that is, how they 'start to stabilize [or settle] into recognizable shape' (Douglas, 1986, p. 111). Functionalist explanation does this by seeing practices 'in relationship to the whole system in which they occur [which] is functionalism's major contribution to society' (Mann, 1984, p. 139).

FUNCTIONALISM IN INFORMATION SYSTEMS RESEARCH

To what extent does IS research employ the functionalist or neofunctionalist paradigm? Are there new opportunities in the IS field for research based on the functionalist or neofunctionalist paradigm? The next sections address these questions.

IS/IT Strategic Alignment Research

To my knowledge, no IS research has explicitly employed the functionalist or neofunctionalist paradigm, with the exception of the email example I gave above. Still, it is possible that the functionalist paradigm figures *implicitly* in IS theory and research.

The MIT research programme entitled 'The Corporation of the 1990s' introduced the IS field to a conceptual model with apparent origins in the paradigm of functionalism. The MIT90s framework (Scott Morton, 1991), which sought to explain how IT contributes to organizational transformation, depicted the elements of strategy, structure, (information) technology, individuals and roles, and management processes arranged in mutual alignment, with management processes as the central element. The model hypothesized that 'IT should affect the tasks in the organization and ultimately its strategy' (Scott Morton, 1991, p. 19), although at that time little evidence in support of the hypothesis had been found.

The justification for this model directly alluded to the concept of homeostasis that figures so prominently in functionalist imagery:

> An organization can be thought of as comprised of five sets of forces in dynamic equilibrium among themselves even as the organization is subjected to influences from an external environment. (Scott Morton, 1991, pp. 19–20)

No explicit sources were cited in support of the MIT90s model, but it bears strong resemblance to the McKinsey 7-S Model, publicized about a decade earlier. The 7-S Model was developed in the late 1970s to explain why Japanese companies seemed so much more effective than their American counterparts (Pascale and Athos, 1981). Fit among three 'hard' Ss (strategy, structure, systems) and four 'soft' Ss (shared values/superordinate goals, skills, staff and style) were prescribed for all organizations that wanted to achieve excellence (Peters and Waterman, 1982). In graphical renderings of the model, shared values/superordinate goals were depicted as the central core through which the other elements were connected.

The MIT90s model stimulated some empirical research outside the MIT research programme, notably the 1994 case study of Yetton, Johnston and Craig (1994), in which business strategy was seen to evolve from the adoption of new IT rather than the other way around. A later product of the MIT90s research, the strategic alignment model of Henderson and Venkatraman (1992), generated even more empirical research and continues to do so to this day.[7] The strategic alignment model brought together four key domains: business strategy, organizational infrastructure and processes, IT strategy, and IT infrastructure and processes. These four domains could be interconnected by different types of relationships, in which two, three or all four domains could be in alignment. Organizational effectiveness was hypothesized to increase as more of the domains became aligned (Henderson and Venkatraman, 1992).

Although the MIT90s and IS/IT strategic alignment models share some common elements with functionalism, closer inspection against Elster's (1983) criteria shows that a few key elements are missing. Let's consider them in turn. The structure to be explained in this case is strategic alignment, and the 'function' that provides benefits to an organization is improved organizational performance.

1. The function is actually a consequence of the structure. *Satisfied*: that improved organizational performance is actually a consequence of IS/IT strategic alignment is demonstrated by research such as Chan *et al.* (1997).
2. The function is beneficial for the organization. *Satisfied*: most people agree that improved organizational performance is indeed beneficial for organizations.
3. The function is unintended by the organization. *Not satisfied*: here is where IS/IT strategic alignment breaks down *as a functionalist explanation*. It is very difficult to claim that the managers of organizations with improved performance do not intend for that outcome to occur. Although organizational performance improvement can occur for reasons unrelated to managerial intentions (e.g. by chance), this contingency does not help functionalist explanation, which must demonstrate a link between the function and the structure (cf. criterion 1).
4. The function (or the feedback loop) is not recognized by people. *Not satisfied*: again, it is most unlikely that managers are unaware of organizational performance, or of steps they take to improve organizational performance, such as actions taken to improve IS/IT strategic alignment (cf. criterion 5).
5. The function maintains itself by a causal feedback loop passing through the organization. *Satisfied*: presumably, managers who are aware that lack of alignment is a problem take steps to improve alignment (Sabherwal, Hirschheim and Goles, 2001).
6. (Stinchcombe's criterion) There are forces that threaten to destabilize the function. *Satisfied*: most people would agree that ability to maintain either strategic alignment or organizational performance at a high-level steady state is problematic owing to changing environmental conditions (Sabherwal, Hirschheim and Goles, 2001) such as competition.

In short, despite superficial similarities, IS/IT strategic alignment models are *not* functionalist explanations, because they fail to satisfy criteria 3 and 4 above. Instead, they are *rational choice* explanations, something that most strategic alignment researchers make clear. For example, Henderson and Venkatraman (1992) specifically referred to the elements of their model as 'domains of strategic *choice*' (p. 99, emphasis added). Chan *et al.* (1997) noted that their model involved 'realized IS strategies', because '*intended* strategies may not be realized' (p. 126, emphasis added). Sabherwal, Hirschheim and Goles (2001) argued that non-alignment persisted for some period of time in case study companies, because '*top executives believed that IS was not strategic and so it did not need to be aligned* with business' (p. 193, emphasis added) and because managers were reluctant to make revolutionary changes to modify the strategic IS management profile.

The functionalist paradigm, then, seems not to have figured prominently in IS research, even implicitly. The question remains whether there are worthwhile opportunities to apply it.

Opportunities in IS Research

Although IS/IT strategic alignment research does not employ the functionalist paradigm, it does suggest at least one important research question that might prove amenable to functionalist explanation. Sabherwal, Hirschheim and Goles (2001) noted that executives' *perception of IS as non-strategic* was a factor in strategic non-alignment. They also argued that significant changes in '*perceptions concerning IS*' triggered revolutions in strategic alignment. Theirs was not the first study to point to negative perceptions of IS/IT's strategic potential, and it will not be the last. Imagine, for example, the potential influence on today's chief executives of the recent *Harvard Business Review* article titled 'IT doesn't matter' (Carr, 2003).

Surely a 'problematic activity' to be explained is the widespread persistence of negative perceptions of IS/IT's strategic potential in the face of incontrovertible evidence that IT does deliver business value (Brynjolfsson and Hitt, 2000) and that IS/IT does appear to be shaping the nature of competition in many industries? Is the beneficial function of this negative 'thought world' about IT that it keeps IT hiring and investment low or that it assuages the anxiety of technology-illiterate executives? Whatever the answer to this question, it is certainly interesting and important to the IS community, and functionalist explanation may be the key.

Functionalist explanation is also particularly useful for illuminating the unintended consequences of information technology use, as the email example showed. This is a topic area that clearly has not received adequate attention by the IS community (Markus and Robey, 2004). In addition, the potential benefit of functionalist explanation in studies of information technology 'framing' (Davidson, 2002), 'appropriation' (DeSanctis and Poole, 1994) and IT use in practice (Orlikowski, 2000) is that it provides a framework for fine-grained analyses of IT features as they relate to social practices. Thus, functionalist explanation provides one way to heed recent calls for putting technology back into information systems research (Benbasat and Zmud, 2003; Orlikowski and Iacono, 2001).

Finally, functionalist explanation can inform studies of specific IS management processes. The evolution of IT governance mechanisms (Sambamurthy and Zmud, 1999), control strategies (Kirsch, 1997), outsourcing arrangements (Lacity and Willcocks, 1998) and so on can all be examined through a functionalist lens. Functionalist explanation can also shed light on IT standards-setting processes (Damsgaard and Lyytinen, 2001) and the emergence of IS 'organizing visions' (Swanson and Ramiller, 1997). In short, functionalist explanation can be applied to many IS research topics and affords a promising approach to the analysis of distinctly IS concerns.

Concerns and Limitations

Although functionalist explanation holds promise for information systems research, several potential limitations should be noted. First, attempts to employ functionalist explanations in IS research are likely to be hindered by methodological challenges. The statistical research methods commonly used to examine IS research hypotheses are not well suited to the analysis of the feedback loops in functionalist explanations. Research approaches that are better adapted to the study of feedback loops, such as systems dynamics (Dutta and Roy, 2002; Forrester, 1961), have only occasionally been used by members of the IS research community.[8]

Second, the basic causal mechanism of functionalist explanation is *negative feedback*, which maintains 'problematic activities' at a constant level. Functionalist explanation does not afford a way to explain behaviour systems characterized by positive feedback, in which activities are reinforced, possibly to the point where a system spirals out of control. For situations that exhibit *positive feedback*, explanations rooted in systems dynamics (Dutta and Roy, 2002; Forrester, 1961) or complexity theories (Anderson *et al.*, 1999; Dooley and Van de Ven, 1999) such as catastrophe and chaos theories (Thietart and Forgues, 1995) or complex adaptive systems theory (Anderson, 1999) are more appropriate.

Third, the use of functionalist explanations in IS is likely to come under attack by strong social constructivists and interpretivists who believe that it is not legitimate to study social phenomena using an 'etic' or outsider's (researcher's) lens (see also Chapters 4 and 9). Strong constructivists argue that the only legitimate social analyses are those that seek to understand ideas and behaviour in 'emic' terms—what these phenomena mean to participants. In response to such a critique, the researcher can only reply (without much hope of convincing) that the functions of functionalist explanations often *are* the meanings attributed to behaviours and events by participants. Recall that, in the case of email use at HCP Inc, the participants, not the researcher, understood and described email as their 'primary means of work-related communication'.

However, functionalist explanations do depart from purely interpretive accounts by showing how, when participants act in accordance with their beliefs, they produce outcomes that they acknowledge to exist, but that they deplore, did not intend to produce and feel powerless to change, in part because they cannot see how their own behaviour contributes to the results. Strong interpretivists generally would not concern themselves with the etic phenomenon of unintended consequences caused by patterns of ideas and behaviour of which participants are unaware.

Functionalism's unconventional blend of emic understanding and etic analysis (interpretation, even) may not satisfy strict constructivists, but it can provide the insight into social dynamics needed for successful intervention. In an applied field like information systems with an eye to improved practice, unconventional approaches should be acceptable, if they work.

A GUIDE TO THE LITERATURE

Talcott Parsons is generally viewed as the leading spokesman of the functionalist paradigm. The core principles of functionalism are developed in his major works, including:

Parsons, T. (1937/1949) *The Structure of Social Action*, New York, NY: McGraw-Hill.
Parsons, T. (1951) *The Social System*, New York, NY: Free Press.
Parsons, T. (1966) *Societies*, Englewood Cliffs, NJ: Prentice-Hall.
Parsons, T. and Smelser, N. J. (1956) *Economy and Society*, New York, NY: Free Press.

Arthur L. Stinchcombe delineated the essential elements of the logic of functional explanations in Chapter 3 of Stinchcombe, A. L. (1968) *Constructing Social Theories*, New York, NY: Harcourt Brace & World.

Jon Elster argued that causal and intentional (rational choice) explanations were more appropriate for the social sciences than were the functionalist explanations that are widely used in biology. In support of his points, he developed a list of criteria that good functionalist explanations have to meet, elaborating on Stinchcombe's analysis, in Elster, J. (1983) *Explaining Technical Change: A Case Study in the Philosophy of Science*, Cambridge: Cambridge University Press.

Mary Douglas used Elster's list of criteria to show that functionalist explanations, while often incomplete, are indispensable in modern social science: Douglas, M. (1986) *How Institutions Think*, Syracuse, NY: Syracuse University Press.

Jeffrey Alexander helped revive interest in Parsonian functionalism and launch the neofunctionalist school of thought in:

Alexander, J. C. (1983) *The Modern Reconstruction of Classical Thought: Talcott Parsons*, Berkeley, CA: University of California Press.

Alexander, J. C. (1985) *Neofunctionalism*, Beverly Hills, CA: Sage.

Alexander, J. C. (1998) *Neofunctionalism and After*, Malden, MA: Blackwell.

Mark Abrahamson provided the historical context of functionalism and neofunctionalism in his useful handbook chapter: Abrahamson, M. (2001) 'Functional, conflict and neofunctional theories', in G. Ritzer and B. Smart (eds), *Handbook of Social Theory*, Thousand Oaks, CA: Sage, pp. 141–51.

ENDNOTES

[1] Some trace functionalism's origins even earlier to Herbert Spencer (circa 1865) (Maryanski and Turner, 2000).

[2] To respond to these critics, scholars such as Lewis Coser (circa 1950–60) extended functionalism into what has been called 'conflict theory', which Abrahamson contends has been squeezed by 'the convergence of neo-Marxian and neofunctional theories' (Abrahamson, 2001).

[3] Heckathorn (1997) mentions Elster's distinction between objective and subjective teleology. Objective teleology, which involves the appearance of purpose in the absence of an intentional actor, is the type indicated here. Subjective teleology is individual rational decision making. To avoid confusion, I reserve the term 'teleological' for objective teleology and use the term rational choice in lieu of subjective teleology.

[4]One authority also attributes neofunctionalist leanings to Jürgen Habermas (Abrahamson, 2001).

[5]Stinchcombe's emphasis on people's motivation to achieve the function is apparently at odds with Elster's insistence that the function must be unintended and out of awareness. However, Stinchcombe's examples convince me that Stinchcombe's functionalist explanation is not the simple 'rational choice' that Elster prefers. Stinchcombe's emphasis is on how rules and other structures 'tend to grow' towards socially important ends rather than on how individuals deliberately set out to create specific rules and structures.

[6]The behaviour pattern collapsed when HCP Inc ran into hard times and the top management team was replaced. This event underscores the pattern's roots in organizational culture rather than in external social or causal forces.

[7]Examples include Chan *et al.* (1997); Palmer and Markus (2000); and Sabherwal, Hirschheim and Goles (2001).

[8]Examples include Kanungo (2003); Abdel-Hamid (1988); Akkermans and van Helden (2002); and Dutta (2001).

REFERENCES

Abdel-Hamid, T. K. (1988) 'The economics of software quality assurance: A simulation-based case study', *MIS Quarterly*, 12(3): 395–411.

Abrahamson, M. (2001) 'Functional, conflict and neofunctional theories', in G. Ritzer and B. Smart (eds), *Handbook of Social Theory*, Thousand Oaks, CA: Sage, pp. 141–51.

Akkermans, H. A. and van Helden, K. (2002) 'Vicious and virtuous cycles in ERP implementation: A case study of interrelations between critical success factors', *European Journal of Information Systems*, 11: 35–46.

Alexander, J. C. (1998) *Neofunctionalism and After*, Malden, MA: Blackwell.

Anderson, P. (1999) 'Complexity theory and organizational science', *Organization Science*, 10(3): 216–32.

Anderson, P., Meyer, A., Eisenhardt, K., Carley, K. and Pettigrew, A. (1999) 'Introduction to the special issue: Applications of complexity theory to organization science', *Organization Science*, 10(3): 233–6.

Benbasat, I. and Zmud, R. W. (2003) 'The identity crisis within the IS discipline: Defining and communicating the discipline's core properties', *MIS Quarterly*, 27(2): 183–94.

Bertalanffy, L. von (1969) *General System Theory: Foundations, Development, Applications*, New York, NY: G. Braziller.

Brynjolfsson, E. and Hitt, L. M. (2000) 'Beyond computation: Information technology, organizational transformation and business performance', *Journal of Economic Perspectives*, 14(4): 23–48.

Carr, N. G. (2003) 'IT doesn't matter', *Harvard Business Review*, 81(5): 41–8.

Chan, Y. E., Huff, S. L., Barclay, D. W. and Copeland, D. G. (1997) 'Business strategic orientation, information systems strategic orientation, and strategic alignment', *Information Systems Research*, 8(2): 125–50.

Damsgaard, J. and Lyytinen, K. (2001) 'The role of intermediating institutions in the diffusion of electronic data interchange (EDI): How industry associations intervened in Denmark, Finland, and Hong Kong', *The Information Society*, 17(3): 195–210.

Davidson, E. J. (2002) 'Technology frames and framing: A socio-cognitive investigation of requirements determination', *MIS Quarterly*, 26(4): 329–58.

DeSanctis, G. and Poole, M. S. (1994) 'Capturing the complexity in advanced technology use: Adaptive structuration theory', *Organization Science*, 5(2): 121–47.

Dooley, K. J. and Van de Ven, A. H. (1999) 'Explaining complex organizational dynamics', *Organization Science*, 10(3): 358–72.

Douglas, M. (1986) *How Institutions Think*, Syracuse, NY: Syracuse University Press.

Dutta, A. (2001) 'Business planning for network services: A systems thinking approach', *Information Systems Research*, 12(3): 260–83.

Dutta, A. and Roy, R. (2002) 'System dynamics', *OR/MS Today*, June: 30–35.

Elster, J. (1983) *Explaining Technical Change: A Case Study in the Philosophy of Science*, Cambridge: Cambridge University Press.

Forrester, J. W. (1961) *Industrial Dynamics*, Cambridge, MA: MIT Press.

Heckathorn, D. D. (1997) 'The paradoxical relationship between sociology and rational choice', *The American Sociologist*, 28(2): 6–15.

Henderson, J. C. and Venkatraman, N. (1992) 'Strategic alignment: A model for organizational transformation through information technology', in T. A. Kochan and M. Unseem (eds), *Transformating Organizations*, New York, NY: Oxford University Press, pp. 97–116.

Kanungo, S. (2003) 'Using systems dynamics to operationalize process theory in information systems research', *Twenty-Fourth International Conference on Information Systems*, Seattle, WA, pp. 450–63.

Kirsch, L. J. (1997) 'Portfolios of control modes and IS project management', *Information Systems Research*, 8(3): 215–40.

Lacity, M. C. and Willcocks, L. P. (1998) 'An empirical investigation of information sourcing practices: Lessons from experience', *MIS Quarterly*, 22(3): 363–408.

Mann, M. (ed.) (1984) 'Functionalism', *The International Encyclopedia of Sociology*, New York, NY: Continuum, pp. 138–9.

Markus, M. L. (1994a) 'Electronic mail as the medium of managerial choice', *Organization Science*, 5(4): 502–27.

Markus, M. L. (1994b) 'Finding a happy medium: Explaining the negative effects of electronic mail on social life at work', *ACM Transactions on Information Systems*, 12(2): 119–49.

Markus, M. L. and Robey, D. (2004) 'Why stuff happens: Explaining the unintended consequences of using information technology', in M. T. Vendelo and K. V. Andersen (eds), *The Past and Future of Information Systems*, London: Butterworth-Heinemann.

Marshall, G. (ed.) (1998) 'Function, functionalism', *Oxford Dictionary of Sociology*, Oxford: Oxford University Press, pp. 241–3.

Maryanski, A. and Turner, J. H. (2000) 'Functionalism and structuralism', in E. F. Borgatta (ed.), *Encyclopedia of Sociology*, New York, NY: Macmillan Reference USA, pp. 1029–37.

Miller, J. G. (1978) *Living Systems*, New York, NY: McGraw-Hill.

Orlikowski, W. J. (1993) 'Learning from notes: Organizational issues in groupware development', *The Information Society*, 9(3): 237–50.

Orlikowski, W. J. (2000) 'Using technology and constituting structures: A practice lens for studying technology in organizations', *Organization Science*, 11(4): 404–28.

Orlikowski, W. J. and Iacono, C. S. (2001) 'Research commentary: Desperately seeking "IT" in IT research—A call to theorizing the IT artifact', *Information Systems Research*, 12(2): 121–34.

Palmer, J. W. and Markus, M. L. (2000) 'The performance impact of quick response and strategic alignment in specialty retailing', *Information Systems Research*, 11(3): 241–59.

Pascale, R. T. and Athos, A. G. (1981) *The Art of Japanese Management: Applications for American Executives*, New York, NY: Simon and Schuster.

Peters, T. J. and Waterman, R. H. (1982) *In Search of Excellence*, New York, NY: Harper & Row.

Sabherwal, R., Hirschheim, R. and Goles, T. (2001) 'The dynamics of alignment: Insights from a punctuated equilibrium model', *Organization Science*, 12(2): 179–97.

Sambamurthy, V. and Zmud, R. W. (1999) 'Arrangements for information technology governance: A theory of multiple contingencies', *MIS Quarterly*, 23(2): 261–90.

Scott Morton, M. S. (ed.) (1991) *The Corporation of the 1990s: Information Technology and Organizational Transformation*, Oxford: Oxford University Press.

Stinchcombe, A. L. (1968) *Constructing Social Theories*, New York, NY: Harcourt Brace & World.

Swanson, E. B. and Ramiller, N. C. (1997) 'The organizing vision in information systems innovation', *Organization Science*, 8(5): 458–74.

Thietart, R. A. and Forgues, B. (1995) 'Chaos theory and organization', *Organization Science*, 6(1): 19–31.

Yetton, P. W., Johnston, K. D. and Craig, J. F. (1994) 'Computer-aided architects: A case study of IT and strategic change', *Sloan Management Review*, 35(4): 57–67.

3
Phenomenology, Screens, and the World: A Journey with Husserl and Heidegger into Phenomenology

Lucas D. Introna and Fernando M. Ilharco

Phenomenology, as a philosophical underpinning as well as a method of investigation, is currently used in a wide range of fields, such as anthropology, sociology, history, management, design, media, psychology, psychiatry, biology, mathematics, philosophy, education and so forth. It has also been used in information systems research (e.g. Boland, 1983, 1985, 1991, 1993; Boland and Day, 1989; Ciborra, 1997, 1998; Dreyfus, 1982, 1992; Haynes, 1997; Ilharco, 2002; Introna, 1993, 1997; Introna and Ilharco, 2000; Introna and Whittaker, 2002; Kjaer and Madsen, 1995; Mingers, 2001; Porra, 1999; Whittaker, 2001; Winograd and Flores, 1986; Zuboff, 1988). Although this chapter is written within this tradition of research, it will endeavour to do something more unusual. It will attempt to provide a coherent, straightforward account of phenomenology, apply it to the analysis of the phenomenon of 'screen', provide a critical assessment of it, and point to some existing work available to those who may want to take up the possibilities it offers. This is an ambitious task to accomplish in one chapter. As a result, many important questions may have to be left unexplored. Nevertheless, we hope the chapter will serve as a platform from which those interested can approach the literature of the phenomenology movement.

Before proceeding, one can legitimately ask: Why invest time and energy in studying phenomenology? We would claim that phenomenology can be seen as a radical answer to the ongoing ideological standoff between a sort of positive naturalism, which argues for general objective accounts of the world as directly given through our observations, and an interpretive approach, which argues for the importance of ongoing socially shared, subjective meaning. Phenomenology provides this radical answer by showing that meaning is not an idiosyncratic, subjectively constructed 'inner' domain, but rather an ongoing, objective public domain of *necessary* relations or references. More formally put, for phenomenology meaning is not 'in' the thing (word, object, action, event, subject etc.). Rather, it is 'in' the nexus of *necessary relations or references* for the thing (word, object, action, event, subject etc.) *to be what it is already taken as*, when taken up in our ongoing activity in everyday life. It is this radical insight that we hope to make clear through this chapter. It is also this radical insight that a widely cited commentator such as Leedy (1997, p. 161) seems to miss when he defines phenomenology, incorrectly, within the subjectivist paradigm—as 'a research method that attempts to understand *participants' perspectives and views* of social realities' (emphasis added).

Phenomenology is still mostly attached to its philosophical origins, namely the works of Husserl, Heidegger and Merleau-Ponty. This philosophical rootedness is characteristic not only of phenomenology but also of all intellectual endeavours. However, in the case of phenomenology, as Sanders (1982) commented when using phenomenology in organizational research, the relative newness of the technique, its dense and complex technical terminology, and the apparent absence of precise methodological procedures contributed to impairing the widespread usage of the approach in many fields of the social sciences. Indeed, phenomenology's cardinal works, namely Husserl's *Cartesian Meditations* (1995) and *The Crisis of European Sciences and Transcendental Phenomenology* (1970a), Heidegger's *Being and Time* (1962) and Merleau-Ponty's *Phenomenology of Perception* (1962), do not themselves give an explicit and systematic account of the phenomenological methods applied. To a great extent, the phenomenological technical terminology and central notions are presented only in their application within specific research concerns. This critique is valid for the works of the phenomenological movement as a whole.

Nonetheless, the phenomenological approach and method of investigation seems to have been a clarified and unproblematic issue among phenomenologists for almost all of the twentieth century. Its phases and technical notions were part of the shared background of the phenomenological movement. It was Herbert Spiegelberg, in 1959 with the work *The Phenomenological Movement: A Historical Introduction*, who first attempted a clear and systematic presentation of the key concepts, phases and respective steps of the phenomenological method of investigation. Spiegelberg's work has become a standard reference point for all phenomenologists. Still, it is doubtful if one can readily access it without a good grounding in the main works of the field; hence the need for this chapter.

As with many other methodological approaches, the phenomenological method has a number of core central traits, which have been used in all phenomenological investigations. On account of the specific issue under inquiry, other features might be used as they prove to be useful to the investigation. In this chapter we attempt to follow the traditional phenomenological approach as synthesized in Spiegelberg (1994). In our discussion and analysis we draw only on the literature of the phenomenological movement. We hope that our exclusively phenomenological approach will provide a significant theoretical and methodological contribution to the information systems field. This is timely, since the phenomenological movement is currently experiencing a new growth period, as is clear from the recent publication of a number of introductory works in the field (e.g. Moran, 2000; Sokolowski, 2000). Before proceeding, we must note that there are many different ways in which one could 'do' phenomenology. One could, for example, explicitly follow the phenomenological method, as we will in the analysis of the screen below. Nevertheless, one could also 'do' it in other ways, such as applying the results of previous phenomenological analysis, or using phenomenological assumptions and insights as grounding principles for one's work; there is simply not just 'one way' to use phenomenology.

The rest of the chapter is structured as follows. We start with a discussion of the key concepts central to phenomenology, pointing out some distinctive features and making some contrasts within the phenomenology movement. We then provide a brief discussion of the phenomenological method. Thereafter, we demonstrate the value of the phenomenological approach and method by doing a phenomenological analysis of the phenomenon 'screen'. This is followed by some critiques of phenomenology as well as references to some other approaches that are related to or emerged from phenomenology. We conclude the chapter by pointing to some existing work in phenomenology that may serve as examples of how phenomenology may be used to inform future research in information systems.

WHAT IS PHENOMENOLOGY?

There is no simple answer to the question of what phenomenology is. We can say, as Husserl did, that phenomenology is 'a return to the things themselves'. But such a cryptic saying only means something if we understand that 'return', 'things' and 'themselves' here have some very specific meanings for the phenomenologist. How, then, will we proceed? One could, for example, give a historical answer by starting with a discussion of Husserl's (1964, 1970a, 1970b, 1995) main works, including his indebtedness to Brentano, and then show how this work was transformed by Heidegger and reinterpreted by Merleau-Ponty, Sartre and Levinas among others. This was done in the massive, now classic work by Spiegelberg (1994 [1959]) and more recently in the excellent, very readable account by Dermot Moran (2000). We could also give an exposition of the 'key concepts' and 'method' of phenomenology, as was done so well by Sokolowski (2000). We will not take either of these routes, however. We will rather present the distinctiveness of phenomenology by developing an account of the claim that phenomenology is a *transcendental* approach to our understanding of the world. In the ongoing evolution of phenomenology, the meaning and source of the 'transcendental' become transformed, redefined and reinterpreted by the various proponents.

Nevertheless, through the notion of 'transcendental' we can relate phenomenology to other approaches and explain why we believe it to be valuable and necessary for the information systems community. We hope to present this discussion in a simple manner with minimal recourse to the technicality of the phenomenological lexicon. To do this in a way that will show the distinctiveness of phenomenology, without becoming simplistic, will certainly not be an easy task. We must also emphasize that this is a very brief account and that any serious engagement with phenomenology requires a more in-depth study, for which the references provided at the end of the chapter are a good guide.

Husserlian Phenomenology

Phenomenology is a transcendental approach to our understanding of the world *as given and taken in ongoing experience.* To understand what this might mean, let us turn to a very mundane situation of experiencing something in the course of our everyday life. Let us take as our example our experience with a typical chair, standing in front of our desk in our office. What makes it possible for us to experience it—take it to be, see it, refer to it and so on—*as a chair* rather than as something else? This may sound like a strange question. However, we must be careful to note that the chair—or any other object, for that matter—is always only *given* to our senses as unordered sensations[1] and only in its aspect or one-sidedness. When we stand in 'front' of it the 'back' is not given to our senses as such. When we stand at the back the front is hidden from our senses. As far as our direct sensory encounter is concerned, we are always only given the unordered flux of perturbations of 'one side' of the chair at any particular time; that is, our senses operate in an unordered flux of one-dimensionality. Yet when we approach the chair we do not *take* it as a confusing flux of sensation, or as one side of a chair. Rather, we take it in its fullness of being, as that which it already is, a chair to sit on, stand on and so forth. Thus, we can ask: What is it that allows us to *take* it in its fullness, *as a chair*, even though we are only always, at any particular point in time, sensually given an unordered flux of an aspect of it?

Phenomenology will answer that it is the 'already there' *sense* that I have of chairs that allows me to take it as a chair, rather than as something else. This 'sense' emerged through my many situated experiences with a multiplicity of 'chair' objects—some made of wood, some of plastic, some of steel—in many different situations—in the bedroom, in the kitchen, outside on the patio and so on. Thus, through all these various situated and ongoing experiences, some 'sense' of what the object chair is—how to take it, see it, refer to it and use it—remained sufficiently stable in order for me to have ongoing situated experiences of chairs 'as chairs', rather than as some unordered flux of an aspect of something. This *ongoing sense* that we have of the world means that every experience we have of things, as the thing that they are, can never be wholly unprecedented, as if from scratch. If this was the case, then our ongoing experience of the world would be deeply perplexing and confusing. However, this is in fact not our normal experience; rather, we experience the world as mostly meaningful and familiar. Thus, in and through all our previous experiences with extended objects and chairs some sense 'remained', became sedimented in some way, which now provides the ongoing horizon or minimal condition of possibility for our ongoing 'taking' of this chair that we are now approaching to sit on 'as a chair' rather as something else. Let us suspend for the moment what this 'remainder' is and how it came about.

In phenomenology we refer to this ongoing persisting sense or 'remainder', that which constitutes the ongoing possibility for the taken extended object to be experienced 'as a chair', as the *transcendental* domain. More formally expressed, we could say 'the transcendental is that which *constitutes*, and thereby renders the empirical possible' (Mohanty, 1970, p. 52). For the more philosophically minded, it is important to make a distinction between Kant's (1965 [1787]) and Husserl's (1964, 1970a, 1970b) use of the notion of the 'transcendental'. For Kant—the originator of the notion—the transcendental is the *a priori categories of mind*—such as sensation and judgement—that make cognition possible as such. For Husserl, the transcendental is the *active, directed, ongoing life of consciousness* that is the necessary condition for our ongoing experience of the world to be meaningful as such.[2]

It is now possible to say that phenomenology, as a transcendental critique, was developed to question the assumptions of naturalism or empiricism, which starts with a world of 'already there' objects without asking the question: 'How is it possible to experience the object (a chair) as the object that it is, "as a chair", in the first instance?' (Mohanty, 1970). Thus, an empirically based science—such as positivism—does not start with that which is *given*—as the world is only given as an unordered flux and in its aspect or one-sidedness—but rather with that which is *always and already constituted*—the world of objects already taken as such by us. Positive empiricists then pose the question 'How can we know these objects' without realizing that the very possibility of experiencing the objects, as such and such an object, already implies a meaningful epistemic encounter that has its source elsewhere. This 'elsewhere' is the already active, already directed, ongoing life of consciousness. It is this active, ongoing, structural correlation—one can almost say ongoing structuration in Giddens' (1984) terms—of conscious life and the world that is the 'remainder' that we have suspended above and to which we will now turn our discussion.

For Husserl, consciousness is not some pre-existing blank slate, space or memory capacity 'in our heads' (an internal *subject* dimension) that somehow 'records' or captures a stream of sensations or representations of the world out there (an external *object* dimension), of which it then somehow makes sense. Rather, consciousness, to be conscious at all, is already an active meaning giving directedness towards the world. To be conscious is always and already[3] to be conscious of *something as this or that something*. Consciousness is always and already an act—an already active *taking* of the given world—that implies, as necessary, some already available sense or meaning that renders the act possible and meaningful. As conscious beings our relationship with the world is not some passive, disinterested, simply 'standing before' the world, being bombarded by an ongoing stream of confusing and unordered sensations. On the contrary, as we go about daily life (even if we sit passively in a chair) we find ourselves as always already *experiencing* the world in its fullness and the objects surrounding us *as something in particular*—as boring, interesting, hard, soft, a tree, a chair, a knife, useful, red, blue, cold, round, far, near and so on. However, such experiencing of the world 'as something' already suggests some simultaneously present sense (unity, meaning, or in Husserl's language a *noema*) of that which is being experienced—as interesting, hard, tree, chair, soft, useful, cold, far and near—that is the necessary condition or transcendental possibility for such an experience to be possible in the first place. Husserl (1969, pp. 233–4) formulates this fundamental ongoing unity of consciousness and the world in ongoing experience as follows:

> But experience is not an opening through which a world, existing prior to all experience, shines into a room of consciousness; it is not a mere taking of something alien to consciousness into consciousness... Experience is the performance in which for me, the experiencer, the experienced being 'is there', and is [already] there as what it is, with the whole content and the mode of being that experience itself, by the performance going on in its intentionality, attributes to it.

To make this discussion a little more specific, let us consider the experience of listening to music, as opposed to encountering objects discussed above. First, we have to note that music is never *given* to us as music. It is *given* to our senses as a flux of unordered[4] sounds. However, when we hear sounds we never *take* them—in ongoing experience—simply as a stream of unrelated sounds; rather, we find ourselves already listening to them *as something*—music, a cry for help, a car braking, some construction noise and so on. '[W]e do not [ever] hear pure meaningless sounds' (Dreyfus, 1991, p. 218). 'We hear the door shut in the house and never hear acoustical sensations or even mere sounds' (Heidegger, 1971, p. 26). As Heidegger argues: 'What we "first" hear is never noises or complexes of sounds, but the creaking wagon, the motorcycle... It requires a very artificial and complicated frame of mind to "hear" a "pure noise", (Heidegger, 1962, p. 207). The things themselves, in their meaningfulness, are much closer to us than all sensations (Heidegger, 1971, p. 26). Thus, listening, the taking of sound as music, or a cry for help, or an accident and so on implies an already there *sense* of what 'music', 'a cry for help' or 'an accident' is, which makes it possible for me to take these sounds as this or that, rather than as a mere flux of unordered sounds.

Furthermore, in order to listen to music as music, I do not only listen, but this listening to music is also already informed by an ongoing *sense* (unity or *noema*) of movement, rhythm, tone, scale, style and so forth. This ongoing active unity or *noema* provides an ongoing temporal horizon that enables me, in the experience of listening (the now), simultaneously to 'retain' the sounds I no longer hear (the past) and in anticipation 'fill in' the sounds that I am not yet hearing but anticipate (the future). Thus, as a phenomenological being I find myself listening to music, not merely hearing sounds. This simultaneous giving and taking in immanent ongoing consciousness are depicted in Figure 3.1 (do not over-interpret the figure, it serves merely as a useful alternative representation).

To sum up: our ongoing, always already directed experience (*noesis* in Husserl's terms) of the world as meaningful (as this or that), which was previously given as a flux of unordered sensation

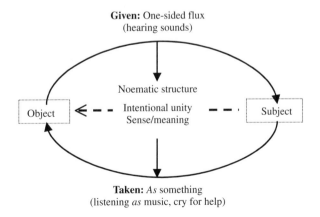

Figure 3.1 Ongoing consciousness as the structural unity of the phenomenological experience

in its one-dimensionality, has as its necessary condition an ongoing transcendental structural correlation or unity (*noema*) that is immediately and wholly implicated in the ongoing experience *but distinct from it*. In all the situated experiences of chairs, the given aspects of particular chairs varied (and could vary infinitely) but the persisting *noematic* sense remained identical.[5] The immediate and simultaneous presence of the identical (*noema*) in the ongoing act of experiencing (*noesis*) the chair through its aspects, possibilities and past experiences is what Husserl refers to as the *intentionality* of consciousness. The always already intentful directedness of consciousness (*noesis*) has as a necessary condition, an already present direction or structural orientation (*noema*), for its directedness to be meaningful rather than random and confused. As mentioned, this state of affairs is itself evident, as we tend to experience our ongoing engagement with the world as mostly meaningful rather than confused and meaningless. The ongoing noematic structure of consciousness is *both medium and outcome* of the intentional activity of consciousness, simultaneously directing and synthesizing. As such, it is active and temporal rather than static and atemporal—it is not a Platonic ideal form. Thus, contrary to the view of the positivists, intentional consciousness is not a subjectively constructed inner and private domain that must be 'eliminated', but rather an always already *public mind* that exists as a completely immanent—wholly present, never absent—ongoing and necessary structural correlation with the world (Sokolowski, 2000, p. 14).

So far we have tended to concentrate only on the experience of a particular object or event in our discussion—the chair and listening to music. However, these objects and events already exist in a *referential whole* in which things refer to each other in such a manner as to constitute a meaningful whole. For example, our experience of the pen on the desk already refers to some sort of writing surface like paper, and the pen and paper refer to the possibility of writing or drawing, which refers to the possibility of communicating, which refers to the need for communication and so on. In this referential whole, where things refer to each other or imply each other, the meaning of something emerges as the nexus of necessary relationships that constitute something as that which it is, a pen in this case. Husserl refers to this as the *external horizon* (or in his later work as the 'life world'). We always *experience* the world within this unfolding horizon of references—its meaning.

Thus, for phenomenology the meaning or sense of something—the phenomena as such—is not the outcome of subjective choices (likes, dislikes, values, beliefs etc.), but rather the outcome of the ongoing nexus of necessary relationships that serve as the transcendental condition of the active, ongoing, already meaning-giving consciousness. As such, the intentionality of consciousness implies an *immediate* relationship between consciousness (the subject) and the world (the object)—an ongoing structural unity—that renders the experience of the world possible in the first place. The theory of the intentionality of consciousness—and human existence—is phenomenology's fundamental contribution.[6] All phenomenologists take some version of this doctrine or theory as self-evident and central to any phenomenological approach. Before we move on we must note that, although we have concentrated on perception—of a chair and music—in our discussion, the intentional nature of the active meaning-giving consciousness is implied in all forms of cognition, such as judging, representing, planning, deciding, remembering, imagining and so forth.

For Husserl, the fundamental task of phenomenology is to *describe* and give an account of the necessary *noematic structural unity* of intentional consciousness—to describe the phenomena as such. For example, if we want to understand the phenomenological meaning of chairs as such—evident in all our experiences of them—we cannot answer this question by looking at this or that particular empirical chair. To our senses the chair can only be known in its 'one-sidededness', or in its 'many-sidedness' in a sequence of observations, but never simultaneously in its 'all-sidedness'. Yet phenomenologically the 'essential' meaning of the chair—its 'sit-upon-ability'—is not known perspectivally. To give an account of its essential meaning, as 'sit-upon-able', we need to give an account of the ongoing noematic structural unity of consciousness and the world that makes such an experience possible through all our diverse 'chair experiences'—hence Husserl's famous saying we must 'return to the things [structural unity] themselves'. How do we 'return to the things themselves'; that is, gain access to the ongoing noematic structural correlation of consciousness and the world? How do we turn consciousness back on itself? Obviously, this is very difficult to do—and Husserl claims that we will always be perpetual beginners.

According to Husserl, we can achieve it by a cumulative process of suspension, referred to as the *epochē* ('suspension of judgement' in ancient Greek philosophy). In every suspension (*epochē*) there is a simultaneous event of reduction—from the Latin *reducere*, 'to lead back'—taking place. In Husserl's (1964, 1970b) work there are a number of suspensions and reductions described. However, we will only distinguish two different levels of reduction here. The first is the *phenomenological reduction*, which is the suspension of the natural attitude and all its suppositions. The second is what is referred to as the *eidetic reduction* (from the Latin root *eidos*, 'essence'), which is the suspension of the empirical world in grasping the essential structural unity of consciousness as such. Let us discuss these in more detail.

Husserl argued that our ongoing experience of the world is one in which one takes the world simply as it is encountered: a horizon full of meaning that we simply draw on as we go about our everyday lives. He called this manner of experiencing the world the *natural attitude* (Husserl, 1964). In the natural attitude we function as naive realists with the belief that the world is as it seems and nothing besides. As we immerse ourselves in the natural attitude of ongoing activity in the world, the transcendental *noematic* structural unity of consciousness operates anonymously, in the background, without ever being thematized or brought to the foreground as such. Thus, in order to gain access to the intentional *noematic* structural correlation of consciousness and the world, we need to suspend the natural attitude. The phenomenological reduction is the taking up of the phenomenological attitude. In taking up this attitude we suspend our supposition of the world as simply there. We 'bracket out'—Husserl's term—all the different manners in which we take the world, *including the theoretical attitude of the scientist.* The phenomenological reduction requires that one suspend all forms of theorizing and generalization, even the supposition that something has to be somehow 'real' or 'concretely existing' to be experienced (Husserl, 1964, p. 154). In the phenomenological reduction we no longer direct our attention to this or that actual thing, event or situation but to the phenomenological *meaning* of these as they *show themselves* across all our intentional experiences. Alternatively, to put it in Sokolowski's (2000) terms, 'we look *at* what we normally look *through*' (p. 50). We often unwittingly take up a 'weak' form of this phenomenological attitude when people ask us to explain the meaning of something 'in general'—for example, the meaning of the notion of 'strategy' in general. We then tend to discard specific instances of strategy and see if we can discern general themes or aspects that are valid for all instances (note, however, that phenomena are not generalizations, see endnote 5). We say 'weak' because in this process of thinking we do not deliberately and actively suspend our presuppositions, as required by phenomenology.

In the eidetic reduction we shift our phenomenological attention to the *essential noematic* structural correlation of consciousness as such—consciousness directed at itself. This analysis is concerned with the essential meaning of human experiences that transcend this or that experience. In doing this analysis we may use the technique of 'free variation,' where we imagine alternative possible meanings (nexus of relationships) and evaluate these against the strictly necessary of our intentional experiences (Husserl, 1995). The essential of the object considered in the reflection 'is constituted by the invariant [meaning] that remains identical throughout the variations' (Lyotard, 1991). The analysis continually draws on the external horizon to explore the intentional structural correlation of consciousness; it uses the nexus of relationships to uncover the essential meaning of phenomena. It is important to note that the reduction is not a 'return' to something 'more real' that is somehow 'behind' that which appears in the natural attitude. It is, rather, the taking up of a *different attitude towards the same* ongoing performance of the world. To make this clearer, we can consider the example of identity. When we talk about a person's identity we are not talking about something other than the multiplicity of ongoing performances (speech and embodied acts) that enact such an identity. Rather, turning to the question of identity is just a matter of adopting a different attitude towards these same acts. Through the reduction we

> reach an understanding of the [ongoing] performance of subjectivity. The world is not something that simply exists. The world appears, and the structure of this appearance is conditioned and made possible by subjectivity [the ongoing intentional correlation of self and world]. (Zahavi, 2003, p. 52)

When we do the phenomenological analysis of the screen below this form of essential reflection will become clearer.

Heidegger and Intentionality as Being-in-the-World

The eidetic reduction as the possibility of a 'direct' access to a domain of pure or absolute transcendental consciousness is the most controversial aspect of Husserl's phenomenology. It must be noted that he also started to turn away from it in his final work, *The Crisis of European Sciences* (1970a). Indeed, one can take the work of Heidegger, Merleau-Ponty and Sartre as a direct existential critique of Husserl's transcendental inquiry (Kockelmans, 1967). This inquiry into the ideal structures of consciousness is often referred to as transcendental idealism. In contrast to this, Heidegger (1962) insisted that the transcendental is always and already grounded in the ongoing practical activity in the world of everyday life. For him, 'all consciousness, all knowledge, all human undertakings, are drawn on an ever present substratum: the world, a world that is always already-there, radically primary' (Thevenaz, 1962, p. 84). Likewise, for Merleau-Ponty (1962) the mind is not a pure intentional structure of consciousness but rather an embodied and always already situated mind.[7] He would argue that our scientific systems of orientation in time and space have their condition of possibility in our being a body—a lived body that is the ongoing horizon of orientation and meaning. For example, for him language already has its source, horizon of meaning, in the gesture.

Heidegger argued that early Husserl did not really break with the Cartesian dualism in as much as he still located the source of meaning in the structure of consciousness, *in the mind* as it were. In today's terms we might say that Heidegger criticized Husserl for his cognitivist tendencies; that is, reducing meaning to some content in the mind. In contrast to this, Heidegger argued that we cannot 'bracket out' the world of everyday practical activity, the referential whole, as this is exactly the ongoing source of all meaning—the ongoing being[8] of beings. One could argue that Heidegger abandoned Husserl's project—as Dreyfus (1991) does—or one could argue that Heidegger extended the work of Husserl, as Moran (2000) and Zahavi (2003) do—a position we would tend to take.

Heidegger's brilliant insight, articulated in division one of *Being and Time*, is that our intentional relationship with the world is *not epistemic*—as Husserl assumed—but rather practical and ontological. By this he means that we do not tend to encounter chairs 'as chairs' in the way that Husserl describes, but we rather tend to encounter them as 'possibilities for', such as 'a possibility for sitting down' or 'for standing on to reach higher' or 'for facing somebody' and so forth. Furthermore, the chair is a 'possibility for' (what Heidegger called an 'in-order-to') only within an already present referential whole where other things refer to it, as a 'possibility for', and it refers to them. Thus, for Heidegger the transcendental domain is not 'purified' consciousness but rather the ongoing, unfolding referential whole in which every thing is what it is—has its being. To describe this radically extended transcendental domain, Heidegger uses the notion of *being-in-the-world*.[9] Heidegger argues that we humans (whom he calls *Dasein*) exist in an ongoing structural openness towards the world in which the self and the world are always already a unity, a being-in-the-world (Heidegger, 1982, p. 297). Thus, we human beings (*Dasein*) are this unity, we are always and already beings-in-the-world—we have this unity as our ongoing being.

Let us consider an example. Whenever we take note of ourselves, we find ourselves *already engaged in practical everyday activity* in which things show up as 'possibilities for' our practical intentions. We should first observe the fact that our human nature is always one in which the things we encounter already *matter* in some way or another—even if they matter only as useless, boring or irrelevant. This is what Heidegger means when he claims that our way of being is that we always and already *care*. It is impossible for us—as always already immersed or 'thrown-into' the world humans—to take a wholly disinterested stance in and towards the world (Heidegger, 1962, p. 176). Thus, Heidegger transforms Husserl's notion of intentionality by insisting that

> intentionality must be understood in terms of the structural features of *Dasein*, specially *Dasein's* transcendence, that is, the fact that *Dasein* is already somehow beyond itself, already dwelling in the world, among things, and not locked up in the privacy of its own consciousness as the representationalist, Cartesian picture assumes. (Moran, 2000, p. 42)

When we encounter tools, they already matter in some way or another. However, these tools *are tools* for this or that purpose only in as much as they already refer to other tools, which also already refer to them as their transcendental condition for being this or that tool. Note that when using the notion 'refer' here, it is used in the sense of a *necessary relation or reference* for the tool to be what it already is *taken* to be when taken up in practical activity. The laptop we are working on, to be a laptop rather than a piece of assembled plastic and silicon, refers to application programs, which refer to operating systems, which refer to hardware, which refer to a power supply—all of which refer to suppliers, which refer to maintenance services and so forth. Dreyfus (1991, p. 62) calls this recursively defining, necessary nexus of relations the *tool or equipment whole*.

When we take up these tools, as tools, we do not take them up for their own sake, we take them up with an already present reference to our projects.[10] We do not simply bang on keys, we use the laptop to type, in order to write this chapter, to do email, to surf the web etc. Moreover, the writing of this chapter refers to the possibility of a book, of which it would be a part. This book refers to editors, which refer to potential publishers, which refer to a potential audience, which refers to research, which refers to further possibilities etc. Furthermore, the writing of this chapter also refers to the publication of our work, which refers to a publication record, which refers to academic status, which refers to the possibility for promotion and so forth. Heidegger (1962, p. 118) calls this recursively defining and necessary nexus of projects, or for-the-sake-of relations, the *involvement whole*. The equipment whole and the involvement whole refer to each other and sustain each other as an ongoing referential whole, horizon of meaning, which Heidegger calls 'the world'.[11] We humans (*Dasein*) dwell in the world in which the world is mostly familiar (it is simply already evidently there, 'ready to hand' in Heidegger's terminology). The phenomenological meaning of the world—in the case of our analysis below, the screen—can only be understood within the always already defining referential whole, the world itself.

Sometimes the world 'breaks down' and then we tend to encounter it as objects or events *as such*—it becomes occurrent or ready to hand in Heidegger's (1962) terminology. When we type and the key gets stuck then we notice it 'as a key', otherwise we merely type. If it remains stuck, the computer becomes occurrent 'as a broken laptop'. However, as we start to take it apart, in an attempt to fix it, it recedes into the background as something I am fixing. The point of Heidegger's account is

> that things show up for us or are encountered *as what they are* only against a background of familiarity, competence, and concern that carves out a system of related roles [recursively defining references] into which things fit. Equipmental things *are* the roles [recursively defining references] into which they are cast by skilled users of them, and skilled users *are* the practical roles [recursively defining references] into which they [become] cast themselves. (Hall, 1993, p. 132)

Thus, our relation with the world is ontological in as much as the world already shows up, or reveal itself to us, as it already is, in and through our ongoing project-edness or behaviour. However, to see this we need to suspend our natural attitude and take up a phenomenological attitude in which we can 'trace' and 'retrace' the referential whole that is the *transcendental* condition for the world to reveal itself as that which it already is.

This transformation of the transcendental by Heidegger, as well as the work of Merleau-Ponty and Sartre among others, has been described as *existential phenomenology* as opposed to the *transcendental phenomenology* of Husserl. Although we tend to follow the major steps of the Husserlian phenomenological method, our detailed analysis within these steps is based more on Heideggerian existential phenomenology. We will give a brief outline of this method in the section below.

THE PHENOMENOLOGICAL METHOD

Like any other method, the phenomenological method of investigation is realized through a methodological circle. However, phenomenology strives to accept and to proceed only within the primacy of human *experience as experienced*; that is, our ongoing intentional structural correlation with the world. As mentioned, our investigation into the essential meaning of the screen below follows the traditional phenomenological method as developed and applied by Husserl and Heidegger, and synthesized by Spiegelberg (1975, 1994). Nevertheless, minor changes were needed to incorporate some of the existential critique developed by Heidegger and others. The main adaptation we introduce to Spiegelberg's synthesis of the method is the role of the traditional etymological critique. We consider the phenomenological account of the etymology of the words not merely as a step of the first phase of the method, but rather as a whole second phase in its own right. Such an adaptation, which to some extent is only a recognition of an important and recurrent phenomenological practice, is clearly supported by the phenomenological investigations of Heidegger (1962, 1977, 1978). The phenomenological method that we apply in the phenomenological analysis of the screen below is therefore structured in the following four[12] phases:

  I. Describing the phenomenon.
 II. Analysing the etymology.
III. Performing the reduction.
IV. Investigating the essence.

It is important to stress the implicit unity when considering these four sequential phases. The phases are united in the basic purpose of 'giving us a fuller and deeper grasp' of the phenomenon

(Spiegelberg, 1975, p. 57), which can only be achieved if all four phases are applied fully. It ought to be clear how the essential concepts of phenomenology, discussed above, relate to the method as we proceed. Nevertheless, this relationship will be explained further as we apply the method to our analysis below. Let us very briefly characterize each of the four phases of the method with reference to our analysis of the phenomenon of the screen to be presented below.[13]

I. *Describing the phenomenon of screen.* This phase aims at returning to the screen as primarily and directly experienced. The purpose is to describe the external horizon of the phenomenon as intuitively and as free as possible from our presuppositions. We are not looking for data in order to explain some preliminary hypothesis, nor are we trying to make sense of some previous intellectual construction about screens. Our central aim is not to explain but to *describe* the screen, as it is, in our ongoing activity in the world.

II. *Analysing the etymology of screen.* We shall trace the origins of the word 'screen'. This analysis is not destined to bring back the meaning of the word *per se*, but rather to bring forth the meaning of the 'thing' itself—that is, of screen—in the antepredicative life of consciousness. In our analysis we will also provide an account of the etymology of the word 'display' as closely related to screen.

III. *Performing the phenomenological reduction on the screen.* In this phase we perform the phenomenological reduction on the consolidated findings of the first two phases. The reduction will aim to *bracket out* the incidental aspects of particular examples of screens in order to reach some essential description of the phenomenon 'screen'. This bracketing process will be guided by our intentional experience of the screening of screens in our everyday encounters with screens.

IV. *Investigating the essence of the screen.* This phase aims at reaching the elements strictly necessary for the phenomenon screen to be what it is. This phase proceeds from the reduced phenomenon of screen presented in the previous phase. It proceeds by stripping it of those elements that, in spite of being common to all appearances of screen, are not strictly necessary. In the analysis the technique of free variation will be used as well as relating and contrasting the phenomenon of screen with closely related phenomena.

The analysis of the phenomenon of the screen, presented below, will proceed by carefully following the phases outlined above. Because the flow of the analysis is a way into the phenomenon of the screen and a method of argumentation (Heidegger, 1977; Husserl, 1995; Merleau-Ponty, 1962), we will, as we proceed phase by phase, add some further discussion of the method where appropriate. In this manner we aim to limit repetition and improve the effectiveness of the discussion. Nevertheless, it must be pointed out that the always provisional nature of the phenomenological method is such that it tends to lead to some repetition of formulations as well as the reconsideration of statements and positions previously taken. We also want to reiterate that following the explicit phenomenological method—outlined above and applied below—is just *one* way to do phenomenology.

A PHENOMENOLOGY OF THE 'SCREENING' OF SCREENS

The odds are that when reading this chapter you will have nearby not simply one but maybe even several screens. Whether at the workplace, at home relaxing with the family, travelling or engaged in entertainment, a growing majority of people find themselves increasingly in front of screens: television (TV) screens, personal computer (PC) screens, mobile phone screens, palmtop computer displays and so forth. It is unlikely that the pervasiveness of screens in contemporary life will be disputed. However, as an example of this fact it is worth noting that the funeral of Princess Diana in August 1997 was followed by an estimated TV audience of 2,500 million (ABC, 1999), which represents more than 40 per cent of the world's population.

What is the meaning of our increasing interactions with screens? In this section we want to demonstrate the importance of phenomenology as an approach and method for enabling us to answer the question of the meaning of screens, in its ongoing screening of our world. We will aim to show that this seemingly 'innocent' technology has powerful ontological implications for our understanding of its pervasive presence in organizations and everyday life.

Phase I: Describing the Phenomenon of Screen

Let us start our analysis by exploring a description of the screen, *qua* screen. As a phenomenological analysis, we do not intend to direct our reflection to the *content* displayed on any particular screen as such, but rather to the meaning of the screen in its ongoing screening. Thus, the focus of our investigation is the screen as a nexus of relationships that provides a concrete way of relating ourselves to and in the world.

It is rather surprising what we encounter from the start. When trying to describe a screen, a computer screen or a television screen, we immediately note that we never seem to look at a screen as a 'screen'. We rather tend to look at screens by attending to what appears on them. What seems evident when looking at a screen is the content presented on that screen—the text, images, colours, graphics and so on—not the screening of the screen. To try to look at a screen and see it as a screen, not taking into account the particular content it presents and all the references with which that same content already appears to us, is apparently not an easy task. We are not familiar with this type of encounter with a screen. Rather, in our familiarity with screens or displays they tend to reveal themselves as things—perhaps surfaces—which function in particular contexts and for particular purposes. That is to say, we simply use screens as we act and relate ourselves to and in the world, mainly within a familiar organizational or institutional context. In the natural attitude screens are familiar 'places', simply there for our use. This familiarity may even lead us to think that the question of the meaning of the screen is odd and perhaps an 'intellectualization' of something quite ordinary. We note this strangeness as we proceed; that is, although we are intimately familiar with screens we tend not to see screens in their screening, *qua* screens. As we move towards suspending the natural attitude and take up the phenomenological attitude—looking at the screen in its screening—what do we note?

Screens in screening present, show, exhibit what is supposed to be *relevant data* in each context, be it a spreadsheet while working at the office, a schedule while walking in the airport or a movie while watching TV. The screen, in screening, finds itself at the centre of the activity. In showing it attracts our attention, often also our physical presence, as it locates our activity. It is often the focus of our concerns in that environment, be it at the office working or at home watching the news. Apparently the screen enters our ongoing activity and engagement in the world—as a screen—when we attend to it by turning it on. When we push the 'on' button the screen locates our attention, we sit down, quit—physically or cognitively—other activities we may have been performing to watch the screen, since it is the place, the location, where what is relevant or supposedly relevant for us at that particular time is happening. Indeed, we rely on it as a transparent, simply there, *ready-to-hand* thing to shape, affect and mediate our own ongoing activity and engagement in the world (Heidegger, 1962).

However, we must note that this screening of the screen—as involving, shaping and mediating our activities—does not sometimes happen and sometimes not. It is not only *when* we turn it 'on' that the screening of the screen is present. On the contrary, *that* we push the 'on' button means precisely that the screening of the screen—its pervasive transparent possibilities—is already suggested and present there in our ongoing activity, our world.[14] In the horizon of our ongoing everyday life—in its dynamic nexus of relationships—other activities and things already refer to it, already suggesting its meaningfulness. For example, we organize our desk around our computer and our living room around our TV. We locate screens where they are visible. We have for example barcodes, text messages, notices at airports and URLs that continually direct us towards the screen. Thus, even if this or that particular screen is off, we are already relying and basing ourselves and our possibilities—the references in which we dwell—on the already present *screenhood* of screens. We will return to this point below.

From our initial attempt at 'seeing' the screen, as it screens, we note that a screen gathers the attention of the people who surround it. The actions of those people are already directly shaped by the presence of the turned-on screens, by the kind of content presented and by the understanding that people surrounding them implicitly assume of that content. The phenomenological description above of a screen points to the notions of *showing relevant data for and about each particular situation*, of *calling for attention*, of *suggesting relevance*, of *acting as mediation between ourselves and the world*, and of *gathering and locating what is appropriate in each particular context*. We now have a first phenomenological description of some of the central meanings of the screening of the screen. It is worth noting at this point that the description of the screen above is also valid for what we know as displays, for example as we find in palmtop displays. In the analysis we will aim to show that there is no fundamental phenomenological difference between a screen and what we refer to as a display[15]—they both have their meaning in-the-world in ongoing screening.

In the next section we will expand our investigation by doing a phenomenological analysis of the etymology of the word 'screen' and the word 'display'. In this phase we will attempt to trace and 'uncover' the paths of meaning of these words by juxtaposing them with the description already given above.

Phase II: Analysing the Etymology of 'Screen'

When doing an etymology of the word 'screen', it is not the intention of phenomenology to argue that a particular meaning of the word screen has a definitive superiority or is the 'real' meaning. What is decisive is that the tracing back of the evolution of the meaning of the word 'screen' enables us somehow to make more evident the realm of *necessary* relations/references in which the word 'speaks' and maintain its meaning. As Heidegger (1977, p. 159) states:

> What counts, rather, is for us, in reliance on the early meaning of a word and its changes, to catch sight of the realm pertaining to the matter in question into which the word speaks. What counts is to ponder that essential realm as the one in which the matter named through the word moves.

Thus, although our phenomenological analysis does share some concerns with linguistic analysis, it goes beyond it. This analysis is not destined to 'bring back' the historical original meaning of the words screen and display, but rather to bring forth 'the [phenomenological] meaning of the thing itself, around which the acts of naming and expression took shape' (Merleau-Ponty, 1962, p. xv).

Screens: calling for attention

'Screen' looks like a rather simple word. It is both a noun and a verb and its contemporary plurality of meanings can be brought together along three main themes: *projecting/showing* (e.g. TV screen), *hiding/protecting* (e.g. fireplace screen) and *testing/selecting* (e.g. screening the candidates) (*Oxford Paperback Dictionary and Thesaurus* (OPDT), 1997, pp. 681–2). What are the meanings that bind this plurality together?

The origins of the word 'screen' can be traced back to the fourteenth century. According to the *Merriam Webster Dictionary* (MW), the contemporary English word 'screen' evolved from the Middle English word *screne*, from the Middle French *escren* and from the Middle Dutch *scherm*. It is a word akin to the Old High

German (eighth-century) words *skirm*, which meant shield, and *skrank*, which meant a barrier of some kind. The word screen also suggests another interesting signification, further away from us in history. It is a word 'probably akin' (MW) to the Sanskrit (1000 BC)[16] words *carman*, which meant 'skin', and *kränti*, which signified 'he injures' (MW). These are possible meanings from which the Middle Age words evolved. The Sanskrit clue suggests that the notions of protection, shield, barrier and separation possibly arose within the older Proto-Indo-European language as metaphors for the concept of skin—possibly that of human (or animal) skin.

Let us now suggest a very brief sketch of the chronological etymological relations that these words seem to have. A barrier or a protection is something raised over and against another something. This 'other' something faces the barrier, as the wind faces the windscreen of a car, which means that the screen protects against something to be excluded that moves towards it. What is moving towards the screen could have been understood as a projection (from the Latin word *projectare*, which meant 'to throw forward') over a surface—just like arrows and bullets were projected over shields, or like heat is projected onto a fireplace screen. The screen protects and shelters (like a skin) because it receives and holds the projection of that which is not to be received 'inside' the cover that the screen provides. But what happens when something stopped by the screen is allowed to pass through? The answer is that it is screened. This means that it is permitted to pass through that barrier, or that it simply passes through it. The screen as a barrier is now understood as a 'system for detecting [for example] disease, ability, attribute' (OPDT, 1997, pp. 681–2). This interpretation links, or so we hope, the three central themes of meaning attached to the word screen: hiding/protecting, projecting/showing and testing/selecting (OPDT, 1997, pp. 681–2). Is there a central intent, distinction or feature common to all these specific meanings of the word screen? We would suggest that the central intent is 'demands for our attention',[17] as summarized in Table 3.1.

From Table 3.1 it seems reasonable to propose that the central intent of the multiple meanings of screen is the *presumed necessary attention* implied in *ongoing screening*, for screening to make sense. We summarize this meaning as *calling for attention*. We now turn our attention to the etymology of the word 'display', which is often used as a synonym for screen with regard to information technology devices, and which we will claim has the same intentional meaning as screen.

Table 3.1   The central intent of the multiple meanings of 'screen'

Meaning	Interpretation	Central intent
Projecting/showing (e.g. TV screen)	Projecting and showing assumes a target or audience whose attention is to be captured. Without such an audience (target), showing (projecting) would not make sense.	Calls for attention of audience/to target
Hiding/protecting (e.g. fireplace screen)	Hiding and protecting assumes something to be excluded from attention. Without exclusion from attention, hiding would not make sense.	Calls for exclusion from attention
Testing/selecting (e.g. screening candidates)	Testing and selecting assumes the attention of those who 'select and test'. Without such attention, selecting cannot be said to 'select'.	Calls for the attention of those selecting

Displaying: evident agreement

The word 'display' entered the English language as a verb in the fourteenth century and as a noun in the seventeenth century (MW). As a verb, display means 'to put or spread before the view' (e.g. *display* the flag), 'to make evident' (e.g. *displayed* great skill), 'to exhibit ostentatiously' (e.g. he liked to *display* his erudition) (MW). As a noun, it means 'a setting or presentation of something in open view' (e.g. a fireworks *display*), 'a clear sign or evidence', an exhibition (e.g. a *display* of courage), an 'ostentatious show', 'an eye-catching arrangement by which something is exhibited' (MW). These notions of showing, in open view and making evident are central to the word display.

What are the necessary conditions for making sense of these diverse meanings? It seems that the central intent is some sense of apparentness, immediately clear to all. Such apparentness has as its condition of possibility the idea of *already-there agreement*. For example, we say 'it is evident to all present here,' meaning that it is impossible for anyone present to disagree with what is taken to be apparent. They in turn are linked to the idea of 'unfolding' and of some sort of agreement.

The work done in this step leads to an idea that is in an important way quite close to the one we had at the end of the previous step. This is the idea of screen as the bringing forth of (or calling forth) attention and thereby implying evident relevance, since 'calling for attention' always implies the supposition, correctly or incorrectly, of some evident relevance. The 'evidence' 'relevance' and 'attention'—emerging from the etymological analysis above—point towards the idea of some already operating *agreement* (implicit or explicit) as their constitutive condition. If the 'attention' mentioned is our attention, as those before the screen, to what do 'evidence', 'relevance' and 'agreement' refer? Is the issue of evidence, relevance and agreement a matter of the *content* of what is on the screen or does screen in its fundamental meaning (or screening) already presume these?

Phase III: Performing the Phenomenological Reduction on the Screen

At this point we must recall that to recover in some way the essential meaning of the screen, as revealed in screening, we must turn our reflection to the phenomenon as it reveals itself from the ongoing structural correlation of self and world. It is now important that we suspend—as a methodological condition of our analysis—the necessity of any particular empirical examples of this or that screen. Performing the phenomenological reduction does this. It means reducing the phenomenon screen to its ongoing appearance in the horizon of the already situated intentionality, disregarding characteristics that we value in it as a particular empirically 'existent' thing, while attempting to preserve its meaning as fully as possible.

As we perform the phenomenological reduction, it is important to note that this intentional 'object', the screen in our already situated consciousness, in its 'screening', is *not* some pure isolated and abstract thing that has meaning in itself as such. For us to grasp the meaning of the screen as screening, we need to have already presumed its world; that is, the nexus of relationships without which it would not have any meaning as such. Thus, the screen, in its essential meaning, always already refers to its functioning in a world in which it makes sense, because it and the other things and activities in the world mutually refer to each other as meaningful. The reduction is a return exactly to this *horizon of meaning*.

Having suspended the supposition of necessary existence in any particular empirical screen, we note that any screen, to make sense as a screen, still seem to require as necessary 'a calling for attention'. Without this 'calling for attention', screens would no longer be screens, merely surfaces or objects. Thus screens, in their screening, seems to be promises of bringing to evidence what is relevant, while simultaneously hiding their claimed physical being behind that same relevance. We see that screens, in screening, function in the flow of our ongoing activity in the world; that is, transparently, as simply there, ready-to-hand beings (Heidegger, 1962). Because the content displayed always 'shows up' within our ongoing activity whole, it is already presumed to be relevant data; that is, data deserving our attention. The reduced phenomenon of screen appears as something devised to attract—or rather that *already* has attracted—our attention and situate our action in the ongoing activity of our world of work, entertainment, travel and so on.

This reflection can be made clearer by realizing the kind of difficulty that one has to go through in order to imagine a situation in which screens do not present relevant data at all. For example, think of experiencing a PC monitor at the NY Stock Exchange showing the ongoing schedule of the trains of some Asian city; or the displays on supermarket cash registers showing air traffic control data. These 'screens' may have an initial curiosity value but will quickly become ornaments in the background—they simply do not screen. These cases demonstrate the difficulty of imagining these surfaces *as screens*, because in order to do that we would need to abandon the essential meaning of the screen, yet still force ourselves to use that same essence to understand an object that looks as though it has lost its meaning as a screen.

Screens display relevant data for us within the involvement whole in which we relate ourselves to the world. The data on screens grabs our attention within our *particular* involvement whole (Heidegger, 1962) in which it refers to our activities and our activities refer to it—within a particular 'form of life'.[18] For example, we can imagine what a man from the fourteenth century might think when confronted with a screen of an automated teller machine (ATM). The surface that we refer to as a 'screen' would merely be a potentially curious object for him. It would not be a 'screen' because he does not already dwell in a world—referential whole—that would render it meaningful as such. The screen would not be a 'screen' for him as it would not call for his attention, it and the content displayed 'on' it would not seem relevant as it is *not already* a screen for him; he would simply not recognize it in its essential meaning. However, for us, who already dwell in the world of bank accounts, the screen in screening is already calling for our attention as a possibility to see our 'bank balance' or to withdraw cash from our account, for example. The data on the screen refer to us, to our residence, our transactions, our financial status, our overdraft facility and so forth; these in turn refer to other aspects of our ongoing activity in the world: can we afford to buy something or not, has our salary been deposited and so on.

Thus, screens in screening claim an ongoing meaning in-the-world as focal interpretive surfaces, presenting, making evident, relevant data for our involvement and action in the world. Screens promise to make evident our ongoing activity in-the-world, because they present an already interpreted and selected 'screened' world to us. This screened world is already consistent with our ongoing involvement in that world, within our form of life. Thus, foremost and primarily screens do not 'show' the data that appears 'on' the screen, but rather *a form of life as such.*

This phenomenological reduced description of screen shows how closely intertwined the ideas of 'attention', 'relevance' and 'world' are in the essential meaning of the screen—as such, it also suggests references to notions of some necessary agreement. However, this is not enough for a fully phenomenological characterization of the phenomenon screen. In order to reach the essential meaning of the screening of screens, we must now try to reach beyond this common ground to identify the *strictly necessary* references for the phenomenon screen to be what it *is.*

Phase IV: Investigating the Essential Meaning of the Screen

To gain access to the essential meaning of the screen is not to generalize. As mentioned above, generalization itself already pre-supposes the existence of some essential meaning for its operation. Moreover, as is evident from our analysis thus far, the notion of 'essence' that we use accounts for some grounded and historical way of unfolding, which evolves and changes in-the-world (Heidegger, 1962, 1977). As such, it does not point to some supposed static concept, object or Platonic idea. Rather, we take the investigation of the essence of the screen, in recognition of the work of Heidegger, to be an attempt to uncover the fundamental meanings, the grounding references, the main and decisive contours, of the growing and pervading presence of screens in our contemporary world.

The way in which screens are screens in-the-world of ongoing activity is of course common to all screens. Nevertheless, it is common not only to the examples analysed but to *all* potential examples of that phenomenon, because the essence is such that without it there is no phenomenon. Imagination, 'by discovering what one can and what one cannot imagine' (Hammond, Howarth and Keat, 1991, p. 76), is the key to the continuation of our analysis. This analysis aims to strip out of our preliminary phenomenon of screening those elements that in spite of being common are not necessary for a screen to be screening. Since we have a pervasive and ongoing experience with screens, we now no longer need empirical observation for discovering the answers we require. Rather, in every new variation in imagination we know that the object we describe is an object of that same kind, a screen, if we recognize it as such, as a screen. Thus, the implicit criterion of recognition—*my ability to recognize the object as the object it is*—is the decisive way of this essential *eidetic* reduction (Husserl, 1970a, 1995; Spiegelberg, 1975, 1994).

First, we note that the same surface can be considered a screen and not considered a screen even if it displays the same data, as is clear from our example of the ATM above. If we have a mirror, with the size and shape of a screen, it displays data—the images it reflects—although we do not consider it to be a screen but a mirror. Nonetheless, we can equally have a screen displaying exactly the same image as the mirror and consider it a screen and not a mirror. So, what is the criterion that is implicit in this imagined experience? Mirrors *reflect*, screens *present*. This means that the kind of data displayed by these different objects have diverse origins. In the case of mirrors, it is merely reflecting back what it receives. However, in presentation there operates a fundamental process of ordering. Presentation always assumes a theme, in the way that a jigsaw puzzle, to be a jigsaw puzzle, assumes a whole that will be its ordering criterion.

Furthermore, the presumed theme of the presentation derives its meaning from an ongoing horizon of activity that already renders it meaningful as a relevant presentation. As Wittgenstein (1967, no. 241, p. 88) argued, words do not refer to something because we agreed it; rather, they already have meaning because we share a *form of life*, a meaningful, ongoing activity whole. Conversely, the screen has meaning not because we have agreed its content, but because in screening it necessarily assumes an already understood meaningful activity whole as its condition of possibility—one could say its already present organizing theme. Thus, we can say that the meaningfulness of the data presented on screens does not depend on the perceiving subject's perspective as such—that is, it is not a matter of an interpretation as such—but rather on the *form of life* in which it already functions as meaningful. Screens present meaningful data—that is, data that was previously already selected in accordance with an already implied meaningful whole—and therefore they gather and locate the attention of the people surrounding them. In watching, one could of course disagree with the relevance of this or that particular data being presented on the screen, but that evaluation itself already suggests a horizon of meaning in which such judgements would make sense.

Screens are not mirrors in that they do not reflect whatever they face. They are a presentation of what is already relevant within the flow of our purposeful action. However, we must also note that in selecting for presentation, in displaying—thus in making relevant or evident—other possibilities are *necessarily always implicitly excluded*. Thus, the screen, as screen, conceals and filters in its revealing. For this to be the case, there is the logical necessity of a *previously agreed grounding* on the basis of which something can be filtered, can be *screened*, at all. To reveal implies to conceal; they both mean to filter; that is, to screen. The revealing and concealing of screening imply an already there, implicitly and fundamentally shared and agreed form of life, on the basis of which the things on the screen become constituted as meaningful and the way the world is (Heidegger, 1962).

We must emphasize that our discussion refers to screens, *qua* screens, which collect and attract attention. The agreement implied in them refers to some shared *ontological* understanding about the 'make-up' of the world, which is the basis on which our own actions with respect to screens gain their references and significance. Obviously, it does not mean that one has to agree with the terms, conditions, analysis or format of what is displayed. The agreement is only with regard to the referential whole within which the screen is a screen; that is, attracts our attention and directs our ongoing activity in that form of life. Thus, by the term 'ontological' here we are referring to the idea that the agreement implied by relevance and attention already suggests that we have agreed to take the world *to be in the terms it is being presented*. For example, we see the news on television *as* the 'news' and take it to be referring to actual events, or we see the arrival time of the train on the monitor and take it to refer to the actual possibility of a train arriving at that time, or we see the numbers on the ATM screen to be the actual amount of money we have to spend and so on.

It is worthwhile noting that the screen as such is first and primordially seeing, watching, perceiving with the eyes. We, as human beings, have a structural tendency to assume the primacy of seeing. Seeing, according to Heidegger (1962, p. 214), is 'a peculiar way of letting the world be encountered by us in perception'. In *everyday practical activity* the human sense of sight performs a central role in our involvement in-the-world (Heidegger, 1962). What is at stake in this supremacy of seeing, so to speak, is not a characteristic or feature of humans, but an ontological conception of being human *in which cognition is conceived as seeing*. This fundamental conception, the ontological primacy of seeing, grounds the way in which screens gain ontological importance as screens—rather than as mere dynamic surfaces.

This priority of seeing, in which cognition is understood as seeing and thus seeing as the access to truth, can be traced back to the early Greek thought of Parmenides (Heidegger, 1962, p. 215) and especially in the work of Aristotle as presented in his treatise *Metaphysics*. The power of the ontological suggestions 'on' screens is evident when we realize that we live in a tradition in which to see is to believe and what is believed is what is true. We will not pursue this analysis here (refer to Introna and Ilharco, 2000). In the phenomenon screen, seeing is not merely being aware of a surface. The very watching of the screen as it screens implies an already there ontological agreement about the nature of the world—as a world that is relevant (and true) to us who share it, in and through the screens we face. Screens, in their screening, already have the attention of those surrounding them because they are focal points of already agreement, because what is displayed already relies on a context of a fundamental, already present agreement. It is exactly this already agreement that we depend on as managers, users, train drivers and so forth when we turn to the screen to reveal our world to us.

To conclude, the phenomenological meaning (Heidegger, 1962, 1977) of screen *qua* screen reveals itself as already ontological agreement. It is this already agreement that calls for our attention, attracts us, makes us look at the screen in its screen-ness and *simultaneously condemns to forgetfulness that which was already agreed*, precisely because it is not an agreement but an already agreement. This already agreement is a form of life in which the screens can be said to be, in a very profound way, its *skin*. As already agreement, the thinking, the bargaining, the transacting, the negotiating that typically precede an agreeing emerge as pre-emptively excluded. It is because this concealed meaning of 'already agreement' is the essential background of 'relevance' and 'calling for attention' that the screen does not show itself, but rather hides itself as it pursues its way in the world. This is where we started. We noted that we do not tend to look at a screen in its screening but rather at what appears on its surface. As such, screens 'screen' our world: concealing and spreading this already agreement. Indeed, it is important to underscore the ongoing *concealing and spreading* of meaning in screening, made possible by the necessary *already agreement* of ongoing screening.

We must emphasize that this analysis of ours only provides the preliminary outlines of a full phenomenology of screens. It still requires further critical consideration to expose suppositions yet to be scrutinized. It also needs more imaginative variation to extend the analysis to other realms of screens and so forth. Nevertheless, we hope that it does serve as a useful illustration of the potential of phenomenology to move us beyond this or that screen, or the way this or that person interprets screens, to the essential meaning of screens as they function in the world of everyday meaningful activity.

Some Empirical Conclusions on the Screening of Screens

Unfortunately, space will not allow us to explore all the possible empirical consequences and implications of our analysis. Nevertheless, we will offer here, for illustrative purposes, some brief comments to point out the empirical relevance of our phenomenological findings.

The power of *already agreement* can, for example, be seen with regard to our general view of television in everyday life. We often refer to people who don't watch television as 'living in another world'. As Fry (1993, p. 13) puts it, the 'television has arrived as the context' and those people without one seem to be out of that context. The power of television to reinforce what is presented just by the presentation itself has important consequences in our daily lives: 'all that is important is revealed on television while all that is so revealed on television acquires some authority' (Adams, 1993, p. 59). However, this power does not belong to the essence of television but rather to the essence of screens. This is also evident from the fact that the kind of data about us that appears on a screen, at the bank, at the office, at the medical doctor, at a public department is often taken as more valid and trustworthy than we are ourselves—as many of us may have found out to our dismay. Indeed, from our understanding of the screening of screens it is clear that this primacy of what is on the screen over what is not on the screen seems to be an issue that needs to be taken into account while designing new systems. Seemingly trivial decisions about entities and attributes to be included / excluded in the database have important ontological consequences for how we will understand our world. These decisions will function as ontological references as they become presented on screens, and will as such mediate the manner in which we relate to and in that world.

It is possible to imagine all sorts of implications of our analysis for the importance of screening; for example the importance of the *form of life* in establishing screens when managing change, or the power of screened information in creating 'facts' through screening as such. Due to space constraints we will not pursue these here. Let us turn now to some critical comments and limitations of phenomenology.

SOME CRITICAL COMMENTS AND LIMITATIONS OF PHENOMENOLOGY

Phenomenology, like all other approaches, has been criticized from various quarters. We will review some of these criticisms and indicate how other approaches emerged or are related to these criticisms.

Phenomenology is often criticized for scholasticism and obscurantism. Critics argue that authors in phenomenology have an excessive tendency to refer back to ancient Greek masters for authority as well as using strange formulations and technical terminology that serves only to hide, obscure or circumvent the debate about its limits and possibilities. There is no doubt that the texts that form the canon of phenomenology are very difficult to access. This may be because they are often read in English as a translation from German or French, which does not always translate well. But more than this, the authors often use ordinary language in a unique and technical manner. This becomes necessary because our normal way of speaking is in the idiom of the 'natural attitude'—which is by its very nature dualistic. For example, in our use of nouns, verbs and adjectives we construct sentences that make us 'see' the world as populated with bounded objects (nouns) that do certain things (verbs) and 'have' certain characteristics or attributes (adjectives). So when Heidegger claims that humans are beings-in-the-world we would normally tend to think of humans as having 'being-in-the-world-ness' as an attribute. However, Heidegger means precisely to say that being-in-the-world is what we are, as such; we are never *not* beings-in-the-world—self and world form a unity from the start and are never not a unity. The difference between these two inter-pretations is profound. Thus, quite paradoxically, phenomenology needs a 'formal' language to talk about something that we all infor-mally already experience, in the background, as it were. However, because this background is *in the background* we do not talk about it; it 'is not what we usually deal with and have words for, so to talk of it requires a special vocabulary' (Dreyfus, 1991, p. 7).

Phenomenology in general, and Husserl's transcendental phe-nomenology in particular, is often criticized as being solipsistic. This criticism infers that phenomenology reduces the reality of the world to some content in consciousness (the mind); that is, that the account of phenomenology implies that we are ultimately 'locked up' in our own consciousness. This is a partial reading and understanding of phenomenology as argued by Zahavi (2003) and Sokolowski (2000). Because phenomenology takes subjectivity seriously and describes the world 'as experienced' does not mean that reality is the product of the inescapable mind. Nor did Husserl's transcendental reduc-tion—the return to the things themselves—imply that the 'source' of reality is somehow 'locked up' in purified consciousness. Both of these views miss the radical innovation of phenomenology, namely the immediate, always already there, unity of the self and the world. For Husserl, as noted above, consciousness is not a subjectively constructed, inner and private domain that must be 'eliminated', rather it is an always already *public mind* that exists as a completely immanent—wholly present, never absent—ongoing structural correlation with the world (Sokolowski, 2000, p. 14). As Zahavi (2003, p. 46) argues:

> To perform the *epochē* and the reduction is not to abstain from an investigation of the real world in order to focus on mental content and representation... The *epochē* and the reduction do not involve an *exclusive turn toward inwardness,* and they do not *imply any loss* (emphasis added).

One could perhaps argue that Husserl is solipsistic in his descrip-tive methodology, in as much as he does want to give an account of the things themselves through a reduction to the noematic struc-ture of consciousness (Moran, 2000, p. 178). Equally, Heidegger argued that the essence of being human is that we are beings who are always and already in-the-world: when we become aware of the world we are already there, committed to things, doing things, expecting things and so forth. This already 'thereness' is the structural unity of world and self, which is the horizon—referential whole—within which things stand out as meaningful. This unity means that it does not make sense to talk about some meaning 'in the mind'. In this same vein, we can see that the debate about idealism and realism does not appeal to phenomenology as it draws on a distinction that phenomenology sees as meaningless or at least not very helpful. Having said this, it must be acknowledged that the fact that phenomenology operates from the first-person perspective, the world 'as experienced', does make it weak with respect to its account of intersubjectivity. Heidegger's account of the intersubjective dimension as 'being-with' is acknowledged to be less innovative than his other work. Also, the work of Schutz (Schutz and Luckmann, 1973) on intersubjectivity has not had the impact that one might have expected. Nevertheless, the influence of phenomenology in the work of social theorists such as Giddens (1984) is widely acknowledged (see also Chapter 8).

Phenomenology is often criticized as being ahistorical, or as not taking history seriously enough (see Chapter 7). This comment is often made together with the claim that phenomenology is an essentialist approach to understanding the world. We will discuss these two claims together. There is no doubt that phenomenology is essentialist: this is exactly its enormous potential. However, what phenomenology sees as 'essential' is different to the general inter-pretation of the notion.[19] Most often essentialism is seen within the context of Platonic essences or ideal forms, which are really existing, timeless, abstract entities of which physical objects are imperfect copies—or, less starkly put, some timeless entity that is the real remainder once we remove the incidental and idiosyncratic. The Platonic need for transcending the specific and the incidental strips the object of its historicity. More significant for phenomenology is the Aristotelian notion of essence, namely those properties that are essential or necessary without which a thing could not exist or be the thing that it is. The phenomenological notion of essence is closer to the Aristotelian notion, in placing the emphasis on the 'necessary conditions (not properties!) for a being to be what it is'. However, it is also radically different, especially in the existential phenomenol-ogy of Heidegger. For Heidegger the essence is not 'in' the object but rather already in-the-world; that is, in the ongoing referential whole that provided the ongoing necessary references for the thing to be what it is already taken to be. The chair is 'a chair' because of all the references, the referential whole or world, that refers to it as such and to which it refers as such. Furthermore, this referential whole is the whole that it is because it exists within the horizon of finite temporal human existence, of memory, activity and anticipation. The unity of self and world is a unity only within finite human temporality. That is why Heidegger's major work is called *Being and Time*: being (essence) does not exist outside of human time. Indeed, it would be extremely difficult, we would argue impossible, to give an account of everyday life without recourse to some form of phenomenological essentialism.

A response to the perceived essentialism, as well as the inadequate intersubjective account in phenomenology, which nevertheless emerged from phenomenology is *ethnomethodology* (Garfinkel, 1967). For ethnomethodology the world is as it appears in the natural attitude. Ethnomethodologists argue that we, as phenomenologists, should not assume to have some privileged access to a world that is 'more real' than it appears to normal everyday persons doing everyday things—for them there is nothing to be gained through the phenomenological attitude. With this in mind, they proceed to examine the everyday practices by which actors make the ongoing ordinary life possible. We would argue that this response may be valid if directed towards early Husserlian phenomenology, but is certainly not valid with respect to existential phenomenology. We cannot pursue this debate here; refer to Rogers (1983) for a detailed discussion of the debate between phenomenology and ethnomethodology.

The most severe critique of phenomenology, in particular Husserlian phenomenology, comes from the deconstructivist movement, in particular from Derrida (1973). Derrida argues that phenomenology operates within the 'metaphysics of presence' that characterizes the western philosophical tradition (see also Chapter 7). By this he means the metaphysical assumption that what is present to me now as such and such a thing is the same as when that same thing was present to me earlier on. Or, differently stated, that there is an *ongoing self-evident presence* that guarantees every re-presentation of every previous present thing as such. For example, if I look at the cup in front of me, look away and then back at the cup, how will I know that it is indeed the same cup? What provides the ongoing temporal horizon for me to take the cup to be the same cup as some moments before? Derrida argues that

> this supposed self-presence is actually the *result of a repeated substitution*. As such, its ground is a nonpresence. Its basis is the absence that allows the substitute to take the place of what it substitutes for. (Mensch, 2001, emphasis added)

Thus, the supposedly self-evident presence operates on the ongoing recalling of what is not present (absence) to guarantee itself here and now. Heidegger realized this, and his later work is indeed a response to this and also the starting point for Derrida's project of *deconstruction*. It must also be said that the deconstruction project also eventually finds itself in a sort of 'metaphysics of absence or otherness', always deferring to a beyond that will never be a presence as such; this is evident in the work of Derrida (1973) and, in particular, the work of Levinas (1991). We will not explore this debate further here; refer to Lawlor (2002) and Mensch (2001) for a detailed discussion of the relationship between deconstruction and phenomenology.

We will note that this lack of self-presence and the need for repeated substitution identified by Derrida are also the key to the *hermeneutics* project. The hermeneutics project, which started with the problem of interpreting ancient texts, moved progressively towards this idea of a fundamental, always already distanciation (see Chapter 4) at the heart of all ongoing experience; that is, the need to continually 'bring back to the present' what has always already 'slipped away' into the past (Ricoeur, 1981). Thus, we find that we are not at all transparent to ourselves, and as such we are continuously interpreting and making sense of our own ongoing presence in the world—in a sense we, and all other human beings, are always an obscure text in need of ongoing interpretation and self-interpretation.

Now that we have outlined some of the critiques against phenomenology and indicated some of the approaches that emanated from these critiques, we will turn to a brief discussion of some work in phenomenology that may be relevant to the information systems community.

SOME REFLECTIONS ON EXISTING RELEVANT WORK IN PHENOMENOLOGY

Albert Borgmann (1984) uses Heidegger's (1977) critique of modern technology—as presented in his famous essay 'The question concerning technology'—to argue that we need to find a 'free' relation to technology. In his essay, Heidegger argues that the essence of modern technology is *Gestell* (often translated as 'enframing'). By this he means that modern technology always already frames our relation to the world in a particular way. He argues that this particular way is one in which everything (even humans) are framed, or rather revealed, as 'resources for' this or that project. Borgmann agrees with Heidegger's analysis of modern technology in arguing that modern technology reveals the world for us as 'devices'. By this he means that modern technology as devices *hides* the referentiality of the world—the worldhood of the world—on which they depend. They do not disclose the multiplicity of necessary conditions for them to be what they are taken to be. In fact just the opposite, they try to hide the necessary effort for them to be available for use. Thus, a thermostat on the wall that we simply set at a comfortable temperature now replaces the process of chopping wood, building the fire and maintaining it. Our relationship with the environment is now reduced to and disclosed to us as a control that we simply set to our liking.

In this way devices de-world our relationship with things, in Heidegger's terminology. By relieving us of the burden of making and maintaining fires, our relationship with the world becomes disclosed in a new way—as one of disengagement. The world of things is not something to be engaged in, instead it is simply available for consumption. Against such a disengaging relationship with things in the world, Borgmann argues for the importance of focal practices based on focal things. Focal things solicit our full and engaging presence. We can think of the focal practice of preparing and enjoying a meal with friends or family as opposed to the solitary consumption of a fast-food meal. If we take Borgmann's analysis seriously, we might conclude that we, as contemporary humans surrounded by devices, are doomed increasingly to relate to the world in a disengaged manner. This might be so, Borgmann argues. However, it is also possible to have a free relation with technology—including modern technology—if we imbed it in focal practices rather than use it, or accept it, as devices. Otherwise we will, as Heidegger (1977) argued, become the devices of our devices.

Phenomenology's critical contribution with respect to technology is not just at the general level as developed by Borgmann. Hubert Dreyfus (1993) used it to develop a devastating critique of artificial intelligence (AI). His work resulted in a complete reorientation of AI, of which the most prominent is perhaps the current 'embodied' paradigm (Steels and Brooks, 1995). Dreyfus, using Heidegger's work, argued against a representationalist approach to cognition and action. He argued that we do not have representations in our mind that guide or direct our actions in the world. Rather, as skilled actors in-the-world we draw on tools 'as possibilities for' without having first to conceptualize the tool, the task and the relationship between them—as assumed in a representationalist account. To put it rather bluntly, skilled action is mindless. Suchman (1987), an ethnomethodologist, also uses this type of Heideggerian argument to show that we do not make plans and then execute it. Rather, the plan only becomes relevant as resources that can be drawn on in situated action when things start to break down.

The work of Dreyfus and Suchman has important implications for IS design and use. For example, organizational actors do not have plans, strategies or goals in their heads that they then implement in action. Rather, as skilled actors they draw on events, reports and communications as 'possibilities for', without having to conceptualize explicitly the strategy, the information and the relationship between them. This was demonstrated clearly in the work of Ciborra (2000). It is also clear that if we take the work of Heidegger seriously, we would tend to think very differently about the role that methodology plays in the design process (Introna and Whitley, 1997; Winograd and Flores, 1986; Rathswohl, 1991).

Phenomenology may also help us to think very differently about the way in which organizational actors use information in decision making, as argued by Introna (1997) and Winograd and Flores (1986). For example, Introna (1997) argues that managers in the world already understand what they need to do and most often use information systems to find ways to articulate and make sense of what they already know. He argues with Heidegger that interpretation can only be based on an already present sense or understanding and not the other way around, as assumed. This claim makes sense if we see that interpretation is the 'unravelling' of the referential whole already present as the necessary condition of meaningful, ongoing, skilful action. Interpretation, and the information to support that, often becomes necessary in moments of breakdown when managers are asked to explain themselves. Likewise, Winograd and Flores (1986) argue that managers find themselves in networks of commitments—Heidegger's notion of thrownness—within which the question is not 'What should we do?' but rather 'What is possible?' given the already there network of commitments—the already there network of commitments that constitute the manager as 'a manager'. Managers in the world find themselves 'always already oriented to a certain direction of possibilities' in which 'relevance always comes from a pre-orientation within a background' (Winograd and Flores, 1986, pp. 147–9). For the manager-in-the-world the information system is just one of the references in a dense, ongoing, referential whole that continuously locates and dislocates possibilities for action.

More generally, phenomenology has also interrogated phenomena such as cyberspace and its relation to embodiment. In his thoughtful book *Designing Information Technology in the Postmodern Age*, Coyne (1995) argues that cyberspace is not an ontological world: mere 'information does not make worlds or space' (Coyne, 1995, p. 177). It is the concerns of everyday life, the people we talk to, the community we are part of and the things that occupy our attention that make a world. In a similar vein, Dreyfus (2001, p. 90) argues:

> Our body, including our emotions, plays a crucial role in our being able to make sense of things so as to see what is relevant, our ability to let things matter to us and to acquire skills, our sense of the reality of things, our trust in other people, and finally, our capacity for making unconditional commitments that gives meaning to our lives. It would be a serious mistake to think we could do without these embodied capacities [and practices]—to rejoice that the World Wide Web offers us a change to become more and more disembodied, detached ubiquitous minds leaving our situated, vulnerable bodies behind.

Don Ihde (2002, p. 15) also concludes that virtual bodies 'are thin and never attain the thickness of flesh'. In the end, when we switch the computer off we are still enmeshed in our daily entanglements, our thrownness, in which we have to make the mundane things work. The 'shortcutting' of the ordinary embodied and situated world through the virtual—the fantasy of the virtual organization—will always eventually have to be made 'real', or grounded, in the thick reality of everyday embodied practices—the world as such. We need to accept that the representation is not the world, the map is not the territory.

It is our argument that phenomenology offers a rich and subtle range of possibilities for information systems researchers. However, phenomenology itself requires a commitment to scholarship and thoughtful thinking, which is always difficult in a world that often requires ready-made solutions rather than thoughtful interpretations.

CONCLUSION

Phenomenology is a response to all forms of empirical and psychological reductionism as well as idealistic theoretical reductionism. Empiricism is based on highly inappropriate suppositions, according to phenomenology. For the empiricists the facts of the world 'speak for themselves', they are given to us as that which they are, for example a chair as a 'chair' and an attitude as an 'attitude'. In other words, the objects, events, states and so on that we observe are simply *given* to our senses as that which they are rather than being constituted through our consciousness of them. Their meaning is already inscribed on their very surfaces, as it were. The world is simply as revealed through our natural attitude. With this supposition in hand, they then proceed to describe, measure and account for the ongoing world in these 'given' terms. These evident, given facts are captured through observation and then constructed into various explanations and theories of the world. Through this process of 'theory making'—which is the 'stuff' of positivism—they proceed to cloak the world with all sorts of theoretical meanings divorced of any sense of actuality—leading many to describe the theory of information systems as irrelevant and meaningless, divorced of practice.

Against this view phenomenology argues that the world is always already meaningful. That we already observe this or that thing in the world requires as a necessary condition an already present horizon of meaning in which 'this' or 'that' shows up as such. The task of phenomenology is to give an account of this necessary horizon of meaning. Through phenomenology we can give an account of the nexus of relationships (in consciousness and in the world) that constitute this meaning as such. Such an account can provide an entirely new foundation from which to direct empirical investigations of the world. Since phenomenology is guided by experience, as experienced, and nothing besides, it will maintain its actuality. Phenomenology is not against empirical investigation. Nor is phenomenology denying that the world exists separate from our experience of it; that is, phenomenology is not anti-realist. It argues rather that such empirical investigation will only make sense if it is grounded in the world, in the nexus of relationships or horizon of meaning, that makes such an investigation meaningful in the first place. The 'real world' of relevance is not merely speaking to more managers if such speaking is not grounded in the world of ongoing and active meaning.

A second supposition of empirical reductionism—in a sense required by the first supposition—is that things have meaning *in themselves*. As said above, their meaning is already inscribed on their very surfaces as such. This supposition leads to a decontextualization of meaning and a reconstruction of meaning through theory making, also as mentioned above. This leads to a theoretical world that is the form of life of scientists—which is a legitimate location of study in its own right. For existential phenomenology the meaning of the thing is always and already in the nexus of relationships of the world. We can only understand managers, 'as managers', by understanding and analysing the nexus of relationships that constitute the manager and on which the manager continues to draw in order to be 'a manager'. The manager is what he or she is only in the ongoing involvement whole of 'being a manager in the organization'. Thus, the meaning making of active consciousness is always and already 'grounded' in the world of ongoing activity. Interpretation of phenomena is not arbitrary or idiosyncratic. Every phenomenological attempt to give an interpretation of something can only be grounded in the world where it has its being, its meaning. Thus, in phenomenology, contrary to the criticism often levelled at interpretivism, anything does not go. Phenomenological interpretation is not the uncovering of the subject's private mind (this is psychological reductionism). It is not just another interpretation or an endless proliferation of interpretations. Interpretivism that is not grounded in phenomenology can indeed be seen as psychologism—and there are quite a number of so-called interpretive studies in information systems that are of this nature.

The challenge of this chapter to the information systems community is to take phenomenology seriously as a path towards meaningful analysis, theory and research. With phenomenology we may be able to face our 'crisis' of rigour and relevance (Benbasat and Zmud, 1999; Keen, 1991); rigour, since we ground ourselves only in the things themselves—ongoing being-in-the-world as the completely immanent (wholly present, never absent) ongoing structural correlation with the world; relevance, since our ultimate authority is the ever-present horizon of meaning, which is the world itself.

A GUIDE TO THE LITERATURE

General Introductions to Phenomenology

Sokolowski, R. (2000) *Introduction to Phenomenology*, Cambridge: Cambridge University Press. Very good general introduction to phenomenology, easy to read.

Stewart, D. and Mickunas, A. (1990) *Exploring Phenomenology: A Guide to the Field and its Literature*, 2nd edn, Athens, OH:

Ohio University Press. A widely referenced introduction to phenomenology in accessible language.

Hammond, M., Howarth, J. and Keat, R. (1991) *Understanding Phenomenology*, Oxford: Blackwell. Slightly more technical introduction to the subject.

Moran, D. (2000) *Introduction to Phenomenology*, London: Routledge. A very detailed introduction to all the main authors in phenomenology, but not the right one to start with.

Husserl

Natanson, M. (1973) *Edmund Husserl: Philosopher of Infinite Tasks*, Evanston, IL: Northwestern University Press. The most widely used introduction to Husserl.

Zahavi, D. (2003) *Husserl's Phenomenology*, Stanford, CA: Stanford University Press. Good introduction with some technical language.

Heidegger

Polt, R. (1999) *Heidegger: An Introduction*, London: UCL Press. A very accessible start to exploring Heidegger's main work.

Dreyfus, H. (1991) *Being-in-the-World: A Commentary on Heidegger's Being and Time, Division I*, Cambridge, MA: MIT Press. Most used introduction to Division I of Heidegger's *Being and Time*.

King, M. (2001) *A Guide to Heidegger's Being and Time* (ed. John Llewellyn), Albany, NY: State University of New York Press. A sophisticated but accessible commentary on Heidegger's *Being and Time*.

Merleau-Ponty

Langer, M. (1989) *Merleau-Ponty's Phenomenology of Perception: A Guide and Commentary*, Basingstoke: Macmillan Press. A good introduction to Merleau-Ponty's main arguments. See also Mingers (2001).

Phenomenology and Technology

Borgmann, A. (1984) *Technology and the Character of Contemporary Life*, Chicago, IL: University of Chicago Press. Good introduction to Heidegger's essay on technology and possible responses to it.

Ihde, D. (1990) *Technology and the Lifeworld: From Garden to Earth*, Bloomington, IN: Indiana University Press. Useful account of how phenomenology can provide ways to analyse technology. See also Rathswohl's (1991) use of this work.

ENDNOTES

[1] We must note that it is not given to us as an extended object. To take it as an object we need already to have separated it from its immediate surroundings and background. Furthermore, to take it as extended we need already to have assumed spatiality. Thus, any taking of an object, even in its aspect, already requires, as necessary, a familiarity with the world as its condition of possibility.

[2] It is important to state that Husserl's work is characterized by an earlier period and a later period. In the earlier period Husserl was more interested in the formal structures of consciousness (this work is often referred to as *transcendental phenomenology*). However, in his later work, especially *The Crisis of European Sciences*, Husserl shifts towards a more *genetic phenomenology* where he emphasizes the active, historical consciousness rooted in the life world. In our discussion and analysis we will tend to focus on this later Husserl rather than the earlier Husserl. It is also the later Husserl that creates the bridge to Heidegger, which is important in our use of phenomenology as an *existential phenomenology* when we analyse the phenomenon of 'screen' below.

[3] The term 'always and already' will be employed frequently and is used in a very specific manner. By this term we mean 'always already', in the sense that it is impossible to find a starting point as such—some point where it all started, as it were. At any point in the past, we may find it is already active and busy. Furthermore, the 'always already' refers to the fact that it is not sometimes active and sometimes not. Rather, it is 'always already' active, engaged and directed. Refer to Heidegger's (1962) introduction of the term in *Being and Time*.

[4] As mentioned above, even the possibility of experiencing sound 'as sound' implies a horizon of temporality that can hold together in the 'now' what has gone before and anticipate what is yet to come.

[5] We must note that the *noemata* are not simply generalizations. The process of generalization itself already presupposes the existence of a *noema* since, for example, 'the abstraction of the general idea "red" [or chair] is arrived at by leaving out of account all those respects in which several red [chair] objects differ in order to hold on to that respect in which they are similar. But the concept of similarity (or even respect) which is in question here itself presupposes the very comprehension (of the essence of 'red' [chair]) which it is supposed to account for' (Macann, 1993, p. 9).

[6] For an excellent in-depth discussion of Husserl's theory of intentionality, refer to Gurwitsch (1967, 1982).

[7] Refer to John Mingers (2001) and Monika Langer's (1989) commentary for a good introduction to Merleau-Ponty's work.

[8] For Heidegger 'being' is not a substance but the ongoing unfolding of the referential whole that reveals something as what it is, its ongoing phenomenological

meaning. Thus, for him being is a *process* not a substance. It would be better to write it as be-ing but this becomes awkward.

[9] Heidegger uses the hyphens in being-in-the-world to indicate the ongoing structural unity of self and world, so that we do not slip back into a natural language in which we speak of the self without immediately also implying an already there meaningful world. This is somewhat awkward but it is important to signal.

[10] We must note that we as humans do not take up projects in a similar way as we do not take up things as objects. Our projects are always already part of our being-in-the-world. We are always ahead of ourselves. When we get up in the morning we already anticipate the day ahead. When we get into our cars we already anticipate the journey. To put it rather abstractly, we are always and already project-ed as a necessary condition of what we already are—as academics, managers etc. We did not decide to take up the project to write this chapter, as much as we found ourselves writing this chapter as that which already made sense for us as academics to do.

[11] Refer to Polt (1999) Chapter 3 for a very accessible account of Heidegger's notion of the world.

[12] Elsewhere we have discussed the method as having five or seven phases (Introna and Ilharco, 2000). This is more in line with Spiegelberg's discussion. However, due to space constraints and considerations of pragmatic use of the method, we will limit ourselves here to only four fundamental phases. These will serve as a consistent way to apply phenomenology.

[13] Unfortunately, due to space limitations we cannot provide a detailed discussion here. We hope that the analysis of the screen will make the method clear. Also, refer to Spiegelberg's (1994, pp. 677–719) account for more detail.

[14] Take careful note again that when we use the term 'world' or 'in-the-world' in our analysis we are using it in the phenomenological sense, i.e. the nexus or referential whole in which things refer to each other as already meaningful, as explained above (Heidegger, 1962).

[15] Indeed, other words we use to refer to screens, such as output device, dumb terminal, cathode ray tube, liquid crystal display, flat panel display and so forth, are multiple modes of showing particular aspects, functionalities or perspectives of screens. They are all phenomenologically related to the phenomena 'screen'.

[16] Sanskrit—the language in which the Vedas, the oldest sacred texts, were written—was an early form of an Indo-Aryan language, dating from around 1000 BC. The Indo-Aryan languages are supposed to derive from the hypothetical Proto-Indo-European language (before 3000 BC) from which also could have evolved Slavic, Baltic, Classical Greek, Latin, Germanic and other families of languages. Old High German, Middle English and Middle Dutch belong to the *West* branch of the Germanic family. Middle French belongs to the Italic (Latin) family (Crystal, 1987).

[17] Elsewhere we have demonstrated this central intent through sound analysis. Due to space limitations we will not pursue such an analysis here (Introna and Ilharco, 2000).

[18] The notion of 'form of life' that we use here refers to a familiar and meaningful ongoing activity whole in which things already appear as meaningful and therefore do not require elaboration by those participating in the form of life—somewhat akin to Wittgenstein's (1967) notion of form of life.

[19]For an excellent discussion on the phenomenological notion of essence, refer to the work of Mohanty (1970, 1997).

REFERENCES

ABC (1999) ABCnews http://archive.abcnews.go.com/sections/world/1997/97diana.html, accessed 29 December 1999.

Adams, P. (1993) 'In TV: On "Nearness", on Heidegger and on television', in T. Fry (ed.), *RVATV? Heidegger and the Televisual*, Sydney: Power Institute of Fine Arts.

Benbasat, I. and Zmud, R. (1999) 'Empirical research in information systems: The practice of relevance', *Management Information Systems Quarterly*, 23(1): 3–16.

Boland, R. J. (1983) 'The in-formation of information systems', in R. J. Boland and R. A. Hirschheim (eds), *Critical Issues in Information Systems Research*, New York, NY: John Wiley & Sons, pp. 363–94.

Boland, R. J. (1985) 'Phenomenology: A preferred approach to research on information systems', in E. Mumford, R. Hirschheim, G. Fitzgerald and A. T. Wood-Harper (eds), *Research Methods in Information Systems*, Amsterdam: North-Holland, pp. 193–201.

Boland, R. J. (1991) 'Information system use as a hermeneutic process' in H. -E. Nissen, H. K. Klein and R. A. Hirschheim (eds), *Information Systems Research: Contemporary Approaches and Emergent Traditions*, Amsterdam: North-Holland, pp. 439–64.

Boland, R. J. (1993) 'Accounting and the interpretive act', *Accounting, Organisations and Society*, 18(2/3): 125–46.

Boland, R. J. and Day, W. F. (1989) 'The experience of system design: A hermeneutic of organizational action', *Scandinavian Journal of Management*, 5(2): 87–104.

Borgmann, A. (1984) *Technology and the Character of Contemporary Life*, Chicago, IL: University of Chicago Press.

Ciborra, C. U. (1997) 'De profundis? Deconstructing the concept of strategic alignment', working paper, Department of Informatics, Oslo: University of Oslo.

Ciborra, C. U. (1998) 'From tool to *Gestell*', *Information Technology and People*, 11(4): 305–27.

Ciborra, C. (2000) *From Control to Drift: the Dynamics of Corporate Information Infrastructure*, Oxford: Oxford University Press.

Coyne, R. (1995) *Designing Information Technology in the Postmodern Age: From Method to Metaphor*, Cambridge, MA: MIT Press.

Crystal, D. (1987) *The Cambridge Encyclopaedia of Language*, Cambridge: Cambridge University Press.

Derrida, J. (1973) 'Speech and Phenomena', in J. Derrida, *Speech and Phenomena and Other Essays on Husserl's Theory of Signs*, trans. D. Allison, Evanston, IL: Northwestern University Press.

Dreyfus, H. (1982) *What Computers Can't Do: The Limits of Artificial Reason*, New York, NY: Harper & Row.

Dreyfus, H. (1991) *Being-in-the-World: A Commentary on Heidegger's Being and Time, Division I*, Cambridge, MA: MIT Press.

Dreyfus, H. (1992) *What Computers Still Can't Do: A Critique of Artificial Reason*, Cambridge, MA: MIT Press.

Dreyfus, H. (1993) *What Computers Still Can't Do: A Critique of Artificial Reason*, 2nd edn, Cambridge, MA: MIT Press.
Dreyfus, H. (2001) *On the Internet*, New York, NY: Routledge.
Fry, T. (ed.) (1993) *RVATV? Heidegger and the Televisual*, Sydney: Power Institute of Fine Arts.
Garfinkel, H. (1967) *Studies in Ethnomethodology*, Englewood Cliffs, NJ: Prentice-Hall.
Giddens, A. (1984) *The Constitution of Society*, Berkeley, CA: University of California Press.
Gurwitsch, A. (1967) 'Intentionality, constitution, and intentional analysis', in J. Kockelmans (ed.), *Phenomenology*, New York, NY: Anchor Books, pp. 118–37.
Gurwitsch, A. (1982) 'Husserl's theory of the intentionality of consciousness', in H. Dreyfus (ed.), *Husserl's Intentionality and Cognitive Science*, Cambridge, MA: MIT Press, pp. 59–71.
Hall, H. (1993) 'Intentionality and world: Division I of *Being and Time*', in C. Guignon (ed), *The Cambridge Companion to Heidegger*, Cambridge: Cambridge University Press.
Hammond, M., Howarth, J. and Keat, R. (1991) *Understanding Phenomenology*, Oxford: Blackwell.
Haynes, J. D. (1997) 'Meaning as perspective: A phenomenology of information systems', unpublished PhD thesis, Queensland: Bond University.
Heidegger, M. (1962) *Being and Time*, Oxford/Cambridge, MA: Blackwell.
Heidegger, M. (1971) *Poetry, Language, Thought*, trans. A. Hofstadter, New York, NY: Harper and Row.
Heidegger, M. (1977) *The Question Concerning Technology and Other Essays*, New York, NY: Harper Torchbooks.
Heidegger, M. (1978) 'On the essence of truth', in M. Heidegger, *Basic Writings*, London: Routledge.
Heidegger, M. (1982) *The Basic Problems of Phenomenology*, Bloomington, IN: Indiana University Press.
Heidegger, M. (1984) *Early Greek Thinking: The Dawn of Western Philosophy*, San Francisco, CA: Harper & Row.
Husserl, E. (1964) *The Idea of Phenomenology*, The Hague: Martinus Nijhoff.
Husserl, E. (1969) *Formal and Transcendental Logic*, The Hague: Martinus Nijhoff.
Husserl, E. (1970a) *The Crisis of European Sciences and Transcendental Phenomenology: An Introduction to Phenomenological Philosophy*, Evanston, IL: Northwestern University Press.
Husserl, E. (1970b) *Logical Investigations*, New York, NY: Humanities Press.
Husserl, E. (1995) *Cartesian Meditations: An Introduction to Phenomenology*, Dordrecht: Kluwer Academic Publishers.
Ihde, D. (2002) *Bodies in Technology*, Minneapolis, MN: University of Minnesota Press.
Ilharco, F. M. (2002) 'Information technology as ontology', unpublished PhD thesis, London: London School of Economics.
Introna, L. D. (1993) 'Information: A hermeneutic perspective', *Proceedings First European Conference of Information Systems*, Henley on Thames, pp. 171–9
Introna, L. D. (1997) *Management, Information and Power*, London: Macmillan.
Introna, L. D. and Ilharco, F. M. (2000) 'The screen and the world: A phenomenological investigation into screens and our engagement in the

world', in R. Baskerville, J. Stage and J. I. DeGross (eds), *Organizational and Social Perspectives on Information Technology*, Dordrecht: Kluwer Academic Publishers, pp. 295–319.

Introna, L. D. and Whitley, E. A. (1997) 'Against method-ism', *Information Technology and People*, 10(1): 31–45.

Introna, L. D. and Whittaker, L. (2002) 'The phenomenology of information systems evaluation: Overcoming the subject object dualism', in E. H. Wynn, M. D. Myers and J. I. DeGross (eds), *Global Organisational Discourse about Information Technology*, Dordrecht: Kluwer Academic Publishers, pp. 155–75.

Kant, I. (1965) *Critique of Pure Reason*, trans. N. K. Smith, New York, NY: St. Martin's Press.

Keen, P. (1991) 'Relevance and rigor in information systems research: Improving quality, confidence, cohesion and impact', in H.-E. Nissen, H. Klein and R. Hirschheim (eds), *Information Systems Research: Contemporary Approaches & Emergent Traditions*, Amsterdam: North-Holland, pp. 27–49.

Kjaer, A. and Madsen, K. H. (1995) 'Participatory analysis of flexibility', *Communications of the ACM*, 38(5): 53–60.

Kockelmans, J. (1967) *Phenomenology*, New York, NY: Anchor Books.

Langer, M. (1989) *Merleau-Ponty's Phenomenology of Perception: A Guide and Commentary*, Basingstoke: Macmillan Press.

Lawlor, L. (2002) *Derrida and Husserl: The Basic Problem of Phenomenology*, Bloomington, IN: Indiana University Press.

Leedy, P. D. (1997) *Practical Research: Planning and Design*, 6th edn, Upper Saddle River, NJ: Prentice-Hall.

Levinas, E. (1991 [1974]) *Other than Being or Beyond Essence*, Dordrecht: Kluwer Academic Publishers.

Lyotard, J.-F. (1991) *Phenomenology*, trans. B. Beakley, New York, NY: SUNY Press.

Macann, C. (1993) *Four Phenomenological Philosophers: Husserl, Heidegger, Sartre, Merleau-Ponty*, London/New York, NY: Routledge.

Mensch, J. R. (2001) 'Derrida–Husserl: Towards a phenomenology of language', in B. Hopkins and S. Gowell (eds), *The New Yearbook for Phenomenology and Phenomenological Philosophy*, Edmonds, WA: Noesis Press.

Merleau-Ponty, M. (1962) *Phenomenology of Perception*, London/New York, NY: Routledge.

Merriam-Webster Dictionary (1999, 2000) http://www.m-w.com.

Mingers, J. (2001) 'Embodying information systems: The contribution of phenomenology', *Information and Organization*, 11(2): 103–28.

Mohanty, J. (1970) *Phenomenology and Ontology*, The Hague: Martinus Nijhoff.

Mohanty, J. (1997) *Phenomenology: Between Essentialism and Transcendental Philosophy*, Evanston, IL: Northwestern University Press.

Moran, D. (2000) *Introduction to Phenomenology*, London: Routledge.

Oxford Paperback Dictionary and Thesaurus (1997) ed. J. Elliot, Oxford/New York, NY: Oxford University Press.

Polt, R. (1999) *Heidegger: An Introduction*, London: UCL Press.

Porra, J. (1999) 'Colonial systems', *Information Systems Research*, 10(1): 38–69.

Rathswohl, E. J. (1991) 'Applying Don Ihde's phenomenology of instrumentation as a framework for designing research in information science', in H.-E. Nissen,

H. K. Klein and R. A. Hirschheim (eds), *Information Systems Research: Contemporary Approaches and Emergent Traditions*, Amsterdam: North-Holland, pp. 421–38.

Ricoeur, P. (1981) *Hermeneutics and the Human Sciences*, Cambridge: Cambridge University Press.

Rogers, M. F. (1983) *Sociology, Ethnomethodology, and Experience: A Phenomenological Critique*, Cambridge: Cambridge University Press.

Sanders, P. (1982) 'Phenomenology: A new way of viewing organizational research', *Academy of Management Review*, 7(3): 353–60.

Schutz, A. and Luckmann, T. (1973) *The Structures of the Life-World*, Evanston, IL: Northwestern University Press.

Sokolowski, R. (2000) *Introduction to Phenomenology*, Cambridge: Cambridge University Press.

Spiegelberg, H. (1975) *Doing Phenomenology: Essays on and in Phenomenology*, The Hague: Martinus Nijhoff.

Spiegelberg, H. (1994 [1959]) *The Phenomenological Movement: A Historical Introduction*, 3rd edn, Dordrecht: Kluwer Academic Publishers.

Steels, L. and Brooks, R. (eds) (1995) *Building Situated Embodied Agents: The Alife Route to AI*, New Haven, NJ: Lawrence Erlbaum.

Suchman, L. (1987) *Plans and Situated Action: The Problem of Human–Machine Communication*, Cambridge: Cambridge University Press.

Thevenaz, P. (1962) *What Is Phenomenology and Other Essays*, ed. and trans. J. M. Edie, London: Merlin Press.

Whittaker, L. (2001) 'Information systems evaluation: A post dualist interpretation', unpublished PhD thesis, Pretoria: University of Pretoria.

Winograd, T. and Flores, F. (1986) *Understanding Computers and Cognition: A New Foundation for Design*, Reading, MA: Addison Wesley.

Wittgenstein, L. (1967) *Philosophical Investigations*, Oxford: Blackwell.

Zahavi, D. (2003) *Husserl's Phenomenology*, Stanford, CA: Stanford University Press.

Zuboff, S. (1988) *In the Age of the Smart Machine*, New York, NY: Basic Books.

4
Hermeneutics in Information Systems Research

Michael D. Myers

Hermeneutics can be defined as 'the theory or philosophy of the interpretation of meaning' (Bleicher, 1980, p. 1). Hermeneutics is primarily concerned with the *meaning* of a text or text-analogue. A text-analogue is anything that can be treated as a text, such as any human artefact, action, organization or culture. The main objective of hermeneutics is human *understanding*: understanding what people say and do, and why. Although there are different kinds of hermeneutics, from 'pure' through to critical hermeneutics, the common thread is that all are concerned with the textual treatment of social settings. The hermeneutic effort consists of an attempt to make clear, or to make sense of, an object of study.

Hermeneutic philosophy has existed for centuries and was originally concerned with the interpretation of the Bible and other sacred texts.[1] In the twentieth century, however, hermeneutics was taken up by social philosophers and applied not just to written texts, but to the interpretation of speech and actions. Social philosophers such as Gadamer, Habermas and Ricoeur looked at how the interpretive techniques of hermeneutics could be applied in the social sciences (Mueller-Vollmer, 1988; Palmer, 1969). Diesing (1991) says that this hermeneutic school of social philosophy 'derives most directly from Heidegger, Gadamer's teacher, but also draws on concepts and logic from the whole German philosophical tradition back to Schleiermacher, Hegel, Kant, and beyond' (Diesing, 1991, p. 105).

More recently, hermeneutic philosophy has been used by sociologists and cultural anthropologists (Agar, 1986; Geertz, 1973). In this case, culture is treated like a text that needs to be interpreted and understood (Frost *et al.*, 1985). The ethnographer or field researcher seeks to discover the meaning of actions or statements in their social and organizational contexts or to explore the socially constructed contexts of institutions and organizations (Berger and Luckman, 1967; Bryman, 1989). As an approach to meaning analysis, hermeneutics has been used in education, medicine, architecture (Vattimo, 1988) and business disciplines such as marketing (Arnold and Fischer, 1994). It has also been applied to the analysis of sociotechnical interactions (Barley, 1986).

In information systems research, the subject of organizational discourse about information technology has become an important theme (Wynn *et al.*, 2002; see also Chapter 7). Hermeneutics can help us understand how information is interpreted and how information systems are used (Boland, 1991). Hermeneutics can also help us to understand the systems development process (Boland and Day, 1989; Hirschheim and Newman, 1991) and the impact of information technology in social and organizational contexts (Boland, 1991; Lee, 1991; Lee, 1994; Myers, 1994; Myers, 1995; Winograd and Flores, 1987). The principles of hermeneutics have been applied to the analyses of the metaphorical nature of theories of information (Boland, 1987). Additionally, hermeneutic philosophy can be used as an approach to interpretive field research (Butler, 1998; Klein and Myers, 1999; Myers, 1997a). This objective of this chapter is to focus on the implications of hermeneutics and hermeneutic philosophy for information systems research, IS research methods and IS practice.

In keeping with hermeneutic philosophy, I think I should acknowledge my own biases and prejudices from the start. I acknowledge that in my own work I have used just one form of hermeneutics, viz. critical hermeneutics. I have used critical hermeneutics in my research work for the past 25 years (going right back to my Master's thesis in the late 1970s and my PhD in the 1980s, both of which were in social anthropology). Therefore this chapter concentrates mostly on this particular form of hermeneutics. However, I recognize that there are important differences between the major strands of hermeneutic philosophy.

Briefly, hermeneutic philosophers range from those such as Dilthey, who advocated a 'pure hermeneutics' and stressed empathic understanding from the 'inside'. This form of hermeneutics is the most objectivist form of hermeneutics: it sees the text or object to be investigated as 'out there' and amenable to being investigated in a more or less objective manner by the scientist (Bleicher, 1982, p. 52).

At the other end of the scale are those who advocate a postmodern hermeneutics. In this case, the idea that there is such a thing as an objective or 'true' meaning to a text is strongly denied. 'Facts' are what a cultural, conversational community agree they are (Madison, 1990, p. 191). Postmodernist hermeneutic philosophers say that a text always goes beyond the author and every reading is a different reading. This form of hermeneutics is the most subjectivist form of hermeneutics. Somewhere in the middle is critical hermeneutics. This agrees that the facts are socially constructed and that there are different if not conflicting interpretations. However, critical hermeneutic philosophers disagree with the idea that all interpretations are equally valid. Some interpretations are better than others. Critical hermeneutics also suggests that there are socioeconomic and political constraints within which human communication takes place. In this case there is an attempt to mediate 'hermeneutically-grounded self-understanding' and 'the objective context in which it is formed' (Bleicher, 1982, p. 150). I discuss the different forms of hermeneutics in more detail later. Suffice to say for now that the philosophical debates among the various protagonists (and between hermeneutic philosophers and other types of philosophy) have been going on for some time and show no sign of abating.

This chapter is organized as follows. In the next section the theory of hermeneutics is defined and some of the key concepts are described. In the following section some key issues are discussed and some of the underlying assumptions of hermeneutic philosophy are contrasted with other approaches. This is followed by a discussion of the implications of hermeneutics for information systems research, IS research methods and IS practice.

THE NATURE OF HERMENEUTICS

Hermeneutics can be treated as both an underlying philosophy and a specific mode of analysis (Bleicher, 1980). As a philosophical approach to human understanding, it provides the philosophical grounding for interpretivism (Klein and Myers, 1999; Myers, 1997b). As a mode of analysis, it suggests a way of understanding textual data. This chapter is concerned primarily with using hermeneutics as a specific mode of analysis.

As was mentioned earlier, hermeneutics is primarily concerned with the *meaning* of a text or text-analogue. The basic question in hermeneutics is 'What is the meaning of a text?' (Radnitzky, 1970, p. 20). Taylor says:

> Interpretation, in the sense relevant to hermeneutics, is an attempt to make clear, to make sense of an object of study. This object must, therefore, be a text, or a text-analogue, which in some way is confused, incomplete, cloudy, seemingly contradictory—in one way or another, unclear. The interpretation aims to bring to light an underlying coherence or sense. (Taylor, 1976, p. 153)

The concept of 'text-analogue' refers to anything that can be treated as a text. The subject matter of hermeneutics is thus extremely broad. Texts include not just written documents, but conversations and even non-verbal communications such as gestures or facial expressions (Diesing, 1991, p. 105). The hermeneutic task consists in understanding what a particular text (such as a ceremony, a video or an event) means. There are several hermeneutic concepts that help to do this: historicity, the hermeneutic circle, prejudice, distanciation, autonomization, appropriation and engagement.

Historicity

One of the most fundamental concepts in hermeneutic philosophy is that of historicity. Wachterhauser (1986) describes the concept of historicity as follows:

> 'Historicity' does not refer to the incontestable but obvious fact that we live out our lives in time. It refers instead to the thesis that who we are is through and through historical. This concept refers to the claim that the relation between being human and finding ourselves in particular historical circumstances is not accidental but rather essential or 'ontological'. This means that what we are cannot be reduced to a noumenal, ahistorical core such as a transcendental ego or, more broadly, a human nature that is the same in all historical circumstances. Rather, who we are is a function of the historical circumstances and community that we find ourselves in, the historical language we speak, the historically evolving habits and practice we appropriate, the temporally conditioned choices we make... In short, hermeneutics defends the ontological claim that human beings are their history. (Wachterhauser, 1986, p. 7)

What this implies is that our understanding of ourselves and others occurs in a historical context where our 'historically informed present informs our interpretation of any topic or subject'. Understanding a phenomenon means being able to talk about it with others in a community (Wachterhauser, 1986).

The Hermeneutic Circle

Another fundamental concept in hermeneutic philosophy is that of the hermeneutic circle. The idea of a hermeneutic circle refers to the dialectic between the understanding of the text as a whole and the interpretation of its parts, in which descriptions are guided by anticipated explanations. As Gadamer explains:

> It is a circular relationship... The anticipation of meaning in which the whole is envisaged becomes explicit understanding in that the parts, that are determined by the whole, themselves also determine this whole. (Gadamer, 1976a, p. 117)

For example, in reading a book we might first of all look at the title and then the table of contents. From this we anticipate what the book is all about (and we might purchase it based on our preconceptions at this point). Then, as we read the introduction, our understanding of the purpose of the book improves. The more we read, the greater our understanding of the whole. But if we get stuck or lose our way, we might step back to look at the whole (the contents pages) to see where we are. This reorientation (from the parts to the whole) enables us to continue reading the part (a particular chapter) once again. The concluding chapter, by definition, 'concludes' or attempts to wrap up the meaning of the whole work. When we have finished reading the book as a whole, our understanding of the subject matter will have changed from the time when we decided to read it. We will have changed as well.

To explain the concept of the hermeneutic circle, Klein and Myers (1999) relate Gadamer's (1976a) example of how we are to translate the meaning of a sentence into a foreign language:

> As a case in question, consider the sentence 'they are playing football.' In order to understand the individual parts of the sentence (i.e. whether football is a round ball, an egg-shaped ball or no ball at all), we must attempt to understand the meaning of the sentence as a whole. The process of interpretation moves from a precursory understanding of the parts to the whole and from a global understanding of the whole context back to an improved understanding of each part, i.e. the meanings of the words. The sentence as a whole in turn is a part of some larger context. If from this context it is clear that nobody is engaged in sport at all, then we can conclude that the meaning of 'they are playing football' must be metaphorical. To apply the metaphor, one needs to interpret 'football' as an issue which is contested which in turn involves a new understanding of the

> meaning of the term 'playing' as involving something abstract which
> is being 'thrown or kicked around.' Also, 'playing' no longer means
> physical movement on a grassy field. (Klein and Myers, 1999, p. 71)

Thus the movement of understanding is constantly from the whole
to the part and back to the whole. Our task is to extend in concentric
circles the unity of the understood meaning. The harmony of all
the details with the whole is the criterion of correct understanding.
The failure to achieve this harmony means that understanding has
failed (Gadamer, 1976a, p. 117).

The idea of the hermeneutic circle can be applied not just to texts,
but to any text-analogue. For example, if an IS researcher is doing
some kind of field research in an organization, then the organization
itself can be treated as a text. The researcher might start by gaining
some general knowledge about the organization (the whole). This
might involve reading the annual reports, newspaper reports and
any other publicly available information (the parts). After doing
this, the researcher might then interview specific people within the
organization about certain subjects or events. As more interviews
are conducted and more information is gathered, the researcher's
understanding of the organization as a whole and its constituent
parts will improve. He or she will gain a better understanding of
how everything (the whole) fits together and why things are the
way they are. The movement of understanding 'is constantly from
the whole to the part and back to the whole'.

However, in-depth field research might also reveal apparent
absurdities or contradictions. For example, a company might have
a mission statement saying one thing, but the actions of the organizational participants might suggest something else. If various
people from different parts and functions of the organization are
interviewed, some contradictions and differences of opinion may
emerge. There may be differences of opinion as to why a certain
event happened (e.g. why the implementation of the ERP system
was scrapped). In this case, the hermeneutic process should continue until the apparent absurdities, contradictions and oppositions
in the organization no longer appear strange, but make sense. From
the perspective of a field researcher, the fieldwork is completed
once all the apparent contradictions are resolved (at least in the
researcher's mind).

We can see that the concept of the hermeneutic circle suggests
that we have an expectation of meaning from the context of what
has gone before. The movement of understanding 'is constantly
from the whole to the part and back to the whole' (Gadamer,

1976a, p. 117). We come to understand a complex whole from preconceptions about the meanings of its parts and their interrelationships.

Ricoeur defines interpretation as:

> the work of thought which consists in deciphering the hidden meaning in the apparent meaning, in unfolding the levels of meaning implied in the literal meaning. (Ricoeur, 1974, p. 13)

This task of unfolding the levels of meaning is at the heart of hermeneutics. The goal of interpretation is 'to produce a reading of the text that fits all important details into a consistent, coherent message, one that fits coherently into the context.' (Diesing, 1991, p. 110).

Prejudice

Another concept that is at the heart of hermeneutics is that of prejudice. Hermeneutics suggests that 'prejudice'—pre-judgement or prior knowledge—plays an important part in our understanding. The basic idea is that our attempt to understand a text always involves some prior knowledge or expectation of what the text is about. In fact, we cannot even begin to understand a text unless we have some understanding of the language in which it is written. Understanding a language involves, at a minimum, prior knowledge of the vocabulary, rules of grammar and social conventions with regard to the appropriateness of what should or should not be said. Thus prior knowledge is a prerequisite for understanding (even though most of this knowledge might be tacit knowledge and taken for granted).

In positivist social science, however, prejudice or pre-judgement is seen as a source of bias and therefore a hindrance to true knowledge; objectivity, according to positivism, is best attained if a social scientist adopts a value-free position and does not let biases interfere with his or her analysis. By contrast, hermeneutics suggests that understanding always involves interpretation; interpretation means using one's own preconceptions so that the meaning of the object can become clear to us (Gadamer, 1975, p. 358). Understanding is thus not merely a reproductive process but a productive process, and interpretations will always keep changing.

Hermeneutics thus suggests that prejudice or foreknowledge is the necessary starting point of our understanding. The hermeneutic maxim is: 'no knowledge without foreknowledge' (Diesing, 1991,

p. 108). The critical task of hermeneutics then becomes one of distinguishing between 'true prejudices, by which we understand, from the false ones by which we misunderstand' (Gadamer, 1976b, p. 124). Of course, the suspension of our prejudices is necessary if we are to begin to understand a text or text-analogue. But as Gadamer points out, this does not mean that we simply set aside our prejudices. Rather, it means that we, as researchers, must become aware of our own historicality (Gadamer, 1976b, p. 125). By this he means that we need to become aware of how our own views and biases are to a large extent determined by our own culture and personal history. Our own ideas and personal experience (education, family situation, job etc.) have a significant impact on how we view the world. Of course, in many scientific experiments it is considered important to know how the research instrument is 'calibrated'. What hermeneutics emphasizes is that in almost all kinds of social research, the research instrument is the researcher. Therefore it is important to know how the researcher approached the research (objectively and subjectively).

This awareness of the dialogue between the text and the interpreter has been brought to the fore in contemporary hermeneutics. The earlier hermeneutic philosophers such as Dilthey ignored this dialogical relationship between the text and the interpreter and attempted to understand the objective meaning of a text in its own right.

Autonomization and Distanciation

Two further concepts that are important in hermeneutics are those of autonomization and distanciation. Ricoeur (1981) makes an important distinction between verbal speech and written text. He says that the author's meaning, once it is inscribed in a text, takes on a life of its own. This process of autonomization takes place whenever speech is inscribed in a text: the text takes on a fixed, finite and external representation. This means that the text now has an autonomous, 'objective' existence independent of the author. Once something is published or in the public domain, it is virtually impossible to take it back. A good example of this is when a politician says something in an interview with a reporter. Many times a politician will 'regret' something that was said or apologize for it, but after the statement is published it is impossible to take it back. Many politicians have been forced to resign because of a statement that has taken on a life of its own.

Closely related to the concept of autonomization is that of distanciation (see Lee, 1994). Distanciation refers to the inevitable distance that occurs in time and space between the text and its original author on the one hand, and the readers of the text (the audience) on the other. A fundamental characteristic of a text is that it is communication 'in and through distance' (Ricoeur, 1991, p. 76). Since the text takes on a life of its own, it becomes dissociated from the original author, the originally intended audience and even its original meaning. Although not all hermeneutic philosophers are agreed on this point, Ricoeur suggests that the goal of hermeneutics is not to get 'behind' the text; that is, to seek to reconstruct the mind of the author or original readers. For example, Ricoeur would say that we can never really understand what Aristotle was thinking when he wrote one of his classic books of philosophy. This is impossible given the distance in time and space between Aristotle and us. No matter how good an imagination we have, we cannot simply abandon our own prejudices, biases, culture and personal history (since many of these things are taken for granted by us and are part of our being). Rather, the hermeneutic task is to make Aristotle's writings our own. The 'text is the medium through which we understand ourselves' (Ricoeur, 1991, p. 87). This leads to the next set of concepts.

Appropriation and Engagement

Hermeneutic philosophers suggest that we only come to understand the meaning of a text if we appropriate its meaning for ourselves; that is, we make it our own. This act of appropriation is essential for understanding to take place. Gadamer suggests that meaning does not reside in 'the subjective feelings of the interpreter' nor in 'the intentions of the author'. Rather, meaning emerges from the engagement of reader and text. As a reader engages with the text, both the reader and text (or the meaning of the text) are changed. This process of critical engagement with the text is crucial.

Forms of Hermeneutics

As I mentioned earlier, there are many different forms of hermeneutics. The early hermeneutic philosophers such as Dilthey advocated a 'pure hermeneutics', which stressed empathic understanding and the understanding of human action from the 'inside'. This is the most objectivist form of hermeneutics: it sees the text or object to be investigated as 'out there' and amenable to being investigated in a more or less objective manner by the scientist (Bleicher, 1982, p. 52).

Bleicher (1982) says that Dilthey failed to take account of the double hermeneutic. Giddens describes the double hermeneutic as follows:

> Sociology, unlike natural science, stands in a subject–subject relation to its 'field of study', not a subject–object relation; it deals with a pre-interpreted world; the construction of social theory thus involves a double hermeneutic that has no parallel elsewhere. (Giddens, 1976, p. 146)

What the double hermeneutic recognizes is that the social scientist does not stand, as it were, outside of the subject matter looking in. He or she does not study natural phenomena such as glaciers or trees from the outside. Rather, the only way a social scientist can study people is 'from the inside'. That is, he or she must already speak the same language as the people being studied (or, at the very least, be able to understand an interpretation or translation of what has been said). The double hermeneutic recognizes that social researchers are 'subjects' and are just as much interpreters of social situations as are the people being studied.

Radnitzky points out that the pure hermeneutics advocated by philosophers such as Dilthey is uncritical in that it takes statements or ideologies at face value (Radnitzky, 1970, p. 20 ff.) He cites Gadamer as saying,

> we don't have to imagine oneself in the place of some other person; rather, we have to understand *what* these thoughts or the sentences expressing them are *about*. (Radnitzky, 1970, p. 27)

In contrast to pure hermeneutics, postmodern hermeneutic philosophers argue that there is no such a thing as an objective or 'true' meaning of a text. 'Facts' are what a cultural, conversational community agree they are (Madison, 1990, p. 191). Postmodernist hermeneutic philosophers say that a text always goes beyond the author and every reading is a different reading. This form of hermeneutics is the most subjectivist.

Somewhere between these two positions is critical hermeneutics. Critical hermeneutics has emerged following the debates between Habermas and Gadamer (Gadamer, 1976a; Kogler, 1996; Myers, 1995; Ricoeur, 1976; Thompson, 1981). Critical hermeneutic philosophers recognize that the interpretive act is one that can never be closed as there is always a possible alternative interpretation (Taylor, 1976). In critical hermeneutics the interpreter constructs the context as another form of text, which can then, of itself, be critically analysed. In a sense, the hermeneutic interpreter is simply creating another text upon a text, and this recursive creation is potentially infinite. Every meaning is constructed, even through the very constructive act of seeking to deconstruct, and the process whereby that textual interpretation occurs is self-critically reflected upon (Ricoeur, 1974).

Critical hermeneutics is thus aware of the double hermeneutic and acknowledges the reflective critique of the interpretation applied by the researcher. As I pointed out in an earlier article (Myers, 1994), critical hermeneutics requires the researcher to become aware of his or her own historicality. This awareness of the dialectic between the text and the interpreter has been brought to the fore in contemporary hermeneutics. Classical or 'pure' hermeneutics ignored this dialectic in the attempt to understand a text in terms of itself.

However, critical hermeneutic philosophers disagree with the postmodern idea that assumes that all interpretations are equally valid (which is itself a normative statement). Some interpretations are better than others. If there are no grounds for judging between alternative explanations, then David Irving's view that the systematic extermination of Jews in German concentration camp gas chambers did not occur is equally valid to the generally accepted historical view of the Holocaust. Critical hermeneutic philosophers reject this position and suggest that we can judge between alternative explanations, even though that judgement may not always be correct and may change over time. The fact that we sometimes get it wrong does not mean that we should suspend our judgement altogether.

Critical hermeneutic philosophers also suggest that there are socioeconomic and political constraints within which human communication takes place. In this form of hermeneutics there is thus an attempt to mediate 'hermeneutically-grounded self-understanding' and 'the objective context in which it is formed' (Bleicher, 1982, p. 150).

A slightly different form of hermeneutics, closely related to critical hermeneutics, is 'depth hermeneutics'. Depth hermeneutics assumes that the surface meaning of the 'text' hides, but also expresses, a deeper meaning. 'It assumes a continuing contradiction between the author's conscious and unconscious mind, a false consciousness, which appears in the text' (Diesing, 1991, p. 130). This form of hermeneutics is a hermeneutics of suspicion (Klein and Myers, 1999). Ricoeur argues that it is possible in certain circumstances to see consciousness as 'false' consciousness. He illustrates the operation of the principle of suspicion with examples of critical analysis from Marx and Freud (Ricoeur, 1976).

An example

To illustrate some of the practicalities of using hermeneutics in IS research, I will take an example from my own work. The completed article on which this is based was published in *Accounting, Management and Information Technologies* (now *Information and Organization*) (Myers, 1994). This interpretive case study was concerned with the failed implementation of a centralized payroll system for the New Zealand Education Department. Although the system did achieve some measure of success, in the end the centralized payroll system was abandoned.

I was attracted to studying this particular project for a few reasons. First, it had achieved some notoriety within New Zealand. The problems with the implementation of this new system were broadcast on national radio and television and publicized on the front page of *The New Zealand Herald*. As this new system affected virtually every teacher in New Zealand, there was wide public interest in it. Second, one of my main research interests at that time was the implementation of information systems. The case fitted perfectly within the scope of this interest. Third, since I had used critical hermeneutics in my earlier research work in social anthropology, I was very interested to see if it could be applied to this area of IS research. My hunch was that it would apply very well, since there appeared to be a variety of opinions about the system and the reasons for failure. For all these reasons, therefore, this case seemed a very good choice.

Unlike ethnographic research, which tends to be very open-ended, I decided to use the interpretive case study method in this instance. I focused on just one question, viz. 'Why did the system fail?' The empirical part of the study was actually the shortest I have ever done in my career, but paradoxically one of the most interesting. The case study material was collected from unstructured interviews, unpublished documents and newspaper and magazine reports.

Once I had gathered all the data, the next step was to write a narrative history of the project. This was fairly straightforward, since I simply recounted the major events over time. This was followed by the case analysis. From a hermeneutic perspective, the case was interesting because of the sharply divergent and sometimes contradictory views of the main protagonists. The project was characterized by conflicting interpretations among the participants about what happened, who was to blame and how successful the project was. In the first instance, my aim in the analysis section was to show how each person's view 'made sense' when considered from their point of view. My analysis juxtaposed some of the conflicting interpretations and my analysis of them, showing how it was possible for two or more people to hold contradictory views of the same phenomenon or event. In the final analysis, I argued that the disaster itself 'made sense' given the social and historical context within New Zealand at the time. The analysis revealed the various interests of the parties and what they were trying to achieve.

In addition to the case analysis, the article also attempted to make a contribution to IS implementation theory. It argued that most existing models of IS implementation were somewhat narrow and mechanistic, and that the implementation of the New Zealand Education Department's payroll system could only be understood in terms of its wider social and historical context. I argued that 'success' is a matter of interpretation.

This example draws attention to a few practical points about using hermeneutics in IS research. First, it is more interesting to use hermeneutics where there are disagreements or contradictory interpretations of the same phenomenon or event within an organization. This gives the researcher something to interpret and explain. Second, prejudice, as used in the hermeneutic sense, is something to build on rather than to be avoided. My previous background and experience, along with my current IS research interests, formed the starting point for this particular research project. In a hermeneutic study there is no need to appeal to a false objectivity. In fact, this research project fitted with my previous experiences and interests. I started with a set of experiences, prior knowledge and interests. However, this is not to say that I had already made up mind as to why the system failed. I really had no idea at the start. The causes for failure required further empirical research.

Third, it is not necessary to discuss every single hermeneutic concept in every paper or journal article. This is because papers and articles are, by definition, quite short. In this particular article I focused on just one hermeneutic concept, that of the hermeneutic circle. I believe it is much better to focus on those issues that seem particularly pertinent to the case at hand, rather than trying to cover everything. Having said this, however, I think it is important for researchers seeking to use hermeneutics to be familiar with the most important concepts, even if they are not discussed in every paper. Otherwise there is a danger that hermeneutics will be used inappropriately and simplistically. Fourth, I think it is important to generalize from the case study or the field study to theory (Klein and Myers, 1999). Hermeneutics is something that enables one to do that and in fact almost requires it. This is because a hermeneutic researcher usually starts out with some kind of theoretical framework that the researcher wishes to explore within the context of a real organization or situation.

HERMENEUTICS CONTRASTED WITH OTHER POSITIONS

In seeking to contrast hermeneutics with other philosophical positions, one of the most obvious contrasts is with positivism. The basic ontological assumption of positivist philosophy is that reality is objectively given and can be described by measurable properties that are independent of the observer (researcher) and his or her instruments. In practice, it is often assumed that the units of analysis that make up reality can be classified objectively into subjects and predicates (subjects are also often referred to as entities or objects). The task of a positivist researcher is thus to be as objective as possible. A positivist researcher should adopt a value-free position and not let biases interfere with his or her analysis. Significant effort is expended trying to improve the reliability and validity of the findings.

By contrast, one of the fundamental assumptions of hermeneutics is that reality is socially constructed. The 'facts' themselves are meanings inscribed in documents, social rules and actions and so on. The task of the hermeneutic researcher is thus to attempt to understand the phenomena through the meanings that people assign to them. Significant effort is expended in becoming aware of one's own preconceptions so that the meaning of the object can become clear. Unlike the positivist researcher who tries to avoid bias altogether, the hermeneutic researcher believes that prejudice is the necessary starting point of our understanding. As Diesing points out,

> The hermeneutic approach does not require detachment or neutrality
> of the scientist. It requires involvement, even participation in the
> culture of the author. Indeed, it denies that neutrality is possible.
> (Diesing, 1991, p. 122)

The critical task of the researcher is thus to distinguish between
'true prejudices, by which we understand, from the false ones by
which we misunderstand' (Gadamer, 1976b, p. 124).

Some scholars understand the fundamental difference between
positivist research and interpretive research (as informed by
hermeneutics) by saying that positivist research is appropriate in
the natural sciences for the study of the natural world. Since natural
scientists study physical objects and processes such as chemicals or
geothermal activity, it is appropriate for natural scientists to be as
objective as possible and to aim for reliability and validity of the
findings. In the social sciences, however, where the subject matter
is people, interpretive approaches such as hermeneutics are more
appropriate. This is because the subject matter itself is what people
say and do. The 'facts' themselves are statements or actions that
occur within a social context. We cannot even begin to understand
the facts if we cannot understand the language in which they are
spoken or created (or at least we must be able to understand a
translation). Therefore both the facts and the analysis of these facts
involves interpreting them within a language and within a social
context, and for this some kind of interpretive or hermeneutic
approach is best.

I believe that this distinction between the natural and social
sciences is useful as a generalization. However, Bernstein (1983)
argues that all of the epistemological assumptions that supposedly
distinguish the human sciences apply equally well to the natural
sciences. He points out that there is a necessary hermeneutical
dimension to all science. Kuhn's historical analysis of the nature
of paradigm shifts in science supports this view (Kuhn, 1996).
Therefore, while I agree that the methods of natural science are
appropriate for the study of the natural world, this needs to be
tempered with the view that there is a hermeneutical dimension to
all science, both natural and social.

We also need to recognize that much social science is in fact
based on positivism (e.g. behaviourist psychology and much of
sociology) and therefore this also tends to water down the distinction between the natural and the social sciences. Many positivist
social scientists believe that the social sciences should more closely
emulate the natural sciences. Bleicher provides an excellent critique

of positivist sociology and positivist social science in general from the perspective of critical hermeneutics (Bleicher, 1982).

A much less obvious contrast can be made between hermeneutics and phenomenology (see also Chapter 3). Both philosophies are quite similar in some respects, in that both can be described as interpretive philosophies; in fact, both hermeneutics and phenomenology can be seen as providing the philosophical grounding for interpretivism. The fundamental contribution of phenomenology, that intentional consciousness is fundamental to human experience, is accepted by all hermeneutic philosophers. However, hermeneutic philosophers believe that phenomenologists such as Husserl and Schutz (Schutz, 1972) have failed to clarify the relationship between consciousness and intersubjectivity.

Phenomenology is sometimes described as a transcendental approach to our understanding of the world. The fundamental task of phenomenology is seen as being to *describe* and to give an account of the content of intentional consciousness—to describe the phenomena as such. 'By means of an essential intuition we explore the intentional structure of consciousness of human experience' (Introna and Ilharco, Chapter 3). The phenomenologist is concerned with essential human experiences that transcend this or that experience. However, Bleicher points out that, since the phenomenologist commences with the self-reflexive subject (i.e. himself or herself), this inevitably leads to a monological conception of intersubjectivity. 'It appears that the phenomenological descriptions of the life-world inevitably lead to the generalization of the phenomenologist's own experience' (Bleicher, 1982, p. 121).

A good example of this can be found in Introna and Ilharco's chapter in this volume (Chapter 3). In describing the phenomenon of the screen, the authors generalize their own experience of screens and assume that this same experience is valid for all. For instance, they claim that 'The screen, in screening, finds itself at the centre of the activity.' As an example of this they say, 'we organize our desk around our computer and our living room around our TV. We locate screens where they are visible.' This claim is unsubstantiated by any empirical evidence—it is simply taken for granted. However, when I was living in Atlanta, Georgia in 2002, I visited many homes of professional people where the placement of the TV screen contradicted this assertion. TVs (and computers) were often hidden away in a rumpus room or study and were most definitely *not* located in the living room. The living room was reserved for conversations with guests while the TV was banished to a less central location. This simple illustration throws into question the claimed universality of the comments made about screens in the chapter. In these southern homes the screen was definitely not the centre of activity (or at least, not while we were there). Bleicher's comment that phenomenological descriptions tend to generalize the phenomenologist's own experience appears to be borne out.

A hermeneutic approach to IS research, by contrast with phenomenology, seeks to go beyond introspection and intuition. Hermeneutics explores the meaning of social phenomena in various social and organizational contexts. Instead of a monologue, we have a multiplicity of conversations and many dialogues (one of which, for example, may be the dialogue between the researcher and the people in a field study).

Another contrast can be made between hermeneutically-informed approaches to interpretive research and what I would call non-dialectical views of interpretive research. One such non-dialectical position is that of the holistic school in ethnography (Harvey and Myers, 1995). Ethnographers of the holistic school attempt to 'go native' and understand other cultures 'in their own terms'. They make a clear distinction between the 'emic' and the 'etic' perspectives. The emic perspective is described as the 'insider's' perspective, while the etic perspective is described as the 'outsider's' (or researcher's) perspective.

From a hermeneutic point of view, however, the idea of a hard-and-fast distinction between the emic and etic perspectives does not make sense. It in effect denies the glossing of the 'insider's' views by the interpretive act of the analyst (i.e. appropriation and engagement). The end result is tantamount to a recourse to objectivity because the need for critical analysis of the dialectics of the interpretive process is taken for granted. The role of the observer is treated as context free, ignoring the fact that every interpretive exploration leads to a new understanding, thus rendering history as the most vital attribute of ethnographic analysis, the history of the material and the history of the interpretation (Harvey and Myers, 1995). Zuboff's study of computer-mediated work (Zuboff, 1988) took the dialectical process of historical critique as fundamental to the ethnographic work being carried out. She argued that 'history would offer only a brief window of time during which such data could be gathered' (Zuboff, 1988, p. xiv; for more on Zuboff see Chapter 7).

Another non-dialectical view of interpretive research is the more positivistic version of grounded theory (especially Glaser, 1992).

According to Martin and Turner (1986), grounded theory is an inductive, theory-discovery methodology that allows the researcher to develop a theoretical account of the general features of a topic while simultaneously grounding the account in empirical observations or data. Many grounded theorists recommend that the researcher should not let his or her preconceptions interfere with the interpretation of the data (Glaser and Strauss, 1967). In fact, Glaser goes so far as to suggest that grounded theorists should not even write a literature review before starting data collection. Critical hermeneutics, by contrast, suggests that prejudice is the necessary starting point of our understanding. Recognition of the dialectical nature of research requires the researcher to confront the data emerging through the research process with the preconceptions (prejudices) that guided the original research design (i.e. the original lenses).

The critical hermeneutic perspective asserts that understanding of an institutional context is not gained by the researcher suspending his or her prejudices. Rather, the researcher is encouraged to become critically aware of them, making them explicit during the research process. Of course, I acknowledge that many grounded theorists (including Strauss) do not agree with Glaser's positivistic version of grounded theory.

The critical hermeneutic perspective leads to the recognition that any interpretive field research is a form of historiography. The researcher is essentially situated in history, the history of the situation and of the interpretation, and is also part of a wider set of social, economic and political relationships. One of the key tasks of a researcher is to be aware of the historical context in which research takes place and to critically reflect this on to the research process itself. In arguing for a reflexive anthropology, Kahn points out that the interpretation of culture(s) 'is in fact part of a process of construction' and says that anthropologists themselves 'are similarly part of a broader socio-historical process' (Kahn, 1989, p. 22).

This awareness of the importance of history leads to criticism of the 'ethnographic present', a standard device used by many anthropologists to describe social and cultural practices. The ethnographic present gives the (false) impression that the activities being described have always existed from time immemorial. The use of such phrases as 'The development process starts out each September' or 'All the members of the development team do not participate' gives the distinct impression that such activities have taken place since the world was created. The ethnographic present is thus ahistorical and neglects to mention when these activities were instituted. The ethnographic present ignores how human actions are always situated in history (Myers, 1997a).

Another contrast that can be made is between critical hermeneutics and critical social theory (see for example Chapters 5 and 6). Unlike many critical theorists, who have focused their research on a critique of class-based societies and capitalist forms of production, a researcher informed by critical hermeneutics does not assume from the outset what the most important oppositions, conflicts and contradictions are in contemporary organizations (see Poster, 1989, 1990). Rather, the interpretive hermeneutics must go hand in hand with a critical analysis of organizations and societies. There is, then, a dynamic interplay between a hermeneutic analysis and theoretical critique, where the critique is firmly grounded in social reality. However, the distinction I have drawn between critical hermeneutics and critical social theory should not be drawn too rigidly. I acknowledge that the work of almost all critical theorists today is informed by hermeneutics, and some scholars have attempted to combine them (Kogler, 1996; Thompson, 1981).

IMPLICATIONS FOR INFORMATION SYSTEMS

Hermeneutics has many implications for information systems research, information systems research methods and IS practice.

In IS research hermeneutics can be used to study the nature of information and information systems (for a brief introduction to the hermeneutic approach to IS research, see Klein and Hirschheim, 1983). For example, Lee (1994) looked at richness in email communications by exploring the wider social and political context within which the email communications took place (see also Chapter 1). Drawing on the hermeneutic theory of Ricoeur (1981), Lee shows that richness or leanness is not an inherent property of the email medium, but an emergent property of the interaction of the email medium within its organizational context. Managers who receive email are not passive recipients of data, but active producers of meaning. Lee's hermeneutic analysis reveals a complex world of social constructions that are evoked through email communications.

Hermeneutics can also be used to study the design and implementation of information systems (Boland, 1985, 1991; Boland and Day, 1989; Winograd and Flores, 1987) and the social, cultural and organizational aspects of systems. Boland (1979, 1985, 1987) was one of the first IS researchers to suggest hermeneutics and phenomenology as a means of looking at the sense-making process in information systems development. Davis *et al.* (1992) used hermeneutics to propose a framework for diagnosing information systems failure. In my own work, I have adopted a more sociological usage of hermeneutics, examining the development and implementation of information systems from a critical hermeneutic perspective (Myers, 1994, 1995; Myers and Young, 1997). In this case the interpretive effort consists in making sense of the organizations as text-analogues, in which the different stakeholders have confused, incomplete, cloudy and often contradictory views on many issues. The aim is to make sense of the whole, and of the dynamic relationship between the organization and the introduction of new information technology.

Butler and Fitzgerald (1997) have also used hermeneutics to study user participation in information systems development. Malhotra, Gosain and Hars (1997) used hermeneutics in their longitudinal study of a virtual community, focusing on the issue of information systems design. More recently, Trauth and Jessup (2000) have used hermeneutics in their analysis of computer-mediated discussions in groups, while Watson-Manheim and Bélanger (2002) used hermeneutic analysis in an in-depth study of communication mode choices in distributed teams. In closely related areas to IS, Winograd and Flores (1987) and West (1997) have looked at the implications of hermeneutics for computer science, and Pospelov (1990) has looked at the implications of hermeneutics for expert systems.

For IS research methods, and especially in-depth interpretive field research, hermeneutics is very useful for making sense of the data (Butler, 1998; Klein and Myers, 1999; Lacity and Janson, 1994; Myers, 1997b). In case studies and ethnographies about information systems phenomena, the 'text' is social and political action: case study notes, interviews and documents record the views of the actors and describe certain events and so on (see Ricoeur, 1981, p. 197 ff). This material needs to be ordered, explained and interpreted in order to 'make sense' of the case. The ordering is done according to the researcher's theoretical position (his or her prejudices or preconceptions) and the researcher's role as interpreter involves the comparison of one text with another (e.g. the statement of an informant with that of a document). The researcher's understanding of the whole has to be continually revised in view of the reinterpretation of the parts.

The idea of the hermeneutic circle draws attention to the way in which we understand an organization as a text-analogue. In qualitative research, the movement of understanding 'is constantly from the whole to the part and back to the whole'; in other words, the more interviews we conduct and the more information we gather, the more we understand the organization as a whole and its constituent parts. This hermeneutic process continues until the apparent absurdities, contradictions and oppositions in the organization no longer appear strange but make sense.

Critical hermeneutics does not accept uncritically participants' own views on a particular topic; rather, it recognizes that the researcher (or at least the developer) attempts to critically evaluate and transform social reality, a reality that is historically constituted (Myers, 1995).

Klein and Myers (1999) point out that there is an inevitable difference in understanding between the interpreter and the author of a text that is created by the historical distance between them. The hermeneutic task consists not in covering up the tension between the text and the present, but in consciously bringing it out (Gadamer, 1976b, p. 133). In interpretive research, therefore, one of the key tasks becomes seeking meaning in context. Various contexts can be explored, the choice largely depending on the audience and the story that the author wants to tell.

The advantage of a hermeneutic approach in qualitative research is that it enables one to portray the complexity of organizations as social, cultural and political systems. In particular, critical hermeneutics requires a researcher to look at information systems and technologies from many different perspectives: we have to look at the meaning of a new information system for various stakeholders in an organization and the value conflicts that there may be; we also have to look at the objective social impacts (autonomization) of information systems (Myers, 1994).

For IS practice, hermeneutics is potentially very relevant during the systems development process. It has been applied to help give a deeper understanding of software quality (Tervonen and Kerola, 1998) and has also been suggested as an approach to teaching the management of information systems development (Westrup, 1994). I believe that the principles of hermeneutics could be used in systems analysis and design and also in post-implementation reviews. However, this is something that requires much more work as such approaches or methods are yet to be developed. Most current IS development methods tend to be normative (West, 1997).

CONCLUSION

Hermeneutics has moved from the periphery to centre stage in contemporary philosophy and social science. It provides the philosophical grounding for interpretivism, and as a mode of analysis suggests how the meaning of a text or text-analogue can be understood. As we have seen, hermeneutics is very relevant for information systems research, IS research methods and IS practice. It is useful in studying the underlying nature of information and information systems (at a philosophical level) and for making sense of the contradictory interpretations of social and historical events (e.g. why a certain system was a failure). It is also useful as a mode of analysis in qualitative research more generally (Myers, 1997b; Myers and Avison, 2002).

I predict that the next breakthrough will come when hermeneutics starts to inform IS development and IS practice. This is because the philosophers have already turned their attention to the relationship between hermeneutics and 'practical reason', initiative and action (Ricoeur, 1991). Critical hermeneutics is directed at the future and at changing reality rather than merely interpreting it (Bleicher, 1980, p. 233). However, considerable intellectual effort is required to make it happen. I believe this may be one of the next frontiers in IS research.

A GUIDE TO THE LITERATURE

A good place to start reading about hermeneutics is to choose one of more of the general introductions. Palmer's (1969) collection of readings on hermeneutics is excellent. *The Hermeneutic Reader* (Mueller-Vollmer, 1988) is another first-rate collection. Both books include selected works by prominent hermeneutic scholars.

From there, the serious scholar will want to look at Gadamer's (1975) book *Truth and Method*, which is regarded as a classic in the field. Gadamer's main concern is the veracity of interpretation; given that we cannot escape our pre-understandings and context, how can we avoid being purely relativistic? Gadamer's solution is to suggest that our prejudices and biases can be made subject to critical scrutiny.

Bernstein's (1983) book is an important landmark in social philosophy. He shows that there is an important hermeneutical dimension to all science (including the natural sciences). Bernstein's work has had a significant influence on Thomas Kuhn (Kuhn, 1996).

A good introduction to critical hermeneutics is the book by John Thompson (Thompson, 1981). Thompson also edited and translated a collection of essays by Ricoeur (1981). This collection presents a comprehensive view of Ricoeur's critical hermeneutics and looks at consequences of his hermeneutic philosophy for the social sciences. Ricoeur is best known for his proposal of a 'hermeneutics of suspicion'. He argues that it is possible in certain circumstances to see consciousness as 'false' consciousness.

Good examples of research articles in IS that explicitly use hermeneutics are those by Boland (1991), Lee (1994) and Myers (1994). Richard Boland was one of the first IS researchers to suggest hermeneutics and phenomenology as a means of looking at the sense-making process in information systems development. Boland's (1991) article argues that the use of information from an information system is always and of necessity a hermeneutic process. Allen Lee's (1994) article shows how the hermeneutic circle can help broaden our understanding of IT. Lee looks at the subject of information richness and shows how a complex world of social constructions may lie behind email communications. My own article (Myers, 1994) examines the failed implementation of a centralized payroll system by the New Zealand Education Department. This article uses critical hermeneutics and contributes to the IS implementation literature.

Klein and Myers' (1999) article suggests a set of principles for the conduct and evaluation of interpretive research in information systems. These principles are derived primarily from anthropology, phenomenology and hermeneutics.

ENDNOTE

[1] For an excellent overview of the early history of hermeneutics, see Bleicher (1980). For a more detailed treatment, including excerpts from some of the earlier and later hermeneutic writers, see Mueller-Vollmer (1988).

REFERENCES

Agar, M. (1986) *Speaking of Ethnography*, Beverly Hills, CA: Sage.

Arnold, S. J. and Fischer, E. (1994) 'Hermeneutics and consumer research', *Journal of Consumer Research*, 21(1): 55–70.

Barley, S. R. (1986) 'Technology as an occasion for structuring: Evidence from observations of CT scanners and the social order of radiology departments', *Administrative Science Quarterly*, 31(1): 78–108.

Berger, P. and Luckman, T. (1967) *The Social Construction of Reality: A Treatise in the Sociology of Knowledge*, London: Penguin.

Bernstein, R. J. (1983) *Beyond Objectivism and Relativism*, Philadelphia, PA: University of Pennsylvania Press.

Bleicher, J. (1980) *Contemporary Hermeneutics: Hermeneutics as Method, Philosophy and Critique*, London: Routledge & Kegan Paul.

Bleicher, J. (1982) *The Hermeneutic Imagination*, London: Routledge & Kegan Paul.

Boland, R. (1979) 'Control, causality and information system requirements', *Accounting, Organizations and Society*, 4(4): 259–72.

Boland, R. (1985) 'Phenomenology: A preferred approach to research in information systems', in E. Mumford, R. A. Hirschheim, G. Fitzgerald and T. Wood-Harper (eds), *Research Methods in Information Systems*, Amsterdam: North-Holland, pp. 193–201.

Boland, R. (1987) 'The in-formation of information systems', in R. J. Boland and R. A. Hirschheim (eds), *Critical Issues in Information Systems Research*, New York, NY: John Wiley & Sons, pp. 363–94.

Boland, R. J. (1991) 'Information system use as a hermeneutic process', in H.-E. Nissen, H. K. Klein and R. A. Hirschheim (eds), *Information Systems Research: Contemporary Approaches and Emergent Traditions*, Amsterdam: North-Holland, pp. 439–64.

Boland, R. J. and Day, W. F. (1989) 'The experience of system design: A hermeneutic of organizational action', *Scandinavian Journal of Management*, 5(2): 87–104.

Bryman, A. (1989) *Research Methods and Organization Studies*, London: Unwin Hyman.

Butler, T. (1998) 'Towards a hermeneutic method for interpretive research in information systems', *Journal of Information Technology*, 13(4): 285–300.

Butler, T. and Fitzgerald, B. (1997) 'A case study of user participation in the information systems development process', *Proceedings of the International Conference on Information Systems*, pp. 411–26.

Davis, G. B., Lee, A. S., Nickles, K. R., Chatterjee, S., Hartung, R. and Wu, Y. (1992) 'Diagnosis of an information system failure: A framework and interpretive process', *Information and Management*, 23(5): 293–318.

Diesing, P. (1991) *How Does Social Science Work? Reflections on Practice*, Pittsburgh, PA: University of Pittsburgh Press.

Frost, P. J., Moore, L. F., Louis, M. R., Lundberg, C. C. and Martin, J. (eds) (1985) *Organizational Culture*, Beverly Hills, CA: Sage.

Gadamer, H.-G. (1975) *Truth and Method*, New York, NY: Seasbury Press.

Gadamer, H.-G. (1976a) 'The historicity of understanding', in P. Connerton (ed.), *Critical Sociology: Selected Readings*, Harmondsworth: Penguin, pp. 117–33.

Gadamer, H.-G. (1976b) *Philosophical Hermeneutics*, Berkeley, CA: University of California Press.

Geertz, C. (1973) *The Interpretation of Cultures*, New York, NY: Basic Books.

Giddens, A. (1976) *New Rules of Sociological Method*, London: Hutchinson.

Glaser, B. G. (1992) *Emergence vs. Forcing: Basics of Grounded Theory Analysis*, Mill Valley, CA: Sociology Press.

Glaser, B. G. and Strauss, A. (1967) *The Discovery of Grounded Theory: Strategies for Qualitative Research*, Chicago, IL: Aldine.

Harvey, L. and Myers, M. D. (1995) 'Scholarship and practice: The contribution of ethnographic research methods to bridging the gap', *Information Technology and People*, 8(3): 13–27.

Hirschheim, R. and Newman, M. (1991) 'Symbolism and information systems development: Myth, metaphor and magic', *Information Systems Research*, 2(1): 29–62.

Kahn, J. S. (1989) 'Culture: Demise or resurrection?', *Critique of Anthropology*, 9(2): 5–25.

Klein, H. K. and Hirschheim, R. (1983) 'Issues and approaches to appraising technological change in the office: A consequentialist perspective', *Office: Technology and People*, 2(1): 15–24.

Klein, H. K. and Myers, M. D. (1999) 'A set of principles for conducting and evaluating interpretive field studies in information systems', *MIS Quarterly*, 23(1): 67–93.

Kogler, H. H. (1996) *The Power of Dialogue: Critical Hermeneutics after Gadamer and Foucault*, Cambridge, MA: MIT Press.

Kuhn, T. (1996) *The Structure of Scientific Revolutions*, Chicago, IL: University of Chicago Press.

Lacity, M. C. and Janson, M. A. (1994) 'Understanding qualitative data: A framework of text analysis methods', *Journal of Management Information Systems: JMIS*, 11(2): 137–55.

Lee, A. S. (1991) 'Integrating positivist and interpretive approaches to organizational research', *Organizational Science*, 2(4): 342–65.

Lee, A. S. (1994) 'Electronic mail as a medium for rich communication: An empirical investigation using hermeneutic interpretation', *MIS Quarterly*, 18(2): 143–57.

Madison, G. B. (1990) *The Hermeneutics of Postmodernity*, Bloomington, IN: Indiana University Press.

Malhotra, A., Gosain, S. and Hars, A. (1997) 'Evolution of a virtual community: Understanding design issues through a longitudinal study', *Proceedings of the International Conference on Information Systems*, pp. 59–73.

Martin, P. Y. and Turner, B. A. (1986) 'Grounded theory and organizational research', *Journal of Applied Behavioral Science*, 22(2): 141–57.

Mueller-Vollmer, K. (ed.) (1998) *The Hermeneutic Reader*, New York, NY: Continuum.

Myers, M. D. (1994) 'A disaster for everyone to see: An interpretive analysis of a failed IS project', *Accounting, Management and Information Technologies*, 4(4): 185–201.

Myers, M. D. (1995) 'Dialectical hermeneutics: A theoretical framework for the implementation of information systems', *Information Systems Journal*, 5(1): 51–70.

Myers, M. D. (1997a) 'Interpretive research methods in information systems', in J. Mingers and F. Stowell (eds), *Information Systems: An Emerging Discipline*, London: McGraw-Hill, pp. 239–66.

Myers, M. D. (1997b) 'Qualitative research in information systems', *MIS Quarterly*, 21(2): 241–2.

Myers, M. D. and Avison, D. E. (eds) (2002) *Qualitative Research in Information Systems: A Reader*, London: Sage.

Myers, M. D. and Young, L. W. (1997) 'Hidden agendas, power, and managerial assumptions in information systems development: An ethnographic study', *Information Technology and People*, 10(3): 224–40.

Palmer, R. (1969) *Hermeneutics: Interpretation Theory in Schleiermacher, Dilthey, Heidegger, and Gadamer*, Evanston, NJ: Northwestern University Press.

Pospelov, D. (1990) 'Hermeneutics in expert systems', *Knowledge-Based Systems*, 3(1): 25–7.

Poster, M. (1989) *Critical Theory and Poststructuralism*, Ithaca, NY: Cornell University Press.

Poster, M. (1990) *The Mode of Information*, Chicago, IL: University of Chicago Press.

Radnitzky, G. (1970) *Contemporary Schools of Metascience*, Goteborg: Scandinavian University Books.

Ricoeur, P. (1974) *The Conflict of Interpretations: Essays in Hermeneutics*, Evanston, IL: Northwestern University Press.

Ricoeur, P. (1976) 'Hermeneutics: Restoration of meaning or reduction of illusion?', in P. Connerton (ed.), *Critical Sociology, Selected Readings*, Harmondsworth: Penguin, pp. 194–203.

Ricoeur, P. (1981) *Hermeneutics and the Human Sciences*, Cambridge: Cambridge University Press.

Ricoeur, P. (1991) *From Text to Action: Essays in Hermeneutics II*, Evanston, IL: Northwestern University Press.

Schutz, A. (1972) *The Phenomenology of the Social World*, London: Heinemann.

Taylor, C. (1976) 'Hermeneutics and politics', in P. Connerton (ed.), *Critical Sociology: Selected Readings*, Harmondsworth: Penguin, pp. 153–93.

Tervonen, I. and Kerola, P. (1998) 'Towards deeper co-understanding of software quality', *Information and Software Technology*, 39(14,15): 995–1003.

Thompson, J. B. (1981) *Critical Hermeneutics: A Study in the Thought of Paul Ricoeur and Jurgen Habermas*, Cambridge: Cambridge University Press.

Trauth, E. M. and Jessup, L. M. (2000) 'Understanding computer-mediated discussions: Positivist and interpretive analyses of group support system use', *MIS Quarterly*, 24(1): 43–79.

Vattimo, G. (1988) 'Hermeneutics as koine', *Theory, Culture and Society*, 5: 2–3.

Wachterhauser, B. R. (1986) *Hermeneutics and Modern Philosophy*, Albany, NY: State University of New York Press.

Watson-Manheim, M. B. and Bélanger, F. (2002) 'An in-depth investigation of communication mode choices in distributed teams', *Proceedings of the Twenty-Third International Conference on Information Systems*, pp. 871–6.

West, D. (1997) 'Hermeneutic computer science', *Communications of the ACM*, 40(4): 115–16.

Westrup, C. (1994) 'Practical understanding: Hermeneutics and teaching the management of information systems development using a case study', *Accounting, Management and Information Technologies*, 4(1): 39–58.

Winograd, T. and Flores, F. (1987) *Understanding Computers and Cognition: A New Foundation for Design*, New York, NY: Addison-Wesley.

Wynn, E. H., Whitley, E. A., Myers, M. D. and De Gross, J. I. (eds) (2002) *Global and Organizational Discourse about Information Technology*, Boston, MA: Kluwer Academic Publishers.

Zuboff, S. (1988) *In the Age of the Smart Machine*, New York, NY: Basic Books.

5
Adorno: A Critical Theory for IS Research

Stephen K. Probert

This chapter considers the work of Theodor Adorno and how it may inform a critical approach to IS research. The theoretical relationship between critical theory, based on the work of Adorno, and positivistic and interpretivistic research work is explored. The main aim of the chapter is to provide a conceptual framework to assist the critical researcher in devising apposite research strategies and programmes. The chapter begins by briefly introducing Adorno and his ideas; the context in which IS development takes place is explored from this critical perspective. A new paradigm for IS research—encompassing both critical and empirical facets of IS research—is then developed. It is argued that critical models of empirical studies may be developed—employing the negative dialectical strategy—to enhance the critical IS research process. These will be models produced by IS researchers (informed partly by empirical studies) who take critical subjectivity seriously. It is concluded that the development and refinement of such models (which can, again, be informed by empirical studies) is the main challenge for the critical IS researcher.

BACKGROUND

The early academic life of Theodor W. Adorno (1903–69) should be considered alongside the increasing dominance of the Nazis in Germany (and Austria) where he originally lived. His father was an assimilated Jew—indeed, his original surname was Wiesen-grund—and he soon adopted his mother's (Catholic) maiden surname for obvious reasons. His early work was conducted in

Germany, famously at the Institute for Social Research, at the University of Frankfurt (i.e. the 'Frankfurt School'). When the Nazis closed the (predominantly Marxist) Institute for Social Research in 1933 he fled to England, and in 1937 he moved to the United States. After the war, he returned to the newly reconstituted Institute for Social Research in Germany, where he remained until his (relatively early) death. A highly relevant aspect of his life—often not discussed greatly—was his exposure to both the continental and the Anglo-Saxon traditions of philosophy and sociology engendered by these geographic movements. There is no doubt that he was heavily influenced by the Germanic philosophical tradition emanating from Kant. Nietzsche and Marx also played a role in the development of his ideas. However, he was also made aware of the traditions of philosophers such as Bertrand Russell while in Oxford, England and sociologists such as Robert Merton while in the United States. These influences are relevant, as Adorno was fully prepared to engage and grapple with these Anglo-Saxon ideas, something that many other continental academics rarely do.

This makes his work especially relevant for IS research, most of which has been driven by an Anglo-Saxon research agenda (positivism)—unsurprisingly, since the majority of IS research is conducted in the United States and given the overwhelming influence of positivistic sociology in that country. Indeed, when this tradition is married with the natural inclinations of researchers from a primarily technical background, it is hardly surprising at all that positivism abounds in IS research. Adorno grappled with the issue of developing research approaches for situations in which social and technical aspects are intertwined.

Below are listed, cryptically, further reasons why the work of Adorno is methodologically relevant to IS research:

1. Adorno has recently been described as 'the most brilliant and versatile member of the Frankfurt School' (Inwood, 1995, p. 7). Habermas, a 'second-generation' member, has attracted quite a few followers in information systems (e.g. Lyytinen and Klein, 1985). If 'respectable' information systems work can be based on the work of Habermas, then *a fortiori* it can be based on the work of Adorno. Indeed, Alvesson and Deetz consider that 'Adorno and Horkheimer's (1979) cultural criticism of administratively induced control contingent upon the conception of progress in the Enlightenment can be read as sounding as close to Foucault as to Habermas's recent writings' (Alvesson and Deetz, 2000,

p. 82; see Chapters 6 and 7 for comparisons). For readers who have already encountered Foucauldian or Habermasian ideas in IS research (or elsewhere), Adorno's research will most likely prove to be both provocative and engaging.

2. Adorno was concerned with power, social structures, cultural issues and so on. These issues are generally accepted as being of importance for IS research. However, his views on these matters were intertwined with considerations on epistemology, ontology, existentialism and various other aspects of philosophy in a holistic manner.

3. Adorno was also concerned with (and developed theories about) the role of technology in modern societies. However, these arguments are subtly different from the more typical or standard arguments about the role of technology in society. These differences will be explored later.

4. Whatever one thinks about Adorno's individual analyses, there is a systemic dimension to his thought. All the individual analyses (be they in critiques of astrology, jazz or administrative systems) are actually tightly interwoven and form a coherent whole. As Jarvis puts it, 'Why does Adorno remain such a powerful force in fields as different as philosophy, musicology and social theory? One reason is the startling inner coherence of his thought. Adorno illuminated an extraordinary range of subjects in his lifetime... Yet despite this, the central motifs of his thought remain remarkably stable' (Jarvis, 1998, p. 1).

The aim of this chapter will not be to develop an understanding of the inner thought of Adorno—that would be far too ambitious in a work of this length (ample references will be provided for the reader who wishes to do this). Rather, it is to show how these thoughts might be relevant to researching the field of information systems, and to provide some practical guidelines for applying these notions.

The field of information systems (IS) and the research topics in this field are highly diversified. Therefore, it is important to note that this chapter is concerned with developing research approaches for applicability in the area of IS practice. IS practice is (of course) a highly diversified field in its own right. One might investigate how a lone analyst programmer develops a small database, how a team develops an ambulance control system, or how the IS strategy group of a large corporation makes decisions as to whether to outsource all (part or some) of that corporation's IS function and its associated information systems. This chapter is attempting to provide a new research perspective for research in these areas.

The main focus of the chapter will be on the need to combine a critical theory approach with empirical findings. This requires an original interpretation of Adorno's approach to critical modelling. This needs to be done in such a way as to be faithful to the optimistic side of Adorno's ideas while being careful not to fall into the trap of using those ideas to support (or encourage) work that is insufficiently critical ever to be realistically considered bona fide critical theory research work. 'Adorno' should not become merely a name to 'tag on' to routine empirical or interpretivistic IS research in order to legitimate it. It will be argued that Adorno's ideas cannot be straightforwardly employed to develop IS research methods; numerous dangers would lie in store for a researcher taking such a simplistic approach. As Crook has argued:

> The nature and extent of Adorno's claim to attention must always be contingent on the degree to which his work can illuminate contemporary developments in culture, polity and society... an assessment must identify core themes in Adorno's analysis which continue to merit attention and to warrant further development. (Crook, 1994, p. 18)

However, it should not be assumed from this that 'bits' of Adorno's thought can, as it were, be taken in isolation and used to tackle research questions in IS. Using Adorno's ideas in this way would be to miss a crucial feature of Adorno's thought: its interconnectedness. This is crucially important, because—unlike some thinkers—no analysis stands entirely in isolation. As Jarvis puts it,

> it is unusually hard to pick and choose in Adorno's work—to select out arguments which still work and to discard those which do not—because all Adorno's arguments have something like a systematic [systemic] relationship to each other. They share a philosophical idiom which gives his work its internal coherence. (Jarvis, 1998, pp. 2–3)

Practically, what this means is that the use of Adorno's ideas on, for example, society cannot be isolated from his ideas on epistemology (or art, for that matter). This might seem off-putting to a would-be user of these ideas, but it need not be so. While it is true that no substantive part of Adorno's body of thought stands in isolation, individual topics can be analysed one at a time quite properly, given a reasonable understanding of his systemic approach. Indeed,

Adorno often did this himself, for example his study of a newspaper astrology column (Crook, 1994). What would be inadmissible would be the use of Adorno's ideas to reinforce—or otherwise 'prop up'—research in a primarily positivist or interpretivist vein.

The relationship with other research in a critical tradition (e.g. a Foucauldian or Habermasian tradition) is more complex. Suffice it to say here that just because the label 'second-generation' may be applied to a theorist, one should not put so much faith in enlightenment progress as to assume that such a theorist has intellectually 'eclipsed' Adorno's ideas. The relationship between Adorno's thought and that emanating from post-war French theorists is a very interesting topic. Those who are familiar with the work of Foucault or Lyotard may well—on first reading Adorno's work—feel a good deal of comfortable familiarity with Adorno's arguments and style of writing. Indeed, Foucault himself came to realize the similarities between his work and Adorno's late in his career (see Chapter 7). There is not space in this chapter to debate the issues of compatibility and incompatibility between the work of Adorno and that of other theorists who are clearly motivated by similar critical aims, and so the would-be Adorno researcher is advised to proceed with caution here, and also to use Chapters 6 and 7 as a basis for comparison and contrast.

THE IS DEVELOPMENT CONTEXT

Adorno considered (as, no doubt, do IS professionals) that the world of economic activity is very real. As Yeates, Shields and Helmy argue:

> Somebody pays for what analysts and designers deliver. New systems have to be justified by the benefits that they deliver. It is easy to use terms like 'the users' and 'user management' ... and forget that they are subtitles for 'the customer'. (Yeates, Shields and Helmy, 1994, p. 2)

The economic activities that generate systems development projects have a key role in determining the analysts' foci of attention in the projects that they are involved with, in that what is considered to be relevant and worth 'analysing' is partly determined by the economic realities inherent in a given situation. The gist of (one important aspect of) Adorno's epistemic approach can be summed up in this quotation:

> While our images of perceived reality may very well be *Gestalten* [*Weltanschaunngen* in soft systems methodology jargon], the world in which we live is not; it is constituted differently than out of mere images of perception. (Adorno, 1977, p. 126)

However, this statement does not presage a return to positivism. Mark Poster summarizes the 'economic/epistemic' problem for IS research thus:

> Since computers are useful objects to industry and government, computer 'scientists' are especially sensitive to the question of the epistemological purity of their discipline. Louis Fein, writing to the *Communications of the Association for Computing Machinery*, insistently articulates his distress with the ambiguous status of his field: 'Like other sciences, our science should maintain its sole abstract purpose of advancing truth and knowledge. It is not clear to me that an organisation can play simultaneously the role of a profession, of an industry, and of a science.' (Poster, 1990, p. 147)

Although Poster is actually discussing computer science, I would argue that these remarks also apply to IS. But IS encompasses all three elements (a quasi-profession, an industry and a sort of quasi-science) and IS practice will always be a matter of 'trading off' between these tensions. Furthermore, there is another crucially relevant factor: the IS professionals themselves. While it is true that IS professionals can be considered to be role occupants, they remain individual people also, as

> one tends to mask one's own genuine self with different masks (personae) and to play various roles and personalities until the mask and one's self become inseparable. . . But in the crucial moments that require definite and significant decisions and action, we are more capable of discerning who we genuinely are. There is no one but ourselves to condemn or appreciate our behaviour. (Golomb, 1995, pp. 24–5)

Although it should be noted that Adorno (1973a) expressed strong doubts about the (critical) utility of the notion of authenticity, it has been found to be useful in understanding the actions of, for example, educational professionals (Cooper, 1983). IS professionals (it is conjectured) do, indeed, sometimes encounter situations in which 'there is no one but themselves to condemn or appreciate their behaviour'; that is, situations that mobilize their own demands for personal authenticity. Therefore IS research needs a research method that can bring about a holistic understanding of all four of these aspects in a given situation, that is:

1. The demands of the IS profession (e.g. adherence to IS methodological precepts or ethical codes).
2. The (economic) demands of industry (e.g. the need to observe externally imposed quality methodologies, or to deliver computer systems 'on time and within budget').
3. The causal effects of the scientific aspirations (or, indeed, pretensions) of the computing industry (e.g. the legitimation of undesirable social consequences on technical grounds).
4. The values and attitudes that (authentic) IS professionals themselves bring (via their personal lives) to the practice of IS.

Put simply, what is needed are techniques for analysing the actual relationships that intertwine between the subjects undertaking IS development projects and the objects in the study (see Figure 5.1). Here, 'objects' should be understood as meaning all the various items (and impersonal 'forces') that need to be analysed (or have an effect) in the organization (the term is not used here in the sense that it is used by the advocates of 'object orientation').

It has long been recognized that the interventions (made by systems analysts) themselves alter the 'current system' in some way or other. What is currently lacking are the critical means to frame our understandings of these situations, owing to the tendency to adhere to a 'binary-opposition' view of IS research methodologies as being 'positivistic' or 'interpretivistic' (see also Chapter 1). The problem with this binary view is that neither approach is adequate for critically analysing the actuality of IS practice, as experienced by IS professionals. The positivistic approaches do not give sufficient emphasis to the active role of the analyst-as-intervener, as the analyst is considered to be 'detached' from personal concerns with the

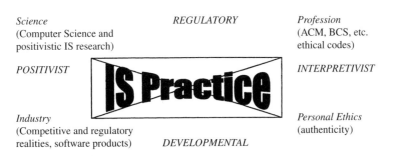

Science	REGULATORY	Profession
(Computer Science and positivistic IS research)		(ACM, BCS, etc. ethical codes)
POSITIVIST	**IS Practice**	INTERPRETIVIST
Industry		Personal Ethics
(Competitive and regulatory realities, software products)	DEVELOPMENTAL	(authenticity)

Figure 5.1   IS practice as a multi-conflictual domain

situation being analysed. The interpretivistic IS research methods (supposedly) have their history rooted in the 'phenomenological' epistemological stance (usually associated with Edmund Husserl, see Bernet, Marbach and Kern (1993) for details; also Chapters 3 and 4). Here, the very appearance of being immersed in a conflict-ridden situation is often reduced to being purely a matter of the IS practitioner's own internal perceptions, rather than being the result of the three other external influences in Figure 5.1, plus the IS practitioner's own perception of the situation. Consequently a 'way out' of this impasse is clearly required. Although we are (often) totally immersed in organizational situations, nevertheless we are all (or most of us at any rate) sometimes able to see problems with the actually existing set of arrangements; that is, we are capable of critically analysing—and transcending, in thought—the current set of arrangements.

IS RESEARCH IN CONTEXT

In many aspects of IS research, it is not possible to isolate the social and technical components of the area under investigation; in any case, it is somewhat reductionistic to attempt to separate the area of investigation into two component parts (social and technical). Here, a sort of 'unified theory' (of technology and society) might prove beneficial because, as Vorisek and Pour argue, 'systems development includes the development of ideas, imaginations and value systems of a company' (Vorisek and Pour, 1994, p. 152). Although it is difficult to summarize Adorno's ideas on the technology/culture dimension, essentially he thought that culture (generally) has become a matter to be administered and that technology has made this possible. The relevance for IS research is that such a view generates a new, possibly more appropriate (but inevitably more complex) theory of the role that technology plays in shaping the culture of organizations (and vice versa). As Scarbrough and Corbett note,

> the relationship between technology and organisation is neither one of 'impacts' [of IT] nor of 'choice' [made by managers] *per se*. Rather, technology and organisation are closely intertwined through flows of knowledge and ideas which transcend the individual organisation but which find expression in, and are reinforced by, political interests and agendas at the organisational level. (Scarbrough and Corbett, 1992, p. 157)

If Scarbrough and Corbett are even approximately right, then it would seem *prima facie* that simplistic distinctions between 'hard' and 'soft' systems approaches to conducting IS research will not provide adequate forms of conceptualization for IS developments and user utilization of the information made available as a result of IS—two notions that themselves may be much more intertwined than is often acknowledged (see e.g. Fitzgerald, 1990; Paul, 1995). As Gardner, Paul and Patel (1995) argue, the need now is for 'tailorable' systems to be put in place; in such systems the concepts of 'developer' and 'user' (and 'technology' and 'organization') are increasingly blurred:

> A computer system is tailorable if it provides a user with control over its operation. This means a user should be able to regulate or operate the system, thus providing ultimate power to direct or manipulate a system's behaviour... A control is understood to be a device or interface widget that enables a user to regulate or operate a system and provides the user with the power to direct or determine its state. (Gardner, Paul and Patel, 1995, p. 187)

So, it appears that IS development should not be conceived as a once-and-for-all activity, but rather as an ongoing, user-definable (and user-achievable) process. Such considerations from the world of IS practice also have important implications for research into IS. A 'binary opposition' view of the distinction between 'positivism' and 'interpretivism' is surely inappropriate when the 'objects' in the research area contain such 'intertwinings' between technical and social aspects; the tailorability of an integrated system is surely an emergent property of the possibilities (and the constraints) created by definite technical 'configurations' and the actual social arrangements pertaining in the situation.

SUBJECTS AND OBJECTS IN IS RESEARCH

Adorno considers that there is a legitimate separation between the subjects (who carry out research) and the objects in the study, but generally this distinction is not made in an appropriate manner:

> The separation of subject and object is both real and illusory. True, because in the cognitive realm it serves to express the real separation, the dichotomy of the human condition, a coercive development. False, because the resulting separation must not be hypostatised, not magically transformed into an invariant. (Adorno, 1978, pp. 498–9)

Actual social arrangements have made us into subjects, so it is not surprising that those IS researchers that celebrate the notion of 'subjectivity' find receptive audiences. However, from an Adornean (negatively dialectical) perspective, this type of subjectivity is hardly something to celebrate—quite the reverse, in fact. Rather, it can be seen as the actualization ('here and now') of a process of social domination. Here and now, we are actually subjects both in the psychological sense (which the interpretivists misconstrue as an ahistorical reality) and in the servile, fawning sense (i.e. the political sense). Therefore interpretivism, far from being 'emancipatory' (in some sense or other), is actually a celebration of our servility—and therefore a reinforcement of it. Adorno considers that the 'subject' makes possible the idea of critique, of a critical interpretation of reality. But the concept of the subject is an intellectual construction—an abstraction—derived from (and not prior to) actual, real, living individuals:

> It is evident that the abstract concept of the transcendental subject—its thought forms, their unity, and the original productivity of consciousness—presupposes what it promises to bring about: actual, live individuals. (Adorno, 1978, p. 500)

Readers may note that there is a very Nietzschean/Foucauldian theme to this argument—as it is (essentially) a Nietzschean argument (e.g. Nietzsche, 1956, pp. 178–80) and this debt is acknowledged by Adorno (1982). Although we can treat the subject as real (or 'standing in for' real, live individuals), in Adorno's view the subject does not 'make the world up' (this is often termed 'constructivism'—Adorno uses the term 'constitute' instead of 'construct', as we saw earlier).

However, Adorno does not argue for a return to 'vulgar objectivism', because this would deny the possibility of a critical interpretation of the objective circumstances. The objective world is real enough, but what we see is always both mediated by concepts (although we may not be aware of this all of the time) and psychologically mediated by forces of domination (as will be discussed shortly):

> What must be eliminated is the illusion that... the totality of consciousness is the world, and not the self-contemplation of knowledge. The last thing the critique of epistemology... is supposed to do is proclaim unmediated objectivism. (Adorno, 1982, p. 27)

In the earlier quotation concerning perceived reality, what Adorno means by 'constituted differently' is that the world is, to a large extent, determined by economic realities, which he sometimes refers to using the term 'exchange':

> The living human individual, as he is forced to act in the role for which he has been marked internally as well, is the *homo oeconomicus* incarnate, closer to the transcendental subject than to the living individual for which he immediately cannot but take himself... What shows up in the doctrine of the transcendental subject is the priority of the relations—abstractly rational ones, detached from the human individuals and their relationships—that have their model in exchange. If the exchange form is the standard social structure, its rationality constitutes people; what they are for themselves, what they seem to be for themselves, is secondary. (Adorno, 1978, p. 501)

Again, these relations are for all practical purposes invariant, but they are in reality historical (and could therefore be changed). Consequently (for practical purposes) the IS practitioner should be seen not purely as some sort of enquiring transcendental subject, but as an economically constituted actuality (quite literally for the time being). Adorno argued that critique is only possible if some status is given to the subject who can become critically aware of these sorts of circumstances (the possibility of such critical awareness is entirely necessary for this argument to be constructed at all). Therefore Adorno preserves a critical role for the subject:

> To use the strength of the subject to break through the fallacy of constitutive subjectivity... Stringently to transcend the official separation of pure philosophy and the substantive or formally scientific realm. (Adorno, 1973b, p. xx)

At the very least, the economic activities that generate systems development projects have a key determining role on the practitioners' foci of attention in IS projects; systems analysts do not generate knowledge purely in the interest of advancing science. What is needed are techniques for analysing the actual relationships that appertain between the subjects developing information systems and the objects in the study. Technically, the qualifying phrase 'in this particular period of human history' should be added to these remarks, but for all critical IS research we may assume or ignore this requirement. The reasoning for this is that information systems (as actual things to study) themselves exist in this particular period of human history (although this is not to rule out *a priori* their existence in future periods). The dialectical nature of actual information systems has been discussed in Probert (1997).

CRITICAL THEORY AND 'TRADITIONAL' RESEARCH METHODS

Much (and probably most) IS research takes the form of empirical studies, while a reasonable number of 'interpretivist' studies are now extant. It has already been argued that neither of these methods can adequately capture the essence of an IS development situation. Adorno's approach to this (general) research problem will now be developed (specifically for IS research).

Positivism

Although much IS research has been carried out in this tradition, Adorno is acutely aware of the limitations of this approach (generally; see also Chapters 1 and 2). Space does not permit a thorough analysis of the epistemological arguments for Adorno's rejection of positivism, so I will focus on three of the methodological arguments for its rejection. First, it is an uncritical method; second, it methodologically prevents genuine thought and reflection on the actual situations being investigated; and third, it presumes that the past is a guide to the future. These remarks provide Adorno's version and can be read together with Allen Lee's arguments in the first chapter.

Positivism as uncritical

Positivism is modelled on the natural sciences; the natural sciences are concerned with the 'facts', which are always (supposedly) value free. In positivism's claim to discover facts lies its strongest appeal. However, the facts about how, for example, a virus does its damage to people cannot be connected to any intention on the part of the virus to cause human suffering; whereas in the social sphere (in which I am taking IS development as residing) deliberate human actions occur. Deliberate human actions arise from intentions—good, bad or indifferent. For example, a medical intervention on a diseased patient arises from an intention to cure the patient. These intentions and the society in which they are both acted out and shaped by is clearly not a value-free arena.

Positivism's claim to discover the 'value-free facts' has to be methodologically grounded in a sort of feigned ignorance of the social issues (the power struggles, the ideological elements and so on) that are actually present in the situations under study:

> In societal and concrete terms, both political apathy and the much-praised scientific neutrality prove to be political facts. Ever since Pareto, positivistic scepticism has come to terms with the specific existing power, even that of Mussolini. Since every social theory is interwoven with real society, every social theory can certainly be misused ideologically or operationalized in a distorted manner. Positivism, however, specifically lends itself, in keeping with the entire nominalist-sceptical tradition, to ideological abuse by virtue of its material indeterminacy, its classificatory method and, finally, its preference for correctness rather than truth. (Adorno, 1976, p. 30)

(Rigour and relevance could easily be substituted for correctness and truth here.) However, this argument is not entirely decisive. Feigned ignorance (of the value aspects) does not necessarily imply genuine ignorance. Put simply, many researchers in the positivist tradition would manifestly not be sympathetic to fascism! However, Adorno's methodological point is entirely apposite in IS research (in my view), much of which makes great use of the 'freedom' allowed by positivism to completely ignore the social issues in IS development (implementation and use, for that matter). However, as Adorno indicates above, although it 'lends itself' to so doing (or 'so ignoring'), it need not necessarily do so.

Positivism as a 'prohibition on thinking'

The entire positivist tradition rests on its claim to be able to prove things; what cannot be proved, cannot be known (a true positivist would/should argue). However, a great many of the social aspects in IS are simply not amenable to being proved in this way. Rhetoric, exaggeration, phoney justifications and face-saving excuses for failure are part and parcel of the IS development world. Few experienced practitioners would deny this, but positivism-as-methodology has no (or very little) access to these features. Methodologically, because such aspects are difficult to prove they must be literally denied by positivists (especially in their published work):

> Especially in the Anglo-Saxon countries logical positivism, originally inaugurated by the Vienna circle, has gained ground to the point of

becoming a virtual monopoly. Many consider it modern in the sense of being the most rigorous faculty of enlightenment, adequate to the so-called technical-scientific age. Whatever does not conform to it is relegated to the status of residual metaphysics, its own unrecognised mythology or, in the terminology of those who know nothing of art, art. (Adorno, 1998, p. 8)

As Adorno argues, that which does not produce fact is (often) not considered to be a bona fide research method (by many people, at any rate). However, although actually to define critical awareness is extremely difficult to do in anything resembling a 'scientific' manner, it is clearly vital in IS research. This is partly (but not entirely) because of the economic context (and the praise/blame, reward/punishment) associated with success or failure in the actual business environment in which IS development takes place. With positivism,

thinking becomes a necessary evil and is broadly discredited. Thinking loses its element of independence. The autonomy of reason vanishes: the part of reason that exceeds the subordinate reflection upon and adjustment to pre-given data. With it, however, goes the conception of freedom and, potentially, the self-determination of human society. (Adorno, 1998, p. 9)

Positivism and change

Finally, an objection can be made concerning positivism that is of clear relevance in IS research. Put simply, positivism tells us about the past (albeit the 'brute facts' about the past), but why should the past be a guide to the future—especially in social analyses? Clearly, with a modicum of reflection, it will be seen that the idea that the past can be guide to the future is an assumption—and a particularly dangerous one in IS research. As Jarvis puts it:

Positivism is criticised, not because it pays too much attention to experience, but because it is not attentive enough. Reports on present and past experience are construed as 'laws' and allowed to legislate over future experience. The putative pure description of positivism carries an ineliminable prescriptive moment within it. Positivism becomes the liquidation of the new, of the possibility that the facts might change. (Jarvis, 1998, p. 88)

Perhaps the key word in all of this is 'change'. If people wish to change the future for the better, then it is necessary to have in mind how they might change it, and in what way, when designing their research programmes. Researchers in the positivistic research tradition may well have such notions in mind when designing their research programmes, but they will not be able to articulate such notions within their research. Strictly speaking, such ideas are at best superfluous and quite possibly entirely absent from positivistic research. In the worst cases, there may be some idea or other along the lines of the powerful exerting greater power over the powerless than hitherto. Even if this is made reasonably obvious in written-up research, positivistic research cannot be criticized on such grounds (by positivists, at any rate).

'Interpretivism'

Of necessity, 'interpretivism' *à la* Checkland (1981), Stowell (1993) (and many others; for example Chapter 4) is not seen as some sort of panacea to positivism by Adorno. Albeit for entirely different reasons, it is seen as equally misguided, as the following quotation makes plain:

> Sociology is only peripherally concerned with the ends–means rela-
> tion subjectively carried out by actors. It is more concerned with the
> laws realized through and against such intentions. *Interpretation is the*
> *opposite of the subjective meaning endowment on the part of the knowing*
> *subject or of the social actor.* The concept of such meaning endowment
> leads to an affirmative fallacy that the social process and social order
> are reconciled with the subject and justified as something intelligible
> by the subject or belonging to the subject. A dialectical concept of
> meaning would not be a correlate of Weber's meaningful under-
> standing but rather the societal essence which shapes appearances,
> appears in them and conceals itself in them. (Adorno, 1976, p. 37,
> emphasis added)

There may well be many 'viewpoints' on any given social situation. While many of these may be entirely reasonable, some may well be riddled with racism, fascism and so on. To passively accept any viewpoint as 'valid' or 'interesting' (or whatever) misses the point entirely; often it is not the viewpoint that matters but the social forces generating the viewpoint that need to be understood. Most people are aware of the kinds of viewpoints expressed by Adolf Hitler and his supporters. These are not in themselves particularly 'interesting' or 'informative' (or whatever). What will be interesting and informative are precisely the specific social and psychological circumstances and affectations that led to the manifestations of such viewpoints—with all their dire consequences when these become 'operationalized'.

The critical researcher needs to be critical rather than passive about the viewpoints expressed in, for example, action research-style IS case studies. Again, a kind of feigned detachment is advocated and effected in interpretivism; namely that the researcher should be indifferent to the views expressed by the actors in the study. The critical researcher is, however, encouraged both to be alarmed at certain viewpoints and encouraged to develop theories concerning the circumstances that have led to their generation. It is important to note that such viewpoints that may cause genuine concern need not be nearly as extreme as the examples given above; the principle remains true.

Positivism and Interpretivism

The force and importance of the anti-interpretivism argument cannot be overstressed or overstated. It is simply impossible (logically and practically) to hang on—in any way, shape or form—to the idea that 'viewpoints' (or whatever one wants to call them) are relevant in any other way than as the objects of research; if one wishes to base one's research on Adorno's ideas. For Adorno, subjectivism provides the ideological basis of fascism—period. Exactly why this should be is rather difficult and complex to explain, but it can be most simply explained logically. If there really are no facts about the matter for a complex social situation, then anything goes—it is all a 'matter of opinion' (or some such phrase). If this is assumed, then it follows that person A's opinion can have no privileged status over person B's, and in that case fascist ideology is absolutely on the same epistemological level as that of the liberal theorist or the critical theorist. The critical theorist has to begin critically, with an inquisitive approach to the viewpoints expressed in a given social situation. This is (partly) what Adorno intends by the phrase 'critical subjectivity'.

It will now be argued that apposite critical theories can, in fact, arise from (reflections on) positivistic research work. Empirical studies can provide important questions and help inform theories in critical IS research. Indeed, without empirical studies it would be quite impossible even to have a basic idea as to what is currently taking place in the IS world. Fads and fashion are well-known phenomena in IS developments in the world of business (and the public sector, for that matter). But the extent of take-up of such phenomena will need to be informed by empirical studies. Therefore to deny the importance of empirical studies would be to make the same sort of (abstract) 'category mistake' as is made by both positivists and interpretivists—to deny the importance of a crucial aspect of actual IS research. The critical theorist cannot hope to provide a critical interpretation of, say, dot-com euphoria (and dot-bomb despair!) without a fairly statistical understanding of the actual situation (which obviously changes over time). One cannot simply armchair-theorize the actual situations in which IS developments take place. However, there is another—possibly more compelling—argument for the critical theorist's being receptive to positivistic studies.

Information Systems in a Critical Context

Concerning the 'culture industry' (the 'industry' that we probably refer to as 'light entertainment', which includes such diverse things as manufactured pop bands and astrology columns in newspapers), Adorno writes:

> One of the justifications of quantitative methods is that the very products of the culture industry are, as it were, planned from a statistical viewpoint. Quantitative analysis measures them by their own standard. For instance, differences in the frequency with which particular tricks recur derive in turn from a quasi-scientific calculation of the effect on the part of the astrologer, who in many respects resembles the demagogue and the agitator. (Adorno, 1998, p. 238)

Earlier in this chapter, it was argued that IS can be considered as a sort of amalgam of quasi-science/industry/quasi-profession. Positivistic studies are probably the most influential studies in informing IS industry developments. They also seem to have an (undue?) influence on professional bodies—and on government-sponsored research initiatives (in Europe at any rate). It must be said at once that a great deal of this informing work is positivistic in nature, rather than genuine empirical research, for example rash predictions about the volume of business that will be conducted electronically in a given number of years' time. It would, I believe, make for an interesting research proposal to investigate the extent to which government, industry and the IS professions are actually influenced by such positivistic research (bona fide or otherwise), but—intuitively at any rate—its influence seems to be significant. Positivist research that, for example, investigates the number of businesses intending to develop 'e-business' websites can help the critical researcher to develop critical research strategies along the lines of investigating the causal influences—rational or irrational—that lead to such (planned) IS developments. But, of course, the causal influences, social structures and psychological affectations (leading to such developments) cannot simply be 'read off' from the statistics; critical interpretation will be crucial. This is the direction for IS research proposed here. However, a large body of interpretistic IS studies exists. Can anything be gained from such studies that is of value to the critical IS researcher? This must be admitted to be a question for further research by the author; nevertheless, a proposal will be made along these lines.

The author has over the years been closely connected with a number of interpretive studies in UK industry. What is remarkable is not the divergence of viewpoints expressed in very different situations, but their similarities. There seems to be an emerging pattern of role playing in such studies. Concerning information issues, one can usually detect intense frustration among the majority of the actors in the studies. Blame transference (for information-related problems) is usually rife, while any notion of problem ownership is almost entirely absent. In psychological terms, very few actors express any feelings that the locus of control is within themselves. More work would be needed to collate and synthesize data from these various studies, but an initial hypothesis would be that the action researcher has a primarily cathartic effect in these situations—confirming the real powerlessness of the majority of the actors studied. This is despite all the claims—often made by action researchers (such as Checkland and Scholes, 1990)—that such actors have been increasingly empowered since the 1970s. Whatever the status of these claims, such issues require a richer analytical framework—in order for appropriate research questions to be posed—than is offered by positivism and interpretivism. Adorno's ideas for understanding the relationship between technology and society are germane here, and so it is to these ideas that we will now turn.

ADORNO, TECHNOLOGY AND SOCIETY

A detailed analysis of Adorno's view on both technology and society would be of value to the would-be critical researcher intending to use the ideas here. However, both topics would really require extensive treatment, not possible within the scope of this chapter.

Therefore, what will be attempted will be a characterization of information systems that adequately captures the nature of an information system in a manner appropriate for the would-be researcher to progress. This analysis will be based on two key ideas, both central to Adorno's thought. These are, first, the notion of instrumental reason; and second, the notion of society as a 'real illusion'.

Instrumental Reason

In the earlier discussion on positivism and change, it was argued that some notion of how things ought to be in the future should (at least) accompany—and potentially drive—an IS research programme. Adorno goes further than this: his whole characterization of reason *per se* is based on an argument that reason cannot be divorced from intention. He argued that philosophers from Husserl right back to Descartes have either ignored or denied this aspect of reason. The thinking behind Adorno's contention is complex, and so a simplified version of this argument will be given here. This discussion is included so that an understanding of the key notion of instrumental reason can be provided, which is germane to the characterization of an information system being developed here.

As society has developed—from the Middle Ages (or earlier) to the late capitalist society of today—humans have been increasingly unable to identify the connections between the causes of reasoning and reasoning itself. However, the stubborn refusal of the causes of reasoning—what Hume called the 'passions'—to disappear from epistemological thought is detectable in modern philosophy from Descartes through to Husserl (Adorno may have first encountered these ideas while reading Nietzsche, for whom they are a central theme). In particular, Adorno considered that Husserl's valiant attempts to do just this, in his phenomenology, had failed (Adorno, 1982). Here, a discussion of phenomenology will be avoided because—for many (especially, but not exclusively, in the IS world)—it is understood to be supportive of *Weltanschaaungphilosophie* (or 'worldview' philosophy); although this is a highly contentious reading (Probert, 1998; but see also Chapter 3). The conclusion Adorno draws is that rather than pursue a philosophical programme of 'pure reason'—where 'pure' means 'uncontaminated'—a programme of dialectical reasoning should be pursued. This programme should set out to elaborate what dialectical reasoning should be (or attempt to be etc.). This is most fully attempted by Adorno (1973b).

The attempts from Descartes through to Husserl to define a 'pure' reason are, Adorno argues, unsuccessful; however, they 'testify' to a desire to define and characterize reason as if it had no context of human intention. (Note: the phrase 'intention' is used herein in its commonplace, everyday sense; it is not used in the technical sense introduced by Husserl.) This desire is the result of various social conditions that have isolated us from properly understanding our own desires; that is, we have become alienated from these in a sense similar (although not identical) to that proposed by Durkheim. The search for a 'pure' reason, devoid of intention, while ultimately unsuccessful, has nevertheless found many receptive audiences over the years, because of the social conditions and conventions that actually operate. What philosophical programmes such as Kant's and Husserl's attempt to achieve has already become the dominant form of modern rationality, precisely because the feeling that (critical) reasoning is linked with desires, many of which have no basis in rationality, is no longer felt by many. What is left ('the residue', to use one of Adorno's phrases) is a reasoning that is practically devoid of any real purposes at all; that is, an instrumental reason that lacks any real aim. Positivism is an example of this. As Jarvis puts it:

> The central argument is that reason has become irrational precisely because of its attempt to expel every non-rational moment from itself. In this way, reason becomes incapable of understanding what makes rationality itself possible, the non-rational element which reason depends upon. The consequence is a kind of rationality which is a tool, blindly applied without any real capacity either to reflect on the ends to which it is applied, or to recognize the particular qualities of the objects to which it is applied. Adorno and Horkheimer call this unreflective rationality instrumental reason. (Jarvis, 1998, p. 13–14)

'Technological' reasoning generally can be seen as a modern extension of instrumental reason; instrumental reason has no purpose whatsoever—until it is given one. This assignment-to-purpose may be entirely arbitrary, but—more generally—it will be related to the preservation of the status quo. Computers and organizational information systems can be seen (for this purpose at any rate) as technological embodiments of instrumental reason. They will need to be paid for, and the justification for so doing will generally be couched in (ultimately) economic terms. In a business context, this justification will naturally be linked to the profit imperative. (In other spheres such as leisure uses, the justification for such purchases will vary accordingly.) Interestingly, it is (fairly) obvious that computers have no purpose(s) until such purposes are assigned, and that the provision of information is just one possible assignation—other purposes could be to edit a video recording or to keep an aeroplane in stable flight. Organizational information systems usually include the application of such technologies—subordinated to the profit imperative.

'Real Illusions'

Adorno's idea of society—as an object of study and as an object to be transformed—is closely related to his epistemological and methodological arguments. As seen earlier, Adorno is critical of Weber; he is also critical of Durkheim. Jarvis summarizes the argument thus:

> Weber argued that social institutions and processes had to be understood through the subjective self-understanding of individuals participating in them, without whom these processes would be nothing at all. The merit of this approach, for Adorno, is its refusal to present social relations which are historical and produced as though they were simply objects 'given' to sociological study in the same way that data are arguably given to natural science. The difficulty with it is that Weber underestimated the extent to which in modern society social relations take on a life of their own. Under capitalism... social relations, which are indeed made by human individuals and which would be nothing without those individuals, have taken on an apparently autonomous and objective existence. It is indeed illusory to think that social relations could be presented as wholly autonomous from the relating individuals. Yet the autonomy of social relations is not simply a mistake, but a 'real illusion'. (Jarvis, 1998, pp. 45–6)

This argument implies that social relations are understandable, because the 'object' of study (society) is locked into fixed, predictable ways of behaving. The logic of the economics of the firm makes profit possible, and will continue to do so for years to come. Accountancy conventions are effectively static. Information systems themselves are locked into this socially rigid situation, and therefore may themselves take on the appearance of being real—which, in a sense, they are. That is, they are real illusions and may be analysed as such without recourse to subjective considerations. It is worth making the point here that Adorno is not concerned with the ways that organizations change as the needs of the market vary; at a fairly deep level the basic logic of the organization and management of the firm does not change, and these basic social-organizational structures are imbedded in the information systems of any firm. Indeed, when traditional systems analysis textbooks talk about analysing the 'current system', the current system really is there to be analysed in this way, and without much recourse to the subjective meanings attributed to people working in the firm. Nevertheless, the current system is a real illusion and therefore—in an equally important way—the current system has no existence that is independent of the social actors in the firm:

> Social relations are no longer interpretable as the sum of the subjects participating in and making them. Durkheim's contribution, against Weber, is to point to this. The merit of his approach is that it testifies to the real preponderance of petrified social relations over individuals... Yet Durkheim, conversely, pays insufficient attention to the illusory character of the objectivity of social relations. (Jarvis, 1998, p. 46)

The world in which IS research takes place is fundamentally one of stable ('petrified') social relations, which could change but almost certainly will not. Thus information systems—as social institutions—are more generally real illusions. This is not to say that information needs are not dynamic (which they often are), but it is to say that the fundamental social processes underpinning information systems use are not dynamic—although in principle they could be. Therefore, for all practical purposes, positivism will be effective in finding out 'facts' about information systems, but it also becomes part of the process that fosters the further petrification of those facts. Methodologically, the critical researcher will need to keep these 'facts' in scare quotes. This will be difficult in practice, as the dominant positivistic view is so prevalent in IS research. Here, the commonplace understanding of IS is simply a subset (or an example of) the commonplace understanding of (reified) society more generally:

> Social appearance, the second nature of petrified social relations, is taken for the essence of society, for all there is or can ever be. For epistemological positivism the notion of essence is a metaphysical relic which must be liquidated; appearance is what there is. For sociological positivism the corollary is that an objective concept of society is a metaphysical relic. (Jarvis, 1998, p. 67)

Of course, an objectively real society is, on this account, not something that can be known—but it can be aspired to. Similarly, merely identifying information systems as real illusions will not be sufficient to change them. As Jarvis puts it, a real illusion 'cannot be dispelled simply by recognising it as such' (Jarvis, 1998, p. 68). Given the versatility of computers, the prospects for information systems development are (typically, given this analysis) simultaneously both encouraging and discouraging. They are encouraging, in that what is often considered to be objectively necessary may be seen as nothing other than the pseudo-imperatives stemming from these real illusions. However, the prospects are discouraging in that such real illusions, these petrified social relations, are very hard to change.

The critical IS researcher may bring a new agenda to the IS research community, by insisting that no description of IS practice is complete without some prescriptions concerning what such practice should be aiming at. Both the positivist and interpretive traditions have, to date, largely ignored what is required from a critical perspective. If Adorno's characterizations of rationality and society are (largely) correct, then there is (or there should be!) the opportunity within IS research to embrace what ought to be, when analysing what 'is', so as to better understand what is actually occurring within IS development and use today.

CONCLUSION

Critical research on IS should be able to link systemically the social aspects (and aspirations) of organizational members (theoretically) with the real economic pressures felt by the managers of those organizations. Many of us are, often, totally immersed in organizational situations; nevertheless, we are sometimes able to see problems with the actually existing set of arrangements. We may well be able to see innovative solutions to those problems, if the organizational culture and the technical infrastructure allow us to (which they may or may not). Therefore, while technical considerations remain essential to successful IS development (because technical personnel will be needed to enable us to solve problems in this way), understanding the often vague and yet undeniable tensions between the cultural and economic aspects of organizations is important if critical IS research is to be carried out:

> People-intensive integrative mechanisms are limited in what they can accommodate. Accessible, well-defined data and a transparent network are therefore the keys to effective development in the coming

years. Developing these resources, however, is not easy. Justifying organisation-spanning networks whose benefits are uncertain and will occur in the future, and whose costs cannot be attributed clearly to any specific suborganisation, is in part an act of faith. Developing common coding systems and data definitions is a Herculean job... although IT may enable the technical infrastructure to connect people and information together more effectively in the networked firm, to realise the benefits we are looking for we need also to have—or to develop—a favourable cultural setting for innovation and change. (Rockart and Short, 1991, p. 215)

This chapter has argued the case for combining a critical theory approach with empirical findings (and vice versa) in such a way as to be faithful to the optimistic side of Adorno's ideas while being careful not to fall into the trap of using those ideas to support (or encourage) work that is insufficiently critical ever to be realistically considered bona fide critical theory research work. The aim should be to produce what can be termed critical models of IS practice. Critical models are 'specific analyses that tactically employ the negative dialectical strategy' (Pickford, 1998, p. ix); they are models produced by IS researchers (informed partly by empirical studies) who take critical subjectivity seriously (informed by e.g. Adorno, 1973b). The development and refinement of such models (which can, again, be informed by empirical studies) is the crucial challenge for the critical IS researcher.

A GUIDE TO THE LITERATURE

Reading Adorno is not easy! There are several reasons for this. First, unless one happens to be fluent in German, what is read will usually have been translated from German. To make matters worse, some commentators are also critical of some of these translations (e.g. Jarvis, 1998). Secondly, Adorno's style of writing is difficult (to say the least). As Jay puts it,

> Adorno refused to present his complicated and nuanced ideas in simplified fashion. Charging the advocates of easy communicability with undermining the critical substance of what they claimed to communicate, he vigorously defied the imperative to reduce difficult thoughts into the conversational style of everyday language. (Jay, 1984, p. 11)

Thirdly, Adorno's work assumes a broad familiarity with the work of many classical figures of European (and occasionally American) thought, such as Marx, Freud, Husserl, Weber, Durkheim, Heidegger and Kant—to name several of the more important figures. Fourthly, Adorno's ideas are themselves complex and (as was discussed in the introduction to this chapter) tightly interconnected.

Finally, Adorno's serious engagements with the aesthetic sphere spill over into his philosophical and sociological engagements. As Brunkhorst explains,

> A person of his time who made a lasting impact on the modern intellect, he was deeply influenced by the burgeoning of modern art around the outset of the First World War. His developing artistic interest merged with his preoccupation with music. Adorno was very close to Schonberg's circle when that was at the height of its influence and was himself an accomplished musician. (Brunkhorst, 1999, p. 144)

Indeed, Jay (1984) characterizes Adorno's philosophy as 'atonal'. If the reader does not have some familiarity with concepts such as *atonality*, he or she may find Adorno's work even more daunting. Adorno simply does not ignore key developments in nineteenth- and twentieth-century thought (and art), but his work does span nearly all of the key ideas that have been explored in the softer areas of IS to date—and yet he produces a unified theory.

Nevertheless, reading Adorno's work presents a challenge, so I shall give some, hopefully helpful, guidelines here. First, most commentators cite *Negative Dialectics* (Adorno, 1973b) or his collaborative work with Horkheimer, *Dialectic of Enlightenment* (Adorno and Horkheimer, 1979) as being his most important (or most influential). Do not *begin* (reading Adorno) with either of these! They are extremely difficult and dense works that represent the apex of his (and Horkheimer's) thought. However, the foundations for these ideas are laid in many more accessible articles such as Adorno (1977, 1978, 1991). To begin to gain an understanding of Adorno's ideas, Jay (1984) provides a useful introduction. I would suggest reading this before beginning on any of the shorter papers listed above. The IS researcher will probably be familiar with the 'hard vs soft' debate and so Adorno's ideas here will be fairly accessible (Adorno, 1976).

A more informal account of these arguments, as well as a basic introduction to many of Adorno's other ideas, can be found in *Critical Models* (Adorno, 1998). The chapters in this book are transcripts from a series of radio interviews in which Adorno does set out to explain his ideas in a clear and straightforward manner. It might be asked why he felt no such compunction in many of his other works. This is probably because to characterize these ideas too simply runs the risk of making the arguments and ideas themselves look simple and naive. This is a difficult problem of which the author of this chapter is well aware!

Having read the above suggestions, there are several paths the reader might wish to take. For those interested in phenomenology, Adorno (1982) is the next step. For those interested in Heideggerian existentialism, Adorno (1973a) would be the logical choice. However, for those who wish to explore the deeper aspects of Adorno's philosophical and sociological thought, then Adorno and Horkheimer (1979) and Adorno (1973b) must—eventually—be tackled. However, I would recommend that Jarvis (1998) and/or Brunkhorst (1999) be read first. Adorno also wrote on other subjects (as mentioned in the introduction) such as art, and Jarvis (1998) provides excellent guidance as to where one may pursue his thoughts on these other themes. Finally, Adorno's work may inspire the reader to investigate some of the other writers from the Frankfurt School; here the classic introductory text would be Jay (1996), who argues,

> For if the Frankfurt School has been so successful in transcending its original context and resonating with the very different concerns of the sixties and the eighties, stubbornly surviving to become one of the mainstays of that uncertain and beleaguered amalgam we can call *fin-de-siècle* socialism, it may still have unexpected things to teach us well into the 21st century. (Jay, 1996, p. xxi)

Its relevance to research in IS may well turn out to be one of these 'unexpected things'.

REFERENCES

Adorno, T. W. (1973a) *The Jargon of Authenticity*, London: Routledge & Kegan Paul.

Adorno, T. W. (1973b) *Negative Dialectics*, London: Routledge.

Adorno, T. W. (1976) 'Introduction', in T. W. Adorno, H. Albert, R. Dahrendorf, J. Habermas, H. Pilot and K. R. Popper (eds), *The Positivist Dispute in German Sociology*, London: Heinemann.

Adorno, T. W. (1977) 'The actuality of philosophy', *Telos*, 31: 120–33.

Adorno, T. W. (1978) 'Subject and object', in A. Arato and E. Gebhardt (eds), *The Essential Frankfurt School Reader*, Oxford: Blackwell.

Adorno, T. W. (1982) *Against Epistemology: A Metacritique*, Oxford: Blackwell.

Adorno, T. W. (1991) 'Resignation', in J. M. Berstein (ed.), *The Culture Industry*, London: Routledge.

Adorno, T. W. (1998) *Critical Models: Interventions and Catchwords*, New York, NY: Columbia University Press.

Adorno, T. W. and Horkheimer, M. (1979) *Dialectic of Enlightenment*, London: Verso.

Alvesson, M. and Deetz, S. (2000) *Doing Critical Management Research*, London: Sage.

Bernet, E., Marbach, C. and Kern, D. (1993) *An Introduction to Husserlian Phenomenology*, Chicago, IL: Chicago University Press.

Brunkhorst, H. (1999) *Adorno and Critical Theory*, Cardiff: University of Wales Press.

Checkland, P. (1981) *Systems Thinking, Systems Practice*, Chichester: John Wiley & Sons.

Checkland, P. and Scholes, J. (1990) *Soft Systems Methodology in Action*, Chichester: John Wiley & Sons.

Cooper, D. E. (1983) *Authenticity in Education*, London: Routledge.

Crook, S. (1994) 'Introduction: Adorno and authoritarian irrationalism', in T. W. Adorno, *The Stars Down to Earth and Other Essays on the Irrational in Culture*, London: Routledge.

Fitzgerald, G. (1990) 'Achieving flexible information systems: the case for improved analysis', *Journal of Information Technology*, 5: 5–11.

Gardner, L. A., Paul, R. J. and Patel, N. (1995) 'Moving beyond the fixed point theorem with tailorable information systems', in G. Doukidis, B. Galliers, T. Jelassi, H. Krcmar and F. Land (eds), *Proceedings of the 3rd European Conference on Information Systems*, Athens, Greece; June 1–3.

Golomb, J. (1995) *In Search of Authenticity*, London: Routledge.

Inwood, M. J. (1995) 'Adorno, Theodor Wiesengrund', in T. Honderich (ed.), *The Oxford Companion to Philosophy*, Oxford: Oxford University Press, pp. 7–8.

Jarvis, S. (1998) *Adorno: A Critical Introduction*, Cambridge: Polity.

Jay, M. (1984) *Adorno*, London: Fontana.

Jay, M. (1996) *The Dialectical Imagination*, Betheley, CA: University of California Press.

Lyytinen, K. J. and Klein, H. K. (1985) 'The critical theory of Jurgen Habermas as a basis for a theory of information systems', in E. Mumford, R. Hirschheim, G. Fitzgerald and A. T. Wood-Harper (eds), *Research Methods in Information Systems*, Amsterdam: North-Holland, pp. 219–36.

Nietzsche, F. (1956) *The Birth of Tragedy and the Genealogy of Morals*, New York, NY: Doubleday.

Paul, R. J. (1995) 'An O.R. view of information systems development', in M. Lawrence and C. Wilsdon (eds), *Operational Research Tutorial Papers 1995*, Birmingham: Operational Research Society.

Pickford, P. (1998) 'Introduction', in T. W. Adorno, *Critical Models: Interventions and Catchwords*, New York, NY: Columbia University Press.

Poster, M. (1990) *The Mode of Information*, London: Polity Press.

Probert, S. K. (1997) 'The actuality of information systems', in J. Mingers and F. Stowell (eds), *Information Systems: An Emerging Discipline?*, Maidenhead: McGraw-Hill.

Probert, S. K. (1998) 'Soft systems methodology and phenomenology', *Systemist*, 20(5): 187–207.

Rockart, J. F. and Short, J. E. (1991) 'The networking organization and the management of interdependence', in M. S. Scott-Morton (ed.), *The Corporation of the 1990s: Information Technology and Organizational Transformation*, New York, NY: Oxford University Press.

Scarbrough, H. and Corbett, J. M. (1992) *Technology and Organization*, London: Routledge.

Stowell, F. (1993) 'Hermeneutics and organisational inquiry', *Systemist*. 15(2): 87–103.

Vorisek, J. and Pour, J. (1994) 'Metainformation system—Tool of systems development', in C. Lissoni, T. Richardson, R. Miles, A. T. Wood-Harper and N. Jayaratna (eds), *Information Systems Methodologies 1994*, Swindon: BCS Publications.

Yeates, D., Shields, M. and Helmy, D. (1994) *Systems Analysis and Design*, London: Pitman.

6

The Critical Social Theory of Jürgen Habermas and its Implications for IS Research

Heinz K. Klein and Minh Q. Huynh

The very concept of critical social theory is often associated with the name of Jürgen Habermas (McCarthy, 1978). According to Jones (2000), using citation analysis as a rough indicator, Habermas is probably second only to Giddens in the frequency with which IS researchers choose Habermas's writings over other social theories to ground their studies. It is therefore highly appropriate to include a chapter in this volume on Habermas's critical social theory and the influence of his ideas on IS research. The boundary of this chapter is drawn rather narrowly around Jürgen Habermas's principal contributions to critical social theory. Our intention is not to give an overview of different traditions and approaches to critical social research, but to explain and analyse the influence of and relevance of Habermas's ideas to IS research since the early 1980s.

The purpose of this chapter is threefold. Our first purpose is to introduce some of the overall goal, fundamental concepts and claims of Habermas's critical social theory (HCST). The objective of this part is to present a judicial selection in an accessible style from the complex and abstract ideas that are often loosely referred to as critical social theory. Our aim is to introduce the basic ideas that are necessary to consult Habermas's original writings for more details and depth of treatment. For this purpose, we shall concentrate on those constructs from Habermas's critical social theory that have received the most attention in information systems (IS) research. Almost all of these can be found in *Knowledge and Human Interest* (Habermas, 1972), and the first part of Habermas's (1981, 1984) *The Theory of Communicative Action* (TCA). As these two references have been particularly influential, they will be the primary sources of inspiration for illustrating the relevance and implications of Habermas's critical social theory in IS research.

Our second purpose is to give some motivating pointers to the parts of Habermas's critical social theory that have not yet received the degree of attention that they might deserve or have not been used at all, but would seem to have considerable applicability in IS research. For this purpose we shall concentrate on the second volume of *The Theory of Communicative Action* (Habermas, 1987). We attempt to offer a high-level view of the content and general direction of Volume II. Our focus will be on explaining a sufficient number of ideas from this work so that it becomes apparent why it is important for IS research and why it should receive more attention in the future. Our third purpose is to illustrate how Habermas's critical social theory has been used in past IS research and to point to some of its implications for IS research, which leads to research questions deserving attention in future work.

Adhering to the guideline from the editors, we organized this chapter to provide the background for HCST as he formulated it in his large synthesis of the TCA. However, the TCA can only be properly understood if seen against certain key ideas from Habermas's prior extensive work. Therefore, following this introduction is a section on the historical context of TCA, which highlights the historical origins, the evolution, the fundamental goals of HCST, and some key concepts of Habermas's Theory of Cognitive Interests (TCI). The selection of material in section two is guided by our judgement of what might be most helpful for a reader who is a newcomer to Habermas, but not to social theories in general. In section three, we then focus on outlining the essence of HCST beginning with an examination of the parts of TCA that serve as its building blocks. Section four selects the most controversial concept of the TCA for more detailed examination: the notion of achieving mutual agreement through rational discourse. It has stimulated two historically important debates on the question how rational social action is possible. These literature debates occurred between Habermas and two of his most articulate critics, Gadamer and Foucault. Section four leads up to the critical reference material on the important issue if and of how reason can overcome prejudice and institutionalized biases. Section five introduces our arguments why HCST is important for IS research, in particular we describe the relevant links of HCST to IS research. We also present a selective overview of critical IS research published in the last two decades. The focus here is on the application and future implications of HCST for IS research. In the conclusion of section five we offer a CST perspective on the shortcomings of past IS research priorities and on possible future directions of critical research in IS.

HISTORICAL CONTEXT

The intellectual and empirical domain of Habermas's critical social theory is the complex of human action that is often called social action after Max Weber (1947, p. 88), who seems to have introduced this notion:

> Action is social in so far as, by virtue of the subjective meaning attached to it by the acting individual (or individuals), it takes account of the behavior of others and is thereby oriented in its course.

Hence, generally speaking, social action is oriented towards fellow human beings in some social context, like bartering, paying their bills, going to school, learning a language and so on. The understanding of the nature of social action as oriented towards other human beings either through communication or means–ends relationships (you see a doctor *in order to* obtain treatment for your discomfort) is the most important starting point for entry to Habermas's critical social theory, both its early and its later versions. Later, in *The Theory of Communicative Action*, Habermas approaches social action by critically reviewing key ideas from the principal social action theories, which were proposed in the nineteenth and twentieth century: Max Weber, Parsons, Adorno, Marx, and Mead and Durkheim. In the earlier version of critical social theory as developed in *Knowledge and Human Interest*, his literature analysis is quite different.

The Basic Design of Critical Social Theory in *Knowledge and Human Interest*

Knowledge and Human Interest critically examines linkages between the analysis of social action at the societal level and major philosophical approaches to reflecting on the nature of social action in society. Hence, one might say that the book attempts to ground social theorizing in certain philosophical traditions (or schools of thought), yet most of its chapters deal with social action in some way. However, the relationship is sometimes difficult to decode without a fair background in the philosophical traditions to which Habermas relates by virtue of his philosophical training. *Knowledge and Human Interest* starts by tracing the trends that led to the crisis in epistemology, which had become apparent with the dismantling of Popper's critical rationalism from within by the post-positivists such as Kuhn and Lakatos (see also Chapter 1). The limitations of critical rationalism along with those of post-positivism had also been made apparent by the attack from the revival of the idealist tradition in the form of hermeneutics (cf. Bleicher's good 1980 survey of pertinent authors like Gadamer and Ricoeur; see also Chapter 4). Habermas traces the origins of this crisis back to Hegel's critique of Kant and Marx's critique of Hegel. So what?

The first part ends with the extremely interesting proposal that certain lines of philosophical analysis (which Habermas calls reflexive philosophy) could be used to understand the formation of human species in society as the result of socially organized work and modes of communication. A key assumption here is that both are not predetermined by any religious eschatology or naturalist laws, but can be interpreted as self-formative. Societal work organization, modes of communication and modes of self-organization through government (forms of domination) evolve in a way that can be influenced by bringing scientific knowledge to bear that itself is created as society evolves. This is the basic idea of 'self-formative' processes. By recognizing this, humans can become the 'blacksmiths' of their own conditions of existence. This idea then gives rise to the fundamental goal of critical social theory: emancipation from unwarranted constraints by influencing societal self-formation so that it is steered towards the most desirable outcomes. Put simply, the research programme of critical social theory is to reconstruct the history of societal evolution and use the knowledge obtained in this way to influence the future course of societal development by feeding the knowledge obtained in this way back into self-formative processes (*Bildungsprozesse*). In a later section we shall return to this fundamental goal of critical social theory, which is, of course, rather problematic and needs further elaboration.

The remainder of *Knowledge and Human Interest* examines the philosophical lines of thought (or traditions) that have battled with each other since the age of enlightenment and could help to justify and realize critical social theory's programme of emancipation. Habermas's strategy is to review the principal insights and difficulties (or even fallacies) of each major philosophical line of thought. He then forms his own opinion by learning from the historical mistakes and retains the best insights for the proposed approach of critical historical reconstruction. This strategy is repeated in *The Theory of Communicative Action* with the major contemporary schools of sociology and in *The Philosophical Discourse of Modernity* (Habermas, 1985) with the philosophical critiques of the Enlightenment ideal of 'freeing humanity from all forms of repression, exploitation, degradation, and alienation' (Schmidt 1996, p. 147).[1] The principal philosophical traditions on which Habermas draws for this purpose in *Knowledge and Human Interest* are those originating from:

1. Hegel and Marx (for Marxist theory of society).
2. Comte and Mach (for positivist theories of social analysis and society).
3. Charles Peirce and Dilthey (for proposing hermeneutics and language analyses as the main approach to the critique of positivism and the recognition of social communication and self-reflection as a central concern for the reconstitution of the human and cultural sciences).
4. Kant and Fichte (to demonstrate the relationship between reason and human interests. In the jargon of management this might be called the relationship between rational action—including knowledge management at the societal level—and goals and values).
5. Nietzsche and Freud (to analyse certain pathologies typical for modern society and question the underlying motives of science and its epistemology). Key themes in this last and extremely interesting third part are how the frustrations for need satisfactions shape society, societal pathologies (including ideologies) and the modes of domination (*Herrschaftsformen*). Habermas uses the ideas of Nietzsche (1844–1900) for two types of analysis. One is fundamentally to question (probe) the process of science and the justification of its methods (in German *hintergehen*, go behind something; *hinterfragen*, probe behind something). The other is to question the generally benign nature of science, which in his time was widely taken for granted. The main benefits of science touted were general enlightenment and emancipation from superstitions and the hazards of nature such as catastrophes like droughts or floods, toil and hardships (e.g. climate, difficult travel etc.)[2]

Clearly, a review of the results of each of these building blocks lies entirely beyond this chapter. It is also unnecessary, because part III as a whole and many (but not all) other passages of *Knowledge and Human Interest* are quite easy to read. A very general characterization of the results of the above five points is the following. At one extreme, the positivist social theories proposed that social action can be studied in similar ways to natural phenomena—a thesis that has most recently been revived by critical realism (Bhaskar, 1989; Mingers, 2002; see also Chapter 10). The most prominent historical examples of this dominance of positivism are the theories of Comte and Ernst Mach and later economics and the behaviourist and behavioural sciences. Examples of other prominent functionalist or positivist social action theories that do not take such an extreme position as economics and behaviourism are Parson's theory of social action and the classical works of Emile Durkheim, Max Weber and George Mead (cf. Habermas, 1981, survey p. xxv, and 1984). At the other extreme are social philosophies that put the historicity of consciousness and its influence on understanding through interpretive (hermeneutic) processes and linguistic interaction at the centre of their forms of analysis (see Chapter 4).

Habermas captures this line of analysis through engagement with Charles Peirce and Dilthey (and later on with Gadamer's philosophy of hermeneutics and Searle's speech act theory). Critical social theory tries to strike a balance by cherry picking from radically different lines of reasoning. It attempts a grand synthesis by picking the most valuable and valid insights from both the positivist and idealist (linguistic-hermeneutic) traditions, to describe its reconstructive programme, to understand societal self-formation and to point to options for improving its self-formative processes in the future. While part of the theory's basic descriptions draw from many ideas and concepts of functionalist thought, its formulation is quite distinctive and to some extent radical. To a certain extent, critical social theory can be considered a theory of social behaviour that defines itself in contrast to most other social theories. According to Habermas, it is a unique framework that clarifies conditions, means, contents, constraints and objectives of all socially organized human behaviour (Habermas, 1984). *The Theory of Communicative Action* Vols I and II include elaborate engagements with the social action theories of Max Weber, Parsons and George Mead.

In a broader sense, critical social theory descended from at least two major streams of thought on human action, which might be labeled the existentialist and the cognitive-rational. Interestingly, both of these streams can be traced back to Kant's critical writings. The existentialist school differentiates itself by its primary focus on the conditions that shape human consciousness, such as 'being' in a given life-world with certain social practices, a unique current culture with its distinct historical origins. The overall goal of this stream is to examine how individual lives are embedded in a web of social practices that are often subconsciously accepted as quasi-natural, given or immutable. However, more relevant to Habermas's work are the ideas from the cognitive-rational stream. This focuses more on human reason (*Verstand*) as opposed to consciousness, but brings aspects of the lived experience into play as a secondary concern that provides background assumptions. It is this fundamental concept that leads us to the Frankfurt School and ultimately to Habermas's seminal works on what has become known as 'his critical social theory' (McCarthy, 1978). Habermas refers to the totality of meanings derived from lived experiences as 'life-world'. This consists of the partly subconscious impressions and meanings retained in human memory and feelings that are taken for granted. They serve as resource to disambiguate social messages and generally make sense of the world.

The Evolution of Critical Social Theory

The historical-conceptual root of the critical social theory literature can be traced back to the works of two major generations of critical social theorists. The first generation consists mostly of members of Horkheimer's Frankfurt Institute of Social Research at the University of Frankfurt. Besides its co-founder, Horkheimer, Fromm, Adorno (see Chapter 5) and Marcuse were among the most prominent members who published in the Institute's journal, *Zeitschrift für Sozialforschung* (1922–39, continued as *Studies in Philosophy and Social Science*, 1939–41). Their works are generally known as the writings of the first generation of the Frankfurt School (of critical theory), as if they were a coherent and systematic critical account of social reality. This is, of course, not true.[3] Arato and Gebhardt (1982) provide a collection of original contributions from the first generation of the Frankfurt School, including a general introduction (pp. ix–xxi) and short biographies (p. 528). Macey (2000) summarizes the principal contributions of each major author.

The two principal contributors of the second generation are Habermas and Karl-Otto Apel, but consult Thompson and Held (1982), Müller-Doohm (2000) and White (1988, 1995a), for a broader range of participants in the debates centred on the ideas of the second generation. By studying under Adorno and then serving as his assistant, Habermas has an indirect connection to the first generation of the Frankfurt School. In the case of Habermas, the experience of fascism and the first-hand observation of subtle forms of repression through capitalist managerial ideologies during the

German reconstruction after the war may have been a motivating force for his keen interest in the value and democratic issues of emancipation.[4] With a sharp eye, Habermas (1962, 1968a, 1968b) described the unsettling tendencies of market capitalism in the newly emerging Federal Republic of (West) Germany under the rubric 'deterioration of the public sphere' (see *Strukturwandel der Öffentlichkeit*, published as *The Transformation of the Public Sphere*). Of course, they would apply even more to the US as the prominent, western-technical society.

The second generation of critical social theorists is separated from the first by three rather different historical events, all monumental in world history. The first event is the rise of Hitler's rule. First-hand experience of totalitarianism in the form of Hitler's fascism was intellectually shattering. The second event was the devastation of the second World War. The war led to large-scale destruction and loss of historically significant buildings due to the Allied Forces' area bombing of all major German cities, including the home town of the Frankfurt School. The subsequent uncritical adoption of western market economics and social policies, which redefined German identity around economic success, was intellectually unsettling. The third important event is the worldwide rise and self-critique of positivism (the so-called post-positivists, e.g. Lakatos, 1970, and Kuhn, 1970) and the successful applications of the natural sciences in engineering and industrial production (including services like medicine, but less so law or education).

The work of the first generation of critical social theory centred on the following six themes: (a) the forms of integration in post-liberal societies, especially corporations as power centres in the state; (b) family socialization and ego development; (c) mass media and mass culture; (d) the social psychology behind the cessation of protest; (e) the theory of art; (f) the critique of positivism and science (Habermas, 1987, p. 378). The writings of the first generation of critical social theorists on these subjects, while provocative, are often over-generalized. Part of the reason for this tendency is that they could not anticipate the large-scale social changes that followed in the wake of rising prosperity after the end of the Second World War. Theoretically, their empirical base was criticized as consisting mostly of anecdotal evidence of contemporary social and economic trends, although Max Horkheimer addressed this weakness when he, together with Lowenthal and Pollock, Fromm, Grossmann and Adorno, began the *Journal of Social Research* as a venue for empirical research (Friedeburg, n.d.). Another issue is that the first generation of critical social theorists could not absorb the epistemological insight generated in the critical debate of positivism, beginning with Popper's critical rationalism and Kuhn's decisive discussion of the nature of scientific revolution. Finally and maybe most importantly, the first generation of critical social theory did not critically reflect their own theoretical foundations based on Marx and Freud. They uncritically relied on many ideas and claims of Marxism that are now widely accepted as irrelevant or dogmatic and uncritically used Freud's theory of the subconscious as a basis for critical analyses (Held, 1980). In fact, it is surprising to discover how 'uncritical' the first generation was towards its own methodological, philosophical and sociopsychological assumptions.

Recognizing the weaknesses from the first generation, the second generation of critical social theorists paid particular attention to achieving a broad and coherent framework. In particular, Jürgen Habermas and Karl-Otto Apel developed their work with a full understanding of the post-positivist debates of the foundations of the philosophy of science, for example the key contributions of Popper, Kuhn, Lakatos, Feyerabend (see Lakatos, 1970), phenomenology and the advances in systems theory, in particular Niklas Luhmann (see *Sozialtechnologie*; Habermas, 1967). Moreover, the second generation of critical social theorists were willing to respond to the critiques of their opponents, in particular critical rationalists and hermeneutic theorists. They continuously modified their conceptual understandings and theoretical contractions in order to retain their critics' insights (Held, 1980). In the case of Habermas, after documenting his evolving thoughts in several seminal preliminary works, for example *Theory and Practice, Knowledge and Human Interest, The Logic of the Social Sciences* (Habermas, 1967) and responding to his critics (Habermas, 1982), this ongoing debate in the literature eventually enabled him to attempt a grand synthesis on which we shall concentrate in this chapter: *The Theory of Communicative Action*, Vols I and II. The second generation has completely moved away from Marxism, the limitations of which are clearly outlined in *Knowledge and Human Interest* and also often highlighted elsewhere. In addition, it has moved away from dependence on Freud's theory of psychoanalysis, except that one of Habermas's central ideas, the need for historical reconstruction of societies' trajectory evolution, heavily relies on Freud's understanding of healing neurosis as an analogy. This will be outlined further below.

Based on this brief history, it is important to note that modern critical social theorists exist who are not associated with the members of the Frankfurt School, be it the first generation of critical social theory or the second. Among these theorists are Held (1980), Poster (1989), Kellner, Feenberg, Foucault (see Chapter 7) and Bourdieu. Moreover, newer approaches to critical social thought have emerged. To some extent they challenge not only the cognitive–rational foundations of the Frankfurt School and those drawing on it, but also all systematic critical theorizing. These are the authors associated with deconstruction and postmodernism (see Rosenau, 1992). These references demonstrate that the diversity and volume of critical social thought have continued to expand. Rather than attempting a broad discussion of different types of critical theory, we prefer to focus this chapter more narrowly on Habermas's critical social theory and its implications for IS research. This permits us to be more accurate and more specific than pursuing the general notion of a critical social theory approach to studying IS and its development as a social phenomenon. Future work will use critical social theory as a base-line and relate it to other forms of critical social analysis, with the intent of identifying some generic principles that might apply to all forms of 'critical' social analysis and design in IS research (Klein and Myers, 2003).

The Man and his Work

Jürgen Habermas was born in 1929 in Düsseldorf, Germany and attended school in a small town, Gummersbach.[5] From 1949–54 he studied philosophy, history, psychology, German literature and economics at the Universities of Göttingen, Zürich and Bonn. In February 1954 he obtained a PhD in the Philosophy faculty of the Friedrich-Wilhelms-University in Bonn for his dissertation on the absolute and the finite in Schelling's thought. The principal dissertation committee members were Erich Rothacker and Oskar Becker.

After finishing his doctorate, Habermas worked as a freelance journalist from 1955 to 1959 and as a research associate with Horkheimer and Adorno at the Frankfurt Institute of Social Research. He received a habilitation scholarship from the German Research Foundation in 1959 and finished his habilitation (qualifying as a German University lecturer) in 1961 at the University of Marburg (see Habermas, 1962). In the same year, the University of Heidelberg called him to his first professorship. In 1965 Habermas presented his inaugural lecture on 'Erkenntnis and Interesse' (see Habermas, 1968b) at the Johann Wolfgang Goethe University in Frankfurt, where he worked as a tenured professor from 1964 to 1971. In 1970 he accepted a call to the Max Planck Institute in Starnberg, which is Germany's most prestigious research centre. From 1971 to 1979, he was the director for the Investigation of the Conditions of Human Existence in the Science–Technology-based World and from 1980 to 1981 the director of Social Sciences. In 1982 he returned to the Johann Wolfgang Goethe University in Frankfurt, where he became Professor Emeritus in 1994.

From 1961 to 1999, Görtzen (2000) lists 43 books by Habermas, of which 150 translations appeared in 25 languages. Most of his books were translated into English, French, Spanish, Italian and Japanese. Translations into other languages are growing.

> If one takes the volume of secondary literature as a yardstick, then Habermas and Heidegger together in the same breath should be named as the world-wide most important philosophers of the 20th century. (Görtzen, 2000, p. 543)

Görtzen's planned, annotated Habermas world bibliography is announced as taking up several volumes. Clearly, any attempt to characterize Habermas's work in the space of a single chapter must be extremely focused by meeting a narrowly defined purpose and cannot do justice to its overall significance for many disciplines.

The Fundamental Goal of Critical Social Theory

The fundamental goal of critical social theory evolved long before *The Theory of Communicative Action* was written and was stated in *On the Logic of the Social Sciences*, 1970 (first published in 1967, and the English translation came out 20 years later; see Habermas, 1988). In this book Habermas challenged the concept of 'division of labour' between the sciences and the humanities, which was widely accepted at the time (see McCarthy, 1978, p. viii). Both are needed to open up possible options for society to coach it collectively on a path towards the ultimate values that make human life worth living and distinguish it from animal existence: freedom, justice, and good taste in all that matters; that is, not only in what we see or hear ('pollution' of language, images and other artifacts, the traditional subject of aesthetics), but also in social affairs. Freedom entails three different aspects: liberation from unnecessary need deprivation and toil, ideological manipulation and other psychosocial compulsions, and liberation from fear. Emancipation is the process through which we as humans individually or collectively remove obstacles standing in the way of achieving freedom to a greater or lesser degree. Emancipation means that more people can achieve their potential to a greater degree. Of course, there will always be limits to emancipation, but Habermas insists that if the best knowledge of both the natural and sociocultural sciences together is marshalled in the right way, it is possible to make progress towards ever greater emancipation by removing 'unwarranted' constraints and compulsions. This is the 'practical intent' of critical social theory.

This section will explain the general argumentation strategy that underlies Habermas's critical social theory research programme in pursuit of this inspiring ideal of a better society. The better society *cannot be* the result of some outside intervention or the manipulative tactics of a Platonian 'philosopher-king' or a privileged mandarin class of enlightened leaders, because this would always be oppressive. Rather, Habermas's idea is that the processes of evolutionary, social self-transformation must be improved 'from within' in a way that will be acceptable to all those who will have to live with the intended and unintended results. Habermas relates to this aspect with the critical social theory concept of 'formative processes' (*Bildungsprozesse*), which include a liberal arts concept of emancipatory education (as opposed to training) that is not limited to general education during adolescence and will continually enlighten public consciousness. Emancipatory discourse and critique have central roles in formative processes.

The following quote encapsulates this idea of a historically oriented critical social theory of societal formative processes with a practical intent:

> The form such a theory could take is that of a 'systematically generalized history' that reflectively grasped the formative process of society as a whole, reconstructing the contemporary social and political situation with a view not only to its past but to its practically anticipated future as well. (McCarthy in Habermas, 1967, p. viii)

This reconstruction deals with the societal self-formative process of society through open and free critique. It is important to recall here that the reconstruction of the self-formative process proceeds with the goal of revealing its historical contingencies that have introduced many deficiencies in any specific society. The critical theorist assumes a role towards society similar to that of a psychoanalytic therapist towards a patient. Habermas develops this analogy in great detail as follows. The approach of the psychoanalytic therapist is to cure neurosis or other psychic pathologies by helping patients to reconstruct influential 'key experiences' (*Schlüsselerlebnisse*) in their life histories, so that they can recognize and then overcome any traumas that were subsequently repressed or subliminated and then caused dysfunctional reactions. The life history is taken as an analogy for the historical evolution of society, and the reconstruction of its events proceeds through reflection and emancipatory discourse relying on the social philosophy concepts summarized in *Knowledge and Human Interest*. In the psychoanalytic model, ultimately the cure is in the patient's recollection of 'forgotten' events and his or her admission that they caused pain and harm (e.g. observing domestic violence, suffering from an uncaring parent etc.). It is the patients themselves (here serving as the analogue to society) who have to overcome their compulsions and distortions. Similarly, it is the citizens themselves who have to overcome the current ills of society. The analyst (or critical theorist in the case of society) can only help them by identifying the past situations that the patients (citizens) 'forgot' (repressed) in order to avoid dealing with certain social conflicts or embarrassing experiences. This repressed memory is supposed to cause the patients' (society's) neurotic behaviour patterns.

By uncovering the 'true history' and psychological repression, the patients (citizens) can emancipate themselves from their neurotic (social) compulsions. In the case of society, the analyst is to reconstruct the societal history for everyone to see. The members of society should understand the reconstructed social history so that they themselves can recognize unwarranted forms of domination with their accompanying self-delusions (sources of 'false consciousness'), which stand in the way of social emancipation. Societal pathologies include ideological distortions and unwarranted forms of domination. Critical social theory is supposed to facilitate emancipatory public discourses that can alter a nation's collective consciousness and lead to political action. Habermas explains the historical details of such a 'self-formative' transformation actually happening in a special moment of history in *The Transformation of the Public Sphere* (1971). This is rightly one of his most famous early publications (and is also easy to read). He claims that after the mid-eighteenth century, discourse in a functioning public sphere was instrumental in bringing about the ultimate victory of liberal democracy in France, England and Germany.

A well-functioning public sphere is one that spreads general enlightenment through citizens' discourse, addressing one another as an audience in a space that is domination free (in particular not subject to norms of 'groupthink', state control, vested interests etc.). Examples were eighteenth-century coffee houses, discussion circles, and later the foundations of an independent free press.[6] The goal of critical social theory is to generalize the principles and social conditions that empowered citizens in the actual historical situation of the seventeenth to nineteenth centuries. They started and eventually succeeded in bringing about democratic reforms overthrowing the aristocratic forms of domination that had existed for centuries, but had lost their traditional legitimacy due to the continuing enlightenment of the age through science and social philosophy.

A difficult issue is how such a critique is possible if critical social theorists are part of the very society that they are trying to reconstruct. How can such social critics set themselves outside the foundation and formative processes that must have shaped their understandings in the first place? Habermas and Gadamer considered this issue in their famous debate over the possibility of developing a 'universal pragmatics' that overcomes Gadamer's 'universality claim to hermeneutics'. This topic is clearly beyond an introduction, but is well summarized in Bleicher (1980, Chapter 8, p. 152) and Foster (1991, Chapter IV, p. 121). The debate ended with important clarifications on both sides that paved the way for identifying a surprising amount of common ground.

To achieve the aforementioned goal of liberating society from its pathologies that get in the way of a commonly shared 'good life', critical social theory sets itself two extremely ambitious tasks. One is to undertake a 'narrative reconstruction' (i.e. to tell the story) of the self-formative processes of society on the basis of a 'systematically generalized history'. The purpose of this effort is to understand the past origins and conditions or causes of the current make-up of society, including its ideological distortions and other deficiencies leading to repressed needs from poverty to alienation, antisocial behaviour and violent crime. Such understanding should bring to public and official consciousness the contingency of the prevailing social conditions, which are normally taken for granted but could be different and better if history had taken a different course. The other task of critical social theory is to influence the formative process of society (internal social change processes), which will shape future societal make-up towards the best possible outcomes as judged by those participating in these processes (Habermas, 1967, pp. viii–ix). The idea here is not to predict likely outcomes, but to uncover alternative and more desirable futures for the human species as a whole than would be available without critical social theory; in Habermas's words: 'reconstructing the contemporary situation with a view not only to its past, but to its practically anticipated future as well' (p. viii). In order to achieve this, Habermas enlisted the best insights from the social philosophies of the eighteenth to the twentieth centuries in *Knowledge and Human Interest* and from the main strands of contemporary sociology in *The Theory of Communicative Action*.

This impressive array of intellectual tools is used to make plausible the idea that the underlying value of societal self-formation could and should be emancipation. Emancipation is the overcoming of unwarranted constraints and the freeing of the mind (human reason) from tutelage, the typical sources of which have been superstition, the church and the state. Unwarranted constraints have two principal origins. One is in the limiting ways by which societies extract their livelihood from nature (through labour); that is, the production technologies that evolved from hunters and gatherers via agriculture-based societies to the mechanization of labour ('smoke stack' technologies) and now knowledge-based production. Each of these technologies sets different constraints for human self-realization; remember Charlie Chaplin's depiction of human alienation in mechanized production in the 1930s. On the other hand, a society without large-scale food storage or trade across climate zones might be closer to nature and have better consensual community processes, but it will suffer from many other fears. For example, it is subject to many more life-threatening exigencies than is one with worldwide access to food resources. Critical social theory tries to have it both ways and for this purpose social philosophy and theory need to check and guide the instrumental machinery of science, lest its values 'colonize' the social community and citizens' participation in public affairs.

In *Technik und Wissenschaft als 'Ideologie'* (*Science and Technology as Ideology*; 1968a, 1974), Habermas describes why science and technology after the nineteenth century have become an 'ideology' supporting certain forms of domination and causing systematic distortions in political discourse. While science at first was a liberating force from superstition, religious doctrines and the normative, institutional power of the church, the ruling elites of scientifically trained managers, capitalists, lawyers and engineers increasingly used the authority of science for secular forms of domination in industry and state administration. This contributed to the displacement of a political (practical) discourse on values as 'irrational'. Consequently, the instrumental imperatives of economics and engineering began to dominate all spheres of life.

Max Weber had already noted and criticized this tendency under the concept of rationalization. Habermas tries to recover the lost memory by broadening the concept of rationality beyond the meaning of purposeful instrumental rationality that it assumed at the beginning of modernity. He does not deny the importance of this type of rationality in serving the instrumental interest in prediction and control, which is essential for a highly productive economy. This instrumental interest is similar to what Max Weber called means–ends rationality and has been captured in the so-called rational choice models, of which linear programming and game theory are common examples. However, he insists that other interests and the knowledge to realize them are no less important. Hence all human knowledge is interest bound, a key insight that Habermas borrows from Nietzsche in *Knowledge and Human Interest*. This idea gives rise to Habermas's theory of cognitive interests. Its main achievement is to broaden the very notion of what counts as knowledge and rational behaviour; that is, human action is rational if it is grounded on some form of knowledge in a broad sense:

> Thus Habermas is not committed to the claim that agents do not sometimes deliberately act instrumentally; his claim is simply that instrumental models do not provide a sufficient basis for a general theory of rational action. (Heath, 2001, p. 13)

By analysing and weighing the fruitfulness of selected core ideas from the lines of philosophical reasoning, which were reviewed in *Knowledge and Human Interest* (see above), Habermas arrived at three cognitive interests that are used to classify human knowledge into three different categories (*Theorie der Wissensformen*: theory of forms of knowledge). The idea of a cognitive interest (also translated as knowledge interest) is that it guides inquiry when seeking knowledge. These interests are characterized by the reasons for which humans seek and apply knowledge *in general*. The three interests are (1) to achieve control of nature and people (outer and inner domination, respectively); (2) improve human understanding; and (3) overcome unwarranted internal and external compulsions (i.e. make progress towards the emancipation ideal of enlightenment: 'knowledge makes us free'.). According to *Knowledge and Human Interest*, these knowledge interests are general in the sense that they apply to all humans as a species. The details of these knowledge interests will be explained in the section on cognitive interest theory (*Theorie der Wisssenformen*).

More than 30 years after the publication of *Knowledge and Human Interest*, Habermas responded to an invitation to comment on the book. In this self-review, he recognized six aspects that needed revision (Habermas, 2000, pp. 12–20). These include the notion of a (human) species history determined by work and communication (in *Knowledge and Human Interest* motivated by Hegel's phenomenology of the spirit) as well as cognitive interest theory. The review also enumerates four aspects that Habermas would still uphold and could make it still worthwhile 'to read the book with systematic intent' (Habermas, 2000, p. 16). They include the material on philosophical hermeneutics, the interpretation of psychoanalysis as a communicative process and with this the idea of systematically distorted communication. (However, Habermas disavowed the transfer of individualistic psychoanalytical pathologies to the development of social institutions.)

We are devoting some space to *Knowledge and Human Interest* in this chapter because of the following three reasons. First, it provides the necessary context for a deeper understanding of the concerns and argumentation strategy of *The Theory of Communicative Action*, which is presented in section three of this chapter. It seems to us that it is easier to appreciate the contributions and argumentation strategy of *The Theory of Communicative Action* if it is interpreted against the background and partial misconceptions of *Knowledge and Human Interest* than if the former were introduced as if the latter had never been published. Second, our historical account of Habermas's influence in IS research would not be complete without at least a brief characterization of some core concepts of *Knowledge and Human Interest*, which have been quoted widely in many disciplines and also in the earlier IS literature. Third, the book has remained useful to communicate some basic ideas of critical social theory to a wider audience (e.g. as in Hirschheim and Klein, 1989), without getting involved in all the conceptual issues surveyed in section three of this chapter.

The Theory of Cognitive Interests: Knowledge and Human Interest

As mentioned earlier, critical social theory is a theory of social behaviour that defines itself in contrast to other social theories.

So what is distinctive in critical social theory? A good approach to explaining its concerns is to begin with Habermas's theory of cognitive interests. This theory is introduced in his book *Knowledge and Human Interest* (1972). At the core of this book is the idea that all human knowledge is related to certain fundamental interests. This leads to a much broader view of the nature of human knowledge than the one adopted by positivism. In building on the knowledge concept of the theory of cognitive interests, Habermas later replaced the relationship between knowledge and interest by focusing on the role of knowledge in rational human action in his theory of communicative action (Habermas, 1984, 1987). As both theories have been used in IS research, we follow here the evolution from theory of cognitive interests to theory of communicative action.

What Habermas calls cognitive interests are the general orientations or strategies that guide how people acquire and use knowledge to pursue their interests in all walks of life, including their occupations (work). In modern societies, many of these interests become institutionalized in the economy, the political institutions, armed forces and the government. Cognitive interest is McCarthy's translation for what Habermas calls *Erkenntnisinteresse*, for which no precise English translation exists. Literally speaking, *Erkenntnis* is the result of a successful investigation or inquiry, to achieve an understanding of something obscure. It has variably been translated as cognition or knowledge (as in the title of *Knowledge and Human Interest*, 1972). *Interesse* corresponds to the English 'interest' as in the phrase 'it is a human interest to plan for the future'. Habermas's theory of cognitive interests attempts to link the roots of human knowledge to two basic processes that are seen as fundamental to human life. One of these is to achieve given ends in labour (or work, work systems and the like) and the other to coordinate social interaction (including but not limited to work coordination) through mutual understanding. Labour is concerned with the material production by which society gains its means of subsistence from nature. The distinguishing characteristic of labour is that its relationships are governed by the value of efficiency and dictated by means–ends rationality. In *Knowledge and Human Interest*, Habermas called this the 'technical interest'. This refers to the desire of human beings to acquire knowledge that will facilitate their technical control over natural as well as social objects (Habermas, 1972). Habermas calls this type of knowledge nomological, of which laws of nature form the principal example.

In work, both physical object and people are typically treated with an instrumental means–ends orientation.

Distinct from this instrumental means–ends orientation is social interaction in the domain of sociocultural life, where people are treated as partners of communication rather than as means to achieve given ends. Habermas sees both (instrumental) action and (social) interaction as elementary types of human action. However, instrumental action is success oriented, whereas social interaction is agreement oriented (*verständigungsorientiert*). They are both of equal importance for the survival of individuals and society as a whole, 'because instrumental action does not provide the "glue" needed to hold together stable human associations. The instrumental model fails to explain how a preponderance of "force and fraud" can be avoided in social interaction, just as it fails to explain how agents can generate the fund of trust needed to sustain shared cooperative activity' (Heath, 2001, p. 17). Therefore, means–ends rationality cannot meet the needs of sociocultural development, which can only proceed by consensual processes of learning and shared sense making. The cognitive interest in social interaction is oriented towards mutual understanding in the conduct of life. This point does not mean that all goals are abandoned, but merely that the stance taken in achieving them changes to a cooperative and agreement-oriented one.

In *Knowledge and Human Interest*, Habermas calls this orientation the 'practical interest'. Whereas the technical interest applies to both people and physical objects in the domain of labour, the practical interest applies only to humans as social communication partners (leaving open the question if and to what extent higher-level pet animals can serve communicative needs). The practical interest manifests itself primarily through ordinary language communication (Berger and Luckmann, 1967), as well as through other media, which extend everyday speaking and reading. Of particular importance are the arts, pictures and so on. The ability to understand comes from cultural socialization, which is necessary to acquire the competence of natural language speaking and understanding and produces accepted social norm and role expectations.

The final knowledge interest that Habermas proposes is the 'emancipatory interest'. It is oriented towards revealing and overcoming internal and external compulsions, which often appear as 'seemingly "natural" constraints' (McCarthy, 1982, p. 58) when in fact they are the result of social forms of domination. Habermas insisted that 'orientations toward technical control, toward mutual understanding in the conduct of life and toward emancipation from seemingly "natural" constraints establish the specific viewpoints from which we can apprehend reality in any way whatsoever'. (Habermas, 1971, p. 311, quoted from McCarthy, 1982, p. 58). However, the treatment of the emancipatory interest at the same level of analysis as the practical and technical interests has always been very controversial, because it is not directly connected to anthropologically recognized forms of human action; that is, work and social exchange. Its treatment was drastically reformulated in *The Theory of Communicative Action*.

The summary of these ideas in Table 6.1 devotes one row to each of the three cognitive interests. First, the *instrumental knowledge* of the engineering sciences relates most directly to the interest in prediction and technical control. Second, the kind of knowledge that the humanities produce, especially history, social philosophy and cultural anthropology, relates to the *communicative interest* (interest in mutual understanding), because it helps us to communicate across different cultures and make sense of the testimonials of the past (historical events and artifacts). As was already explained, such understanding of history is obviously essential for recognizing societal ills and improving the formative process to change society for the better, to realize the 'practical intent'. Therefore, Habermas calls it *practical knowledge* by relating to Aristotle's meaning of 'practical' where praxis means political action. Finally, ordinary practical communication may be error prone due to misunderstandings or purposeful deceptions. Such misunderstandings could be checked by entering a discourse to clarify any dubious claims. *Knowledge and Human Interest* refers to this third interest concerned with 'truth seeking or claims justifying' as the *emancipatory interest*. Discourses suspend ordinary communication and proceed on a meta-level, reflecting on what was said. Any discourse in this sense aims at overcoming the distortions and imperfections of ordinary communication.

The fundamental differences among the three cognitive interests are also summarized in Table 6.1. The key to their differences is explained in the following five aspects:

1. The applicable domain aspect suggests three real-world elements that underlay a specific cognitive interest (Habermas, 1972).
2. The purpose of inquiry provides the reasons behind a cognitive interest inquiry.
3. The science aspect suggests how disciplines can be classified according to their underlying cognitive interest (Habermas, 1972).

Table 6.1 Summary of the main distinctions of Habermas's cognitive interests

Cognitive interest	Applicable domain	Purpose	Sciences	Inquiring methods	Associated social action types
Technical	Work	Explanation, prediction and control	Empirical analytic, especially natural science and engineering sciences	Empirical analytic methods of science	Purposive rational or teleological (instrumental and strategic action)
Practical	Interaction	Achieving mutual understanding, sharing of meanings	Historical hermeneutic, as used in history and literature analysis	Interpretive	Three communicative action types
Emancipatory	Reflection and critique of work and social interaction	Agreement by 'the force of the better argument'[1]	Psychoanalysis, philosophy, critical social sciences	Reflection, critique of ideology and discourse, assumption analysis	Discursive action

Note: [1]The 'force of the better argument' refers to the 'power of reason' in what might be called a 'rational discourse', i.e. an open debate, which is domination free and potentially unlimited, but in practice always limited by deadlines and resources.

4. The inquiry method (process) aspect gives the methodological framework of the inquiry. Together with aspect 3, the inquiring methods define what counts as knowledge. Habermas uses the phrase 'social and cultural sciences' to indicate his wide definition of the nature of science to embrace also the type of knowledge that is usually associated with the liberal arts and humanities.
5. The social action aspect reveals the connection between a type of social action and the cognitive interest with which it is associated (McCarthy, 1978; Bernstein, 1976).

As illustrated in Table 6.1, cognitive interests determine the cognitive strategies that guide systematic inquiry. They therefore provide a means to categorize processes of systematic inquiry and purposes. Since cognitive interests manifest the activities of human life, namely labour and social interaction, they are also related to social actions in general.

Because of its provocative and stimulating ideas, the theory of cognitive interests has drawn numerous criticisms. Where do these interests come from and why are there exactly three? One of the fundamental problems with the theory is its reliance on many assumptions. For instance, Habermas suggested that the interest in mutual understanding is intrinsic in the make-up of the human species, which needs to rely on communication to coordinate work (for providing the means of livelihood) and interaction in groups (for maintaining solidarity and social harmony). This *a priori* assumption met with widespread criticism, which ultimately convinced Habermas to look for a different foundation for critical social theory. However, much of the original thrust of the theory of cognitive interests has been retained in the reformulation. In particular, this includes the very broad concept of the nature of human knowledge, which is apparent from Table 6.1 and contrasts with the positivist ideal of knowledge. As positivism disavows reflection as a valid form of inquiry, its ideal of knowledge is confined to serving the technical interest. This is the reason that prediction and explanation in positivism are treated as identical.

In search for a better foundation for the issues associated with the emancipatory interest, Habermas turned to discourse theory. With discourse theory he tries to explain how agreement between actors can be reached without relying on an interest in mutual understanding. The new form of critical social theory was called the theory of communicative action because of the central role that agreement-oriented action (discourse) assumes in it. However, discourse theory introduced a new controversial notion: the force of the better argument that would ultimately—over longer periods of time—reveal and establish the truth. In the following section, we are going to introduce discourse theory along with the social action typology, the notion of lifeworld and system dichotomy as the cornerstones of the theory of communicative action.

THE BUILDING BLOCKS OF HABERMAS'S THEORY OF COMMUNICATIVE ACTION

We selected the theory of communicative action as the primary focus for this chapter, because it incorporates the most important insights of approximately 30 years of research by Habermas. It was not the result of a single grand design, but has continuously evolved since it was first promised in the preface 'Zur Logik der Sozialwissenschaften' (Habermas, 1967; see also Habermas, 1984, p. XLI) through debate and controversy with supporters and fundamental critics of Habermas's project.

The most fundamental difference between *Knowledge and Human Interest* and *The Theory of Communicative Action* is that the latter book fully realizes the implications of the so-called linguistic turn. In *The Theory of Communicative Action* Habermas no longer speaks of 'cognitive knowledge interests'. Instead he grounds the fundamental concepts of success-oriented vs agreement-oriented action (*verständigungsorientiertes Handeln*) in ontological and linguistic notions:

> with the choice of a specific sociological concept of action we generally make specific 'ontological' assumptions. And the aspects of possible rationality of an agent's actions depend, in turn, on the world relations that we thereby impute to him. (Habermas, 1984, p. 85)

In order to sketch the ideas of the theory of communicative action following this quote, we need first to explain the relationships that Habermas introduces between (1) knowledge and rationality; (2) rationality and different social action types; and (3) action types and world relations (ontology) that are implied (or 'imputed') in different types of social action. We refer to these three topics as the first three building blocks of the theory. We shall take them up in that sequence. For the second relationship the following will concentrate on Habermas's typology of social action and for the third the three-world ontology associated with the social action types in addition to the lifeworld.

A more complete outline of the theory of communicative action requires two more building blocks. The fourth is the concept and role of discourse theory for understanding how disagreement can be overcome when it arises in communicative action. These four building blocks make up the very core of the theory. Since it is mostly the action typology and discourse theory that have been the primary inspiration for critical social theory research in information systems, we will focus on these first four major components as the primary building blocks of the theory of communicative action in greater detail. However, the fuller implications of the theory cannot become clear without a fifth building block: the system–lifeworld distinction. Unfortunately, it turned out to be impossible to deal systematically with this fifth complex of ideas within the space limitations here. We shall therefore introduce the indispensable lifeworld concept together with Habermas's three worlds under the third relationship. Later on in the chapter, we shall relate to the system–lifeworld differentiation that is associated with Habermas's concern for lifeworld colonization in an informal way and return to it briefly in the conclusions. Given that so far we could find only one IS research paper that made explicit use of the system–lifeworld distinction (Broadbent, Laughlin and Read, 1991), we believe that this limitation is defendable for an introductory chapter at the current state of knowledge. A separate publication will in due time expand the summary of the theory of communicative action as stated here. Such an expansion needs to introduce the meaning, implications and controversy surrounding Habermas's system–lifeworld differentiation.[7]

The Relationship between Knowledge and Rational Action

The theory of communicative action is primarily concerned with rational human action, but proposes a much broader concept of rationality than is typically presumed in economics, engineering and other disciplines that adopted Weber's ideal of instrumental action as the defining type. This raises the fundamental issue of what should count as rational action. *The Theory of Communicative Action* Vol. I begins with this fundamental issue and answers it by relating rationality to grounding one's action in knowledge, which provides good reasons for what one does (or avoids doing).

This then leads Habermas to define rational action as that which is consciously based on knowledge. Knowledge is defined broadly enough (as was already indicated in Table 6.1) so that it can support all types of human action. The link between knowledge and rational action is constructed through explicitly discussing the different uses of language in each of the action types. Language has the most prominent and unrestricted role in communicative action:

> The concept of communicative action presupposes language as the medium for a kind of reaching understanding, in the course of which participants, through relating to a world, reciprocally raise validity claims that can be accepted or contested. . . With this model of action we are supposing that participants in interaction can now mobilize the rationality potential. . . expressively for the cooperatively pursued goal of reaching understanding. (Habermas, 1984, p. 99)

In the section on discourse theory we shall come back to the question of what kind of claims participants in communicative action typically raise.

The next step of the theory of communicative action is to reduce 'the profusion of action concepts employed (for the most part implicitly) in social-scientific theories' in essence to 'four basic, analytically distinguishable concepts' (Habermas, 1984, p. 85). By 'profusion of action concepts', Habermas has in mind the many different action types (Habermas, 1984, pp. 85 and 94–7) that were proposed in sociology (beginning with Aristotle's teleological action and continuing to Max Weber; see Klein and Hirschheim, 1991 for their importance for information systems development), contemporary sociology (especially those related to George Mead's interactionism), Goffman's analyses of self-expression, linguistics (which construes speaking as a kind of action), economics and its application in decision and game theory models. After a lengthy analysis of pertinent literature, Vol. I proposes four action types, which have already been widely described and quoted in the literature.[8] They are teleological, normatively regulated, dramaturgical and communicative action, summarized in Table 6.2. They will also be addressed in more detail in the context of Table 6.3.

Before going into further detail, it is important to note that these four types are not of equal weight. The fundamental distinction is between purposefully rational types of action (called *teleological*) and *communicative* types of action. In fact even this simple binary distinction is partly misleading, because Habermas claims that all action types are either in different ways dependent on communicative action or a special case of communicative action

Table 6.2 *The role of language in four models of action*

Action type	Ontological relation(s)	Manifested through	Direction of fit	Nature of language (see Habermas, 1984, pp. 94–5)
Teleological action	Objective world	Claims to power and any means of establishing control oriented to achieving success as defined by self-interest	World to language if successful	**Restricted** to one of several media to influence opponents to accept beliefs that are in the speaker's interest
Normatively regulated	Objective and social worlds	Consensus an accepted social norms and values	Bi-directional	**Restricted** to language as the medium for the transmission and reproduction of social norms and cultural values
Dramaturgical	Subjective and objective worlds	Experiences, feelings, desires; cognitive elements assume a subordinate role in favour of expressive functions of language	Language to world	**Restricted** to language as the medium of self-expression, i.e. 'the presentation of self in relation to an audience' (Habermas, 1984, p. 95)
Communicative action	Subjective, objective and shared social worlds	Language or other forms of expression	Depends on illocutionary point	**Restricted** —language is the medium of uncurtailed communication to negotiate common definitions of the situation through mutual critique and evidence giving with an orientation to achieving agreement

(see last column in Table 6.2). The theory of communicative action calls the first three action types—teleological, normatively regulated and dramaturgical—in various places 'one-sided' (Habermas, 1984, p. 94 with further details p. 95) and even 'parasitic' on communicative action, because their language use is restricted in various ways. Communicative action is the only action type that allows for completely unrestricted communication. This is important, because only domination-free and mutually unrestricted communication opens up the possibility of bringing to bear any type of evidence to achieve authentic consensus by unleashing the full 'force of the better argument'. We shall return to this important point further below.

The purposefully rational intent of teleological action is most familiar to those who studied economics and decision-making theory. Habermas distinguishes two types of teleological action, instrumental action and strategic action. These roughly correspond to economic action in the context of anonymous markets (instrumental action) and action analysis in game theory (e.g. strategic action, which Keen, 1981, applied to user resistance behaviour) or analysis of firms' competitive behaviour in oligopolies. Human action is strategic when it is directed towards other social actors ('opponents' or 'competitors') and their (strategic) counter-actions have to be taken into account to calculate the best strategy. Teleological action is instrumental if it is applied to nature, or more generally any domain that is treated as a non-social domain of action ('nature or machines', such as calculating the best route for a salesperson or finding the best place to build a bridge over a waterway). However, the 'non-social domain' includes the application of technical knowledge to predict and control human behaviour if the affected people are treated as 'warm bodies' only or as a mere statistical mass. Examples would be a mass marketing campaign or the calculation of force needed in war to dislodge an entrenched defence battalion.

The different roles of language that each action type implies are introduced in the context of Table 6.2. This tabulation will need to be expanded substantially for communicative action with the analysis of language use in discourse theory (see Table 6.4 later).

The Basic Action Typology of *The Theory of Communicative Action* Vol. I

Habermas derives his social action theory from observing two human tendencies. One of these is striving for success, based on

Table 6.3   Habermas's basic typology of action (adapted from Thompson and Held, 1982, p. 263)

Domains of action	Type of action		Type of social action
	Purposive-rational or teleological	*Communicative*	
	One or more actors are oriented towards their own success	These actors (at least two) are oriented towards *mutual agreement*	
Non-social	Instrumental action	N/A	Action
Social	Strategic action	Communicative action	Social interaction

command of resources and power, and the other is coming to mutual understandings in ordinary life and in the coordination of actions through partnership (Habermas, 1979, 1982). In daily life the human activities most closely aligned with these strivings are work and social interaction, except that work may involve agreement-oriented social interaction for coordination to achieve shared social ends. Habermas's basic action typology as shown in Table 6.3 provides the foundation for his later version of critical social theory. It amounts to a critique of the narrow definition of economic or purposive rationality. The purposive rationality definition takes the calculative optimization of means–ends relationships as the guiding principle of human action, which is presumed in most economic theory of human action and corresponds to the technical interest.

Three clarifying points need to be made before discussing Habermas's simplified typology in Table 6.3. First, his typology of action represents ideal types (McCarthy, 1978; Habermas, 1982, p. 266). It is an attempt to simplify complex social behaviours to core definitions and to highlight their principal differences. Second, actions oriented towards success have a powerful means–ends relationship and are based on technical knowledge (McCarthy, 1978). Actions oriented towards agreement, in contrast, are concerned with agreed norms of behaviour, reciprocal expectations and mutual understanding and values. Third, the distinction between action and interaction in the last column may seem confusing at first and has caused debate in the literature (see the two chapters by Giddens and Habermas in Thompson and Held, 1982).

> Evidently I expressed myself so unclearly in earlier works that Giddens basically misunderstands my concepts of action. As [Table 6.3]

... shows, I am far from equating action with interaction. (Habermas, 1982, p. 263)

The point is that Habermas calls all actions directed towards achieving success and taking into account only the interests of the acting agent purposive-rational action (left column) regardless of whether they are oriented towards people (opponents) or matter (a non-social domain, see the upper row in Table 6.3). The success of these types of actions is measured by a means test to determine how closely they achieve the desired objectives. If purposive-rational action is an intervention in the physical world and proceeds by applying technical rules, Habermas refers to it as instrumental action. The success of instrumental action is achieved by applying engineering-type, empirical technical knowledge and it is measured by means tests. In distinction, actions oriented to success, that is, purposive-rational actions,

> are termed strategic only if they are understood as following rules of rational choice and can be appraised from the standpoint of the efficiency of influencing the decisions of rational opponents. Instrumental actions (as well as their corresponding tasks) can be combined with the social actions as elements of roles; strategic actions are themselves a class of interactions. (Habermas, 1982, p. 264)

Thus, both strategic and instrumental actions follow decision rules to maximize individual interests, and their success can be measured in terms of their efficiency in achieving the desired objective. Both instrumental and strategic actions share the idea of control in the sense of affecting objects (human and non-human) in an environment in such a way as to achieve given ends, but strategic action requires the understanding of human behaviour to anticipate strategic counter-action (as in a chess game). This aspect is absent from instrumental action, which only requires that an actor has knowledge of and is able to apply natural laws. In the case of strategic action, knowledge of social norms or empirical knowledge about human behaviour is necessary to predict the outcomes of this kind of action and, based on this prediction, to choose an 'optimal' strategic action (see Hirschheim, Klein and Lyytinen, 1996). The fundamental difference from instrumental action is that strategic action needs to predict the likely reactions of rational opponents, which have a will and intelligence of their own and are not 'passive' like natural objects. Therefore, strategic action is associated with knowledge of social situations and social values.

In light of this, it is somewhat surprising that Habermas reaches the conclusion that strategic action 'remains, as regards its onto-logical propositions, a *one-world* concept' (Habermas, 1984, p. 88). Yet the term interaction is appropriate for strategic action, because natural laws and technical rules are insufficient to act rationally in such situations. With rational opponents we can interact through language even if we do not aim at reaching agreement, but make a claim to power ('surrender, you are surrounded'). In instrumental action no success can be achieved using language alone: a horse will not talk no matter how much it is threatened and a river will not stop flowing if one issues a command. The linguistic medium of strategic action is the reason why the outcome of a court trial is much less certain than the outcome of a chemical intervention. Strategic action is more complicated than instrumental action, because its success depends on wielding social power. The outcome of the struggle between two strategically acting opponents depends on the power resources available to each plus their cleverness in apply-ing them against their opponents' strategies. Strategic actions can be subdivided into openly strategic action, like social behaviour in market situations (Ouchi, 1979) or war, and covertly strategic action, such as deception in some forms of negotiation, advertising and political actions.

The other main form of social action in Table 6.3 is communicative action. It takes place through language and aims to achieve mutual understanding. It focuses on agreement, a common understanding of norms, meaning and values, and on maintaining social rela-tionships (Habermas, 1979). In communicative action, people reach understanding through having a common background of values, norms and assumptions about the world. It is based not only on shared experiences and on evidence taken for granted, all of which can be expressed in ordinary language, but also on gen-eral knowledge of shared norms, conventions, habits and accepted worldviews. Participants in communicative action may only be partially conscious of all the background assumptions they make, which may not be easily articulated unless special effort is spent on explaining them. As non-human objects (i.e. natural objects or artifacts), which are defined to make up the non-social domain, do not have the command of language, by definition communicative action is not applicable to them. If a dog is trained to follow com-mands, it is not through agreement (e.g. by appealing to its sense of duty to comply because 'you do not bite the hand that feeds you'), but through stimulus response conditioning.

An important question is what happens if the assumed consensus about the background assumptions that were taken for granted breaks down in communicative action. This can easily happen through misunderstanding or discovery of differing opinions and perceptions regarding ends and the best means to achieve them. Clearly this is a common situation in daily life. Two reactions are possible. One is to end the cooperation (at least for the time being) or even to start fighting, each person pursuing their own ends, no matter what. This is the defining moment when communicative action ends and strategic action starts. Before it comes to that, the parties typically try to argue their point and either convince each other or discover new common ground through their cooperative interactions. That is the second option, which Habermas calls *discourse.*

It is important that discourse be interpreted as an open-ended debate and not as mere rhetoric to embarrass opponents (unless such embarrassment is employed to get opponents to reconsider their positions). Without engaging in discourse in an open-ended way, it is impossible to discover new common ground or negotiate compromises in good faith. If one party has already made up their mind that the ends are not negotiable, then the willingness to compromise or move to new ground is missing and what on the surface appears as communicative action is really covert strategic action (see Figure 6.1). In covert strategic action two situations are possible:

> In the case of *systematically distorted communication*, at least one of the participants is deceiving *himself or herself* regarding the fact that he or she is actually behaving strategically, while he or she has only apparently adopted an attitude oriented to reaching understanding. (Habermas, 1982, p. 264, italics in original)

If at least one of the participants is consciously misleading the other side about his or her intent not to comply with the conditions of communicative action, then Habermas refers to this as *manipulation* (see Figure 6.1).

If the conditions of manipulative or systematically distorted communication do not apply when disagreements arise, then communicative action can continue and seek to restore agreement by engaging in discourse, the preconditions of which are discussed below. What is important in the current context is that when the participants engage in discourse, the topic of the ongoing ordinary communicative action (perhaps a conversation on how to address shared concerns at work) must be 'suspended' so that the communication can move to a different level to examine the causes

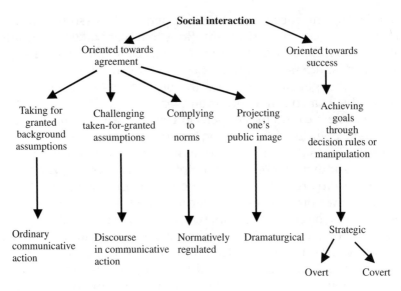

Figure 6.1 *Habermas's complete social action typology (adapted from Habermas, 1982, p. 264 and 1984, p. 333)*

of emergent disagreements or misunderstandings. Because of this break in the usual and ordinary flow of communicative action and in order to emphasize the importance of discourse to maintain agreement, some of the IS literature introduced *discourse as a separate action type—discursive action—*based on Lyytinen (1986, p. 144). However, this is an analytical device, because the orientation to agreement is maintained during discourse. Discourse is therefore part and parcel of communicative action; in the theory of communicative action, communicative action incorporates discourse. However, Habermas pays special attention to discourse, clearly implying its importance, and in a personal conversation with Lyytinen agreed that it could be conceived as an action type, as shown in Figure 6.1.

In the following, our focus will mainly be on social interactions and therefore instrumental action is omitted from Figure 6.1. Tables 6.1 to 6.3 are sufficient for its characterization—no further subtypes exist. In contrast, the breakdown of the action types associated with the agreement orientation are communicative, normatively regulated, dramaturgical and, on the meta-level of communicative action, discursive action. Habermas elaborates these distinctions in the first part of The *Theory of Communicative Action*, Vol. I. To repeat: discursive action arises in the context of communicative action when background assumptions become problematic to one of the participants and therefore is a contingent component of any ongoing communicative action in which it is embedded. Discursive action is contingent on problems of understanding or acceptability arising from what is said in the communicative exchange. Because of its importance for achieving agreement in light of differences and conflicts, it is shown here separately for analytical reasons.

Communicative action and discursive action both depend on language. Communicative action is generally oriented towards maintaining smooth social relationships through greetings, pleasant comments and other forms of casual conversations. Perhaps more importantly, when the conversation turns to more serious matters, communicative action uses language to influence perceptions, preferences and attitudes. It also explores possible bases for agreements or compromises, interpretations of shared norms, values and the meanings of observations and experiences (Habermas, 1979). In order to make themselves understood when agreement breaks down in communicative action, people need to fall back on whatever common background of assumptions they may have about the world. Without such shared background knowledge (e.g. between strangers of different cultures), discourse may very well fail and communicative action end—as was already explained.

Habermas refers to common background knowledge as a shared or at least partly overlapping lifeworld. The lifeworld provides a stock of knowledge and meanings related to shared experiences, formative events, norms, conventions, habits and accepted worldviews. They are taken for granted and seldom articulated; in fact, they can never be fully articulated. The lifeworld knowledge provides the first, hermeneutic pre-understanding in any conversation. In principle, lifeworld knowledge can be expressed in ordinary language. It is tied to the 'forms of life' (Wittgenstein) that make up people's daily routines: getting ready for breakfast, being a member (or coach) of a baseball team, being a boss (or a secretary), being a parent and so on. Whatever fills people's lives contributes to a stock of background knowledge that becomes part of their lifeworld. This knowledge is an essential resource in communicative action and in discourse that we will discuss in detail in the next section.

Dramaturgical action refers to actions that stylize the expression of one's own experiences with a view to the audience. Since all agents can disclose parts of their own subjectivity, for example intentions, thoughts, feelings and so on, in order to evoke a certain image in public, interactions among agents involve a mutual access to their own intersubjectivity. In other words, interactions represent an 'encounter' and 'performance' in which participants form a visible public for each other and perform for one another. Since the notion of dramaturgical action is used primarily in phenomenologically oriented descriptions of interactions, it has often been overlooked in past IS research. However, with the advent of the Web and the widespread use of multimedia forms of communication, dramaturgical action has become quite relevant and should be developed into a theoretically generalizing approach. This is one area with specific opportunities for further research development.

Normatively regulated action refers to action oriented to norm conformance. Norms represent an agreement on common values in a social group. Normatively regulated actions are those that comply with a norm by fulfilling expected behaviours. Based on a normative sense, members in a social group are entitled to expect a certain behaviour.

Habermas's Three-World plus Lifeworld Ontology Implied in the Action Typology

The description of the action types up to this point needs clarification with regard to two aspects: the implied ontology and the details of discursive action (discourse) that makes the achievement of agreement possible in communicative action. The above introduction of the action types relied on such phrases as physical world, relating to one's own subjectivity, knowledge of shared norms, conventions or habits. These phrases imply a certain make-up of the ontology, for example a world of shared norms and values or the existence of consciousness in feeling and thinking subjects, but not outside them. Such an ontology of subjective and social worlds exists in a practical sense because it can be referred to in speech and it can be observed to have some real effects on the behaviour of the agents involved. Social norms of reciprocity, traffic law or the tax code are obvious examples of how shared norms influence human behaviour.

We can gain a deeper understanding of different types of social action as previously introduced if we focus directly on their 'world relations'; that is, the kind of assumptions they make about the world towards which they are oriented. All types of action make ontological presuppositions. Recognizing such presuppositions is a key to revealing the nature of human rationality that guides agents' performance and actions, because it is knowledge about these

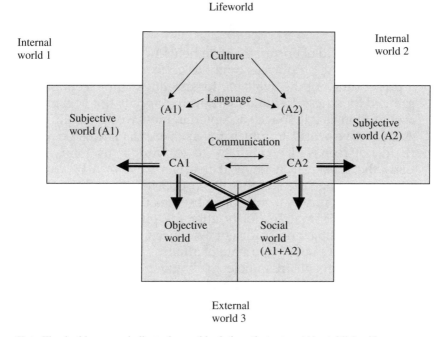

Note: The double arrows indicate the world relations that actors (A) establish with their utterances (CA)

Figure 6.2   *World relations of communicative acts (adapted from Habermas, 1987, p. 127)*

worlds that distinguishes rational actions from random behaviour or 'thrashing about' with 'shots in the dark'.

Habermas discusses his ontology in the context of Figure 6.2. It is built around two rational subjects, A1 and A2, engaging in some form of interaction, which could be any of the action types in Figure 6.1. Habermas insists that the lifeworld has a different status than the other three worlds depicted in Figure 6.2 as rectangles. At first we will follow this conceptual strategy, but will reconsider it towards the end of this section.

To interpret this figure, let us consider the example where an employee phones a supervisor to say, 'I am sorry that I cannot participate in the meeting scheduled for later this morning, because I do not feel well enough to go to work. I probably have the flu because my joints ache and the thermometer showed that I have a fever.' We shall reuse the same example later to introduce the basics of discourse theory.

At first sight, this statement makes reference to the following three worlds:

1. A shared world of norms: the statement implies the general norm that usually all employees ought to go to work on weekdays at a preset time and be available for meetings, but exceptions are granted for illness. It sounds silly even to specify this background assumption as it is so well accepted in most western cultures.
2. A subjective world to which the speaker has exclusive access: 'I do not feel well enough to go to work', 'my joints ache'. Only the speaker can know if this is a truth or a lie, but this does not change the fact that this proposition does have a truth value. For example, if someone observes the employee playing a tough tennis match shortly after the phone call, this would count as credible and sufficient evidence for a false claim about the employee's subjective state of affairs.
3. Objects and events in an objectively given or taken-for-granted external world to which A1 and A2 and possibly more agents have shared access: a meeting, a time frame (this morning with the precise time and location assumed known by the hearer), a measurement (of body temperature where 'mild' implies a temperature one or two degrees higher than 98.6°F, indicating fever). In principle, any statement about this world can be objectively tested by direct inspection or demonstration.

An important aspect to recognize about this sentence is that it refers to very concrete objects in one of the three worlds. However, it implicitly draws on lifeworld experience for interpreting them. For instance, only in western-type medicine using thermometers do we know what a mild body temperature means or have the norm of punctuality and reliability in work schedules. Because of the relative degree of concrete structure of worlds 1, 2 and 3, Habermas separates them from the lifeworld, which remains diffuse even though any problematic aspect can be retrieved from the lifeworld and through analysis in speech, then becoming part of one of the other worlds. However, we would argue the reverse is also true. Experiences and observations in any of the three worlds recede into the lifeworld as they lose their immediacy in the ongoing back and forth of life.

Language performs very different functions in different types of action. Table 6.2 summarized the role of language in four models of action. It is important to note that in the first three action types, communication is limited and one-sided. In teleological action, communication relates only to those matters that are important to realize self-interest. In pursuit of their self-interests, agents block or ignore all repartee and counter-arguments. Normatively regulated action communication merely serves to reproduce normative agreements that are presumed as unproblematically pre-existing. In the employee phone call example, an appeal is made to the norm that only sickness is an excuse for remaining home. The caller is not in any way questioning the standard under which work takes precedence over other needs. The use of language in dramaturgical action is highly stylistic, serving the portrayal of an image with aesthetic appeals to emotions and feelings. The speaker acts as a 'performer' whose intent is to entertain or move the audience and not to engage in a dialogue. Only communicative and discursive actions are open to all sorts of arguments, draw on all functions of language equally and in doing so relate to all three worlds depicted in Figure 6.2.

So far we have assumed that all the claims made during communicative action are not problematic: that the employee, indeed, is expected to participate in the meeting (which could be a misunderstanding) or that the employee's excuse stated over the telephone is truthful. Each speaker shares the knowledge and background assumptions that are made. To use another example, two fishermen making a mutually acceptable plan as to when and where to meet in an area they both know from past fishing trips can proceed without much trouble. They can coordinate their actions with agreement-oriented communication, since both have the same kind of experience of where fishing is good at certain times of year and where it is convenient to meet. However, only a minority of life situations are so simple. Just consider the issue of family vacation planning, when the younger members want to go skiing and the older ones prefer to go to a place where it is warm in the winter. While agreement-oriented communication in such situations is quite common, it does involve challenging one another's assumptions and claims (e.g. 'I need to go skiing, because it will help me with my gym grades', which might be true in Austria but not in the US) and searching for common bases of agreement ('they have a sunroom and heated pool at the ski resort' or 'you can go water-skiing instead'). Even more difficult are matters involving extensive interactions, such as policy formation from the lowest level of an organization all the way up to the highest level of government policy. How communicative action is possible in the face of misunderstandings, differing perceptions and preferences and goal conflicts is the topic of discourse theory.

Before approaching the subject of discourse theory in a general way, it is important to understand how, in the context of a family or friendship group, mutual understanding can be restored if misunderstandings and other disagreements arise. Basically this requires explaining controversial words (like a new word that a family member learns 'from the outside', such as school or the workplace). In terms of lifeworld, every family and friendship group has access to a history of 'shared lived experiences' that is understood and taken for granted by all members of the group. As we have seen, Habermas refers to the stock of meanings and values that can be derived from these experiences as the *lifeworld*. This is the fourth world in Habermas's ontology of social action.

People acquire their initial lifeworld experiences first in the home, then in childcare groups and friendship circles, followed by school and other types of institutionally based interactions (play groups, clubs, neighbourhoods, churches etc.). After schooling, professional training, on-the-job experiences and membership roles in sociopolitical formations like political parties and interest groups are extremely important to form lifeworld experiences. Habermas uses the metaphor of an onion to illustrate how the lifeworld expands during everybody's life span from a core to ever larger and also more ambiguous spheres (see Schutz and Luckmann, 1974). Nevertheless, everyone's lifeworld is the most concrete thing that helps us learn new meanings by relating them to past ones and trying to identify how they are different. Within a society it is assumed that the general culture and its history transmit a basic stock of experiences that all members take for granted even though they may be biased. For instance, the view of Napoleon's reign is quite different in the UK and France. In general, Napoleon is seen as evil in the UK yet in France he is held as a hero and deserves a monument.

With reference to Schutz and Luckmann (1974), Habermas emphasizes that 'the lifeworld is given to the experiencing subject as unquestionable' (Habermas, 1987, p. 130). More generally, he then suggests

> identifying the lifeworld with culturally transmitted background knowledge, for culture and language do not normally count as elements of a situation. They do not restrict the scope for action and do not fall under one of the formal world-concepts by means of which participants come to some understanding about their situation. (Habermas, 1987, p. 134)

In Figure 6.2, placing the label of 'lifeworld' outside all boxes is supposed to indicate that lifeworld knowledge is *a priori*, given as preceding the definition of the situation. It remains 'at the back' of the communicating partners. In distinction, the two labels for the internal world 1 and 2 refer to the two boxes for the 'subjective world'. In the employee example, we anticipated this point by illustrating that the sentence refers to very concrete entities in the world, and some of these must be interpreted against prevailing background knowledge from the lifeworld. Layder (1997, pp. 99–104) clearly points out that Habermas's lifeworld concept is ontologically intended to be identifiable as a segment in the real world, and that it is not merely an analytical distinction. (We shall return to this point in the next section.) So if the lifeworld, at least up to a point, is a distinguishable fourth world, why does the earlier schema in Figure 6.2 display the lifeworld outside the other three worlds and why are no arrows pointing to it? This connotes the idea that the lifeworld is a diffuse background that works subtly and unnoticeably behind (*a tergo*) our speech. It can never be made explicit in its totality yet forms an important experiential basis for our consciousness. The scheme in Figure 6.2

> is meant to illustrate that the lifeworld is constitutive for mutual understanding as such, whereas the formal world-concepts constitute a reference system for that about which mutual understanding is possible: speakers and hearers come to an understanding from out of their common lifeworld about something in the objective, social or subjective worlds. (Habermas, 1987, p. 126).

For what follows, it is important to keep in mind the double roles of the lifeworld. On the one hand, it is the ultimate resource for forming attitudes, preferences and many other kinds of meanings (like general beliefs about what is true and right). On the other hand, the lifeworld also imparts the ability to convey these meanings to others who share the same or similar lifeworlds; that is, to communicate. However, as soon as an element of the lifeworld is moved from the background into the focus of (linguistic) foreground attention, it loses its lifeworld status. The reason is simply that anything that is explicitly articulated can also be subjected to doubt and questioning. If this happens, the lifeworld item loses its unquestioned and unproblematic status. The following quote speaks to this insight:

> The unproblematic character of the lifeworld has to be understood in a radical sense: *qua* lifeworld it cannot become problematic, it can at most fall apart. The elements of the lifeworld with which we are

naïvely familiar do not have the status of facts and norms or experiences concerning which speakers and hearers could, if necessary,
come to some understanding... The lifeworld forms the indirect
context of what is said, discussed, addressed in a situation; it is, to
be sure, in principle accessible, but it does not belong to the action
situation's thematically delimited domain of relevance... *the lifeworld always remains in the background*. (Habermas, 1987, pp. 130–31,
with references to Searle, 1979 and Schutz and Luckmann, 1974, p. 4;
emphasis in original)

For the remainder of the chapter, the lifeworld is treated as the
fourth world along with the three worlds shown in Figure 6.2. This
means that the lifeworld is assumed to have real existence and not
just an analytical distinction.[9] Instead of going into a long conceptual argument to justify it, which can be found in Layder (1997),
let us simply point to the fact that the experiences that build up
the stock of meanings making up the lifeworld from our childhood
belong to the most 'real' to which we humans have direct access. By
and large, we have little difficulty in identifying what comes from
within our lifeworld and what from outside. For example, tax law
gobbledygook, the definition of the number i for the square root of
−1 and the fourth dimension of time in relativity theory typically
come from outside the lifeworld, but bratwurst, pretzels and beer
for lunch come from within the lifeworld of the Bavarian country
boy just as the World Series (which is not worldwide), hamburgers
and doughnuts come from within for the typical American. Of
course, as we move through life, we assimilate an ever-broader set
of things into our lifeworld, which thereby expands. But the same
is true of Habermas's other three worlds. For example, neither the
objective world nor the social world of norms and values remains
what we thought it was during childhood and adolescence, but
this does not make it unreal or deprive it of existence. Finally,
if Habermas's system–lifeworld distinction is to hold up against
some of its less unfounded criticisms, it is difficult to see how this
can happen without emphasizing the ontological status of both.
However, we must admit that the conceptual difficulties to which
these considerations point are by no means resolved in critical
social theory. At the same time, we must keep in mind that all social
theories suffer from similar ambiguities and potential contradictions in their conceptual apparatus. Which theory is preferable is a
matter of complex judgements regarding their relative insights and
fruitfulness and it is not a question of their absolute compliance
with some predefined standard of clarity.

Much more could be said to clarify the ontological status and theoretical construct of the lifeworld, for example how it relates to Wittgenstein's forms of life, the philosophy of consciousness (Schutz and Luckmann, 1974) and Foucault's existential studies of complex, distributed power relationships. However, for our current purposes it is sufficient to recognize that the stocks of meanings in a lifeworld are an important resource for agreement-oriented communication.

The lifeworld concept has some interesting implications for IS research. This is so because it is a prerequisite for introducing Habermas's concern that the success-oriented, teleological, societal macro systems of the economy (consisting of markets and money) and government (public systems of administrative power) could overpower ('colonize') the lifeworld. If so, IS could become accessories to certain social tendencies that undermine the resources of the lifeworld, making agreement-oriented communicative action more difficult, thereby producing a consensus deficit in modern societies. This raises an important research issue for IS: whether the net effect of the growing spread of IT into all walks of life is one of social integration by providing more opportunities for authentic communicative action or not. In the latter case, IS become 'Darth Vader's stormtroopers' of an all-powerful ideology of instrumental reason. The effects of such an ideology could threaten the solidarity bases (social integration processes) of society by intruding on the lifeworld of millions of people with purposeful rational (mis)information that follows the logic of instrumental and strategic action in profit-seeking commerce and power-seeking politics. We shall take up this issue in the conclusion under the concept of the lifeworld–systems distinction and Habermas's hypothesis of lifeworld colonization tendencies in modern societies.

For now, we turn from the importance of lifeworld as a prerequisite for mutual understanding to the explicit linguistic assumptions and processes that Habermas identifies as 'general presuppositions of communicative action' (Howe, 2000, p. 18). These are the types of speech that we employ when shared understanding is in jeopardy and we start challenging the validity of each other's claims to cognitive truth or normative rightness. Typically, we respond with arguments and reasons to redeem our claims in communicative action by clarifying and supporting them with further evidence. (The word 'redeem' is used by analogy to redeeming a monetary claim, as may be represented by a draft or cheque by cashing the claim against an account.) These questions are addressed in discourse theory.

Discourse and Universal Pragmatics: Towards a Theory of Communication

Discourse theory is important because it is necessary to explain how agreement in communicative action can be restored if it is disturbed by misunderstandings, disagreements over tacit background assumptions or deceptive manoeuvres. Recall that in the theory of communicative action Habermas insists that the most important part of human behaviour is agreement oriented. If consensually oriented action were the exception rather than the rule, then the theory of communicative action would no longer be very interesting. As disagreements are commonplace, it must explain how agreement can be achieved and maintained; that is, how misunderstandings can be corrected, tacit assumptions revealed, deceptions detected and addressed. This is at the core of discursive action, which arises out of ordinary speech. If restoring of agreement were not possible in spite of common disagreements, then there would be no such thing as communicative rationality and emancipation. This would mean that the enlightenment goals of critical social theory (emancipation) would be completely beyond reach because they would be devoid of any rational grounds. The general conditions and assumptions that give natural speakers the competence to achieve the astounding results (*Leistungen*) of discursive action through language use are called universal pragmatics. Habermas's discourse theory is concerned with identifying and reconstructing universal conditions of possible understandings (Habermas, 1979), but here we shall consider universal pragmatics and discourse theory (Habermas also speaks of the theory of argumentation, see Habermas, 1987) together. A very salient concept of discourse theory is the notion of an ideal speech situation or 'rational discourse', because it allows us to distinguish between a fallacious (distorted) and a valid (authentic) social consensus. Later sections explain this cornerstone of discourse theory and introduce some of its implications.

Discourse always proceeds on a meta-level; that is, above the ongoing conversation in which some claim has become problematic and threatens the mutual acceptability of what is being said. At the most basic level of explanation, discourse theory is concerned with the following assumptions. Some of these are evident from the earlier example of the sick employee's phone call. These include:

- The intelligibility of utterances (the phone call was audible and used a language shared between speaker and recipient).

- The social appropriateness of what is being said (e.g. it is not appropriate to explain or even question the meaning of toast).
- The sincerity of the speaker (that the speaker means what he or she says).
- The truth of what is being claimed. (Habermas, 1979)

In the most basic sense, Habermas speaks of discourse when one party in an ongoing conversation starts to feel that that he or she is no longer 'on the same wavelength' as the speaker. The listener mentally wants to stop and check one or more of the assumptions or claims advanced. To clarify this notion, we may say that in the sense of phenomenology (see Boland, 1985), one or more parties in communicative action 'bracket' the ongoing speech and start questioning one or more of its assumptions or inspecting its background. In such a case the graceful flow of conversation is interrupted and we can speak of switching to discourse. For stylistic reason, we will use the phrases 'discursive communication' and 'discursive action' interchangeably with 'discourse'. In discourse, the assumptions that might have lead to the breakdown are carefully examined to test their validity. To indicate the need for discourse, often such phrases are employed as 'time out' or 'wait a minute', 'let's look at this more carefully', 'what exactly do you mean by saying. . .', 'why do you believe this' and so forth. We all have observed such turns of conversations in committee meetings.

Generalizing from the above simple characterization discourses, Habermas's discourse theory is concerned with identifying and reconstructing universal conditions of possible understandings (Habermas, 1979). These conditions are illustrated by examples of rules described below. Discursive action is potentially powerful for initiating social learning exactly because it aims at revealing taken-for-granted assumptions or beliefs, which may not have been entirely conscious to the speaker either. Often it is exactly these unspoken assumptions that have to be read 'between the lines' that stand in the way of reaching understanding if they differ between the participants (one or more).

In the previous example of the employee's phone call, the claim of 'not feeling well' because of a legitimate illness could be questionable in the supervisor's mind if the employee was seen last night 'dancing up a storm'. In anticipation of such a challenge, the employee included counter-evidence: 'the thermometer showed that I have a fever', which is typically acceptable evidence for illness and a fever could easily start overnight. In a court of law, the claim whether someone was sick or not would be settled in a theoretical discourse by calling on expert evidence. The highest form of theoretical discourse, for instance, is an academic debate about the validity of theory, as is carried on in the journals of all disciplines. The simple sick call example also exhibits reference to 'rightness of norms of action'—that it is socially appropriate to call in sick. However, moral discourse is ultimately concerned with establishing an agreed set of ethics that is acceptable to all those having to live with it. This is very different from Kant's idea of establishing a universally valid ethical standard (i.e. the general law of morals). Moreover, Habermas's 'generalizable' set of ethics must be continuously adjusted to changing circumstances, by repeated discourse. No agreement is cast in concrete, as new evidence and unpredictable new circumstances emerge all the time.

The power of discourse rests on the 'force of the better argument' to overcome misunderstandings, self-delusion and social conflict—a catchphrase that was used in Table 6.1 in the context of the emancipatory interest. Discourse theory is the appropriate background where this important idea should be explained. We begin with summarizing the kind of claims that can become the subject of a discourse, because they are potential causes for disagreement. According to *The Theory of Communicative Action* Vol. I, there are five different types of argumentation, which can be employed in corresponding discourses. They are summarized in Table 6.4 (see Habermas, 1984, p. 23; the following five points are based on Habermas, 1984, pp. 10–24):

1. *Theoretical discourse*:   What I am saying or writing is justifiable by good reasons. I can redeem the claims I make with credible and convincing evidence. Theoretical discourse thematizes truth and efficiency claims; that is, it explicitly recognizes the difficulties of providing sufficient evidence for truth and efficiency claims. This type of discourse is most highly developed; some parts of it may apply second-order (predicate calculus) and higher-order logic. It serves as a model for the other types of discourse.

2. *Practical discourse*:   What I am saying or writing in this situation is socially appropriate or at least acceptable (for example, handing out a written reply to a wedding toast is *not* socially appropriate no matter whether it is true or not and how clearly or politely it is worded). I can defend the values and norms of rightness that I propose for governing social order in a rational discourse as serving the generalizable social interest.

Table 6.4   *Types of argumentation (adapted from Habermas, 1984, p. 23)*

Reference dimensions Forms of argumentation	Problematic expressions	Controversial validity claims
Theoretical discourse	Cognitive-instrumental	Truth of propositions; efficacy of teleological actions
Practical discourse	Moral-practical	Rightness of norms of action
Aesthetic criticism	Evaluative	Adequacy of standards of aesthetic and authentic value
Therapeutic critique	Expressive	Truthfulness or sincerity of expressions
Explicative discourse	—	Comprehensibility or well-formedness of symbolic constructs

3. *Aesthetic criticism*:   I have reflected the adequacy of the standards by which I judge the quality of aesthetic experiences (this painting goes well with your colonial furniture) conveyed by nature and works of art (e.g. performing, visual, literature) in terms of culturally established standards of value and their critical discussion. I strive for authenticity in appreciating aesthetic experiences in nature and culture. My claims to good taste can be supported by reasons that the hearer finds at least intelligible and plausible. (Habermas explicitly recognizes that for this sort of discourse to be successful, it has to rely to some extent on conventionally agreed taste alignments. This is the reason why the word 'criticism' rather than discourse is used.)

4. *Therapeutic critique*:   What I am saying or writing is justifiable by self-reflection. It is assumed that I am free from illusions such as may arise from self-deceptions, fallacious evidence supporting vested group interests, or from ideologies ingrained in national culture or social class identity (e.g. only aristocracy or management is fit to govern).

5. *Explicative discourse*:   My forms of expression are familiar to the audience I am addressing. My means of expressions (natural language, mathematical or other symbolisms) follow established rules and the interpretation of my expressions makes sense in terms of customary, accepted conventions. I actually do mean what I am saying or writing (irony excepted, where it is assumed

that the hearer can perceive that I mean the opposite of what I am saying).

At any point, one or more of these claims can be become question-able, causing communicative action to 'derail'. When this happens, the ongoing conversation must be suspended so that attention can turn to evaluating (redeeming) the problematic claim. In the earlier schema of Figure 6.1, we referred to this as discourse in communicative action (and McCarthy, 1978, pp. 272–333 called it a theory of communication). The following quote speaks to the central importance of the idea of universal pragmatic for achieving the goals of critical social theory.

> In short Habermas' entire project, from the critique of contemporary scientism to the reconstruction of historical materialism, rests on the possibility of providing an account of communication that is both theoretical and normative, that goes beyond a pure hermeneutics without being reducible to a strictly empirical-analytic science. (McCarthy, 1982, p. 272)

Habermas's attempt to articulate and support a universal theory of communicative competence both philosophically and empirically is by far the most complex and controversial part of his theory of discourse. Under the heading of universal pragmatics, he explains what it means to reach mutual understanding and how this is possible by 'the force of the better argument'. To come to an understanding with someone is 'to bring about an agreement that terminates in the inter-subjective communality of mutual compre-hension, shared knowledge, reciprocal trust and accord with one another' (McCarthy, 1978, p. 290). Howe (2000, p. 22) points out that when Habermas speaks of coming to an understanding, he seems to create a link between *truthfulness* (sincerity and veracity), *truth* and *shared knowledge* through his concept of a rationally motivated consensus. Such a rational consensus can be achieved

> in practical discourse only if it is possible to call into question and, if necessary, modify an originally accepted conceptual frame-work (metaethical, metapolitical discourse). Here too the adequacy of the language system in which phenomena are described, data selected, and arguments formulated and criticized is a condition of the rationality of the consensus. (McCarthy, 1978, p. 316)

Interpretation plays a major role in a moral political argument. For explaining the problem of understanding meaning, Habermas draws on a variety of hermeneutic theorists, including Gadamer (Habermas, 1984, pp. 102–41). Again, McCarthy (1978, p. 316) elaborates, with a quote from 'Theories of truth' (pp. 251–2):

> The consensus-producing power of argument rests on the supposition that the language system, in which the recommendations requiring justification, the norms, and the generally accepted needs cited for support are interpreted, is adequate.

In previous quotes the phrases 'the force of the better argument', 'rationally motivated' agreement and 'rational consensus' are all equivalent to the concept of a 'rational discourse'. They mean that the agreement is based only on the weighing of evidence, not on power or other social forces (status, prior block voting agreements etc.) that could distort judgements. While a full treatment of the issues raised by this idea is beyond the scope of this chapter, a clearer definition of the notion of rational discourse is in order.

THE MEANING OF THE RATIONAL DISCOURSE CONCEPT

We have already noted the importance of the rational discourse concept. This section will further clarify the problematic notion of a rational discourse. Based on this, the next section will then sketch its implications for both computer support of rational discourse and the theory of democracy. The key ideas for this are Habermas's *system–lifeworld* distinction and his *lifeworld colonization* thesis.

The *rational discourse concept* is a central piece of discourse theory (which in turn is a core part of the theory of communicative action), because Habermas has always recognized that communicative action (or the practical interest) could lead to a 'fallacious consensus'; that is, one that is inauthentic and does not stand up to evidence. In order to counteract such common social tendencies, Habermas insists that any consensus achieved in communicative action can only claim 'generalizability' (to be valid and apply to all affected) if it is validated by an informed and voluntary (authentic) consensus achieved through a debate that satisfies the conditions of a rational discourse as stated below. The intent of these conditions is to ensure that all viewpoints and all arguments supporting and contesting each viewpoint have an equal chance of being heard. Most simply, a rational discourse is defined by the ideal conditions that should characterize an informed, democratic, publicly open debate. In such a debate no force should influence the outcome except the force of the better argument. In practice, there are many alternatives to the rational discourse approach to decision making, for example when the executive calls a meeting to 'discuss' a decision with his subordinates although in fact his mind is already made up; when a group merely looks for a solution that makes everyone 'feel good'; or when a solution is developed on the basis of 'not upsetting anyone'.

While the first formulations of the rational discourse concept are in Habermas (1973, p. 255 and 256) and Apel (1973, p. 425), we found the clearest explanation in Habermas (1983). There he formulates the requirements of a rational discourse that include the rules of argumentation by Aristotle, Popper and Hare, but go in important ways beyond them. Habermas's definition of rational discourse employs a set of rules organized into three levels, which he refers to as a 'catalogue of presuppositions of argumentation' and is based on Alexy (1978, p. 37). The three levels into which the catalogue is organized are *logical-semantic, procedural* and *performative* presuppositions. The performative rules amount to a clarification of what it means for a discourse to be 'domination free'. The following are examples and not a complete catalogue. The idea is to illustrate that such rules in principle can be formulated, and that work in philosophy and linguistics has proceeded to a point where such a catalogue could actually be drawn up and subjected to debate:

1. Examples of rules at the logical-semantic level, free of ethical content:
   — No speaker may contradict himself.
   — Every speaker who applies predicate F to object A must be prepared to apply F to all other objects resembling A in all relevant aspects.
   — Different speakers may not use the same expression with different meanings.
2. Examples of procedural rules, which must assure cooperation and sincerity:
   — Every speaker may assert only what he really believes.
   — A person who disputes a proposition or norm not under discussion must provide a reason for wanting to do so.
3. Examples of rules to assure social symmetry (power balance) in the conditions of discourse. As examples of these rules we paraphrase the four conditions of a rational discourse as proposed in Habermas (1973, p. 255 and 256). Interestingly, Apel's (1973) foundational article on the grounding of ethics in discourse has proposed very similar conditions for defining an

'ideal speech situation' or an ideal communication community, which Habermas has referenced in various places.

— All potential participants in a rational discourse must have an equal opportunity to begin a discourse at any time and to continue it by making speeches and rebuttals, and by questioning and answering. Habermas calls this an equal chance to use communicative speech acts.

— For all participants there must be an equal opportunity to interpret, to assert, to recommend, to explain and to justify as well as to question or to give evidence for or against the validity claim of any of these forms of speech. The purpose of this condition is to assure that in the long run, no presupposition or opinion can escape from becoming the centre of discussion and criticism.[10]

— All participants are presumed to be equally able to express their attitudes, feelings and intentions. These Habermas calls representative speech acts. They serve as a guarantor against self-deceit, illusions and insincerity of members among the speech community towards one another.

— All participants are presumed to be equally able to give and refuse orders, to permit and prohibit, to promise or ask for promises, to account and ask for accounting and so on. Habermas refers to these as regulative speech acts. They guarantee that the formal chance of equal distribution of opportunity to begin or continue a discourse is realized.

It has been widely recognized that the full realization of these conditions is not possible. Nevertheless, IS research has often assumed the existence of these conditions, at least in approximation, in a rather naive way. This applies most notably to the literature bodies of decision support, group decision support, knowledge and information management and computer support of cooperative work (CSCW). In principle, there are typically two lines of reasoning to address the issue of rational discourse implementation. First, from a practical perspective, it would be sufficient if the implementation of a rational discourse eliminates the worst inequities and assures a reasonable amount of fairness in the arena of communal debate, such as might be realized in a well-functioning parliament. The *second* argument is philosophically deeper: it is to some extent self-defeating to deny the practical approximation of a rational discourse, because through that denial, one is already engaging in a discourse. As Apel (1973) points out, anyone entering a dialogue presupposes in principle the possibility of a rational discourse;

that is, the willingness to engage in dialogue is an indication of the willingness to submit oneself to the counter-factual norms of ideal speech, communication that is unimpeded by the usual cognitive, emotional and social barriers to rationality (see Klein and Hirschheim, 2001 for a convenient summary of these barriers to rational discourse).

> He who enters a discourse implicitly recognizes all possible claims of the members of the communication community which can be justified by reasonable arguments. . . and at the same time he commits himself to justify his own claims against others by arguments. In addition, all members of the communication community (and that implicitly means: all thinking beings) in my opinion are also obliged to consider all virtual claims by all virtual members, i.e., all human 'needs' insofar as they could make claims to fellow human beings. (Apel, 1973, p. 425)

From the discussion in this section, both Habermas's careful definition of rational discourse and its powerful potential for critique should have become apparent. The next section addresses some of the implications following from the acceptance of its status as a counter-factual supposition in various types of speech. As an aside, it might be noted that these implications led to very fruitful philosophical debates after Habermas's publications (1976, 1977, 1979).

Further Implications of the Rational Discourse Concept

The three areas that we shall single out for a brief introduction to the further implications of the rational discourse concept are *epistemology*, especially the notion of truth, the *grounding of ethical norms* and the *emancipatory* goals of critical social theory; that is, the possibility of social critique.

In light of the previous explanation of the rational discourse concept, it is obvious why Habermas defines truth as 'warranted assertability' (Habermas, 1973). This means that a statement is true if it has been validated by a rational discourse and such a discourse is not limited to factual propositions but includes claims of rightness (ethics) and fairness (theory of justice). Heath (2001) summarizes the applicability of the rational discourse concept to the validation of ethical norms through moral-practical discourses as follows:

> A norms is valid if and only if all affected can accept the consequences and side effects its general observance can be expected to have for the

satisfaction of everyone's interests. (Heath, 2001, p. 227, paraphrased from Habermas, 1990, p. 65)[11]

Heath's further discussion of this 'universalization principle' from Habermas's discursive grounding of ethical norms explains why the latter's theory of language and discourse successfully defeats the counter-arguments of the two major lines of thoughts of non-cognitivism; that is, subjectivist-relativist and naturalist theories of moral judgement. According to Heath (2001, p. 218),

> Habermas has shown that there is no reason to think that practical discourses *must* become bogged down in intractable moral disputes, but he has at this point done nothing to show that they will not in fact become so.

For further treatment of the conceptual issues involved with applying discourse theory to the grounding of moral norms so that communicative action can become the basis for democratically legitimating the normative basis of social order, refer to McCarthy (1978, Chapter 4, p. 272), Heath (2001, Part II) and Warnke (1995).

Regarding the goal of Habermas's critical social theory of critically reconstructing the societal history with the practical intent of improving formative processes through critical discourses, Habermas explicitly recognized that the various discourses must be institutionalized so that they do lose their sporadic character and can 'become a systematically relevant learning mechanism for a given society' (McCarthy, 1978, p. 292). For example, an independent philosophy research community has systematically questioned mythical and religious worldviews and the roots for this kind of discourse can be traced back to Athens' classical period. With the founding of secular universities since the beginning of the fifteenth century, an ongoing discourse has emerged to check propositional truth claims in the natural sciences and efficiency claims in the engineering sciences through means tests. The institutionalization of expectations that certain types of discourses will be initiated is not limited to university-like structures. A historical example of this is how practical political validity claims came under general scrutiny as a public sphere developed in seventeenth-century England and subsequently in continental Europe and America (see Habermas, 1971).

In spite of some empirical base for the historical effectiveness of institutionalized approximations to rational discourse, very powerful objections have been raised to the very possibility of rational discourse from hermeneutic philosophy and Foucault's study of power. Some of these objections were first formulated in the Gadamer–Habermas and Foucault–Habermas debates (see Heath, 2001, Chapter 6, p. 219; see also Chapters 4 and 7).

Gadamer's hermeneutic philosophy assigns a central role to the historical roots and contingency of our understanding. All understanding begins it with some pre-understanding, which is shaped by the cultural heritage and traditions in which we happen to grow up. How, then, can a discourse possibly challenge all assumptions if its participants will always be limited by the pre-understandings with which they enter the discourse? This question was at the core of the Gadamer–Habermas debate on how discourse could overcome the mental prison of our traditions to which all our interpretations and sense making are chained. This debate confronted Gadamer's claim of the 'universality of hermeneutics' with Habermas's notion of 'universal pragmatics' of discourse theory. In a more recent turn, the issues at stake in this debate have been radicalized into the challenge of justifying socially critical thinking itself, especially if such thinking is carried on with the 'practical intent' of social change, when the outcomes of such changes are unknown and therefore risky (see Müller-Doohm, 2000, p. 71).

Another line of research that challenged Habermas's critical social theory to justify its notion of critique through rational discourse came from Foucault's detailed studies of distributed power. In studying the evolution of medical history, he found that power is not lodged in a central institution that can be criticized and eventually toppled. Rather, power is vested in the practices of collectivities (discursive formations) that determine what counts as legitimate evidence and acceptable forms of arguments through so-called regimes of truth. How is rational discourse possible if invisible regimes of truth govern its agenda and procedures rather than the linguistic philosophers' rules of the type outlined in the previous section?

Habermas has spent considerable effort and time in responding to both of these challenges, not only in articles, but also through modifying his evolving theoretical constructions. This is most visible in his double engagement with Foucault (Habermas, 1985). Even a cursory introduction to these issues is not a matter for a first exposure to critical social theory. It is also unnecessary, because excellent introductory treatments exist (see also Chapter 7). Howe (2000, pp. 18–38) or more fully McCarthy (1978, pp. 272–333, 'A theory of communication') both provide excellent introductions to

Habermas's universal pragmatics, which are prerequisites for following the Gadamer–Habermas debate (see Bleicher, 1980, Chapter 8, p. 152, and Foster, 1991, Chapter IV, p. 121). For readers with a decision theoretic background, Heath (2001, pp. 173–218) engages in an interesting game-theoretic interpretation of Habermas's discourse ethics. Foster (1991) examines more fully the controversies surrounding the Gadamer–Habermas debate. Schmidt (1996) gives great insight into the Habermas–Foucault debate.

However, what are some of the practical implications of these theoretical controversies that lead to concrete research issues from an IS perspective? Clearly, if critique is impossible, the project of the enlightenment to emancipate humanity from its many miseries is impossible. In *The Theory of Communicative Action* and his most recent work, Habermas sees the interplay of the forces of instrumental reason and communicative rationality in two different segments of complex modern societies. The domain of communicative and discursive rationality is the lifeworld, a concept already described. The efficiency imperative of instrumental reason gives rise to large system structures that are supposed to be responsive to democratic will formation nurtured in consensually oriented lifeworld communications. These are the systems structures of institutionalized instrumental action of administrative and economic powers such as hierarchies, clans and markets (see Ouchi, 1979). It is in the public sphere of the lifeworld that rational discourse is to realize its emancipatory potential via public critique, supposedly free of the worst distortions that these structures produce. However, if the public sphere deteriorates, if markets, hierarchies or clans exert manipulative or even domineering influences in the lifeworld meanings, the public sphere can no longer fulfil this function and it becomes 'colonized' by the technical interests of the system structures of the economy and other institutions, in particular the bureaucracies of public administration.

The importance of the lifeworld for articulation and interpretation in communicative action had already become apparent in the context of introducing the ontological assumptions of different types of social action (see Habermas, 1987, pp. 124–35). The meanings of a shared lifeworld are necessary for explaining how speakers can overcome disagreements by explaining themselves in terms of shared lifeworld experiences and concepts. We now can understand how the meanings of the lifeworld can grow through ongoing discourses that challenge outdated or distorted meaning complexes in the lifeworld. A well-functioning public sphere is the arena of large-scale social learning driven by the engines of rational discourses on public issues of interest.

However, Habermas's theory of communicative action goes much beyond this important aspect when explaining how societal evolution tends to lead to the uncoupling of lifeworld and system by replacing sacred traditions with rational structures of legitimation that are based on explicit reasons. Habermas examines the bureaucratic dysfunctions that this causes under the concept of 'lifeworld colonization'. The discussion of the origins of lifeworld colonization and its potential problems for society is at the core of Vol. II of *The Theory of Communicative Action*.

While this point appears to be rather abstract, it does have concrete implications for IS research. Traditional IS research focused primarily on purposive action and therefore IS were primarily 'system reinforcers'. In principle, the theory of communicative action supports a positive orientation to this, because the realization of technical interests is very important for the material welfare of humanity. Nevertheless, from viewpoint of the theory of communicative action we must also insist that purposeful rationality must not be realized at the expense of the communicative rationality of social processes of reproduction, integration and transformation. From this perspective, it is therefore disappointing that it was only with the evolution of IS from reporting and control systems to various forms of decision support and computer mediated communication that IT started to become a potential factor in the lifeworldly communicative processes of social and consensus formation. Yet, as was mentioned, this literature fails to examine whether these technologies are used in a social context that is conducive to rational consensus formation. If not, we must harbour the suspicion that they are merely a new technology of manipulation and domination. With this observation we have moved to one of the important implications of the theory of communicative action for IS research. We shall return to it at the end of the next section and place it in a broader context.

APPLICATION OF COMMUNICATIVE ACTION THEORY IN INFORMATION SYSTEMS RESEARCH AND UNRESOLVED ISSUES

So far we have described the historical context of critical social theory, the conceptual roots of Habermas's critical social theory and the cornerstones of its later formulation in the theory of communicative action. In this section, we shall focus on the links between the latter theory and IS research. We shall trace the evolution of critical research in IS by selectively looking at past studies. Based on our observations of the literature with which we are familiar, this section will then examine some of the theoretical, substantive, methodological and philosophical implications and issues that we see arising from the theory of communicative action for IS research. We start by considering the methodological implications of the fundamental purpose of Habermas's critical social theory for IS research: the critical reconstruction of societal evolutionary processes of self-formation.

The Affinity of Critical Historical Reconstruction Methodology to IS Research

In attempting a narrative reconstruction of the evolution of society, the theory of communicative action faces the same methodological dilemmas that have surfaced in all previous grand theories that have been proposed in the applied social and cultural sciences since the turn of the nineteenth century. This is not surprising, because for its reconstruction Habermas attempts no less than to reconceptualize and integrate 'the explanatory and interpretive, functionalist and narrative elements required for social theory' (see Habermas, 1967, p. ix) based on prior theoretical frameworks that had similar goals. More specifically, to achieve the proposed reconstruction, the theory of communicative action builds on the classics of social theory, in particular Max Weber, Talcott Parsons and George Herbert Mead. Therefore, its insights into the methodological issues of social research may be expected to be directly applicable to a number of applied social sciences including, but not limited to, IS. For example, it is only since the late 1980s (Hirschheim and Klein, 1989) that IS researchers have discovered the potential value of the kind of knowledge that interpretive research can reveal to complement the type of nomological knowledge that is the trademark of positivist research. Given that Habermas explicitly called for both types of research as early as 1967 (see Habermas, 1967), the methodological debate in IS research could benefit from the insights generated in the methods debate of critical social theory over the last 35 years.

The Evolution of IS Research Using Habermas's Critical Social Theory

The first published articles creating an explicit link between IS and Habermas's critical social theory were Mingers (1981) and Klein and Lyytinen (1985). Since then, a small trickle of critical social theory papers has continued to appear by a small number of authors. Only recently has the number IS researchers working with Habermas's critical social theory increased sharply, along with wider interest in other theoretical bases for 'critical' IS research, as shown in Table 6.5.

Table 6.5 provides a highlight of past IS studies related to critical social theory in the past two decades. The tabulation is based on the limited literature to which we could gain easy access. Hence, we do not claim that our conjecture on the evolution of critical IS research is statistically representative. Our objective here is to take a snapshot of how critical IS research has evolved over time. Drawing on this snapshot, we offer our observation and interpretation of the applications and implications of critical social theory in IS research. Then, we describe the most fundamental IS research issue on which Habermas's critical social theory framework leads us to reflect.

Up to this point all studies of which the authors are aware apply intensive (qualitative) research methods with an interpretive flavour. However, in principle quantitative methods should also be applicable in carefully designed circumstances. Such designs need to be sensitive to the many, intimate connections of critical social theory to hermeneutic philosophy. Habermas implies in several places that his broad theoretical conceptions could and should be confronted with concrete empirical knowledge. Unfortunately, he himself did not address directly the difficult question of how this should be done. Rather, he seems to imply that historical and sociological studies can be brought to bear. This is partly illustrated in *The Transformation of the Structural Sphere* (1991) and 'Technology and science as ideology' (1970). In fact, in view of the importance of Habermas's work for both societies as whole and smaller units of analysis within the societal macro-context, how Habermas himself has dealt with the serious methodological issues of providing empirical evidence for his far-reaching theorizing is unsatisfactory. However, he might subscribe to the opinion of Horkheimer, the founder of the Frankfurt School. Horkheimer wanted 'to pursue the

Table 6.5 Summary of the key applications and contributions of Habermas's critical social theory in IS research

Year	Contribution	Principal references that apply critical social theory (CST) in IS research	Major strand
1980 to 1985+	Introducing and adopting CST for use in IS research	Mingers (1981): Introduces the work of Habermas as a starting point for the discussion of the relevance between CST and applied system thinking. Jackson (1982): Differentiates between soft systems methodology and CST based on Habermas's work. Mingers (1984): Applies some of the ideas in Habermas's CST as the basis to revealing the weaknesses in subjectivism and soft systems methodology. Mumford *et al.* (1985): Discusses the theoretical foundations of various IS research programmes, including the CST research agenda.	Introduction of CST into IS research
1985 to 1991+	Justifying CST as a theoretical foundation for IS research	Lyytinen and Hirschheim (1988): Discusses IS as rational discourse. This is one of the first cases where Habermas's theory of communicative rationality can be applied in IS research. Hirschheim and Klein (1989): Critiques the positivism and argues for the alternative view based on CST. Jackson (1991): Charts the origins and nature of critical systems thinking. Mingers (1992a): Applies Habermas's theory of knowledge-constitutive interests as the basis for the reflection on the history and future of operational research.	Conceptual justification of CST

(continued overleaf)

Table 6.5 (continued)

Year	Contribution	Principal references that apply critical social theory (CST) in IS research	Major strand
1991 to 1995+	Applying CST in IS field studies and in the development of IS research methodology	Broadbent, Laughlin and Read (1991): Illustrates a critical theory analysis of recent financial and administrative changes in a healthcare system. Forester (1992): Presents the first empirical study from Habermas's CST perspective. Mingers (1992b): Reviews the developments in critical management that draw on the work of Habermas. Lyytinen (1992): Discusses the application of critical theory as an alternative conceptual framework in the study of IS. Hirschheim and Klein (1994): Discusses the potential emancipatory role of participation in IS development methodologies. Argues for the reconstruction of design ideals and ways to handle value-laden issues in IS.	CST's influence on the conceptualization of IS development
1996 to 1999+	Setting CST as an alternative theoretical foundation for IS research and systems development	Hirschheim, Klein and Lyytinen (1996): Sets the theoretical foundation of CST in the research on IS development. Klein and Truex (1996): Introduces CST as the theoretical foundation for IS discourse analysis. Jackson (1997): Discusses the contribution of critical systems thinking in the emerging discipline of IS Ngwenyama and Lee (1997): Examines the use of email communication from a CST perspective.	CST's influence on IS research methodology

			Critical studies in IS
1999 and beyond	Operationalizing the CST framework and applying it in empirical IS research	Klein and Myers (1999): Develops a set of principles based on CST and integrates them as a guideline for the assessment of IS research. Klein and Huynh (1999): Applies the CST framework in discourse analysis and language action coding. Cecez-Kecmanovic, Webb and Tayler (1999): Presents two case studies of Web-based teaching and learning through the lens of CST. Cecez-Kecmanovic and Janson (1999): Presents an approach to understanding the application of IS using communicative action theory. Cecez-Kecmanovic (2001b): Shares her experience and knowledge on how to conduct a critical study. Kanungo (2001): Examines the emancipatory effects of Village Community Support Systems in India. Heng and de Moor (2003): Applies Habermas's communicative theory to the study of a GRASS (Group Report Authoring Support System) project.	

great philosophical questions using the most finely honed scientific methods, reformulate the questions during the work on the subject, state things precisely, think of new methods and yet never lose sight of the general'. In his inaugural speech, he referred to the example of a study begun by the Institute on a social group that was especially important and characteristic in societal-theoretical terms, namely qualified workers and employees in Germany. The findings of the study were, at the beginning of the 1930s, suitable to 'influence' and 'change' not only the theoretical considerations, but also their relationship to societal practice (Friedeburg, n.d.).

However, anyone who has not followed the past development of 'critical' IS research literature may ask with some bewilderment why critical social theory deserves serious consideration when formulating new research agendas and alternative approaches in IS research. After all, the fruitfulness of using Habermas's critical social theory as a theoretical basis for IS research is far from clear, because they appear to have rather different concerns and goals. Critical social theory, as a philosophy, primarily addresses itself to theorizing about the evolution of societies as a whole from their humble origins as tribal societies in the distant anthropological past to their present-day formations. Specifically, one may wonder how the broad focus of critical social theory relates to building better IS and promoting their enlightened use.

ANALYSIS OF THE PRINCIPAL RELATIONSHIPS OF HABERMAS'S CRITICAL SOCIAL THEORY TO IS RESEARCH

While at first sight this characterization of critical social theory and the theory of communicative action appears to be far removed from the practical day-to-day concerns of building and using information systems, the following three theoretical comments on the key concerns of the theory of communicative action should give us pause before we simply dismiss the above as irrelevant social theorizing. First of all, two major goals of the application of information communication technology (ICT) in building IS are (1) to increase productivity and (2) to support various forms of social compliance through administrative or managerial measurements and reports. Both of these IS goals are related directly to central concerns of critical social theory in general and the theory of communicative action in particular. Increasing productivity relates directly to overcoming unwarranted constraints in the labour process, whereas the use of IS to support social compliance relates to 'forms of domination'. Critical social theory does not deny the need for a social contract of government *à la* Locke, Kant and Rawls (1971, pp. 221, 235) justifying legitimate forms of social control. Secondly, the support of human communication appears to have become a prominent form of IT applications as network technologies are ever more ubiquitous. This relates directly to the privileged position that the theory of communicative action assigns to communicative social action. Finally, critical social theory emphasizes the roles of different types of knowledge (or information in a broad sense) in the self-formative processes of society, which by implication *a fortiori* also applies to other types of social systems, especially organizations. Therefore, critical social theory and the theory of communicative action in particular deal directly with core phenomena of IS research; that is, information, knowledge and essential human interests.

Theoretically, we have just argued that critical social theory is very relevant and appropriate to the context of IS research. As shown in Table 6.5, Habermas's critical social theory has been adopted and used in IS research. What is the status of this adoption? Where is critical IS research heading? What are some of the issues facing critical IS researchers? These are some of the important questions that we are going to discuss next. Based on our observation of past literature related to critical IS research, we drew Figure 6.3 to depict how the absorption of critical social theory in IS research has progressed during the last two decades. On the Y-axis is the major focus and on the X-axis is the time line. As shown,

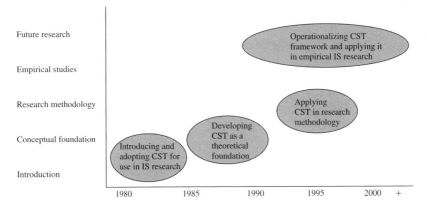

Figure 6.3   *The progress of the adoption of critical social theory (CST) in critical IS research*

it appears that progress moves from the general explanation of the potential of critical social theory to more concrete theorizing about topics directly relevant to IS research—ranging from IS design and research methodology to empirical studies. However, the theorizing has not used the full breadth of critical social theory. Only one study, that of Broadbent, Laughlin and Read (1991), drew on Habermas (1987) and none on his recent writing. Therefore, a return to more conceptual work appears to be needed.

Substantively, our observations show that most adaptations of Habermas's ideas to IS have been conceptual. There have not been many empirical investigations to confront the theory with observations of human behaviour, let alone to test its implications or to try it out in practical applications. This suggests a need for future work with a focus on applying Habermas's ideas in a real-world setting and assessing their impact in bringing about changes to improve the world. According to Ngwenyama and Lee (1997), the change focus is a characteristic that sets critical research apart from other types of social research. Thus, critical research does not end with good explanations of social phenomena, but it reaches beyond mere explanations to reveal and criticize unjust and inequitable conditions.

Methodologically, our observations point out a number of issues related to the application of critical social theory in IS research. Methodology is generally considered to be the overall strategy of conceptualizing and conducting research. If critical social theory is suitable to become a viable IS research approach, it has to provide essential linkages between critical theory constructs, empirical methods and research questions within the context of a particular research situation. Given this premise, the first issue is concerned with the relationship between research questions and chosen theories. Should research questions be driven by a choice of theory and not the other way around? If so, then the critical social theory research approach may not be able to set a research agenda and pose specific research questions. But then, of course, on what grounds should IS research questions be formulated? Clearly, theories and practice interact and research questions emerge from these interactions. Critical social theory is one of the key players on the theory side, because its broad theoretical social framework is a good lens that brings many shortcomings of real IS development and use to attention.

The second issue is concerned with the appropriate tools for conducting a critical social theory research study. Should more specific critical research methods be developed for specific critical research theory domains? From Table 6.5, it appears that language action analysis is one of the very few tools available. The article by Cecez-Kecmanovic (2001a) on how to conduct a critical study is also a helpful step towards recognizing the special methodological status of critical IS research. However, most critical social theory studies of IS have relied on traditional methods, such as ethnography, action research and case studies. The challenge is how to experiment with promising applied research methods, learn from their use and then identify what makes them appropriate.

The third issue is concerned with the development of generic principles and methods for critical research. This effort has to draw from a broader context of methodological debate on the nature of scientific methods rather than *ad hoc* applications of various methods and their tools. Therefore, the construction of research methods that are appropriate for critical social theory research 'needs to address a much broader range of issues beyond the narrow view of specific critical empirical methods' (Cecez-Kecmanovic, 2001a, p. 158). Only through such a legitimizing process can critical research gain credibility and claim its results to represent generally recognized 'truths'. (For some interesting details on how to do critical research, see Cecez-Kecmanovic, 2001a).

Philosophically, our observations of the IS research literature in general impress on us the need to reflect on the fundamental role of IS for individuals, organizations and society. This is a question that is by no means limited to critical research, using Habermas or other social theorists, but cuts to the very core of the nature of information systems as artifacts, contrived sociotechnical systems or emergent clusters of societal practices and subsystems. By implication, it also cuts to the core of the mission of IS research for the citizenry and the institutions of society from government to private business. The question points to a dualistic identity for IS. On the one hand, information systems by their nature are part of the systems differentiation of societies. This is so because their technological, science-based methods have the tendency to better support purposive rational action systems than communicative action of a lifeworldly character. We might call this the IS mission of supporting purposive rationality. If this mission captures the true nature of IS, then it is not surprising that many findings from past studies reveal that most information systems tend to serve the technical interest of instrumental rationality. Presumably, then, it would be rare to see information systems used to support the need for social integration through consensually oriented communication. This has been demonstrated over and over again in studies with rather different theoretical lenses, ranging from Markus's (1983) classical analysis of four cases, to the application of Giddens' structuration theory to the use of CASE tools (e.g. Orlikowski and Baroudi, 1991; see also Chapter 8), from grounded theory analysis of CMM-based system development (Ngwenyama and Nielsen, 2003) to Broadbent, Laughlin and Read's (1991) critical theory analysis of introducing MIS in the British National Health Service (NHS), from the application of transaction cost theories in outsourcing cases (Hirschheim and Sabherwal, 2001) to the plain description of ERP implementation effects (Truex, 2001). Control appears to be the name of the game in many guises.[12]

However, this is only half of the story, because it ignores the fact that IS also can and to some extent have supported decentralized, consensual communication. We might call this the information media mission of IS. The popularity of email from first graders to grandmothers is vivid testimony that IS can support communicative action and that the need for assuming an information media mission is widespread. Yet the bulk of IS research and development appears to ignore this other, more human side of IS, which may be dubbed its media face. The conclusions briefly outline the challenges that this raises for future IS research.

CONCLUSIONS: CHALLENGES FOR FUTURE IS RESEARCH BASED ON HABERMAS'S CRITICAL SOCIAL THEORY

If the previous concerns about the overbearing effects of IS as instruments of control and compliance have *prima facie* value, then a primary research challenge is to provide evidence for and against this concern, which arises directly from the theory of communicative action, especially Habermas (1987). Two points of anecdotal evidence may lend some urgency to this claim. First, the intruding nature of advertising in the realm of personal computing has already been noted. Of course there are possible antidotes, such as firewalls and pop-up screen blockers, which are likely to become more widespread as users become savvier. The question is how many users have these capabilities? The digital divide hypothesis becomes relevant in this context. On the organizational level we noticed that Temple University, one of the major public universities in the US, along with others has started to enforce email address standards that limit personal choice. Temple also uses not-so-subtle means of 'encouragement' to get all instructors to integrate Blackboard (a Web-based course management software application) into their course designs and conduct. We have seen similar assessment criteria on tenure and promotion dossiers from other universities ('Does the instructor show evidence of innovative use of technology support for her teaching strategy?'). If this is happening at academic organizations that traditionally upheld the value of autonomy in the classroom and free expression, then one wonders what is going on in industries that, along with armed forces, have always been at the forefront of controlling their staff and labour force. While these examples are not necessarily bad and may serve legitimate efficiency needs, the point is that this was never fully debated. The control decisions are made administratively, bypassing consensus formation.

Moreover, they might foreshadow more advanced practices that are clearly objectionable, An example of this is the use of spy software in advertising or tracking all interactions with course software like Blackboard and then providing summary measures in 'dossiers' that prospective employers request from students and administrators from faculty with their annual activity reports. This raises the question of whether we are slipping into Foucault's version of an Orwellian control society. This is an urgent research issue for two reasons. One is an external reason, because citizens and society alike are entitled to be informed whether many small IT changes add up to a policy that affects the nature of the society in which we live. The second reason is internal to the IS community. The mission of IS teaching and research will be different if IS primarily are to support instrumental and strategic action or if they are to devote equal effort and resources to supporting communicative action. For example, in the infrastructure developed by AIS for the IS research community, communicative action is clearly in the driver's seat. Therefore, the mission that IS plays for the external stakeholders cannot be without deep and lasting effects on the field's self-understanding (identity) and interpretation of its fundamental mission. Let us be more concrete on how this issue can be theoretically approached.

Research Challenges at the Level of Society

The counter-argument to the above scenario is obviously that IT is supposedly neutral and the social practices determining IT use can be democratically debated and controlled, even though so far this has not happened. If IT is neutral, its uses in the longer run will 'naturally' balance out between purposive rational and communicative uses. No new checks and balances are needed.

To cross-check this optimistic projection of the long-term effects of IT, we need to consider two potential counter-arguments. One comes from Habermas directly, the other from Foucault's analyses of social practices. From the perspective of Habermas's theory of communicative action, personal IS use could provide the unintended gateway for intruding system imperatives accelerating lifeworld colonization. As was pointed out above, the preliminary signs that this is happening are already visible. IS research should observe them carefully and alert societal decision makers so that counter-actions can be taken while the seeds of unwarranted and partly concealed domination are still in their tender blossoming stages.

Using the theoretical lens of Foucault as an alternative framework of analysis, we should learn from studying personal IS uses whether IS tend to serve as instruments for self-discipline and surveillance (see Chapter 7). This is particularly worrisome, as the technical interest is then invading the lifeworld 'from the inside out', like a social virus. If so, personal computer use could be the Trojan horse for system-induced self-discipline, as is required for the effective functioning of systems of coordination through the steering media of money and power. Counteracting this tendency is much more difficult than dealing with systems intrusions from the outside, as there is no clear centre of power for these tendencies. Enlightening education (as part of mandatory, introductory IS courses reaching large numbers of future citizens), debate and reflection at the level of individuals and small group opinion formation appear to be the only antidotes.

Does this mean that IS research will forever be limited to support the imperatives of steering media money and administrative power, and IS research condemned to remain the handmaiden of a societal panopticum, *à la* Foucault? Clearly, past performance needs not be indicative of future results. However, if this is to change—and it has not in the last 20 years (see Klein and Lyytinen, 1985 and Lyytinen and Klein, 1985)—we need nothing less than a fundamental debate on the vision and mission of the IS discipline with subsequent action as, for example, proposed in Hirschheim and Klein (2003) and Klein and Lyytinen (2003).

Research Challenges Transcending the Level of Society and Organizations

With the emergence of the Internet, IS entered the arena of being a public information media. Eventually it might be on par with—if not superior to—print, radio and television. Consider the introduction to Dahlberg (2001):

> The Internet's two-way, decentralized communications are seen by many commentators as providing the means by which to extend informal political deliberations. Indeed, a cursory examination of the thousands of diverse conversations taking place everyday online and open to anyone with Internet access seems to indicate the expansion on a global scale of the loose webs of rational-critical discourse that constitute what is known as the public sphere.[13] However, some commentators argue that online discourse is not presently fulfilling its deliberative potential.

The many experimental cyber-communities that do engage in serious debates and the many individualized discourses of email list servers clearly demonstrate that the potential for deliberative, communicative functions of IT does indeed exist. Heng and de Moor (2003) review a number of examples of such communities. However, for whatever reasons, such serious communicative functions of the Internet have not yet materialized on a larger scale. We find this surprising, because the communicative functions of IT have been highly touted since the inception of the computer (e.g. Hedberg, 1975; Sackman, 1967). If so, it is also part and parcel of the American credo that public information distribution should be governed by policies that serve the better good of all. Historically, the values that were supposed to be advanced in public policies governing information technology, from print to radio and television, were those associated with the notion of a free press; that is, freedom of inquiry, expression of the greatest diversity of opinion (marketplace of ideas) and universal access. From the press these were transferred to other media that played a similar role as communication technology advanced: radio, television and to some extent the telephone. *A fortiori* they should have also been extended to the new IT. Yet, as was previously noted, that has not happened so far.

We believe that an important research issue for IS as a field is to understand why this has not happened and whether it should happen in the future (see Hirschheim and Klein, 2003 for some further elaboration of this research issue). If the answer to the last question is affirmative, then IS research should have something to say about the ways it can be made to happen through appropriate IT designs. This does not mean that IT would have to stop serving the masters that it is serving now: specific interest groups, such as the management of corporations and owners of the communications industry. However, this influence would then become more democratically moderated. It is obvious that there would also be beneficial side-effects of dealing with the general issue of lifeworld colonization if the information media nature of IS with its corresponding value base were recognized and implemented on a large scale, both at the organizational and societal levels.

Research Challenges at the Level of Organizations

In order to outline some of the implications of Habermas's critical social theory for IS research at the organizational level, it is convenient to distinguish between products and processes of IS development. Products are specific systems designed to support concrete application domains, for example Mowshowitz (1976) distinguished between IS applications to control deviance and those that support the coordination of diversity. The theory of communicative action suggests distinguishing between IS applications that support the various types of social action, which were summarized in Figure 6.1. The result of an earlier extensive literature analysis using this action typology was that very few IS applications exist that support unrestricted communicative action; that is, both ordinary conversations and discourses of various kinds (Hirschheim, Klein and Lyytinen, 1996). We suspect that this result still holds in spite of the many changes that the spreading use of Internet applications has brought about. The more detailed examination of Habermas's work in this chapter suggests that the following critical comments should be added to the 1996 IS literature analysis.

Earlier, this chapter noted that the ITC industry markets a number of IS products with the claim that they improve various forms of organizational communication. This gives the impression that a new wave of IS products is on the way to bolster communicative action and with this could overcome the heavy instrumental bias of past IS applications. The literature that we have in mind here goes by various names. In essence it covers applications from the now classical (group) decision support systems to modern groupware and CMC (computer-mediated communication). Its functionality is concerned with providing memory aids (data bases, data warehousing), discovering and feeding relevant information (e.g. query macros and data mining), performing complex analysis (decision models), displaying results in more comprehensible form (human–computer interface and computer–human interaction), 'empowering' users by designing more flexible and more intuitive interfaces with greater than usual functionality, and facilitating synchronous and asynchronous communications. The latter include multimedia conference systems, web-based teaching support and online course designs employing both synchronous and asynchronous communication features. The most advanced software products offer any combinations of the previous features and organizational frameworks have been proposed combining multiple products with various functionality in comprehensive knowledge and information management systems (KMS and IMS).

However, as was pointed out, facilitating social consensus formation uncritically may actually reinforce existing systematic distortions and power plays if the social prerequisites for overcoming barriers to effective social communication through discourse are not carefully checked. The key message of one earlier section was that discourses, computer supported or otherwise, could only contribute to socially authentic (valid) communication if the procedure and symmetry preconditions of rational discourse are at least approximated. Heng and de Moor (2003) provided an informative prototype of how this could be accomplished in the *inter*-organizational arena. We are convinced that the same principles could be used to develop *intra*-organizational applications. Did anybody see a recent prototype for this? The point is that 'what is good for the goose is good for the gander'. Any computer support for rational discourse must carefully check these conditions and in the case of intra-organizational support, they need to be considered carefully at the stages of organizational requirements determination, systems implementation and post-implementation use evaluation.

So far, this has happened at best sporadically, as in the case of so-called brainstorming or nominal group support systems, which provided anonymity as a possible safeguard against social distortions. At best, they provided occasional flashes of insights into the darker side of organizational life; at worst these systems were 'islands' in a sea of instrumental and strategic action systems and hence could not effectively counteract pre-existing institutionalized biases, blind spots, groupthink and power structures, but gave them an air of liberal appearance. In most cases of communication support system implementations, concerns with checking the procedure and symmetry conditions for rational discourse never even crossed the minds of the organizational system sponsors, implementers and users. Yet the few isolated studies investigating these issues clearly indicated that even such simple systems as list servers and email lend themselves easily to covert strategic action, undermining trust and the motivation to engage in future discourses (e.g. Cecez-Kecmanovic and Janson, 1999; Cecez-Kecmanovic, Treleaven and Moodie, 2000). We therefore propose to generalize the following research question to apply to all kinds of ICT applications that are concerned with improving social communication, not just KMS:

> A principal research question that remains to be explored is: to what extent and under what conditions would the technology for KMS with specified characteristics, that embodies the suggested features and design principles, assist participants to realise their communicative rationality potential and learn to interact heedfully, and thereby increase their chances to share knowledge and create a collective stock of knowledge? (Cecez-Kecmanovic and Janson, 1999, p. 10)

This research question points to an important area that is in urgent need of broad-based empirical inquiries. How widespread and how serious are systemic communicative distortions? Are they the exception or the rule? If distortions exist, do they have a major impact or affect the outcomes only at the margin? Maybe the impacts of distorted communications at the organizational level are not as serious as on the macro-societal level? Which user groups are in the driving seat and which are disenfranchised? We simply do not know the answers to such questions and, of course, they cannot be obtained from sending out questionnaires or conducting telephone interviews with study participants whom the research team has never met. In an earlier era of IS applications development, similar issues were investigated under the banner of user participation in systems development. However, these classical results are no longer directly relevant to the current organizational situations, as the modes of systems design and implementation have changed drastically—which takes us to process considerations.

In 1994 one of the authors made a concrete proposal for advancing human emancipation through IS development at the organizational level through extending the classical principles and methods of sociotechnical systems (including soft systems) development (Hirschheim and Klein, 1994). While this proposal reads cumbersomely from the current perspective and may have had some infelicitous formulations that can easily be misunderstood (see the sharp critique by Wilson, 1997), its core thrust still stands as a challenge to IS research: how can the IS research community contribute to emancipatory goals at the organizational level? The goals of emancipatory information systems development confront researchers and practitioners with the question of how IS can be designed and implemented that are not authoritarian or manipulative, improve instrumental rationality and communicative rationality where each is most appropriate, yet also help most those who are underprivileged. This ethical imperative is consistent with Rawls' (1971) theory of justice. Unfortunately, very little has happened along those lines even though there is a tremendous need, not only in developing countries but also in the developed nations, their inner cities and marginalized rural areas. Again, IS research has been silent. Even independent university research has shown little interest in this area. The principles of adopting such an 'emancipatory' approach to IS development have received little attention and funding. They need to be further elaborated, tested and kept in tune with advances in the economic and technical powers of IT.

Interestingly enough, the two projects of which we have become aware both happened in developing countries. One was reported at the 2001 ICIS conference, and the other came to the attention of one the authors through a personal visit to the University of Pretoria. As a summary of both projects is easily available at http://www.mis.temple.edu/hkklein/ (also Phahlamohlaka and Friend, 2003) and http://www.mssrf.org/ (also Kanungo, 2001), we limit ourselves to quoting the fundamental value under which the M S Swaminathan Research Foundation's Information Village project was conducted:

> Recall the face of the poorest and the weakest man whom you have seen, and ask yourself, if the steps you contemplate are going to be of any use to him. Will he gain anything by it? Will it restore to him control over his own life and destiny? (M. K. Gandhi)
>
> (Quoted from a website document on '*Information Village Research Project, (IVRP)—Union Territory of Pondicherry*', supported by the International Development Research Centre (IDRC), Canadian International Development Agency (CIDA), Canada, accessed in 2002. This website is no longer active.)

This Gandhi quote reads like a paraphrase from Rawls' theory of justice and provides a beautiful example of the possibility of intercultural convergence of ethical arguments through communicative action. What could be further apart in theoretical and cultural lenses than the traditions on which Gandhi, Habermas and Rawls built their life's work? Yet they arrive at the same fundamental value. One wonders what IS as a field would be like today if industry and IS research had heeded this value when it all started with the first commercial applications of IT in the early 1960s. It seems we have lost about 40 years in which we could have better served humanity.

A GUIDE TO THE LITERATURE

Recommended Original Readings for the Principal Stages of Critical Social Theory

On the Frankfurt School's background to Habermas's work: **Held (1980)**; Arato and Gebhardt (1982).

Leading up to *Knowledge and Human Interest*: Habermas (1970, **1972, 1991**).

From *Knowledge and Human Interest* to *The Theory of Communicative Action*: Habermas (1973, 1975, 1979).

Beyond *The Theory of Communicative Action*: Habermas (1990), especially the essays on 'Reconstruction and interpretation in the social sciences' and 'Discourse ethics: Notes on a program of philosophical justification'; Habermas (1977, 1996).

Recommended Secondary Literature

On Habermas's theoretical contributions up to *The Theory of Communicative Action*: **Howe (2000)**; Heath (2001), Chapters 1 and 2, especially recommended for readers with background in game theory; **McCarthy (1978)**.

On Habermas's theoretical contributions beyond *The Theory of Communicative Action*. The relationship of the following references to IS research is by no means obvious and is itself part of a research programme to broaden the theoretical foundations of IS research by aligning them with the exciting, fundamental developments in contemporary philosophical debates: White (1995a, 1995b); Heath (2001) beyond Chapters 1 and 2; d'Entrèves and Benhabib (1997).

After d'Entrèves' introductory overview, the most relevant contributions from an IS perspective appear to be essays 2, 5 and 7.
On applying Habermas's critical social theory in empirical studies: Cecez-Kecmanovic (2001a); Klein and Myers (1999); together with Morrow and Brown (1994).
General reference on terminology: Macey (2000).
Note: Bold items are recommended for a first introduction to Habermas's critical social theory.

ENDNOTES

[1]Of course, this argumentation strategy is not without its dangers, as Schmidt (1996, p. 148) clearly points out with reference to Rajchman (1991, p. 28).

[2]As principal sources for this part on the 'Unity of knowledge and interest', Habermas in *Knowledge and Human Interest* relies on Freud and Nietzsche. Interestingly, Freud is by far the most frequently used basis for details. However, Habermas's interpretation of Nietzsche is critical for transferring Freudian, psychoanalytical, 'critical' thought patterns to the societal level. This includes diagnosing the nihilist effects that the scientific enterprise—its enlightenment process—had on eroding the legitimatization of traditional norms and values. The erosion of traditional norms and meanings included not only the destruction of religious doctrine and the moral authority of the church by appealing to God and his word (which science reduced to simply one of many possible myths), but also the grounding of the authority of government and public morality (*Sittlichkeit*) in shared views of world order. Nietzsche is also important for the critical reflection that the orientation of the scientific enterprise, in particular its causality thinking, is not so much towards inquiry and understanding but towards 'gaining power' over matter (*Bemächtigung der Dinge*). Ultimately this gaining power includes not only prediction and control of nature, but also people. Habermas transfers this insight to defining the 'technical interest' and in *The Theory of Communicative Action* it is teleological action through which humans pursue and realize this interest in gaining power over matter and people.

[3]http://www.uta.edu/huma/illuminations/ and http://www.helsinki.fi/~amkauppi/hablinks.html (last accessed 27 November 2003) provide useful overviews of critical social theory in general and Habermas's recent work, respectively. Both websites contain many useful links, for example the Habermas bibliography, annotated references, and critical reviews by serious authors such as Mark Poster or Andrew Feenberg (http://www-rohan.sdsu.edu/faculty/feenberg/marhab.html).

[4]For further personal information on Habermas see http://www.nyu.edu/classes/stephens/Habermas%20page.htm (last accessed 27 November 2003).

[5]The following information on Habermas is drawn and translated from Görtzen, 2000.

[6]From this perspective it is obvious why Habermas is deeply concerned about the deterioration of the public sphere through new forms of dominations and distortions such as economic power concentration, manipulating advertising

interests that intrude on the content of information media, ideological control of the now so-called free press, and the general population's lack of access to and educational ability to participate in the debate of important public policy issues. Science and technology have become an ideology (see the explanation later in this section) that complicates public policy issues to the point of placing them beyond the understanding of most citizens. Choices are then made by experts, who fall victim to the hidden assumptions underlying their own decision-making technologies. For more elaboration and on how this might apply to IS as a field, see Hirschheim and Klein (2003) and Habermas (1971, 1974).

[7]Associated with such an expansion will be the following claim. If critical empirical studies were to apply the ideas that emerged from the system–lifeworld debate (which is related to Foucault's work) in the context of considering all of the above five theoretical building blocks of the theory of communicative action as are introduced here, then this could bear substantial fruits for future critical social theory research in information systems.

[8]Unfortunately, the general definition of the action types is sometimes not quite correct. For example in an award-winning paper (Ngwenyama and Lee, 1997), the reviewers failed to notice that the teleological action type is misconstrued. (However, this slight error does not affect the principal point of the paper.)

[9]The observation that the lifeworld is difficult to articulate does not force the conclusion that therefore it has no ontological existence. It seems not only more fruitful but also more consistent with the overall structure of the theory of communicative action to assign a distinct existence to the lifeworld. Layder's (1997, p. 105) social domain theory provides support for this view. If it were not so, then the lifeworld would merely be an analytical aspect of 'one whole life'. But this then would also shed doubt on the ontological separation of the other three worlds and, given that, the whole system of distinguishing different action types would begin to crumble.

[10]Habermas (1973, p. 256) also says that this second postulate of equal speech opportunity 'describes the formal conditions for all discourses if these are to possess the force of rational motivation'. What is presumably meant here is that no other force should be more effective than that of the logically and empirically superior argument—*sine ira et studio*.

[11]We chose to quote Heath (2001) because he provides further discussion and his paraphrase is clearer than Habermas's original formulation, as follows: 'Thus every valid norm has to fulfill the following condition: (U) *All* affected can accept the consequences and side effects its *general* observance can be expected to have for the satisfaction of *everyone's* interests (and these consequences are preferred to those of known alternative possibilities for regulation)' (Habermas, 1990, p. 65).

[12]If there is a need to dispel any doubts about this judgement, then it could be addressed by engaging in a major coding effort of the research literature of the last 10 years or longer using an action type framework, as was explained here and further elaborated in Hirschheim, Klein and Lyytinen (1996). It could score numerically which action types have been supported the most and the least in industry practices, government, other non-profit organizations and IS research. Such data coding could be very valuable in shedding light on the issue of where the priorities have been in the past in IS research and various domains of practice. This could then provide a basis for reflecting, from a

socially responsible perspective, whether the resource allocation is in need of rebalancing, as Hirschheim and Klein (2003) have suggested.

[13] Proponents of the idea that cyberspace may, under the right social conditions, offer a renewed public sphere include Aikens (1997), Fernback (1997), Hauben and Hauben (1997), Kellner (1999), Moore (1999), Noveck (1999), Rheingold (1993) and Slevin (2000).

REFERENCES

Aikens, S. (1997) 'American democracy and computer-mediated communication: A case study in Minnesota', doctoral dissertation in social and political sciences, Cambridge: Cambridge University.

Alexy, R. (1978) 'Eine Theorie des praktischen Diskurses', in W. Oelmüller (ed.), *Normenbegründung, Normendurchsetzung*, Paderborn: Uni-TB.

Apel, K.-O. (1973) 'The apriori of the communication community and the foundations of ethics', English trans., in K.-O. Apel, *The Transformation of Philosophy*, London: Routledge and Kegan Paul.

Arato, A. and Gebhardt, E. (eds) (1982) *The Essential Frankfurt School Reader*, New York, NY: Continuum.

Berger, P. and Luckmann, T. (1967) *The Social Construction of Reality: A Treatise in the Sociology of Knowledge*, Garden City, NY: Anchor Books.

Bernstein, R. (1976) *The Restructuring of Social and Political Theory*, London: Methuen.

Bhaskar, R. (1989) *Reclaiming Reality*, London: Verso.

Bleicher, J. (1980) *Contemporary Hermeneutics: Hermeneutics as Method, Philosophy and Critique*, London: Routledge and Kegan Paul.

Boland, R. J. (1985) 'Phenomenology: A preferred approach to research on information systems', in E. Mumford, R. Hirschheim, G. Fitzgerald and A. T. Wood-Harper (eds), *Research Methods in Information Systems*, Amsterdam: North-Holland.

Broadbent, J., Laughlin, R. and Read, S. (1991) 'Recent financial and administrative changes in the NHS: A critical theory analysis', *Critical Perspectives on Accounting*, 2: 1–29.

Cecez-Kecmanovic, D. (2001a) 'Doing critical IS research: The question of methodology', in E. M. Trauth (ed.), *Qualitative Research in IS: Issues and Trends*, Hershey, PA: Idea Group Publishing, pp. 158–80.

Cecez-Kecmanovic, D. (2001b) 'What enables and what prevents knowledge sharing via computer-mediated communications?' *Journal of Systems and Information Technology*, 5(1, June): 115–34.

Cecez-Kecmanovic, D. and Janson, M. (1999) 'Communicative action theory: An approach to understanding the application of information systems', *Proceeding of 10th Australasian Conference on Information Systems*, Wellington: University of Wellington, pp. 183–95.

Cecez-Kecmanovic, D., Treleaven, L. and Moodie, D. (2000) 'CMC and the question of democratisation: A university field study [CD-ROM]', *Proceedings of the 33rd Hawaii International Conference on Systems Sciences HICSS'2000*, Hawaii: IEEE Computer Society.

Cecez-Kecmanovic, D., Webb, C. and Tayler, P. (1999) 'Being flexible by being WISE: Two case studies of Web-based teaching and learning', in M. Khosrowpour (ed.), *Managing Information Technology Resources in Organizations in the Next Millennium*, Hershey, PA: Idea Group Publishing, pp. 730–34.

Dahlberg, L. (2001) 'Extending the public sphere through cyberspace: The Case Minnesota e-democracy', *First Monday*, 6(3, March), http://www.firstmonday.dk/issues/issue6_3/dahlberg/index.html#author.

d'Entrèves, M. and S. Benhabib (eds) (1997) *Habermas and the Unfinished Project of Modernity: Critical Essays on the Philosophical Discourse of Modernity*, Cambridge, MA: MIT Press.

Fernback, J. (1997) 'The individual within the collective: Virtual ideology and the realization of collective principles', in S. G. Jones (ed.), *Virtual Culture: Identity and Communication in Cybersociety*, London: Sage, pp. 36–54.

Forester, J. (1992) 'Critical ethnography: On fieldwork in Habermasian way', in M. Alvesson and H. Willmott (eds), *Critical Management Studies*, London: Sage, pp. 46–65.

Foster, M. (1991) *Gadamer and Practical Philosophy*, Atlanta, GA: Scholars Press.

Friedeburg, L. V. (n.d.) 'History of the Institute of Social Research (Summary)', http://www.ifs.uni-frankfurt.de/english/history.htm.

Görtzen, R. (2000) 'Habermas: Bi(bli)ographische Bausteine: Eine Auswahl' (Bi(bli)ographic building blocks: A selection), in S. Müller-Doohm (ed.), *Das Interesse der Vernunft: Rückblicke auf das Werk von Jürgen Habermas seit 'Erkenntnis and Interesse'* (Human interest of reason: Reflections on the opus of Jürgen Habermas since 'Knowledge and Human Interest'), Frankfurt an Main: Suhrkamp, pp. 543–83.

Habermas, J. (1962) *Strukturwandel der Öffentlichkeit*, trans. in 1989 as *The Structural Transformation of the Public Sphere: An Inquiry into a Category of Bourgeois Society*, Berlin: Luchterhand.

Habermas, J. (1967) 'Zur Logik der Sozialwissenschaften' (The logic of the social sciences), *Philosophische Rundschau*, 14(5): 1966–67.

Habermas, J. (1968a) *Technik und Wissenschaft als Ideologie* (Technology and science as ideology), Frankfurt an Main: Suhrkamp.

Habermas, J. (1968b) *Erkenntnis und Interesse* (Knowledge and human interest), Frankfurt an Main: Suhrkamp.

Habermas, J. (1970) 'Technology and science as ideology', in J. Habermas, *Toward a Rational Society*, trans. J. Shapiro, Boston, MA: Beacon Press.

Habermas, J. (1971) *Der Strukturwandel der Öffentlichkeit: Untersuchungen zu einer bürgerlichen Kategorie der Gesellschaft*, 2nd edn, Berlin: Luchterhand.

Habermas, J. (1972) *Knowledge and Human Interest*, London: Heinemann.

Habermas, J. (1973) 'Wahrheitstheorien' (Theories of truth) in H. Fahrenbach (ed.), *Wirklichkeit und Reflexion: Festschrift für W. Schulz*, Pfüllingen: Neske, pp. 211–65.

Habermas, J. (1974) *Technik und Wissenschaft als 'Ideologie'* (Technology and Science as Ideology), 7th edn, Frankfurt an Main: Suhrkamp.

Habermas, J. (1975) *Legitimation Crisis*, Boston, MA: Beacon Press.

Habermas, J. (1976) 'Was heißt Universalpragmatik?' (What is universal pragmatics?), in K.-O. Apel (ed.), *Sprachpragmatik und Philosophie*, Frankfurt an Main: Suhrkamp, pp. 174–272.

Habermas, J. (1977) 'Modernity, an unfinished project' in M. d'Entrèves and S. Benhabib (eds), *Habermas and the Unfinished Project of Modernity: Critical Essays on the Philosophical Discourse of Modernity*, Cambridge, MA: MIT Press, pp. 38–55.

Habermas, J. (1979) *Communication and the Evolution of Society*, London: Heinemann.

Habermas, J. (1981) *Theorie des Kommunikativen Handelns*, Frankfurt an Main: Suhrkamp.

Habermas, J. (1982) 'A reply to my critics', in J. Thompson and D. Held (eds), *Habermas: Critical Debates*, Cambridge, MA: MIT Press.

Habermas, J. (1983) *Moralbewussten und Kommunicatives Handeln*, Frankfurt an Main: Suhrkamp.

Habermas, J. (1984) *The Theory of Communicative Action: Reason and the Rationalisation of Society (Vol I)*, Boston, MA: Beacon Press.

Habermas, J. (1985) *The Philosophical Discourse of Modernity: Twelve Lectures*, Frankfurt an Main: Suhrkamp.

Habermas, J. (1987) *The Theory of Communicative Action: The Critique of Functionalist Reason (Vol II)*, Boston, MA: Beacon Press.

Habermas, J. (1988) *On the Logic of the Social Sciences*, trans. S. Web Nicholsen and J. A. Stark, Cambridge, MA: MIT Press.

Habermas, J. (1990) *Moral Consciousness and Communicative Action*, trans. C. Lenhardt and S. Nicholsen, Cambridge, MA: MIT Press.

Habermas, J. (1991) *The Transformation of the Structural Sphere*, trans. T. Burger and F. Lawrence, Cambridge, MA: MIT Press.

Habermas, J. (1996) *Between Facts and Norms: Contributions to a Discourse Theory of Law and Democracy*, trans. W. Rehg, Cambridge, MA: MIT Press.

Habermas, J. (2000) 'Nach dreißig Jahren: Bemerkungen zu *Erkenntnis und Interesse*', in S. Müller-Doohm (ed.), *Das Interesse der Vernunft: Rückblicke auf das Werk von Jürgen Habermas seit 'Erkenntnis und Interesse'* (Human interest of reason: Reflections on the opus of Jürgen Habermas since 'Knowledge and Human Interest'), Frankfurt an Main: Suhrkamp, pp. 12–20.

Hauben, M. and Hauben, R. (1997) *Netizens: On the History and Impact of Usenet and the Internet*, Los Alamitos, CA: IEEE Computer Society.

Heath, J. (2001) *Communicative Action and Rational Choice*, Cambridge, MA: MIT Press.

Hedberg, B. (1975) 'Computer systems to support industrial democracy', in E. Mumford and H. Sackman (eds), *Human Choice and Computers*, Amsterdam: North-Holland.

Held, D. (1980) *Introduction to Critical Theory: Horkheimer to Habermas*, Berkeley, CA: University of California Press.

Heng, M. and de Moor, A. (2003) 'From Habermas' communicative theory to practice on the Internet', *Information Systems Journal*, 13(4): 331–52.

Hirschheim, R. and Klein, H. K. (1989) 'Four paradigms of information systems development', *Communications of the ACM*, 32(10): 1199–216.

Hirschheim, R. and Klein, H. K. (1994) 'Realizing emancipatory principles in information systems development: The case for ETHICS', *MIS Quarterly*, 18(1): 83–109.

Hirschheim, R. and Klein, H. K. (2003) 'Crisis in the IS field? A critical reflection on the state of the discipline', *Journal of the Association for Information Systems*, 4(5): 237–93.

Hirschheim, R. and Sabherwal, R. (2001) 'Detours in the path toward strategic information systems alignment: Excessive transformations, paradoxical decisions, and uncertain turnarounds', *California Management Review*, 44(1): 87–108.

Hirschheim, R., Klein, H. K. and Lyytinen, K. (1996) 'Exploring the intellectual structures of information systems development: A social action theoretic analysis', *Accounting, Management and Information Technology*, 6(1/2): 1–64.

Howe, L. (2000) *On Habermas*, Belmont, CA: Wadsworth/Thomson.

Jackson, M. (1982) 'The nature of soft systems thinking: The work of Churchman, Ackoff, and Checkland', *Journal of Applied Systems Analysis*, 9: 17–27.

Jackson, M. (1991) 'The origins and nature of critical systems think', *Systems Practice*, 4(2): 131–49.

Jackson, M. (1997) 'Critical systems thinking and information systems research', in J. Mingers and F. A. Stowell (eds), *Information Systems: An Emerging Discipline*, London: McGraw-Hill.

Jones, M. R. (2000) 'The moving finger: The use of social theory in WG8.2 conference papers, 1975–1999', in R. Baskerville, J. Stage and J. I. DeGross (eds), *Organizational and Social Perspectives on Information Technology*, Dordrecht: Kluwer Academic Publishers, pp. 15–31.

Kanungo, S. (2001) 'On the sustainability of rural information systems: Analysis of preliminary experimental evidence', presentation at the *Twenty-Second International Conference on Information Systems*, 01TRP12, New Orleans.

Keen, P. (1981) 'Information systems and organizational change', *Communications of the ACM*, 24(1): 24–33.

Kellner, D. (1999) 'Globalization from below? Toward a radical democratic technopolitics', *Angelaki: Journal of the Theoretical Humanities*, 4(2): 101–13.

Klein, H. K. and Hirschheim, R. (1991) 'Rationality concepts in information systems development methodologies', *Accounting, Management and Information Technologies*, 1(2): 157–87.

Klein, H. K. and Hirschheim, R. (2001) 'Choosing between competing design ideals in information systems development', *Information Systems Frontiers*, 3(1): 75–90.

Klein, H. K. and Huynh, M. (1999) 'The potential of the language action perspective in ethnographic analysis', in O. Ngwenyama, L. D. Introna, M. D. Myers and J. DeGross (eds), *New Information Technologies in Organizational Processes: Field Studies and Theoretical Reflections on the Future of Work*, Dordrecht: Kluwer Academic Publishers, pp. 79–98.

Klein, H. K. and Lyytinen, K. (1985) 'The poverty of scientism in information systems', in E. Mumford, R. Hirschheim, G. Fitzgerald and T. Wood-Harper (eds), *Research Methods in Information Systems*, Amsterdam: North-Holland, pp. 131–62.

Klein, H. K. and Lyytinen, K. (2003) 'Knowledge creation and transformation in networks: The case of relevancy of information systems research', manuscript submitted for review.

Klein, H. K. and Myers, M. D. (1999) 'A set of principles for conducting and evaluating interpretive field studies in information systems', *MIS Quarterly*, 23(1): 67–93.

Klein, H. K. and Myers, M. D. (2003) 'On the foundations of critical IS research', working manuscript.

Klein, H. K. and Truex, D. P. (1996) 'Discourse analysis: An approach to the analysis of organizational emergence', in B. Holmqvist, P. B. Andersen, H. K. Klein and R. Posner (eds), *The Semiotics of the Work Place*, Berlin: W. DeGruyter, pp. 227–68.

Kuhn, T. (1970) *The Structure of Scientific Revolutions*, 2nd edn, Chicago, IL: University of Chicago Press.

Lakatos, I. (1970) 'Falsification and the methodology of scientific research programmes', in I. Lakatos and A. Musgrave (eds), *Criticism and the Growth of Knowledge*, Cambridge: Cambridge University Press, pp. 91–196.

Layder, D. (1997) *Modern Social Theory: Key Debates and New Directions*, London: UCL Press.

Lyytinen, K. (1986) 'Information systems development as social action: Framework and critical implications', PhD thesis, Department of Computer Science, University of Jyvaskyla, Finland.

Lyytinen, K. (1992) 'Information systems and critical theory', in M. Alvesson and H. Willmott (eds), *Critical Management Studies*, London: Sage, pp. 159–80.

Lyytinen, K. and Hirschheim, R. (1988) 'Information systems as rational discourse: An application of Habermas' theory of communicative rationality', *Scandinavian Journal of Management Studies*, 4(1): 19–30.

Lyytinen, K. and Klein, H. (1985) 'The critical social theory of Jurgen Habermas as a basis for a theory of information systems', in E. Mumford, R. Hirschheim, G. Fitzgerald and T. Wood-Harper (eds), *Research Methods in Information Systems*, Amsterdam: North-Holland, pp. 219–36.

Macey, D. (2000) *The Penguin Dictionary of Critical Theory*, London: Penguin Books.

Markus, M. L. (1983) 'Power, politics and MIS implementation', *Communications of the ACM*, 26(6): 430–44.

McCarthy, T. (1978) *The Critical Theory of Jürgen Habermas*, Cambridge, MA: MIT Press.

McCarthy, T. (1982) *The Critical Theory of Jürgen Habermas*, 2nd edn, Cambridge, MA: MIT Press.

Mingers, J. C. (1981) 'Toward an appropriate social theory for applied systems analysis: Critical social and soft systems methodology', *Journal of Applied Systems Analysis*, 7(1): 41–9.

Mingers, J. (1984) 'Subjectivism and soft systems methodology: A critique', *Journal of Applied Systems Analysis*, 11: 85–103.

Mingers, J. (1992a) 'Recent developments in critical management science', *Journal of the Operational Research Society*, 43(1): 1–10.

Mingers, J. (1992b) 'Technical, practical, and critical OR: Past, present, and future?' in M. Alvesson and H. Willmott (eds), *Critical Management Studies*, London: Sage, pp. 91–109.

Mingers, J. (2002), 'Realizing information systems: Critical realism as an underpinning philosophy for information systems', in J. DeGross (ed.), *International*

Conference on Information Systems, Barcelona: Association of Information Systems, pp. 295–303.

Moore, R. (1999) 'Democracy and cyberspace', in B.N. Hague and B.D. Loader (eds), *Digital Democracy: Discourse and Decision Making in the Information Age*, London: Routledge.

Morrow, R. and Brown, D. (1994) *Critical Theory and Methodology*, Thousand Oaks, CA: Sage.

Mowshowitz, A. (1976) *The Conquest of Will: Information Processing in Human Affairs*, Reading: MA: Addison-Wesley.

Müller-Doohm, S. (ed.) (2000) *Das Interesse der Vernunft: Rückblicke auf das Werk von Jürgen Habermas seit 'Erkenntnis and Interesse'* (Human interest of reason: Reflections on the opus of Jürgen Habermas since 'Knowledge and Human Interest'), Frankfurt an Main: Suhrkamp.

Mumford, E., Hirschheim, R., Fitzgerald, G. and Wood-Harper, T. (eds) (1985) *Research Methods in Information Systems*, Amsterdam: North-Holland.

Ngwenyama, O. and Lee, A. (1997) 'Communication richness in electronic mail: Critical social theory and the contextuality of meaning', *MIS Quarterly*, 21(2): 145–67.

Ngwenyama, O. and Nielsen, P. (2003) 'Competing values in software process improvement: An assumption analysis of CMM from an organizational culture perspective', *IEEE Transactions on Engineering Management*, 50(1): 100–12.

Noveck, B. (1999) 'Transparent space: Law, technology and deliberative democracy in the information society', http://webserver.law.yale.edu/infosociety/papers/democracy.html.

Orlikowski, W. and Baroudi, J. (1991) 'Studying information technology in organizations: Research approaches and assumptions', *Information Systems Research*, 2(1): 1–28.

Ouchi, W. G. (1979) 'A conceptual framework for the design of organizational control mechanisms', *Management Science*, 25(9): 833–48.

Phahlamohlaka, J. and Friend, J. (2003) 'Community planning for rural education in South Africa', *European Journal of Operational Research*, 152(3): 684–95.

Poster, M. (1989) *The Critical Theory and Poststructuralism: In Search of a Context*, Ithaca, NY: Cornell University Press.

Rajchman, J. (1991) 'Habermas' complaint', in J. Rajchman, *Philosophical Events: Essays of the 80s*, New York, NY: Columbia University Press.

Rawls, J. (1971) *A Theory of Justice*, Cambridge, MA: Harvard University Press.

Rheingold, H. (1993) *The Virtual Community: Homesteading on the Electronic Frontier*, Reading, MA: Addison-Wesley.

Rosenau, P. M. (1992) *Post-Modernism and the Social Sciences*, Princeton, NJ: Princeton University Press.

Sackman, H. (1967) *Computers, System Science and Evolving Society*, New York, NY: Wiley Interscience.

Schmidt, J. (1996) 'Habermas and Foucault', in M. d'Entrèves and S. Benhabib (eds), *Habermas and the Unfinished Project of Modernity: Critical Essays on the Philosophical Discourse of Modernity*, Cambridge, MA: MIT Press, pp. 147–71.

Schutz, A. and Luckmann, T. (1974) trans. R. M. Zaner and H. T. Engelhardt, *The Structures of the LifeWorld*, London: Heinemann.

Searle, J. R. (1979) 'Literal meaning', in J. R. Searle, *Expression and Meaning*, Cambridge: Cambridge University Press.

Slevin, J. (2000) *The Internet and Society*, Cambridge, Polity Press.

Thompson, J. and Held, D. (1982) *Habermas: Critical Debates*, Cambridge, MA: MIT Press.

Truex, D. (2001) 'ERP systems as facilitating and confounding factors in corporate mergers: The case of two Canadian telecommunications companies', *Systèmes d'Information et Management*, Special issue on project management, 1(6): 7–21.

Warnke, G. (1995) 'Communicative rationality and cultural values', in S. White (ed.), *The Cambridge Companion to Habermas*, Cambridge: Cambridge University Press, pp. 120–42.

Weber, M. (1947) *The Theory of Economic and Social Organization*, New York, NY: Free Press.

White, S. (1988) *The Recent Work of Jürgen Habermas: Reason, Justice and Modernity*, Cambridge: Cambridge University Press.

White, S. (1995a) 'Reason, modernity, and democracy', in S. White (ed.), *The Cambridge Companion to Habermas*, Cambridge: Cambridge University Press, pp. 3–16.

White, S. (ed.) (1995b) *The Cambridge Companion to Habermas*, Cambridge: Cambridge University Press.

Wilson, F. (1997) 'The truth is out there: The search for emancipatory principles in IS design', *Information Technology and People*, 10(3): 187–204.

7
Foucault, Power/Knowledge and Information Systems: Reconstructing the Present

Leslie P. Willcocks

> We have been able to see what forms of power relation were conveyed by various technologies (whether we are speaking of productions with economic aims, or institutions whose goal is social regulation, or of techniques of communication)... What is at stake, then, is this: How can the growth of capabilities be disconnected from the intensification of power relations? (M. Foucault, 'What is enlightenment', Rabinow, 1984)

In this chapter we look at the work of Michel Foucault and its relevance to the information systems (IS) field. This introduction will give an insight into Foucault's style of thought and his intentions. The second section then provides an overview of the evolution of his work, while the third describes Foucault's fundamental concepts and contributions. There follows a fourth section in which the major critiques of his work are presented and discussed. The fifth section details applications and possible developments of Foucault's ideas in the IS field. A reader wishing to grasp Foucault's concepts and their relevance to IS could usefully focus first on sections three and five, then come back to gain a deeper understanding of his intentions and motivations and how his work evolved.

What drove Michel Foucault and what were the characteristics of his thought? Habermas (see Chapter 6) recalls at their first meeting in 1983:

> The tension... between the almost serene scientific reserve of the scholar striving for objectivity on the one hand, and on the other,

the political vitality of the vulnerable, subjectively excitable, morally sensitive intellectual.

Though his self-selected title at the Collège de France was professor of the history of systems of thought, Foucault was himself far from being a systematic thinker. He once described his work as a Swiss cheese: readers found themselves in the holes and it was up to them to find their way out, choosing their own direction. Here we come up against the unfinished character of his work. Indeed, Foucault quite deliberately described his practices as 'analytical work' rather than theory, and his analysis of power relations as 'not a theory, but rather a way of theorizing practice' (Kritzman, 1988). Part of this was his own sense of the provisional, socially constructed nature of knowledge. One can also feel Nietzsche's affinity, but also influence. As just one example, Nietzsche's dictum 'What is the history of truth but that of our irrefutable errors?' sits easily in the heart of much of Foucault's work. Then again, Foucault's thought was less continuous development and more a move from one crisis to another. While he often reinterpreted his own positions to create seeming consistency, as we shall see it is also possible to view his work as responding to at least three major intellectual crises, each pushing him in significant new directions.

Foucault's impulse is also to think 'from the outside' (Foucault, 1998), constantly to question accepted interpretation and method, in fact at times to provide the opposite interpretation, surface subjugated knowledges, construct counter-memory, offer a new, provisional method, to see what can be learned from this. In this, at his best, he constantly fights against the self-images of the age. At his not so best, he provides an intellectual gymnasium with endless sets of formidable exercises whose intents are not clear, sometimes because they reflect Foucault's own, often painful debates with himself.

One also needs to understand his later view of history revealed, Nietzschean quote and all, in a 1971 essay:

> the world of effective history knows only one kingdom, without providence or cause, where there is only 'the iron hand of necessity shaking the dice-box of chance'. Chance is not simply the drawing of lots, but raising the stakes in every attempt to master chance through the will to power, and giving rise to the risk of an even greater chance. (Foucault, 1984)

Foucault also harboured a deep-seated drive to transgress, both intellectually and politically. Intellectually he was influenced by, but wanted to depart from, the dominant traditions of thought of his time. In their excellent book, Dreyfus and Rabinow (1983) catch some of this in their subtitle: 'Beyond Structuralism and Hermeneutics'. But it is also Marxism, phenomenology, pyschoanalysis, humanism, postmodernism among many others that Foucault questions, and moves on from. Frequently, and confusingly, the critique is merely implicit, simply through the different direction in which he chooses to take his work.

Part of this transgression is his personal resistance against all forms of labelling. Part of it is, as Gilles Deleuze (1995)—who knew him well—points out, that Foucault 'always evokes the dust or murmur of battle, and he saw thought itself as a sort of war machine'. Moreover, Foucault's suspicion of all systems of thought requires him, like Nietzsche, not to become an -ism himself. In the retreat from Grand Theory, Foucault chooses to avoid universal claims and tries to demonstrate the usefulness of empirical research in limited, neglected, often novel fields. Transgressing again, and by trade a philosopher, Foucault found his way into, for example, writing history, social studies, cultural interpretation, studying medicine, madness, prisons and sexuality, influencing many fields; but as we shall see, as the wages of transgression, also receiving plenty of criticism therefrom.

Politically Foucault, like the postmodernists he did not want to be identified with, has been criticized for offering intellectually little that is constructive, apart from, in his case, the possibility of resistance. In practice, his massive cross-disciplinary influence in revitalizing the sorts of questions asked and methods adopted in, for example, urban planning, criminology, education, mental health, management studies, architecture, social work and public policy belies this interpretation. At the same time, he constantly stressed that power relations were not merely negative but productive as well. However, though in sympathy with those at the margins of normalized society—as illustrated by his political and gay activism—Foucault's own intellectual edifices of disciplinary society, bio-power and governmentality did in fact create a Weberian 'iron cage' effect, in which the human subject seemed surprisingly passive, given the sort of independent, transgressive thinker that Foucault himself was. As we shall see, following a crisis, this led to Foucault's final focus on an ethic for and care of the self.

One must also take Foucault's own, late assessment into account: that the direction his work took was always towards where the present danger lies to individual and society. In this sense his major works were attempts to understand 'the history of the present' (Foucault, 1984), to point out that what is accepted as normal, natural and true in fact arises from historical contingency, from power relations, from constructed social and intellectual regimes, historical narratives and political ideologies that determine what knowledges, truths and actions are possible. In one of his late essays, with a reinforced focus on what it is to be a subject, Foucault (1983a) put it like this:

> Maybe the target nowadays is not to discover what we are, but to refuse what we are... we have to promote new forms of subjectivity through the refusal of this kind of individuality which has been imposed on us for several centuries.

This is the sort of individuality, Foucault argues, that, as subjectification, sees us policing ourselves.

With this picture of Foucault in mind, the chapter proceeds by first describing the development of Foucault's work, then examines in detail its fundamental concepts and contributions. We then review critiques of Foucault's work, before focusing on its use and usefulness in the information systems field. On the latter point, Foucault himself wrote little directly about information and communications technologies (ICT), and indeed little about technological artifacts and tools, though he recognized that the technologies in which he was interested were physical in part, for example in the architecture of prisons, schools or clinics. However, he did write much about procedures, techniques, processes and behavioural/disciplinary technologies, for example the confession, the examination, prison rehabilitation regimes and 'technologies of the self'. This may well have led to his relative neglect among information systems researchers, though a similar omission does not seem to have done any harm to the reception of the work of Giddens (Chapter 8) and Habermas (Chapter 6), also in this book. Part of this may well be that Foucault comes less packaged, with fewer schemas that are easy to adopt. That said, some of his work, especially the image of the Panopticon, has been translated directly into, for example, studies of surveillance technologies (Lyon, 1994, 2003), the use of information and databases (Poster, 1990) and discipline, information use and technologies at work (Webster, 1995; Zuboff, 1988).

However, the chapter will argue that Foucault's contribution can be much richer than this. For example, Foucault was well aware, not least from his reading of Heidegger, of the long-term 'greatest danger' (Heidegger's phrase) from technology, as well as from Weberian rationalization (though Foucault, 1983a, prefers to investigate 'specific rationalities') and the disciplining and normalization inherent in bio-power. Had he lived into the so-called Information Age, he might well have made the connections between these and the key roles of media-, military- and work-based information and communication technologies forming this present danger, arising, in Heidegger's 'essence of technology' (1977) and in Virilio's (2002) view, as technocratic thinking and imagination become social imagination itself. A Foucauldian perspective leads to a key question here: how indeed can the growth of technological capabilities be disconnected from the intensification of power relations? Therefore a major part of the chapter will assess the contribution that Foucault's social theory and philosophy has made and can further provide in the study of ICT and information systems.

THE WORK: AN OVERVIEW

Michel Foucault was born in Poitiers, France in 1926. In 1948/9 he graduated in philosophy, then psychology from the Ecole Normale Supérieure, Paris, gaining further qualifications in these subjects up to 1952. From 1952–55 he taught philosophy at the university of Lille, while also working as a researcher and unofficial intern (Miller, 1993) at the Sainte-Anne Hospital in Paris, giving him clinical experience that would help him in his later books on psychology, medicine and asylums. His first book, *Mental Illness and Psychology*, appeared in 1954. While largely ignored, it also prepared some of the way for his next, more famous text. Foucault spent five years in teaching positions in Sweden, Poland and Germany, allowing him to research and write most of *Madness and Civilization: A History of Insanity in the Age of Reason*, before returning to France in 1960, presenting it successfully for his doctoral thesis in 1961 (Foucault, 1988).

Meanwhile Foucault had become professor in psychology at Clermont-Ferrand University, a post which, combined with a sabbatical at Tunis University for two years, he held until 1968 when he was appointed professor and head of department of the new university in Vincennes, Paris. This period saw the French publication of three major works, the first being *The Birth of the Clinic: An Archaeology of Medical Perception* in 1963 (Foucault, 1973). There followed *The Order of Things: An Archaeology of the Human Sciences* in 1966 (Foucault, 1970) and *The Archaeology of Knowledge* in

1969 (Foucault, 1972). He also produced a number of books and essays on art, literature and philosophy, including on Roussel, Blanchot, Magritte (Foucault, 1983b) and Bataille.

In 1970 he was elected Chair of the History of Systems of Thought at the Collège de France, the highest-ranking French academic institution, a post that he held until his death on 25th June 1984 from AIDS-related illness (see Eribon, 1991; Macey, 1993; and Miller, 1993 for detailed biographies of Foucault). His yearly courses at the Collège de France provided a wealth of fascinating detail into his intellectual concerns across the years from 1970–84, covering such themes as criminology, power/knowledge, aesthetics, governmentality, sexuality, ethics and care of the self. The highly interesting 1976 lectures were first published in French in 1997, and published in English (Foucault, 2003) as the start of a series.

Between 1969 and 1975 Foucault became more politically active with groups such as the Prison Information Group in France, and also went to Poland and Iran, the experiences finding their way into essays on repression and revolution. He gave interviews and edited texts, including the nineteenth-century memoir of a murderer, Pierre Riviere, but no major work appeared until *Discipline and Punish: The Birth of the Prison* in 1975 (Foucault, 1979). This represented a methodological turn from archaeology to Nietzschean genealogy signalled earlier by the important 1971 essay 'Nietzsche, genealogy, history' (reprinted in Rabinow, 1984). Also pursuing a genealogical history of the present, *The History of Sexuality Volume 1: An Introduction* quickly followed in 1976 (Foucault, 1978), as the first of a six-part series. However, Foucault reconsidered this project and only two later volumes appeared in 1984, after his death, as *The Use of Pleasure* and *The Care of the Self* (Foucault, 1985a, 1986). These two books include a more active individual actor, but, through a Nietzschean genealogy, the series consistently deconstructs western concepts of sex and soul, and its historical regimes of ethics, truth and identity.

If the above constitute Foucault's major works, then across his life he was also a prolific essayist and interviewee. The more important work here is represented in Foucault (1996, 1997a, 1997b, 1998, 2000) and in Bouchard (1977), Gordon (1980) and Kritzman (1988).

Development

How to make sense of this oeuvre? Foucault himself provided many commentaries. A provisional, insightful accounting of the previous

15 years and his developing interests occurred in the 1976 lectures, where he talked of:

> the essentially local character of the critique... resembling a sort of autonomous, non-centralized theoretical production... that does not need a visa from some common regime to establish its validity.

In this he sought the 'insurrection of subjugated knowledges', by which he meant, first, buried scholarly blocks of historical knowledges present but masked in the functional and systematic ensembles that claimed status as sciences, and secondly, local knowledges disqualified as non-conceptual, insufficiently elaborated, naive, hierarchically inferior or below the required level of erudition and scientificity. By 1976 the project of his 'disorderly and tattered' genealogies was to couple together scholarly erudition and local memories in order to rediscover struggles and 'the raw memory of fights' and 'make use of that knowledge in contemporary tactics' (Foucault, 2003).

On a broader, late view:

> My objective... has been to create a history of the different modes by which in our culture, human beings are made subjects. My work has dealt with three modes of objectification which transform human beings into subjects. (Foucault, 1983a)

The first are 'modes of enquiry that try to give themselves the status of sciences'. Foucault cites as examples the objectivizing of the speaking subject in philology and linguistics; of the labouring, productive subject in analyses of wealth and economics; and of the sheer fact of being alive in biology or natural history. Secondly, he has studied the objectivizing of the subject in 'dividing practices'. For Foucault, the subject is objectivized by being divided inside himself or divided from others. Examples include 'the mad and sane, the sick and healthy, the criminals and the "good boys"'. Finally, he cites himself as also studying in his current work (1983a): 'the way a human being turns him- or herself into a subject. For example, I have chosen the domain of sexuality—how men have learned to recognize themselves as subjects of "sexuality".'

Foucault's own assessment, then, is that his work is concerned with analysing classification, dividing and self-subjectification practices across three fields of subjectivity, namely the body, population and the individual (Foucault, 1983a, 1985a, 1985b; Rabinow, 1984). He was interested in highlighting and taking part in three types of struggle: against forms of domination, against forms of exploitation that separate individuals from what they produce, and—which he saw as contemporaneously increasingly more important—against forms of subjectivity that tie the individual to him- or herself, and in this way submit the individual to others (Foucault, 1983b). However, this is to smooth out the discontinuities, inconsistencies and changes of direction that are inevitable over a 30-year publication span. For purposes of exegesis, our own organization and understanding of the evolution of his work are shown in Figure 7.1.

Essentially, Foucault was concerned with truth, knowledge, power, ethics, the subject and relations between these, though his specific emphasis and focus varied at different points in his life. All these issues were present in the first major work, *Madness and Civilization*, albeit in a somewhat confused fashion, as he himself later admitted. The truth axis and scientific classification practices were studied in *The Birth of the Clinic* and *The Order of Things* in the 1960s, while truth and knowledge received attention in the later 1960s, in *The Archaeology of Knowledge*. These represented 'a historical ontology of ourselves in relation to truth through which we constitute ourselves as subjects of knowledge' (Foucault, 1983a). The power axis, power/knowledge and dividing and self-subjectification practices were the subject of *Discipline and Punish* and *The History of Sexuality Volume 1* in the mid-1970s. These represented 'a historical ontology ... in relation to a field of power through which we constitute ourselves as subjects acting on others' (Foucault, 1983a). The ethical axis, self-subjectification practices and developing an ethic and care for the self receive the greatest attention in *The History of Sexuality* taken as a whole from 1976–84. Foucault (1983a) saw this as 'a historical ontology in relation to ethics through which we

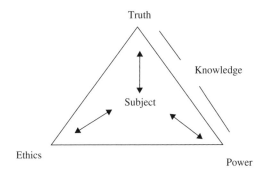

Figure 7.1 *Foucault's domains, 1954–84*

constitute ourselves as moral agents' (for a discussion of 'ontology' see Chapter 1).

This is of course too programmatic a view. In practice, Foucault's thinking evolved as a result of, and developing critiques against, many influences and through a series of changes in direction. His early intellectual milieu at the Ecole Normale saw the influences of Marxism (including Louis Althusser), Hegelian phenomenology, structural linguistics, existentialism, Freud, Merleau-Ponty and the science historian Georges Canguilhem. By the early 1950s Foucault's intellectual interests were in the history of science, philosophy and psychology (Miller, 1993). In a final interview, Foucault (1985b) also cited Heidegger as:

> for me, the essential philosopher... I began to read him in 1951 or 1952; then in 1952 or 1953... I read Nietzsche... My whole philosophical development was determined by my reading of Heidegger. But I recognize that Nietzsche prevailed over him.

In practice, Dreyfus (2003) demonstrates structural similarities in the thought of Foucault and Heidegger, but Foucault never wrote anything on Heidegger and it is difficult to identify anything like an explicit influence except in his very early work.

To a considerable degree *Madness and Civilization* represented the results of a crisis of working through all, and rejecting some of, these influences to create a distinctive, historically-based critique of western/Enlightenment reason animated by a shift from philosophies of consciousness and liberal, idealist notions of the subject. If vestiges of hermeneutics are found in that work, then this is (over?) reacted against in the work of the 1960s, with a shift towards quasi-structuralism and semiology discernible in *Birth of the Clinic, The Order of Things* and *The Archaeology of Knowledge*. Important influences on the development of his archaeological approach here were also Bachelard's and Canguilhem's theories of historical discontinuity, and critiques of presentism and progressivism in the history of science. Out of this came a whole conception of knowledge and discourse, fully developed in *The Archaeology of Knowledge*.

By 1970, Foucault was distancing himself from the label 'structuralist':

> I have been unable to get it into their tiny minds that I have used none of the methods, concepts or key terms that characterize structural analysis. (Foucault, 1970)

At the same time, when asked in a 1996 interview when he stopped believing in 'meaning', he replied that the break came when Levi-Strauss for societies, and Lacan for the unconscious, demonstrated that:

> 'meaning' was probably only a surface effect, a shimmer, a foam, and that what ran through us, underlay us, and was before us, what sustained us in time and space, was the system. (Quoted in Eribon, 1991)

Strictly speaking Foucault, though tempted by structuralism, was never a structuralist and later backs away from his strong claims in *The Archaeology* that discourse is a rule-governed, autonomous and self-referring system. His focus was to seek not a-temporal structures but 'historical conditions of possibility' (Foucault, 1973). More seriously, by 1969 he ran into an intellectual and methodological crisis. Despite his rising social and political interests (partly fuelled by the 1968 Paris uprisings), in *The Archaeology* discourse and archaeology had become separated from the influences that social institutions have. The causal power attributed to the rules governing discursive systems was unintelligible and provided no basis for a critical analysis that could bear on Foucault's social concerns. According to Deleuze (1988, 1995), the 1968 Paris events were a radicalization, stripping bare all power relations. From then Foucault moved from archaeology, discourse and knowledge through Nietzsche, towards genealogy, power relations and power/knowledge. Six years after *The Archaeology*, *Discipline and Punish* represented the decisive fruition of the working through of these concerns. Genealogical method allowed him to thematize the relationship between truth, knowledge, values and the social institutions and practices in which they emerge. Form rediscovered itself as a combination of forces. History, social institutions and practices regained their motor.

However, a still further crisis emerged. After *The History of Sexuality Volume 1* in 1976, Foucault did not publish any books for eight years. In that time he was reorienting his research around modes of subjectification. Deleuze (1995) suggests that Foucault found himself intellectually and personally in an impasse within power relations, locked in what he had discovered about power making us speak and see, and needing some opening, a way forward. This he found in his later two volumes of *The History of Sexuality* in focusing on technologies of the self, ethics and care of the self, partly influenced by the Nietzschean *Will zu Macht* in its constructive sense of 'that which uses'. Here Foucault focuses on a more active individual subjectivity, less imprisoned in and less constructed through scientific discourse and power relations, more geared to self-knowledge supporting work of self on the self, to constitute a self-stylization able to separate from subjectification practices. The goal, however, is not dissimilar from what in fact on my reading, though said in his penultimate book, it always was. It is the effort to think one's own history, to 'free thought from what it silently thinks and so enable it to think differently' (Foucault, 1986). Ironically, for a social theorist famous for his notions of disciplinary society, normalization and bio-power, liberty, resistance and selfhood remained a living pulse throughout his work.

FUNDAMENTAL CONCEPTS AND CONTRIBUTIONS

Within this overview of Foucault's work, we will now focus on fundamental concepts, with the main attention given to those offering most potential in information systems studies.

From Madness and Civilization to The Archaeology of Knowledge (1960–69)

Foucault's studies focused on one overall discourse, that of the human or social sciences, for example psychology, penology, criminology, demography, sexology, sociology and economics. His stock-in-trade was the overturning of received interpretations about established 'knowledges'. Foucault's purpose was not to determine the truth and progress of these human science disciplines, but to examine the social effects of the knowledges they produced. For him, discourses that aimed to reveal the 'truth' of madness and abnormal personality, the criminal or human sexuality both created and controlled the very objects they claimed to know.

The trajectory of this part of his contribution can be first picked up in *Madness and Civilization*, which describes how towards the end of the eighteenth century the 'insane' were singled out from other marginalized groups, for example beggars, whores, robbers and invalids, who earlier themselves had been the objects of the 'great incarceration' in workhouses, hospitals and prisons throughout Europe. In institutionalized asylums insanity could be studied systematically, in practice through observation and classification, rather than through dialogue with the insane. For

Foucault, this departure was hardly the victory it was often presented as for humanism and enlightenment. The lunatic swopped physical chains in hospitals for normative judgements, examination, labelling and the need for self-confession that affirmed the analysis. Foucault's 'central intuition' is that madness is an invention of psychiatric reforms that offered an 'insidious new form of social control'. Psychiatric knowledge is coordinated with power, whose purpose is to correct and normalize under the guidance of rational reason, whose boundaries were defined by its polar opposite, insanity.

In this we can already see the Foucauldian critique against liberal and Enlightenment (and also Marxist) beliefs in social progress, driven by the advance of human reason in scientific disciplines. There are also the contours of a disciplinary-based modern society that his subsequent studies on medicine, prisons and sexuality elaborate. Thus his 1963 book, *The Birth of the Clinic*, deals with the development of (French) medical practice from 1760–1810. In its Preface, Foucault (1973) declares: 'this book is about space, about language, and about death; it is about the act of seeing, the gaze'. In a very short period of time, the body and life (through examination) and death (through autopsy) became the objects of a new, explanatory clinical gaze. A new scientific discourse was established backed by a medical profession, physicians selected on competence criteria and able to make decisions, new relationships between patient and doctor based on questioning, observation and a clinical gaze that evaluates and calculates in its constant search for the pathological. For Foucault (1973), the emerging structure of the anatomo-clinical method, in which space, language and death are articulated, 'constitutes the historical condition of a medicine that is given and accepted as positive'. This is important, because Foucault places medical science as the formative discipline in providing an exemplary, fundamental and general view for all subsequent human sciences of how human existence can be the object of organized, positive knowledge.

The development of classification practices highlighted in these two books receives central, if different, attention in Foucault's 1966 book *The Order of Things*. Here, Foucault focused on the analysis of discourse moved as far as possible from its social setting, to discover the rules of its self-regulation. At the same time, after bigger game, he expanded his domain of investigation to cover the central sciences of humanity—in Foucault's classification those disciplines formed in the nineteenth century dealing with labour (economics), life (biology) and language (linguistics). The book is ambitiously subtitled 'An Archaeology of the Human Sciences'. It arose, according to its Preface, out of a passage from a fictional story by Borges of a Chinese encyclopaedia whose bizarre classification of animals 'shattered... all the familiar landmarks of my thought—our thought... breaking up all the ordered surfaces and all the planes with which we are accustomed to tame the wild profusion of existing things'. The taxonomy demonstrated not just the exotic charm of another system of thought, but 'the limitation of our own, the stark impossibility of thinking *that*'.

The book conducts an *archaeology*, by which Foucault meant a method of historical inquiry examining the statements of (primarily human science) discourses and statement processes, in order to uncover the discursive practices that constitute fields of knowledge. Archaeology is the mapping of the enabling conditions for the production of truth and knowledge, a 'reordering of events... not perceived before' in order to lay bare 'the empirical conditions under which (expert) statements come to be counted as true' (Hacking, 1986). Along with the later *The Archaeology of Knowledge*, the book applies archaeology to research *discourse*, whose meaning Foucault expands from 'a regulated order of talk' to cover also chains of statements, institutionalized statement processes and the historically and culturally determined rules that regulate the form and content of the order of talk.

A still grander concept is that of the *episteme*: a structured field of knowledge, conditions and historical and cultural patterns that determine what counts as knowledge, truth and reality, and what is conceivable during a specific period. Foucault posits how knowledge in the areas of nature, economics and language was differently shaped during the Renaissance, the 'classical' period from the mid-seventeenth century to the French Revolution, and through the modern episteme from the nineteenth century to the present. He finds coherence in systems of knowledge within an episteme, but discontinuities across epistemes, even in seemingly similar knowledge areas. Knowledge is contextually bound in history and culture; the movement of history is discontinuous, not cumulative. It is marked by periods of stabilized knowledges then changes in direction (a parallel is sometimes drawn here between Foucault's episteme and Kuhn's presentation of stabilized paradigms in the natural sciences broken by occasional major shifts in directions). The Enlightenment ideal of progressive knowledge is questioned and found wanting.

In particular, Foucault stresses, from the 1800s the configuration changes entirely. As the modern episteme forms:

> a profound historicity penetrates into the heart of things, isolates and defines them in their own coherence, imposes upon them the forms of order implied by the continuity of time.

The 'imposition of order' hints at the irony of the book's title. In fact for Foucault, so far as there is a truth it is in the disorder of things. Furthermore, in the modern episteme knowledge of life, language and work gains an anthropological foundation as 'man' becomes the centre of the fields of knowledge. In this interpretation, if it is from 'man' that the order of things now emanate, then he is 'probably no more than a rift in the order of things'. Controversially, and against liberal and Enlightenment ideals:

> man is only a recent invention, a figure not yet two centuries old, a new wrinkle in our knowledge, and... he will disappear again as soon as that knowledge has discovered a new form. (Foucault, 1970)

Foucault's next book, *The Archaeology of Knowledge*, is his only attempt at systematic theoretical analysis, in this case developed from the historical dissections represented in his earlier works. According to Foucault (1972), he was engaged in an approach and method 'by which one throws off the last anthropological constraints; an enterprise that wishes, in return, to reveal how these constraints could come about'. *The Archaeology* presents this archaeological method in detail and the theory of discourse on which it is based. However, the analytic approach proceeds to accord discursive formations considerable autonomy in order to concentrate on the rules, laws and systems through which they achieve internal self-regulation. Here he also oversteps his own intentions of 'modest empiricism' to give a quasi-structuralist causal role to the observed formal regularities of discursive formations, making them conditions and rules of these formations' existence. As Dreyfus and Rabinow (1983) note, the result is the strange notion of regularities that regulate themselves. They argue, convincingly, that archaeology is ultimately a methodological failure, awaiting a reattachment to social practices and concerns.

The Shift to Genealogy

Two important bridging essays followed in 1971. The first, 'The Discourse on Language', was an inaugural lecture summarizing the archaeological project and introducing genealogy as a complementary approach. The lecture is useful for delineating the rules of exclusion through which the production of discourse is 'controlled, selected, organized and redistributed' (Foucault, 1972). These rules take the form of prohibition, division, rejection and the opposition between 'true' and 'false'. Increasingly he sees the latter assimilating the others, and views the delineation of 'true' discourse from 'false' as manifesting a 'will to knowledge... reliant upon institutional support and distribution [which] tends to exercise a sort of pressure, a power of constraint upon other forms of discourse'. If truth, knowledge and the subject were the major concerns so far, from now on power relations and their significance would take an increasingly prominent position.

The shift of focus to the complex articulations between truth, forms of knowledge and power relations, together with the development of the genealogical method of analysis, is registered almost as a manifesto in the beautifully written 1971 essay 'Nietzsche, genealogy, history'. Influenced by Nietzsche's writings, not least *On the Genealogy of Morals* (1887), Foucault (1984) maps how genealogy, against more traditional histories, is applied to investigate 'the history of an error we call truth':

> To follow the complex course of descent is to maintain passing events in their proper dispersion, it is to identify the accidents, the minute deviations—or conversely, the complete reversals—the errors, the false appraisals, and the faulty calculations that gave birth to those things that continue to exist and have value for us; it is to discover that truth or being does not lie at the root of what we know and what we are, but the exteriority of accidents.

Foucault also emphasizes the need to study the body. The task of genealogy, as an analysis of descent, is 'to expose a body totally imprinted by history and the process of history's destruction of the body'. Therefore 'effective history' shortens its vision to those things nearest it: the body, nervous system, nutrition, digestion and energies. Moreover, as 'an effective history', genealogy 'seeks to re-establish the various systems of subjection... [and] the hazardous play of dominations'. Moreover, 'genealogy has to fight the power-effects characteristic of any discourse that is regarded as scientific' (Foucault, 2003). In all this we can see Foucault's later focus on the microphysics of power. However, according to Foucault (2003), archaeology is retained as 'the method specific to the analysis of local discursivities' (i.e. producing knowledge of discursive formations), while genealogy 'is the tactic which, once it [archaeology] has described these local discursivities, brings into play the desubjugated knowledges that have been released from them'. In practice, given Foucault's later interests, genealogy holds the key, not least to his subsequent interpretive analytics (Dreyfus and Rabinow, 1983) of power relations, knowledge, bio-power, disciplining, subjectivity and governmentality.

Disciplinary Society

Foucault's most accessible and influential book is probably *Discipline and Punish: The Birth of the Prison*. It charts how from the late eighteenth century and reaching its apogee in the twentieth century, the primary objects for punishment, but also, from then on, rehabilitation, increasingly became the soul, conscience and thought, rather than the body of the criminal. The character of the shift is indicated by some of the book's section headings: 'the gentle way in punishment'; 'docile bodies'; 'the means of correct training'; 'hierarchical observation'; 'normalizing judgement'; 'the examination'; and 'panopticism'. These constitute discipline, the key concept here, and a generalizable technique, a 'physics' or an 'anatomy' of power, a technology, not an institution. The emphasis is on disciplining and correcting abnormal behaviours, bodies and minds, rendering them obedient, docile, trained and useful. The construction of a 'micropower', starting from the body as an object to be divided into units and then trained, is the key to disciplinary power. Disciplining through the control and organization of space and time was also an essential constituent of this technology.

As an icon of these developments, Jeremy Bentham's 1791 prison design of the *panopticon* (inspection house) particularly caught Foucault's imagination and has been highly influential in subsequent organization, technology and work studies. The prison consists of a central tower and a courtyard surrounded by an outer ring of cells. The few in the tower could watch the many in the cells, while the observed could not communicate with each other, nor see the observers, but lived knowing they could always be observed by their guards. As the final step in architectural and technological perfection, the panopticon includes a system for observing and controlling the controllers. However, Foucault (1979) points out that for him, it is a generalizable model, a way of defining power relations in terms of the everyday life of people, a mechanism of power reduced to its ideal form: 'a figure of political technology that may and must be detached from any specific use'. Bentham offered this model of efficient surveillance for all buildings where activities needed supervision. This attracted Foucault, because his argument was that the new prison regimes emerged so quickly as an inseparable part of wider developments in the emergent capitalist society. According to Foucault, disciplinary power was increasingly adopted, for example, in schools, factories, hospitals, asylums and military barracks and came to permeate the social body. If not the cause of capitalism's emergence, the rise of disciplinary power and technologies formed preconditions for the directions that capitalist societies took.

Power/Knowledge

If the rise of disciplinary society was one big idea, another of Foucault's was recasting the concept of power and linking power inextricably with knowledge. In fact, as Foucault (1983a) himself points out, he rarely used the word power by itself. Most often he employs power to refer to power relations or power/knowledge. For Foucault, the shift is partly due to historical changes in power, but also due to inadequacies in, for example, modern humanistic and Marxist accounts. The juridico-discursive model that Foucault (1983a, 2003) dismisses sees power as possessed, flowing from a centralized source from top to bottom and primarily repressive in its exercise. Against this, and against Marxist and many other conceptualizations, Foucault presents power as exercised rather than possessed, needing to be analysed as moving from the bottom up, as not primarily repressive or coercive but productive, in that 'it produces reality, it produces domains of objects, and rituals of truth' (Foucault, 1979). Furthermore:

> Power is the implementation and deployment of a relationship of force... the continuation of war by other means. (Foucault, 2003)
>   Power must be analyzed as something that circulates... that functions only when it is part of a chain. It is never localized here or there, it is never in the hands of the some, and it is never appropriated in the way that wealth or a commodity can be appropriated... Power is exercised through networks, and individuals do not simply circulate in those networks: they are in a position to both submit to and exercise this power. They are never the inert or consenting targets of power, they are always its relays. In other words, power passes through individuals. (Foucault, 2003)

In this conceptualization, power relations permeate and constitute the social body. With power relations rooted in the system of social networks, there is little room for the assumption of authentic human interests or a self outside power relationships. Human beings are essentially social and cultural products. Though 'there are no relations of power without resistances'—the obstacles and impediments that power or force meets in its motion—nevertheless the individual is one of power's first effects (Foucault, in Gordon, 1980). Moreover, institutions like the state, family, sciences and prisons represent power in particular concentrations. They do not produce but instead relay—that is, receive, coordinate and disperse—power.

A further distinctive development is Foucault's compacting of power relations and knowledge so that they are inextricably linked (but not equatable). Given the trajectory of his work, it is an elegant, timely and remarkably effective conceptualization. The mistake made by some here, as Foucault later recognized, was to assume that Foucauldian knowledge was a mask for power, a 'thin mask thrown over structures of domination' (Kritzman, 1988). This is definitely *not* Foucault's position. Power produces knowledge and discourse, and discourse and knowledge have power and truth effects:

> Power and knowledge directly imply one another... there is no power relation without the correlative constitution of a field of knowledge, nor any knowledge that does not presuppose, and constitute power relations. (Foucault, 1979)

Genealogy studies how power/knowledge is exercised, how strategies and tactics of power/knowledge are conducted and with what outcomes. Applied to the development of modern society, it uncovers how a specific, historically contingent relationship among truth, ethics, power and knowledge formed in individuals, groups, systems and institutions to produce disciplinary society.

An allied concept, also studied genealogically, is that of *bio-power*, seen as a particular kind of power that has developed since the seventeenth century, which operates by disciplining individuals and regulating populations in ways never before experienced. Somewhat rhetorically, Foucault states that for millennia man remained what he was for Aristotle: a living animal with the additional capacity for a political existence. But 'modern man is an animal whose politics places his existence as a living being in question' (Foucault, 1978).

The concept figures prominently in the first volume of *The History of Sexuality*. Bio-power developed in two forms. The first, an anatomo-politics of the body, was centred on the body as a machine, its disciplining, optimization of its capabilities and its integration into systems of efficient and economic controls. The second, a bio-politics of the population, focused on the species body; that is, the body imbued with the mechanics of life and serving as the basis for propagation, mortality, level of health and life expectancy. Their supervision was effected through the development of very diverse institutions and a series of interventions and regulatory controls:

> The old power of death that symbolized sovereign power was now carefully supplanted by the administration of bodies and the calculated management of life. (Foucault, 1978)

Moreover, a '*normalizing* society is the historical outcome of a technology of power centred on life' (Foucault, 1978). Among all the techniques, practices, knowledges and discourses discussed by Foucault, normalization is at their core and is seen by him as unique to the modern era, and dangerous, taking the form of 'a strategy without a strategist'.

For Foucault, these several developments are important for understanding how the discourse of sexuality proceeded across the last two centuries. Moreover, sexuality is a key area for study because, at the juncture of the 'body' and the 'population', sex became a crucial target of power organized around the management of life rather than the menace of death.

By the late eighteenth century, a new discourse and technology of sexuality had emerged and sex became a state concern, requiring the social body and individuals to put themselves under surveillance. Foucault points to four power/knowledge strategies providing the means for disciplinary control over sexual desire and practice. These were, in his words, the 'hysterization of women's bodies', 'the pedagogization of children's sex', 'the socialization of procreative behaviour' and the 'psychiatrization of perverse plea-sure'. In simpler terms, 'the hysterical woman, the masturbating child, the Malthusian couple and the perverse adult' became objects of knowledge and targets for social control.

Disciplinary technologies, normalizing society, bio-politics and developments in the human sciences are linked inextricably with— indeed foundations of—*governmentality*. For Foucault (1983a), to govern is 'to structure the possible field of action of others'. From the seventeenth century he sees western European countries rational-izing their management of social problems with new government techniques such as surveys, health regulations, centralized welfare and 'statistics' (the science of the state). In the face of big demographic and economic changes, the welfare and security of the population, not the act of government itself, became the new object for government. Modern governmentality became based on new knowledges and techniques of normalization, regulation and control of bodies. It moved from an earlier art of government to a new political science and techniques of government, turning on the themes of population and political economy (Foucault, 1991). In this expanded concept of governmentality, Foucault rejects a unified view of the state for one of a network of institutions, practices, procedures and techniques in which power as strategic relations circulates. Once again, his concern is with how power/knowledge produces subjects and specific forms of subjectivity, in this case with practices of government and practices of self woven together.

Technology

From the early 1970s the word *technology* is increasingly to be found in Foucault's writings. It is normally used in phrases such as 'technologies of power', 'political technology of the body', 'disciplinary technologies' and 'technologies of the self'. Foucault often elides the word technology with those of *techne* and also technique, but power always resides in his concept of technology whether referring to behavioural technologies or to technology as architectures, buildings, physical artifacts and how space is defined and used. Foucault rarely seeks to define his use of the word technology. In an interview called 'Space, knowledge, and power' (Rabinow, 1984), while discussing the study of architecture, Foucault offers, somewhat elliptically, the following:

> What interests me more is to focus on what the Greeks called *techne*, that is to say, a practical rationality governed by a conscious goal... if architecture, like the practice of government and the practice of other forms of social organization, is considered as a *techne*, possibly using elements of sciences like physics... statistics, that is what is interesting... The disadvantage of this word *techne*, I realize is its relation to the word 'technology' which has a very specific meaning... one thinks of hard technology, the technology of wood, of fire, of electricity. Whereas government is also a function of technology: the government of individuals, the government of souls, the government of the self by the self, the government of families, the government of children and so on.

An interesting comparison can be made with Heidegger, who was interested in the products and tools of the *natural sciences* and focused on 'the essence of technology', or what Dreyfus (2003) calls technicity; that is, the new technocratic thinking and style of practices that have emerged, distinguished from the techno-logical devices that these practices produce and sustain (see also Chapter 3). For Heidegger, it is the essence of technology (the technological understanding of being)—that is, the domination of nature by the natural sciences, not technology—that causes our distress. For Foucault, too, to judge technology by its tools and its production is to miss the point. In his later work, however, he is looking at modern *human sciences*, the practices and power relations by which they are founded, the knowledge and behavioural tech-nologies they produce; these operate allied to structures, designed space and use of tools and artifacts. Moreover, the operation of these new methods (technologies?) of power 'is not ensured by right but by technique, not by law but by normalization, not by punishment but by control' (Foucault, 1978).

Furthermore, these technologies of power function anonymously—they are implemented by everyone and no one—and autonomously—for, as Foucault once commented in an interview, 'while people know what they do, and may know why they do what they do, they do not know what what they do does'. Given this distinctive, historically recent blending of knowledges, disciplinary technologies and bio-power, power/knowledge emerges as the key concept in Foucault's philosophy of modern technology. However, this philosophy of technology is particularistic. Unlike Heidegger, he does not attempt a general account of the 'essence' of modern technology, but rather reveals specific histories of technological practices overlooked in other accounts of modern forms of power.

Several points occur here. First, it is important to stress that Foucault does not deny that technologies of power/knowledge can have beneficial features: 'my point is not that everything is bad, but everything is dangerous... if everything is dangerous, then we always have something to do' (Foucault, 1983a). Secondly, especially in his later work, Foucault indicates that modern subjects can and do subvert the conditions of their own subjectivity. In the later volumes of *The History of Sexuality*, for example, the individual is increasingly positioned as the personal space where both active and passive and regulated and resistant possibilities for human agency surface in the context of material practices (Katz, 2001). The self-subjectivation practices, or 'technologies of the self' as Foucault calls them, take on a more active, used dimension, less geared to relations of power and discourse, more geared to bending force back on itself, and so to self's work on the self. One can begin to read Haraway's (1991) cyborg manifesto, 'I would rather be a cyborg than a goddess', into the direction that Foucault's work was taking.

Thirdly, Best and Kellner (2001) point out that while Foucault (1970) heralds the 'death of man' and the coming of posthumanism, he sees this as a merely conceptual transformation from one episteme to another, whereas the shift to posthumanism is also a *material* matter of new technologies erasing the boundaries between biology and technology. They correctly point out that, more generally, Foucault provides no analysis of information and communications technologies, and little consideration of the hybrid landscape of techno-bodies. This is not that surprising given the periods he studied, when he was writing and the social theory and philosophy of technology founded on power/knowledge and technique that he formulated. More importantly, Best and Kellner have to concede that Foucault considers both the enmeshment of the body in systems of discipline and surveillance and ethical technologies of the self that cultivate 'new passions and new pleasures'. While the genealogy of information and communications technologies has yet to be written, Foucault, as Poster (1990) recognized, provides a considerable amount of the necessary groundwork.

Fourthly, Deleuze (1995) stresses that Foucault was one of the first to say that we have been shifting from disciplinary societies to what Deleuze calls *control societies*. These no longer operate by, for example, physically confining people but through continuous control and instant communication enabled by developments in material technology. In this rendering, what has been called 'information society' can also be read as control society. If this is correct, then Foucault's power/knowledge, discourse, bio-power and governmentality remain as thoroughly applicable concepts, as Foucault intended them to be.

Moreover, Deleuze points out that if each kind of society corresponds to a particular machine—for example simple mechanical for sovereign societies, thermo-dynamic machines for disciplinary societies and cybernetic machines and computers for control societies—then 'the machines don't explain anything, you have to analyze the collective arrangements of which the machines are just one component'. In other words, the machines do not determine different kinds of society, but do express the social forms capable of producing them and making use of them. And of course, the shift to new forms of society can be exaggerated, as we have seen in the rhetorics of postmodernism and in the Internet, digital and knowledge economies. A stronger possibility is of hybrids of continuity and change occurring, with new ICTs being put to multiple uses, not least having widespread reinforcement and amplifying effects wherever disciplinary practices inhabit the social and individual body.

CRITICAL ASSESSMENTS OF FOUCAULT

So far we have given a largely sympathetic account of Foucault's work, to provide an understanding of its content and his intentions. Not surprisingly, it has generated a great deal of criticism, only the main points of which can be noted. Here, his 1945 school report, quoted in Eribon (1991), might usefully be borne in mind: 'is better than his grades—will have to free himself of a tendency to be obscure'. Responding to many criticisms through his interviews, articles and book prefaces over the years, Foucault argues that his intentions and the nature of his projects have been regularly misunderstood or misrepresented.

Foucault (1991) also suggests that he provokes a wide, diverse group of people because he does not have a unitary position. He also crosses disciplinary boundaries, self-accuses his style of 'not being naturally clear' and assumes of the reader an often undue familiarity with a wide range of philosophical debates, ideas, theorists and contemporary issues. As catch-all rebuffs to accusations of lack of rigour, consistency and accuracy, he frequently suggests that he is well aware that all he ever created were fictions, though not without truth-effects: 'those who say that for me the truth does not exist are simple-minded' (Foucault, 1996). Moreover, in *The Archaeology of Knowledge* he writes: 'Do not ask who I am, and do not ask me to remain the same: leave it to our bureaucrats and our police to see that our papers are in order.'

In all this Gutting (1994) is useful in pointing out that too many interpretations deny Foucault's specificity—each work is specific to itself—and his marginality—he works at the limits of thought, trying to rethink the limits of reason. Gutting suggests that it is more profitable to regard Foucault as an intellectual artisan who was particularly adept at crafting three sorts of intellectual artifacts: histories (e.g. madness, prison, sexuality), theories (e.g. language, power relations) and myths (these take different forms from book to book but, for Gutting, are invariably about societal monsters versus transgressing heroes). Burrell (1998) and Prado (2000) also usefully point out that as a product of a long European philosophical tradition, Foucault's writings are not fully coherent to the Anglo-American eye. (Actually, this downplays the considerable criticism from French/continental sources, from Sartre, Habermas through to Baudrillard, that the provisional nature of his work, internal contradictions and Foucault's position taking have always attracted.) Moreover, he does not develop theoretical propositions in the conventional sense and his iconoclasm takes him into positions that are not readily defensible.

These latter limitations are readily seized on by critics such as Merquior (1985), Herman (1997) and Tallis (1997), who react against Foucault's seeming dismissal of rationality and the Enlightenment inheritance, and also against his inherent pessimism. Herman points out that every instance of western man's search for knowledge 'turns out to be simply a construction of discourses of power, or "practices" of discipline and domination over unperceived victims'. As we have seen, it is of course an 'iron cage' pessimism that Foucault recognized and attempted to redress in his later work.

If one wishes to use Foucault, there are problems inherent in the fact that he did not develop a fully worked-out methodology. Why prefer its results to any other interpretation? This is a point that Kendall and Wickham (1999) have tried to address in their book on using Foucault's methods (see also Gaventa and Cornwall, 2001). Standard and revisionist historians have been split over problems with Foucault's sometimes unscholarly use of historical materials and evidence and questionable argumentation, conclusions and interpretations (Gutting, 1994; Jones and Porter, 1994). As two examples, on several accounts the importance Foucault gives to the 'ship of fools' in *Madness and Civilization* and the panopticon in *Discipline and Punish* is belied by their historical unimportance as actual events. Thus Hamilton (1996) points out that even according to Bentham's *Works*, the original design was never built and only six panopticon-style prisons can be traced subsequently, in the USA and the Netherlands. He concludes that 'an entire school of social history has been based on a patent nonfact'.

In general, such strictures on Foucault's use of archival evidence and rather free use of examples as rhetorical devices are sometimes accurate. Moreover, as Roy Porter has pointed out on 'the great confinement' and the institutionalization of madness, Foucault's generalizations from specific French experiences do not always carry well into other countries (Gutting, 1994). But on the panopticon, as we have seen, Foucault used it as a generalizable model reduced to an ideal form. On the ship of fools, Gutting (1994) points out that Foucault's use of the ship is almost entirely concerned with its mediaeval literary and artistic significance, and it is central to his argument only as a striking symbol of what he thinks was the status of mediaeval madness.

Many of Foucault's procedures create problems that someone using his thought must address. Smart (2002) wonders how ultimately the Foucauldian researcher can avoid questions of truth and meaning and the need to differentiate between accurate (i.e 'true') and distorted descriptions and interpretations. Furthermore, Mills (2003) points out that Foucault's disinterested stance belies the fact that, while he argues against relying on cause and effect to describe events, he smuggles these notions into his argument implicitly. Foucault places great emphasis on researching practices empirically and describing the results, but the way he assembles elements from the past into a narrative creates some form of explanation, however provisional. Donnelly, in Gane (1986), sees Foucault as coming perilously close to arguing from origins and using notions of causality, ironically 'precisely the fallacy genealogy is contrived to correct'.

Foucault's conception of power poses difficulties for many commentators and has provoked a very large literature indeed. If power is capillary, ever-present and everywhere, then all social and cultural phenomena become reducible to power relations. As for Nietzsche's will to power, important as the conceptualization is, power relations become an all-too-encompassing, somewhat blunt, repetitive instrument for explaining social phenomena. Power becomes all too like the night in which all cows are black. One notion that suffers as a result is that of agency. While Foucault does focus on the possibility of resistance, he locates resistance within power itself and severely restricts agency. In fact, Foucault is hard put to identify just what it is that resists. As we have seen, by the mid-1970s he himself comes up against the question of whether there is anything beyond or outside power. In his later work, as social theorists who use him have to do, he struggles to escape the impasse that he has created for himself within power relations.

McCarthy (1991) and Honneth (1993), looking to advance critical social theory, are particularly acute on these and other deficiencies in Foucault's conception of power. McCarthy attacks Foucault's one-dimensional ontology: truth and subjectivity were reduced in the end to effects of power. This can give valuable, otherwise neglected insights into the politicization of truth and subjectification. But, for both McCarthy and Honneth, the costs for social theory of such de-differentiation are considerable. Distinctions at the heart of critical social analysis—between just and unjust social arrangements, legitimate and illegitimate uses of political power, strategic and cooperative interpersonal relations, coercive and consensual measures—all become marginal. Fraser (1989) also argues that Foucault calls too many different sorts of things power and leaves it at that, seemingly oblivious to a whole body of Weberian social theory and its careful delineations of authority, force, violence, domination and legitimation. As a consequence, the potential for a broad range of normative nuances is surrendered and 'the result is a certain normative one-dimensionality'. One can add that one ironic consequence is that Foucault's own analyses are frequently as totalizing and homogenizing as any modern theory he attacked.

For Best (1994), one problem with Foucault's work is that, unlike Habermas (see Chapter 6), he never developed the means to distinguish among different forms of knowledge and power. His failure to distinguish between (in Habermas's terms) instrumental and emancipatory interests is in fact a methodological axiom, not an oversight. Foucault refused to develop the normative framework necessary to make such distinctions and to uphold positive values (Habermas, 1987). While he clearly opposed the present form of society and wanted to achieve political impact, he simultaneously sought a methodological detachment from normative commitments and questions of validity of his analyses (Bernstein, 1991). A result is that Foucault could not state, for example, why his ideas would not replicate domination in another form, why they could be considered true, how acceptable and unacceptable forms of power can be distinguished, why we should change constraints or from what standpoint we can make a whole string of judgements. As Best (1994) points out, the unavoidable result of this atheoretical pragmatism is the contradiction of having strong normative commitments while denying that they exist. Both Bernstein (1991) and Taylor (in Couzens Hoy, 1986) see Foucault's unstable position on the ethico-political perspective informing his critique as ultimately incoherent, with hard issues left unresolved.

A comparison can be made with Habermas, a critical theorist pursuing 'the unfinished project of modernity'. In fact the

Foucault–Habermas debates are enlightening on both thinkers (see Ashenden and Owen, 1999; Kelly, 1994; also Chapter 6, this volume). Foucault himself revealed that if he had been more familiar in the 1950s and 1960s with the current of thought running from Max Weber to Habermas: 'I would not have said a number of stupid things I did say and I would have avoided many of the detours... when, meanwhile, avenues had been opened up by the Frankfurt School.' What Foucault and Habermas differ about, but also share part of, is the Enlightenment inheritance:

> The thread that may connect us to the Enlightenment is not faithfulness to its doctrinal elements, but rather the permanent reactivation of an attitude—that is of a philosophical ethos that could be described as a permanent critique of our historical era. (Foucault, in Rabinow, 1984)

But if they all share the value placed on critique, what Foucault sees and values in the Frankfurt School (see also Chapter 5) contrasts markedly with what Habermas sees there. For Foucault the school avoids the 'blackmail' of the Enlightenment's conception of reason; that is, one should be for reason or else be irrational. But against Habermas, Foucault does not think that one must construct a theory of what rationality really is in order to undertake an analysis of seeming rationality that is shown by critical investigation to be veiling deep irrationality. For him, human beings develop forms of rationality in specific historical conditions. Thus Foucault is interested in the historicity of reason, while Habermas is interested in the theory of reason (Hoy and McCarthy, 1994).

Habermas (1987) and other critics raise four objections to Foucault's work up to 1977. Foucault studies underlying practices rather than what agents say and do, and thereby generates a kind of presentism; his approach is unreasonable because it violates universal validity claims; it is context bound rather than context transgressing; and Foucault does not account for the normative dimension of his analysis. From 1977 to 1984 Foucault's reformulation and response were that practices are to be understood as the way agents themselves problematize the forms of knowledge, power and ethics, in accordance with which they are constituted. A genealogy is reasonable because it tests the universality of a given, specific validity claim. Genealogy transgresses rather than transcends limits in the present. And the normative dimension of his work is a novel conception of freedom within relations of power (Tully, in Ashenden and Owen, 1999).

Some critics (for example Bernstein, 1991 and Hoy and McCarthy, 1994) still have problems with this reformulated position, while Tully offers reasons for preferring Foucault's approach over that of Habermas. While we cannot pursue the debate further here, it is interesting to note that one of Foucault's pertinent objections to Habermas is the utopian nature of his theory of communicative action, positing as it does a state of communication where games of truth could circulate freely, without obstacles, without constraint and without coercive effects. For Foucault this is too big an abstraction from what is really going on in terms of power relations and the possibilities of concrete freedom within them in communicative games. Foucault conjectures that, unlike himself, what drives Habermas to build his theory on such utopian foundations is the (incorrect) assumption that power is bad in itself and one must free oneself from it.

Foucault's positions on discourse and knowledge have also produced criticisms (see also Habermas's position on discourse in Chapter 6). Of course, his own substitution of power/knowledge configurations for discourses as systems of scientific statements was itself an act of self-criticism. It marked an important shift towards incorporating non-discursive factors into the explanation of historical change. His alternative picture of discourse sees the enmeshing of power, truth and practices and the positioning of human beings in these historical configurations. He posits a relational and historical conception of discourse. But while he consistently stresses that his main objects of inquiry are discursive practices, he never really formalizes his conception of discourse satisfactorily, in a way that would allow exploration of the boundaries and interconnections between discursive and non-discursive elements (Howarth, 2000; Mills, 2003). That said, Foucault does produce dispositive analysis (Andersen, 2003). This asks the general questions: how are forms linked together as functional elements of an apparatus (discourse, self-technology, architecture, institutions). And how are discursive and technological elements generalized in a schematic that develops as a strategic logic (legal/illegal; security/insecurity; desired/undesired behaviour). The separation of apparatus and strategic logic may well be useful in analysing, for example, the new use of information technologies employing old or innovative strategic logics in particular workplaces.

However, in looking at applications of Foucauldian discourse analysis to organization studies, Reed (1998) also registers some major criticisms. He finds that Foucauldian discourse analysis is necessarily tied into a conception of power that cannot hold the explanatory load it is required to bear. There is an inadequate treatment of the agency/structure relationship. The lack of analytical differentiation between social action and structural constraint leads to a form of 'totalism' in which social actors become the products, rather than the creators, of the discursive formations in which they are trapped. Furthermore, for Reed, Foucauldian discourse analysis remains wedded to an ontology where discourse is treated as nothing more than a social construction. This means that it cannot begin to understand, let alone explain, 'how material and social constructions are constrained and facilitated by the relatively stable and intransitive properties of the very materials and agents through which they are made possible'. Reed suggests that a realist approach to discourse/organizational analysis provides the most promising way out of the explanatory cul-de-sac into which Foucauldian analysis has driven organizational studies.

Finally, Foucault has had a mixed reception among feminist theorists. Feminist critiques of Foucault tend to coalesce around his analysis being androcentric (centred on male experience alone), his rhetoric masculine and his vision pessimistic (see for example McNay, 1994; Mills, 2003; and Sawicki, 1994). For example, he proposes a martial imagery to emphasize the dynamics and non-systematicity of power and knowledge. However, feminist theorists often point out the epistemological dangers of building militarism and violence into our very tools of theoretical analysis. Foucault's rejection of modern foundationalist epistemologies and their philosophies of the subject downplays the active subject. Lacking an adequate theory of agency, he struggles with developing an adequate foundation for the politics of resistance. At the same time, and taking into account the gender-specific nature of his work, many feminist theorists have tried to modify and make Foucauldian ideas work for them, not least because they find his analysis of power relations productive. Moreover, 'he compels us to reconsider the value of the emancipatory practices handed down to us within Western capitalist patriarchal traditions' (Sawicki, 1994).

FOUCAULT IN AN 'INFORMATION AGE': APPLICATIONS AND DEVELOPMENTS

Given this massive influence and response across so many other diverse disciplines and areas of intellectual endeavour, it is surprising to find Foucauldian methods and concepts discussed so little, let alone digested and used, in the information systems field. By 'information systems' here I am referring to those academics, researchers, teachers, students and indeed practitioners who gravitate around conferences such as ICIS, ECIS, HICSS, PACIS and ACIS, tend to be members of the Association for Information Systems or related/similar bodies, write research papers and books consciously within an IS discipline and publish in a self-defined group of 'IS' journals that may be global, regional or national in stretch. However, there are also some academics who work on issues related to information and communication technology (ICT) from an adjacent or associated perspective, and sometimes consciously connect with the above, for example researchers in organization studies, sociology, cultural studies, philosophy of technology, innovation studies, strategic management and critical accounting. Foucault tends to be more influential among these latter groupings.

In this section we will consider the reasons for this relative neglect in IS; where Foucauldian perspectives, concepts and methods have been applied; with what results; and how Foucault can be made increasingly relevant to what we shall call information systems studies (IS). Foucault himself somewhere refers to Nietzsche's observation that while thinkers are always shooting arrows into the air, the key thing is for others to pick them up and shoot them in another direction. In other words, Foucault himself would expect from others a development, not mere replication, of his work.

The objective in what follows is not to give a comprehensive review of the literature but to illustrate main Foucauldian uses and themes in the IS context. In his books, Foucault was fond of dramatic illustrations of key ideas: witness the execution that starts *Discipline and Punish*, the panopticon, the ship of fools or the use of Borges and Velasquez in *The Order of Things*. Let us start, then, in a Foucauldian manner by saying that while Foucault never wrote explicitly about ICT, one book he might have written on the subject is—ironically, given the above—the most cited and celebrated in the whole of the IS field, namely Zuboff's 1988 book *In the Age of the Smart Machine*.

Foucault and the Automate/Informate Debate

The most cited aspect of Zuboff (1988) is its major premise: ICT can be designed and applied to automate or informate work. The former option builds on ICT's potential for speed and consistency, but creates deskilled blue- and white-collar jobs, minimizes job satisfaction, can displace physical labour and increases the decision making, discretion and remoteness of management. Informating, on the other hand, derives from the enormous transparency given by ICT-assisted information generated from an organization's underlying production and administrative processes.

Informating enables much greater ICT potential to be exploited and more commercial advantage to be gained. Undoubtedly changes in technology greatly increase what is possible. But, Zuboff argues, what subsequently happens depends on transformations, profound discontinuities in fact, in how knowledge, authority and technique are managed, and implies a comprehensive conscious strategy. This includes the empowerment of employees, with more knowledge and new intellective skills, enabling them to operate in decision making and with discretionary judgement—always formerly accepted as the preserve of managers. The dilemma is posed by Zuboff as a stark and ultimately political question. Will managers move from drivers of largely bodily labour to drivers of learning? Do and will managers utilize ICT to support, and even reinforce, existing political, social and organizational structures and processes, or transform these and their own positions within them in order to gain the full pay-offs from ICT investments?

Elsewhere, we have argued that there are other options that these very flexible technologies make possible and that have been pursued (Willcocks, 1989). For example, ICT have been used to both informate and increase control over lower-level labour, and over managers as well. The informating capacity can be used to facilitate a more embedded and repressive means of control in organizations (Knights and Murray, 1994; Orlikowski, 1991; Willcocks and Mason, 1987). In situations of high skills shortages, perhaps due to lack of training investment, automation may well be an economically rational short- and long-term decision. Labour control issues may not be uppermost in managerial minds when ICT are being designed and implemented. At the same time, Zuboff would seem to be correct about the potential transformative capacity of ICT in organizations, and the complex, not least political reasons why it frequently might not happen. At the date of her writing she was also probably justifiably pessimistic on her central message. One of her management interviewees' questions—whether we are all going to be working for a smart machine or have smart people around the machine—seems to be answered already by her own evidence and book title.

However, the real strengths of the book are less immediately striking than its high-profile, too simple 'automate or informate' theme. Zuboff provides a rich historical dimension, placing IT in the context of long-term developments in the nature of management and work organization. The theme of ICT as historical discontinuity may have been overdone for the 1980s (Willcocks and Mason, 1987), but even then there was plenty of evidence to suggest that ICT had yet to be applied in ways that went to the core of operations in workplaces.

Zuboff also supplies a highly useful categorization of skills and a detailed, rewarding analysis of how ICT applications can require skill and work redistribution. If skills can be divided into intellective, working-with and working-on, then the first two—involving mental work and communicating with others—have been traditionally identified with managerial activity. Working-on skills are applied in manual labour and may be knowledgeable (tacit skill) or 'indifferent' (needing little training or 'know-how'). If ICT are to 'informate' then manual is replaced by mental labour and working-with skills throughout the organization. Information becomes available to all through the screen rather than through, and being the preserve of, managers. Skill patterns become transformed. Hierarchical structures are less appropriate. Zuboff patiently documents how and why this so rarely happened in her case studies.

A further strength of the book is the detailed discussion of the political issues raised by the application of advanced ICT systems, often missing from books ostensibly about the human aspects of ICT (Willcocks and Mason, 1987). The struggle for one's interests, the fear of the new and unpredictable, the need to extend old, or develop new, forms of control are rehearsed in the cases for all categories of employee. More broadly, Zuboff provides an unusual degree of fresh insight into the processes of computerization and people's responses and experiences, to the level of physiological reactions, anxieties, touch, smell and sight.

In all this, though not heavily referenced, the influence of Foucault is quite striking. Zuboff's concept of power is not exactly that of Foucault but, for her, power is a key concept, does circulate and is intimately related to skills and types of knowledge. Like Foucault, she downplays conspiracy and instead stresses contingency and expediency in how things turn out. Her approach in taking a long-run historical perspective on the labouring body and skill in production and white-collar work, on managerial authority (called by her the 'spiritual dimension of power') and in presenting ICT as a potential discontinuity—all these echo the shape of Foucault's work in many places. In many ways Zuboff maps a long-run, complex, Foucault-like discourse on management, work, technology and struggles, into which ICT are finding their way.

Foucault is also influential in Zuboff's concentration on technique, which she calls the material dimension of power. The debt then becomes explicit in the related two chapter headings, namely 'The information panopticon' and 'Panoptic power and the social text'. Her focus on bio-power and the microphysics of power—how power produces bodies and minds—is also Foucault's in *Discipline and Punish*. Interestingly here, in her excellent research methodology, she gives a central place to phenomenology, a move that Foucault would have needed to make if he had wanted to explore bio-power further at the material level in institutional settings. The automate/informate dilemma is also one that points, Foucauldian-like, to 'the present danger': will we reinforce present disciplinary, panoptic tendencies through ICT applications, or will we take up other options in relation to the new boost in power and possibilities that these technologies can offer. Ultimately the pessimism in her findings, and to some extent her conclusions, also remind one of Foucault's own dilemmas with disciplinary/bio-power.

However, something interesting then happened to the direction that the informate/automate debate took. As Zuboff's book became a bestseller, its Foucauldian influences and themes fell away almost completely and the automate/informate dilemma came to be posed as a choice for managers and, indeed, capitalist societies to make. Partly this was because of how the book was sold, with a simplified central message, an 'informate' challenge, indeed, that Zuboff asks managers to step up to in her last chapter. But interestingly, there is some inconsistency between on the one hand the rich historical discourse and constraints she describes, and on the other the levels of active *choice* she then assumes for managers.

In practice, Zuboff's work was adopted by the Harvard Business School where she was, at the time, an associate professor. Harnessing the School's reputational effects and its powerful marketing and self-referencing capability, the book's public messages were pushed into certain directions rather than others. Arguably, the book was used to support Harvard's own 'can do', 'born again', transformative philosophy of management, in which a dichotomous before/after, from/to message is transmitted to trainee managers and businesses alike. Simple, powerful messages are likely to be more influential than the twists and turns of a long, rich and complex book that most have probably read about, rather than read all the way through. Power/knowledge circulates, people, institutions and documents are its relays—knowledge and power produce each other indeed.

Ultimately the meaning of Zuboff's book was diluted and rendered complementary to, for example, Walton (1989), also a product of Harvard. Walton's work went on to figure prominently in another book highly influential in IS, namely *The Corporation of the 1990s* (Scott Morton, 1991). This proceeded to offer dichotomous thinking in contrasting bad/good 'control' versus 'commitment' strategies in ICT use and, in an un-Foucauldian manner, failed to problematize commitment strategies and their political and control implications. A more informed view here was provided by Deetz (1998) and Townley (1993), who saw the cultural or normative controls that operate as alternatives to bureaucratic rules and direct supervision as new technologies of power developed within knowledge-intensive organizations.

A related, influential development was the neo-Zuboffian, 'don't automate, obliterate' message of Hammer and Champy's writings on reengineering the corporation, with heavy use of ICT. Grint and Willcocks (1995) point out that Hammer and Champy work with a negative, unitary view of power, and while the objective of reengineering is ostensibly to render the corporation a-political, in fact successful reengineering, supported by labour 'empowerment' strategies, is designed to make managerial power and control more complete. The inherently political agenda is signalled by the marked violence in the language used, the dismissal of 'resistance to change', the determination to banish social, cultural and historical issues by starting with a blank sheet of paper and, the use of management-determined ICT designs to support the shape and process of the transformed corporation. On this view 'informate' is too small a step and 'transformate' is necessary (see also Scott Morton, 1991), but only a more radical view of power relations would seek to fully problematize the intentions, approaches and outcomes. Those in IS studying such phenomena could more than usefully adopt Foucauldian concepts and modes of analysis.

Information Systems as a Discipline

Ironically again, the Foucauldian elements of Zuboff's book have been remarkably *uninfluential* in information systems, a relatively immature discipline crying out for applicable theory. But Zuboff's influence, taught as she is on every conceivable type of IS programme, has hardly stretched to the founding of a Foucauldian school of IS. Despite her demonstration of his applicability, why *not* Foucault now?

The operational word here may well be discipline. For decades a string of scholars and articles have registered 'discipline anxiety' for IS. This comes from its relative newness as an area of study and its hybridity, based as it is on an amalgamation of computer science, operational research, management studies, economics, organization studies and strategic management, to name a few. The definitional phrase that comes to mind is the one that Richard Whitley used for management studies: a fragmented adhocracy. How can one discipline and gain intellectual respectability for a knowledge field that lacks discipline?

A natural tendency is look to another accepted reference discipline for already approved methods, procedures and standards, for definitions of what qualifies as knowledge and truth (see also Chapter 1 of this volume). One unfortunate outcome in IS is that methods and approaches have often been adopted uncritically (that is, failing to address the debates that surround them in their own discipline, e.g. transaction cost theory in economics) or may be inappropriate for the specific research task. This can lead to unnecessary defensive polarities developing and an over-expectation on what a particular approach can deliver. For example, if scientific rigour and methods are applied in IS, one is sometimes led to believe that something like god can be seen in the statistics. (On the other hand, some interpretivists have been known to treat a 'fact' like a cow: if you look at it for long enough it will go away).

For historical reasons—not least because of the hard, technology component of IS, the general dominance of the procedures of the natural sciences infiltrating into the social sciences and the large influence of North American academic practices in IS—the IS tendency has been to focus on quantitative, statistics-based methods and procedures derived from natural sciences. Speculatively, one might also observe that as an immigrant culture, the USA naturally gravitated towards a set of disciplinary procedures that could be learned and applied as techniques largely devoid of contextual, cultural, historical and processual understandings of what was under study.

The rise of IS as a discipline has yet to be charted satisfactorily and, I would suggest, may well benefit from a Foucauldian analysis. IS awaits its genealogist, though Introna (2001) makes a thought-provoking start in his paper on evolving regimes of truth from 1977 to 2000 at one of the major IS journals, namely *MIS Quarterly*. He shows the mechanisms used to produce truth and how contingent they were, as well as how, through intentional and unintentional moves, these regimes of truth were continually shifting, opening spaces for certain types of research to become legitimate and others not. It is a matter of some pertinence here that the widespread acceptance of certain types of qualitative, interpretive and case research in major IS journals has been a relatively recent phenomenon. In such an unstable situation, given their cross-disciplinarity and provisional methods, Foucauldian-type studies, at best, could only be marginal to how the IS discipline has been developing.

The debate on what would constitute IS as a discipline has been running for some time. After 2000, faced with the sheer rising diversity in research methods being adopted in the field, there has been renewed 'discipline anxiety' and fresh debates in several major IS journals over establishing the rules, procedures for what counts as knowledge and how it can be legitimately produced. Introna (2003) makes an interesting Foucauldian intervention in pointing out that what constitutes acceptable research methods, processes for producing the truth and a definable knowledge base are not matters of what is right or rationally superior, but are inherently political questions from the start. Moreover, participants are not simply disciplining others in the process of creating 'the IS discipline', but also disciplining themselves. Introna (2003) also points out that if IS proceeds to constitute itself as a regime of truth, then it will need to follow Foucault (in Gordon, 1980) in establishing five things. These are:

- Types of discourse it accepts and makes function as true.
- Mechanisms and instances that enable one to distinguish true and false statements.
- Means by which each is sanctioned.
- Techniques and procedures accorded value in the acquisition of truth.
- Status of those charged with saying what counts as true.

On these counts, one would suggest that if IS is not yet externally or even self-regarded as a discipline, it has been remarkably successful at disciplining itself, and that this process deserves much more detailed, perhaps Foucauldian study. One must also ask why a diversity of approaches, as long as they import critical debates and perspectives, should be regarded as dysfunctional, especially given the evolutionary shifts in the objects of study. There may well be a strength to be built from multidisciplinarity. In a Foucauldian move, Introna himself offers a transgressive thought. Why this haste to be an academic discipline? If it is a matter of survival, then at a time when knowledge regimes are shifting, becoming an 'academic' discipline may well be a distinct disadvantage.

FOUCAULT AND IS: APPLICATIONS

Having said all this, some within IS have made a strong case for Foucault, and indeed have used aspects of his work. Introna (1997) effectively utilizes Foucault's power/knowledge in harness with Clegg's (1989) conceptualization of circuits of power in order to explicate several case studies of ICT implementation and use. Brooke (2002a, 2002b), in discussing what it means to be 'critical' in IS research, argues that Foucault can be used to move beyond the Habermasian framework employed in earlier IS work. As a related point, initially Habermas was presented somewhat uncritically in IS, but a healthy critique of his use has grown up (see also Chapter 6), which Foucault's work can readily fuel. Brooke (2002a) herself offers a point of reflection for IS in which she argues that Foucault opens up the topics of emancipation and power relations to critical inquiry in ways that Habermas cannot.

For her, this derives from Foucault challenging an idea central to critical theory when he suggests that relations of power are not something bad in themselves, nor something from which one can or must be emancipated. It also derives from his argument that any production of knowledge contains within itself the potential for contradictory outcomes. In practice, extending an argument made above, Brooke (2002a, 2002b) makes a crucial point for the future conduct of IS studies. The scientific and positivistic heritage of IS does tend to favour the adoption of approaches that are more easily 'modelled'. And any line of research seeking to use a normatively articulated framework will tend to favour a Habermasian approach rather than a Foucauldian one. But, to paraphrase Brooke's argument, when it comes to applying critical theory who guards the guards? From a Foucauldian perspective, it is not enough to apply particular methodological frameworks, we also have to subject them to ongoing critique, and Foucault's work supplies means for doing this.

Among other IS researchers using Foucault we may also point to Probert (1993), who employs what Dreyfus and Rabinow (1983) have called Foucault's interpretive analytics, and who has sought to follow Foucault's stipulations that 'we have three axes whose specificity and whose interconnections have to be analysed: the axis of knowledge, the axis of power, the axis of ethics' (quoted in Rabinow, 1984).

Davies has also sought to apply Foucault in several pieces of empirical research. For example, Davies and Mitchell (1994) adopted a research perspective that sought to understand technology formation as a power/knowledge object used within a sociopolitical context, but also looking at 'how technological forms affect the predomination of discourse of power, allowing for the "truth" of an object's utility value to emerge as a product of its own structural form and the value of the form according to the group world-view adopting it'. The authors argue, with Burrell (1998), that Foucault's genealogical method, focus on history and concept of power/knowledge are of high relevance to studying organizational forms currently emerging, particularly in relation to the control of information effects induced by the increasing reliance on information technologies within organizations.

While Davies and Mitchell do not adopt Foucault as comprehensively as they might, they do demonstrate how his work on the regulatory nature of discourse within contextual histories can be used productively in IS studies, in this case that of IT manipulation in an Australian state government department. Following Foucault, they point to the constraining regulations by which discourse is inevitably tied. They take three interacting forms, shown in Figure 7.2.

The three principles of exclusion are immediately external to a discourse and define and legitimize meaning and rationality within discourse. The three principles of limitation operate to classify order and distribute the discourse to allow for and to deal with irruption and unpredictability. Finally, the three principles of communication create the ritual framework (akin to an ideology) of the context of any discourse, with the ritual framework being more dominating than the merely external principles.

While these constructs may seem somewhat abstracted, the researchers do bring them to life in applying them to a concrete case, namely the purchasing of office support systems. By applying all the concepts, the research shows how one system is adopted in preference to another, predominantly through the prior regulations of discourse supporting the continuance of the superior technical knowledge and power of the IT function. The researchers successfully show how applying Foucauldian principles to analysing the

EXCLUSION

Prohibition	Division	Truth power
Taboos	Legitimate participation	True vs false

LIMITATION

Commentary	Rarefaction	Disciplines
Meaning rules maintained	Identity rules maintained	Belief rules maintained

COMMUNICATION

Societies of discourse	Social appropriation	Systems of regulation and control
Social group	Maintain or modify	Production and manipulation

Figure 7.2   *Principles of discourse regulation (adapted from Davies and Mitchell, 1994)*

discursive context of IT use in an organization can provide in-depth insight into the role of power and politics, and whether IT is used augmentatively to reinforce the status quo or transformatively.

A later Foucauldian study of an ICT needs analysis project was also carried out by Davies, as Harvey (1998). The study usefully demonstrates how the history of power relations in an IT decision context influenced discourses regarding the acceptability of solutions. Historical dominance was demonstrated through how visibility was controlled, how counter-discourses were silenced and how surveillance was applied. What is interesting in this study, that of Davies and Mitchell (1994) and that of Zuboff (1988) is how they all extend and enhance interpretive research methods through using Foucault. Doolin (1998) argues that this is a necessary move in order to counter potential shortcomings in the treatment of technology in interpretive research on information systems.

Let us look at this proposition. Interpretivism in IS research has been criticized for its failure to explain the unintended consequence of action, which cannot be explained by reference to the participants and is often a significant force in shaping reality (but see Chapter 4 for counter-arguments). Orlikowski and Baroudi (1991) and Tinker (1998) also point to its frequent neglect of historical change and a failure to recognize the inherent conflicts and contradictions in social relations. For Tinker (1998) and Knights (1995), interpretive IS research can become more critical—questioning and deconstructing the taken-for-granted assumptions in the status quo—by becoming more politically informed and examining ICT and organizations in a wider societal, historical, economic and ideological context. While Doolin (1998) concedes that critical theory and critical hermeneutics inform a style of critical ethnography that is in fact well developed in the IS literature, he is interested, like Knights (1995), in exploring what Foucault might add.

This depends on how ICT are characterized. Doolin uses Bloomfield (1995), Latour (1994) and Knights and Murray (1994), among others, to position ICT as part of processes in which both technology and organization become redefined. Social relations are instantiated and mediated through technology and organizations are made relatively cohesive and stable by the way they are intimately bound up with the technical. Technology is society made more durable (see Chapter 9). Bloomfield (1995) puts this well:

> Technology does not *impact* on organizations or society: a change in social relations, tasks, skills and knowledge is already prefigured in the way that the technology is conceived and constructed. Machines do not *control* social relations: they presuppose, mediate and reinforce them.

Of course, Bloomfield, Knights and Murray are considerably influenced by Foucault and bring to bear a valuable conceptualization of technology that is only implicit in his work. They also stress the need to be sensitive to the exercise of power, in studying technology without reducing technological developments to technological or managerial imperatives. In seeing reality as materially heterogeneous and relational, they find it valuable to employ Foucault's relational notion of power. This is because ICT increasingly mediate how power circulates, is exercised and what it produces. Thus Orlikowski (1991) also suggests that the mediation of work processes by information technology creates a disciplinary matrix of power, knowledge and control.

For our purposes, Doolin (1998) is highly useful in illustrating this theme of information systems as a calculative and disciplinary technology. He does so by reference to his own Foucauldian study of power relations and effects involving the deployment of a hospital 'casemix' IS. A casemix system is an IS that links detailed information on individual patient clinical activity with associated costs, for use by managers and service providers as a basis for contracting and for revealing the relative efficiency of clinical resource usage. The intention is to place clinical activity under scrutiny and to persuade clinicians to conform to 'normal' work practices. Potentially Doolin found that the IS could increase hospital management control directly and indirectly. Direct control was attempted by monitoring and making visible the financial implications of clinical decisions. Managers could then use the information to make stronger truth claims in their attempts to contain clinical resource usage. Surveillance through the system also had the potential to engender a degree of self-control in clinicians' behaviour, leading to rational decision making and more efficient usage of resources.

However, following Foucault, resistance by the clinicians was always possible. Disciplinary technologies such as comparative surveillance IS are not exclusively constraining, but instead open up a new discursive space for action. In practice clinicians often appropriated and manipulated the information and rhetoric of the system, diverting disciplinary practices to their own ends, principally in arguing for more resources. Indeed, some senior clinicians explored the possibilities offered by the casemix system in assuming new roles as clinician managers. However, the IS increased the transparency of professional knowledge, expertise and work processes. Its deployment provided management with the technology and the rational justification for increased intervention in medical practice. Moreover, casemix information became the currency of debate, the principal media through which claims to legitimacy and control were processed. Taking a Foucauldian view, Doolin points out that in reproducing the practices associated with the casemix IS, clinicians internalized the norms and values inherent in the particular discourse in which casemix is grounded, opening up the possibility of their self-control as self-disciplined subjects. Thus IS utilization could have more subtle power effects than deliberate strategies to modify clinical behaviour through strengthening general management in or imposing computerized surveillance.

Foucault and IS in Organization and Management Studies

As Doolin's case study illustrates, IS as a discipline may learn a great deal more on the applicability of Foucault if it addresses more seriously the altogether more developed debate and application of his work to be found in organization studies and associated areas (OS/MS). Foucault has had a long-standing presence in sociology and OS/MS because his concepts and contribution have such clear applicability to researching work organizations. Moreover, from the early 1980s as ICT were increasingly used in organizations, it became a necessary move to embrace the analysis of how they are utilized and embedded in the social bodies, practices and institutional arrangements of organizations. The same argument can be made from the perspective of information systems studies, of course. This section is not intended as a comprehensive but rather as an illustrative view of OS/MS use of Foucault in studying ICT and organizations. Note also that some OS/MS work has been discussed at earlier points in this chapter and will not be repeated here.

The maturity of OS/MS Foucauldian debate and use is well demonstrated in the articles collected by McKinlay and Starkey (1998) and Carter, McKinlay and Rowlinson (2002). These carry penetrating papers that seek to critique, develop and utilize Foucault's work in, for example, human resource management (see also Townley, 1993), power and politics in organizations and production, managing managers, accounting, reading organizational analysis into Foucault, developing a Foucauldian historical dimension in the study of organizations, the relationships between discipline and desire, the epistemic nature of management, and the need to deconstruct management studies underpinned, like influencing disciplines, as it is by rationality, agency and causality.

Foucault has also done much to breathe new life into labour process theory, not least in OS/MS researchers emphasizing how individual subjectivities and identities are constructed and reconstructed through discourses operating in the workplace (Knights, 1990; Knights and Vurdubakis, 1994) There has also been an expansion of the concept of power (Clegg, 1989, 1998), with Hardy and Leiba-O'Sullivan (1998) positioning Foucault as providing the fourth dimension of power, extending the three defined by Steven Lukes. All this illustrates a strong Foucauldian pedigree in OS/MS, one that is directly applicable to any work in IS where ICT are studied in organizational contexts.

Even more pertinent to our purposes is the OS/MS accumulated evidence gained from applying Foucault to the study of information and communication technologies. Many of these attempts focus on new managerial technologies aimed to broaden the scope and deepen the intensity of the managerial gaze, but, Foucault-like, invariably with complex, often unanticipated outcomes. Surveillance, control and legitimation are facilitated by giving complex, ambiguous phenomena 'hard' numerical values (Morgan and Willmott, 1993), for example in ICT use in activity-based costing systems where the managerial gaze extends into supplier networks and market information. ICT facilitate enumeration, which can underpin categorization, and thus what is made visible. Such technologies privilege formal quantitative information, aiding in the construction of calculative realities (Bloomfield and Coombs, 1992).

However, developments in ICT to monitor and scrutinize can also facilitate panopticon-like control, making individuals within an organization both calculable and calculating with respect to their own actions. For example, Sewell and Wilkinson (1992) investigate these propensities in the context of JIT (just-in-time) manufacturing and total quality control regimes. They point to the development of what Webster and Robins (1993) call 'a panopticon without walls', where responsibility can become delegated to groups but individuals become enlisted in their own control through their belief that they are subject to constant electronic surveillance through collected, retained and disseminated information. McKinley and Starkey (1998) also point to how the extension of JIT supplier relationships accelerates the concentration and widens the scope and speed of corporate knowledge acquisition, and that this is knowledge combined with economic power that is not reciprocal: 'there is no parallel gaze by consumers or supplier companies into the internal transaction costs of the organization'. Webster and Robins (1993) suggest also that these developments are not restricted to the labour process or the factory but are more societal, to the point where one can speak of a more generalized 'social Taylorism' made more possible through information and communication technologies.

Bloomfield, Knights, Willmott and colleagues have done much important work in developing Foucauldian studies of ICT and organization. It is not possible to do justice to the richness of their work, but good examples can be found in Knights, Murray and Willmott (1997), Bloomfield *et al.* (1997) and Bloomfield and Coombs (1992). A particularly representative work is that of Knights and Murray (1994). This book has the great merit of providing a real in-depth theoretical and empirical examination of the politics of systems development. It focuses on the theory over the first five chapters, then applies the preferred theoretical perspective to a major systems project undertaken at a UK life insurance company. It devotes some five chapters to this single longitudinal case study.

In the theory sections the book provides a Foucauldian-informed critique of the major theoretical perspectives on ICT development and implementation. From this Knights and Murray then develop a political processual model of organizational change. At its centre stands politics as Foucauldian power/knowledge relations. These are enacted in specific conditions of possibility, the social construction of which is also part of an organization's political processes. For analytical purposes these four conditions of possibility are separated out as:

- *Organizational*—structure, practices, culture.
- *Subjectivity and security*—subjectivity/identity and individual insecurity management (see also Knights, 1990).
- *Sociopolitical and economic conditions*—general and local contextual factors prevailing, including those affecting gender and race relations.
- *Technological possibilities*—solutions and innovations that can be developed from a given technology, given constraining aspects of local conditions.

Knights and Murray also supply the useful definition of ICT that Foucault never provided, in order to inform their Foucauldian analysis. They see ICT as a set of human and non-human artifacts, processes and practices ordinarily directed towards modifying or transforming natural and social phenomena in pursuit of human purposes. This involves:

- Technological artifacts, such as computers, hardware.
- Technological knowledge, particularly systems development skills.
- Technological workers and managers engaged in particular systems development, as well as IS specialists.
- The culture of technology: signs, symbols and values brought to bear in discussing, using and developing technology.

In this analytical framework, the organization is likened to a pinball machine. While recognizing the limitations of the analogy, the researchers suggest that the political process stands in the middle of the machine and is bombarded by steel balls energized in different parts of the organization. These bounce against the motor of political process and are shot back to bounce against other conditions of the organization. Though a little uncritical of Foucault, as opposed to every other theoretical approach, Knights and Murray (1994) do provide, as they show in their case study, operationalizable analytical tools that can be very useful to IS researchers.

Foucault, ICT and Surveillance

Perhaps the most obvious and influential use of Foucault has been in surveillance studies, not merely in manufacturing and service work organizations but across society at large, including in all manner of institutional settings. There is a large literature on the theme of ICT roles in surveillance, with Lyon (1988) and Dandeker (1990) being representative of a number of writers in the late 1980s discussing the 'electronic panopticon', the 'carceral computer' and 'the electronic eye'. Poster (1984) is also influenced enough by Foucault to posit an emerging 'mode of information' by whose social conduits and databases members of developed economies are organized and controlled.

Webster (1995) also links surveillance technologies with the nation state's 'governmentality' role over the security needs, rights and duties of its citizens. For him, the panopticon is not an exact metaphor. Following Giddens, a lot of surveillance information does feed back to people and allow them reflexively to monitor their own position, prospects and lifestyles. He is drawn instead to De Landa's (1991) depiction of the 'machine vision' of military surveillance, where power and the accumulation of information are intimately connected, manifested in things like telecommunications interceptions, satellite observations and automatic intelligence. De Landa sees the military dream of machine vision as an extension of earlier panoptic techniques. Now humans and their eyes do not have to operate physically in the surveillance tower. Moreover, surveillance has extended from the optical to the non-optical regions of the electro-magnetic spectrum. Not just computing and telecommunications, but the discovery of infrared and ultraviolet radiation, radar, radio and microwave technology have opened new resources to be exploited as well as new zones to be policed. De Landa offers the word 'panspectron' to communicate the ambition of total surveyability vested in the 'new non-optical intelligence-acquisition machine'. This is a highly pertinent issue, not least for IS studies, if De Landa is correct in suggesting that historically, earlier technologies developed in the military have been transmitted through a series of relays to the civilian worlds.

Lyon (1988) registers related concerns in his early work on the rise of the information society. He suggests that dreams of electronic democracy must be tempered with a recognition of technological and political realities. He recognizes, even for the late 1980s, that the 'carceral computer' is 'a present reality, both in direct state administration and control, and in the potential for linkage with private databases'. However, as yet the dangers had not been sufficiently recognized or resisted by citizens, and some predictions of total social control by computers may be ahistorical 'in that past technological dystopias have not come into being, and may also be based on inadequate social theories'.

If Lyon (1988) points to the 'present danger', then the subsequent direction that much of his work takes suggests that in his estimation, with rising use of ICT, the danger has become very real. Thus Lyon (1994) is entitled *The Electronic Eye: The Rise of Surveillance Society*. For him the most socially pervasive question raised by the new technologies has become the garnering of personal information to be stored, matched, retrieved, processed, marketed and circulated using powerful computer databases and related technologies. His position is that the electronic eye may well blink benignly, but important questions must be asked about under what circumstances and by what criteria the current computer-aided surveillance capability may also become undemocratic, coercive, impersonal and even inhuman.

In later work and edited volumes, Lyon and colleagues provide rich, detailed studies of these and related questions (see for example Lyon and Zureik, 1996; Lyon 2003). In all this, it becomes difficult not to read the influence and relevance of Foucault's work, among others. Thus, in these volumes some take the phenomenon of electronic surveillance as contributing to a postmodern condition in which several 'virtual selves' circulate within networked databases, independent of their Cartesian counterparts who use credit cards and are identified by social insurance numbers (Lyon and Zureik, 1996). This raises questions of how identity and selves are constructed, sorted and controlled, privately and publicly. In the same volume, Mowshowitz sees the widespread use of databases as promoting 'endogenous' forms of social control, where virtual individuality, group conformity and other-directedness will reside in the data themselves. For Poster, databases have become the new text in Foucault's sense of discourse.

In all this, researchers point also to limitations in both Foucault's work and in applying it to surveillance studies (see also Chapter 6). Thus Gandy, writing on 'Coming to terms with the panoptic sort', enlists also Giddens' synthesis of Marxian, Weberian and Foucauldian theory to emphasize surveillance as a modern institution, and the role of the 'dialectic of control' and knowledgeable human agents in all surveillance situations (Lyon and Zureik, 1996; see also Chapter 8 in this volume). Zureik (in Lyon, 2003) concludes that surveillance in the workplace is ubiquitous and increasingly based on network control technologies. He suggests that the concept of panoptic power is important, but that more than one theoretical perspective is needed to analyse how in specific contexts empowerment and disempowerment, skilling and de-skilling, control and autonomy exist, and indeed can coexist, depending on technological deployment, gender and authority structures (but see also Knights and Murray above).

Lyon (1993) asks in what ways electronic surveillance displays panoptic features. He finds plenty of evidence of ICT being used to accumulate coded information for the internal pacification of nation states, as well as for panoptic control within workplaces, including what Zuboff calls 'anticipatory conformity', where standards of management had been internalized by employees. He also cites evidence of the spill-over of panoptic surveillance into society at large in the establishment of, for example, more 'efficient' network market-places, something that Poster (1990) refers to as a 'superpanopticon', because the panoptic has few technical limitations.

But, partly following Giddens (see Chapter 8), Lyon also sees analysts of electronic surveillance picking up from Foucault a relatively undifferentiated view of power and panopticism, and therefore of panopticism's ICT-facilitated spread across different types of institutions. At the same time he concedes that the reality of contemporary electronic surveillance is that, increasingly, disciplinary networks do, for example, connect employment with civil status or consumption with policing. But if Poster's 'superpanopticon' is accurate, does it nevertheless impose Foucault-type norms, incorporate bio-power, discipline subjects? Maybe, Lyon suggests, all it can do is provide a structure, and one within which real choices are still made. Ultimately Lyon finds the panopticon wanting as an explanatory concept. Electronic surveillance does contribute to social control via invisible inspection and categorization. But seeing the panopticon in a 'totalizing' way deflects attention from other modes of social ordering (Lyon, 2003). Lyon (1993) also comments that Foucault's failure to admit any basis of 'outrage' against the panopticon inhibits the development of a properly critical theory of electronic surveillance.

Maybe one of the mistakes in contemporary surveillance theory, as in other disciplines, is to represent Foucault's work too one-sidedly by the panopticon and its admittedly strong metaphorical power. As we have seen, Foucault is much richer than this. For example, in summarizing his own work he defined four major types of technologies, each a matrix of practical reason, each associated with a certain type of domination (Deetz, 1998). Foucault presents technologies of production, of sign systems, of power and of self. He also suggests that these may interplay in particular sites. In addition he worked with a generic mode of discipline, of which the panoptic represents merely one type. One way forward for electronic surveillance studies may well be to readdress Foucault's work more fully. In addition, Dandeker (1990) suggests that, given the uneasy relations in Foucault between an idealist history of knowledge, class struggle and the functional or technical imperatives of modern societies, his insights may be used to complement those generated by other, especially Weberian, strands of social theory.

From Mode of Information to Network Society and Cyberstudies

In this final section, we look briefly at Foucault's abiding relevance in the face of developments in ICT and their uses in the twenty-first century. Poster (1984, 1990, 1995) was among the first to suggest that Foucault provides key ideas (on signification, power/knowledge, subjectification, discourse) for the development of a critical theory of the newly emerging 'mode of information'. Poster suggests that the reversal of priorities that Marx saw in the factory, whereby the dead (machines) dominate the living (workers), is being increasingly extended by the computer to the realm of knowledge. He posits three stages in the mode of information:

- Face-to-face, orally mediated exchange, characterized by symbolic correspondences.
- Written exchanges mediated by print, characterized by the representation of signs.
- Electronically mediated exchange, characterized by informational simulations.

Given the attributes and applications of ICT, an increasing, distinctive characteristic in the latter electronic stage is that the self becomes decentred, dispersed and multiplied in continuous instability. If Poster (1990) subsequently utilizes several postmodernist thinkers to analyse the emerging mode of information, he finds how information is structured and used through databases and their relation to society best disclosed by Foucault's analysis of discourse: 'the linguistic quality of the database, its implications for politics, can best be captured by a theory, like Foucault's, that problematizes the interdependence of language and action'. As we have seen, Poster sees electronic circuits of communication and the databases they generate as constituting a superpanopticon, a system of surveillance without walls, windows, towers or guards.

New ICT used in surveillance result in a qualitative change in the microphysics of power. However, Poster observes, technological change is only part of the process. The populace, through social security cards, driving licences and in their consumerist activities, for example, have been disciplined to surveillance and participating in the process. For Poster (1990, 1995), when Foucauldian discourse analysis is applied to the new mode of information, it yields the uncomfortable discovery that the populace participates in its own self-constitution as subjects of the normalizing gaze of the superpanopticon. Moreover, databases are often seen not as a threat to a centred individual or to privacy, but as the multiplication of the individual, the constitution of an additional self, one that may be acted on to the detriment of the 'real' self without that 'real' self ever being aware of what is happening. For Poster, then, while recognizing the deficiencies of Foucault's work, the concepts and methods for exploring discourse, subjectification, disciplining, knowledge and power relations remain key to critical study of ICT, and indeed the Internet (Poster, 2001), in the emerging mode of information that they facilitate.

Munro (2000) also recognizes how Foucault has been drawn on to analyse the power relations involved in computer information systems. As a partial corrective, he argues not that disciplinary modalities of power have disappeared, but that they are subject to infiltration and mutation where ICT are transforming social relationships and allowing other forms of power to be brought to bear. The examples he includes are how the Human Genome Project is bringing to bear bio-technologies such as genetic screening and cloning. He also cites Deleuze's (1995) depiction of moves towards a 'control' society, for example from schools to continuing education, from prisons to electronic tagging. New forms of 'resistance' are also possible, for example computer piracy and viruses or sabotage of information databases. New social divisions are developing, including the information haves and have-nots, and new institutions, consisting of series of connected nodes or stations that work by circulating information flows as much as wealth and goods. He points to the power of networks and how these new institutions do not rely on enclosure or visual surveillance. Instead, power operates through the regulation of flows rather than the imposition of exercises (Deleuze, 1995).

Munro posits the rise of network power in contrast to panoptic power. The differentiation he makes is along the dimensions of techniques, space, time and the body (Table 7.1). At the level of technique, power relations become more centred on access to and control over information and the electronic text. Time–space constraints disappear, with real-time and connected nodes creating new circuits of power. Following Virilio, the body becomes motile; that is, more dependent on communications prosthetics, for example the mobile phone or portable computer. Whereas the docile body was the object of disciplinary power, the prosthetic body is the object of network power.

Munro argues that sticking doggedly to Foucault's original conceptualizations of disciplinary power can lead to errors in analysis in these new conditions. However, this is possibly to underestimate the extent to which the new ICT themselves are conditioned in the first place, and may subsequently be infiltrated by disciplinary power (Finlay, 1987a, 1987b). Munro's is a good formulation, but over-dichotomous in its presentation of developments. And as with computer surveillance studies, his argument also relies on not granting to Foucauldian analysis the full richness of Foucault's ideas and formulations.

In documenting what they call 'changes in the technoscape', Robins and Webster (1999) argue that the information revolution does not represent a profound break from the past, but a continuation of capitalism in many similar forms. Moreover, the prevailing virtual culture 'lacks critical edge with respect to the capitalist dynamics of the network society' (see also Feenberg, 2002). If this is the case, then not only is Foucault not outdated, as some have

Table 7.1   *Panoptic vs network power (after Munro, 2000)*

Dimension	A panopticon	A network

Techniques	Dressage
	The panopticon—visual
	   surveillance
		Control of flows
		The panspectron—data
		   surveillance

Space	Confined cells	Connected nodes (stations)
Time	Timetable	Global 'real time'
The body	Docile body	Motile body

suggested, but means of critical questioning such as he provides are vitally needed in the study of contemporary ICT.

In looking at contemporary developments one can trace Foucault's influence into work on bio-power and technology. Hayles (1999) rightly points out that the absorption of embodiment into discourse imparted interpretive power to Foucault, but also limited his analysis in significant ways. The universalization of the Foucauldian body is a direct result of concentrating on discourse rather than embodiment. Building on Foucault's work while going beyond it requires an understanding of how embodiment moves in conjunction with inscription, technology and ideology. But, as we have seen, this is something that Zuboff's work largely achieves, while Sofoulis (2002) rightly points out Foucault's influence on Haraway (1991) and her subsequent development of his notions of bio-power and bio-politics in her post-Foucauldian notions of the 'informatics of domination' and 'techno-biopower'. Quinby (1999) has also reoriented Foucault's work on subject formation. She uses it to develop how 'technoppression' can occur in the pursuit of the programmed perfection enabled by digital and biotechnologies. A Foucauldian perspective is useful in questioning the race to human bodily perfection through technological means.

Finally, one can point to some interest in Foucault's work among those studying the Internet. The questioning here is whether the Internet and 'cyberspace' are or will become a form of more intensive control and power relations—precisely Foucault's concern registered at the head of this chapter. The literature so far tends to have different interests and emphases (see also Chapters 3, 4, 6 and 9). Three examples will suffice. Thus Aycock (1997) is interested in applying the later Foucault and his notions of technologies of the self to examine how online identities can be fashioned. Winokur (2003) applies yet again the concept of the panopticon and concludes that the codes of cyberspace are not clearly a disciplinary discourse. Boyle (1997) is interested in legal issues, surveillance, levels of censorship and the development of digital libertarianism. He argues that digital libertarianism is often blind to the effects of private power, but also to those of the state's own power in cyberspace. In practice he finds that the state can often use privatized enforcement and state-backed technologies to evade some of the supposed practical and constitutional restraints on the exercise of legal power over the Net. He also argues that technical solutions to these dilemmas are neither as neutral nor as benign as they are often perceived to be.

CONCLUSION

This chapter has argued for the abiding relevance of Foucault's work and the usefulness of incorporating and developing further his thinking into contemporary information systems studies. This should be done as a critical act in three senses. First, Foucault should not be applied uncritically. Following Barratt (2003), he should be worked with rather than copied. This chapter has pointed to the provisional, unfinished nature of many of his concepts and formulations, but also to how these can and have been addressed in the study of ICT, for example with the use of ethnography (Zuboff, 1988) and social construction approaches (see Chapter 9). Secondly, Foucault has been shown to be a critical and usable weapon in a field not over-full of such tools. Moreover, as we saw in the case of the Foucault–Habermas debates, Foucault can be used to sharpen our critique of other, explicit or implicit social theories and philosophies perhaps borrowed from reputationally stronger reference disciplines and used uncritically in a relatively new IS field. Finally, as we saw, Foucault can be employed in the ongoing debate over the nature of, and what it is to construct, an IS discipline.

One of the warnings given by this chapter, and one that it has attempted to address by its content, is not to import, uncritically, just a social theorist's high-profile, easy-to-use frameworks. That is to surrender to a technique fetishism that ill serves the complexity of both social theory and the phenomena to which it is applied. In practice what is difficult in a thinker like Foucault, as in for example Adorno (see Chapter 5) and Habermas (see Chapter 6), is what is most productive. Thus Foucault contributes methods and concepts that can be developed and operationalized, but he also urges us to transgress, to rethink and even to reverse interpretations, to redis-cover what seems familiar and obvious, to recognize continuities and discontinuities by taking histories, discourses and long views seriously in IS.

He also reminds us, uncomfortably, of our epistemological frailty and ontological uncertainties, and from this can sensitize us to how much human use of ICT is a will towards control, certainty and 'knowledge' in the face of considerable risk and ambivalence. If Foucault does not deal explicitly with ICT as hardware and soft-ware, he does provide a useful corrective against narrow definitions of technology and ICT applications. Instead of privileging material technology, he privileges the behavioural and social technologies encoded and imbedded in material technologies. This provides an important corrective to recent 'digital economy' rhetorics about the transformative power of ICT in themselves. Furthermore, his work suggests that all participate in the technologies that surround us, whether these are invisible or visible, whether we know it or not. Despite how he is generally presented, Foucault also urges us to acknowledge indeterminacy. There is, for example, nothing inevitable about technology trajectories. In acknowledging indeterminacy in the history of technology we may note with Scranton (1995) Foucault's comment:

> nothing is fundamental . . . [there] are no fundamental phenomena. There are only reciprocal relations, and the perpetual gaps between intentions in relation to one another. (Foucault, 1996)

Whither Foucault? Baudrillard (1987) urges us to forget him, but this chapter argues for his abiding relevance. However, while Foucault's work still awaits the further application it deserves in the IS field, it is strange that his theorizations of knowledge, power and discourse have not been utilized more productively in, for example, deconstructing knowledge management and related systems. In the ICT context knowledge awaits its geneaologist, and this may be one of the richer veins still to emerge from Foucault's potentially important contributions to IS studies—yet another way of deconstructing, in order to reconstruct, the present.

A GUIDE TO THE LITERATURE

The most accessible single major work by Foucault pertinent to IS studies is his *Discipline and Punish* (Foucault, 1979). There are many collections of Foucault's articles and interviews now, and these provide valuable complementary reviews and extensions of his work. Among the most informative and wide-ranging are the three-volume *Essential Works* (Foucault, 1997b, 1998, 2000). Foucault (1996) offers a series of interviews and provides a view of Foucault as interlocutor. *Society Must Be Defended* (Foucault, 2003) communicates well the absorbing nature of his lecture series at the Collège de France, and gives fresh insight into his mid-1970s thinking and interests. A view from the engine room, as it were.

Prado (2000) provides the most accessible, philosophically inclined introduction to Foucault's work. Dreyfus and Rabinow (1983) offer an indispensable review and interpretation of the development of Foucault's thought and approaches, and also include two chapters commissioned from Foucault himself that comment on power and his most recent studies of sexuality and ethics. These are valuable not least because they were written shortly before his death. Deleuze (1988) is always insightful on Foucault because Deleuze knew him and his work so well. There are several good biographies, each recommendable (Eribon, 1991; Macey, 1993; Miller, 1993).

There are few sources on using Foucault's methods. Among these are Kendall and Wickham (1999) and Gaventa and Cornwall (2001). For a broader view see Alvesson and Deetz (2000). The best single source on Foucault as used in organization studies is, at the time of writing, McKinley and Starkey (1998). See also the special issue on Foucault of *Organization*, edited by Carter, McKinlay and Rowlinson (2002). And on Foucault and IS, though difficult, long and sometimes frustrating, Zuboff (1988) really does repay careful attention.

REFERENCES

Alvesson, M. and Deetz, S. (2000) *Doing Critical Management Research*, London: Sage.

Andersen, N. (2003) *Discursive Analytical Strategies: Understanding Foucault, Koselleck, Laclau, Luhmann*, Bristol: Policy Press.

Ashenden, S. and Owen, D. (eds) (1999) *Foucault Contra Habermas: Recasting the Dialogue between Genealogy and Critical Theory*, London: Sage.

Aycock, A. (1997) 'Technologies of the Self: Foucault and Internet Discourse', *Journal of Computer Mediated Communication*, 1(2): 25–38.

Barratt, E. (2003) 'Foucault, HRM, and the Ethos of the Critical Management Scholar', *Journal of Management Studies*, 40(5): 1069–87.

Baudrillard, J. (1987) *Forget Foucault*, New York, NY: Semiotexte.

Bernstein, R. (1991) *The New Constellation*, Cambridge: Polity Press.

Best, S. (1994) 'Foucault, postmodernism and social theory', in D. Dickens and R. Fontana (eds), *Postmodernism and Social Enquiry*, London: UCL Press.

Best, S. and Kellner, D. (2001) *The Postmodern Adventure: Science, Technology and Cultural Studies at the Third Millennium*, London: Routledge.

Bloomfield, B. (1995) 'Power, machines and social relations: Delegating to information technology in the National Health Service', *Organization*, 2(3/4): 489–518.

Bloomfield, B. and Coombs, R. (1992) 'Information technology, control and power: The centralization and decentralization debate revisited', *Journal of Management Studies*, 29(4): 459–84.

Bloomfield, B., Coombs, R, Knights, D. and Littler, D. (eds) (1997) *Information Technology and Organizations*, Oxford: Oxford University Press.

Bouchard, D. (1977) *Language, Counter-Memory, Practice: Selected Essays and Interviews by Michel Foucault*, New York, NY: Cornell University Press.

Boyle, J. (1997) 'Foucault in cyberspace: Surveillance, sovereignty and hard-wired censors', *University of Cincinnati Law Review*, 66: 177–205.

Brooke, C. (2002a) 'What does it mean to be 'critical' in IS research?' *Journal of Information Technology*, 17(2): 49–58.

Brooke, C. (2002b) 'Critical perspectives on information systems: An impression of the research landscape', *Journal of Information Technology*, 17(4): 271–85.

Burrell, G. (1998) 'Modernism, postmodernism and organizational analysis: The contribution of Michel Foucault', in A. McKinlay and K. Starkey (eds), *Foucault, Management and Organization Theory*, London: Sage.

Carter, C., McKinlay, A. and Rowlinson, M. (eds) (2002) 'Special issue and introduction: Foucault, management and history', *Organization*, 9(4): 515–26.

Clegg, S. (1989) *Frameworks of Power*, London: Sage.

Clegg, S. (1998) 'Foucault, power and organizations', in A. McKinlay and K. Starkey (eds), *Foucault, Management and Organization Theory*, London: Sage.

Couzens Hoy, D. (ed.) (1986) *Foucault: A Critical Reader*, Oxford: Basil Blackwell.

Dandeker, C. (1990) *Surveillance, Power and Modernity*, Cambridge: Polity Press.

Davies, L. and Mitchell, G. (1994) 'The dual nature of the impact of IT on organizational transformations', in R. Baskerville, S. Smithson, O. Ngwenyama and J. DeGross (eds), *Transforming Organizations with Information Technology*, Amsterdam: North-Holland.

Deetz, S. (1998) '(Re)constructing the modern organization', in A. McKinlay and K. Starkey (eds), *Foucault, Management and Organization Theory*, London: Sage.

De Landa, M. (1991) *War in the Age of Intelligent Machines*, New York, NY: Swerve Editions.

Deleuze, G. (1988) *Foucault*, London: Athlone Press.

Deleuze, G. (1995) *Negotiations: 1972–1990*, New York, NY: Columbia University Press.

Doolin, B. (1998) 'Information technology as a disciplinary technology: Being critical in interpretive research in information systems', *Journal of Information Technology*, 13(4): 301–12.

Dreyfus, H. (2003) ' "Being and Power" revisited', in A. Milcham and A. Rosenberg (eds), *Foucault and Heidegger: Critical Encounters*, Minneapolis, MN: University of Minnesota Press.

Dreyfus, H. and Rabinow, P. (1983) *Michel Foucault: Beyond Structuralism and Hermeneutics*, 2nd edn, Chicago, IL: University of Chicago Press.

Eribon, D. (1991) *Michel Foucault*, London: Faber and Faber.

Feenberg, A. (2002) *Transforming Technology: A Critical Theory Revisited*, Oxford: Oxford University Press.

Finlay, M. (1987a) 'Technology as practice: And (so) what about emancipatory interest', *Canadian Journal of Political and Social Theory*, 11(1–2): 198–214.

Finlay, M. (1987b) *Powermatics: A Discursive Critique of New Communications Technology*, London: Routledge and Kegan Paul.

Foucault, M. (1970) *The Order of Things: An Archaeology of the Human Sciences*, London: Tavistock. Original French version 1966.

Foucault, M. (1972) *The Archaeology of Knowledge and the Discourse on Language*, London: Tavistock. Original French versions 1969 and 1971 respectively.

Foucault, M. (1973) *The Birth of the Clinic*, London: Tavistock. Original French version 1963.

Foucault, M. (1978) *The History of Sexuality Volume 1: An Introduction*, New York, NY: Pantheon Books. Original French version 1976.

Foucault, M. (1979) *Discipline and Punish: The Birth of the Prison*, London: Peregrine. Original French version 1975.

Foucault, M. (1983a) 'The subject and power', in H. Dreyfus and P. Rabinow, *Michel Foucault: Beyond Structuralism and Hermeneutics*, 2nd edn, Chicago, IL: University of Chicago Press.

Foucault, M. (1983b) *This Is not a Pipe*, Berkeley, CA: University of California Press. Original French version 1973.

Foucault, M. (1984) 'Nietzsche, genealogy, history', in P. Rabinow (ed.), *The Foucault Reader*, London: Penguin. Original French version 1971.

Foucault, M. (1985a) *The Use of Pleasure: The History of Sexuality Volume 2*, New York, NY: Pantheon. Original French version 1984.

Foucault, M. (1985b) 'Final interview', *Raritan*, Summer: 8.

Foucault, M. (1986) *The Care of the Self: The History of Sexuality Volume 3*, New York, NY: Pantheon.

Foucault, M. (1988) *Madness and Civilization: A History of Insanity in the Age of Reason*, New York, NY: Random House. Original French version 1961.

Foucault, M. (1991) 'Governmentality', in G. Burchell, C. Gordon and P. Miller (eds), *The Foucault Effect: Studies in Governmentality*, Brighton: Harvester Wheatsheaf.

Foucault, M. (1996) *Foucault Live: Collected Interviews 1961–1984*, New York, NY: Semiotexte.

Foucault, M. (1997a) *The Politics of Truth*, ed. S. Lotringer, Boston, MA: Semiotexte/MIT.

Foucault, M. (1997b) *Essential Works of Michel Foucault 1954–84: Volume 1, Ethics*, London: Penguin.

Foucault, M. (1998) *Essential Works of Foucault 1954–1984: Volume 2, Aesthetics*, London: Penguin.

Foucault, M. (2000) *Essential Works of Foucault 1954–84: Volume 3, Power*, New York, NY: New Press.

Foucault, M. (2003) *'Society Must Be Defended'. Lectures at the Collège de France 1975–76*, New York, NY: Picador. Original French version 1977.

Fraser, N. (1989) 'Foucault on modern power: Empirical insights and normative confusions', in N. Fraser (ed.), *Unruly Practices*, Minneapolis, MN: Minnesota Press.

Gane, M. (ed.) (1986) *Towards a Critique of Foucault*, London: Routledge and Kegan Paul.

Gaventa, J. and Cornwall, R. (2001) 'Power and knowledge', in P. Reason and H. Bradbury (eds), *Handbook of Action Research*, London: Sage.

Gordon, C. (ed.) (1980) *Foucault: Power/Knowledge: Selected Interviews and Other Writings 1972–77*, Brighton: Harvester Wheatsheaf.

Grint, K. and Willcocks, L. (1995) 'Business process reengineering in theory and practice: Paradise regained?' *New Technology, Work and Employment*, 10(2): 99–109.

Gutting, G. (ed.) (1994) *The Cambridge Companion to Foucault*, Cambridge: Cambridge University Press.

Habermas, J. (1987) *The Philosophical Discourse of Modernity: Twelve Lectures*, Cambridge: Polity Press.

Hacking, I. (1986) 'The archaeology of Foucault', in D. Hoy (ed.), *Foucault: A Critical Reader*, Oxford: Blackwell.

Hamilton, R. (1996) *The Social Misconstruction of Reality*, New Haven, CN: Yale University Press.

Haraway, D. (1991) *Cyborgs and Women: The Reinvention of Nature*, New York, NY: Routledge.

Hardy, C. and Leiba-O'Sullivan, S. (1998) 'The power behind empowerment: Implications for research and practice', *Human Relations*, 51: 451–85.

Harvey, L. (1998) 'Visibility, silencing and surveillance in an IT needs analysis project', in T. Larsen, L. Levine and J. DeGross (eds), *Information Systems: Current Issues and Future Challenges*, Amsterdam: North-Holland.

Hayles, K. (1999) *How We Became Posthuman*, Chicago, IL: University of Chicago Press.

Heidegger, M. (1977) *'The Question Concerning Technology' and Other Essays*, New York, NY: Harper and Row.

Herman, A. (1997) *The Idea of Decline in Western History*, New York, NY: Free Press.

Honneth, A. (1993) *The Critique of Power: Reflective Stages in a Critical Social Theory*, Cambridge, MA: MIT Press.

Howarth, D. (2000) *Discourse*, Buckingham: Open University Press.

Hoy, D. and McCarthy, T. (1994) *Critical Theory*, Oxford: Blackwell.

Introna, L. (1997) *Management, Information and Power*, London: Palgrave.

Introna, L. D. (2001) 'Truth and its politics: Evolving regimes of truth at the *MISQ*', in D. Howcroft and A. Adam (eds), *(Re)Defining Critical Research in Information Systems, Proceedings of the CRIS Workshop*, Salford: University of Salford, pp. 45–55.

Introna, L. (2003) 'Disciplining information systems: Truth and its regimes', *European Journal of Information Systems*, 12: 235–40.

Jones, C. and Porter, R. (1994) *Reassessing Foucault: Power, Medicine and the Body*, London: Routledge.

Katz, S. (2001) 'Michel Foucault', in A. Elliott and B. Turner (eds), *Profiles in Social Theory*, London: Sage.

Kelly, M. (ed.) (1994) *Critique and Power: Recasting the Foucault/Habermas Debate*, Cambridge, MA: MIT Press.

Kendall, G. and Wickham, G. (1999) *Using Foucault's Methods*, London: Sage.

Knights, D. (1990) 'Subjectivity, power and the labour process', in D. Knights and H. Willmott (eds), *Labour Process Theory*, London: Macmillan.

Knights, D. (1995) 'Refocusing the case study: The politics of research and researching politics in IT management', *Technology Studies*, 2(2): 230–54.

Knights, D. and Murray, F. (1994) *Managers Divided: Organizational Politics and Information Technology Management*, Chichester: John Wiley & Sons.

Knights, D., Murray, F. and Willmott, H. (1997) 'Networking as knowledge work: A study of strategic interorganizational development in the financial service industry', in B. Bloomfield, R. Coombs, D. Knights and D. Littler (eds), *Information Technology and Organizations*, Oxford: Oxford University Press.

Knights, D. and Vurdubakis, T. (1994) 'Foucault, power, resistance and all that', in J. Jermier, D. Knights and W. Nord (eds), *Resistance and Power in Organizations*, London: Routledge.

Kritzman, L. (ed.) (1988) *Foucault, M: Politics, Philosophy, Culture: Interviews and Other Writings 1977–1984*, New York, NY: Routledge, Chapman and Hall.

Latour, B. (1994) 'On technical mediation: Philosophy, sociology, genealogy', *Common Knowledge*, 3(2): 29–64.

Lyon, D. (1988) *The Information Society: Issues and Illusions*, Cambridge: Polity Press.

Lyon, D. (1993) 'An electronic panopticon? A sociological critique of surveillance society', *Sociological Review*, 41(4): 653–78.

Lyon, D. (1994) *The Electronic Eye: The Rise of Surveillance Society*, Cambridge: Polity Press.

Lyon, D. (ed.) (2003) *Surveillance as Social Sorting*, London: Routledge.

Lyon, D. and Zureik, E. (eds) (1996) *Computers, Surveillance and Privacy*, Minneapolis, MN: University of Minnesota Press.

Macey, D. (1993) *The Lives of Michel Foucault*, London: Verso.

McCarthy, T. (1991) *Ideals and Illusions: On Reconstruction and Deconstruction in Contemporary Critical Theory*, Cambridge, MA: MIT Press.

McKinley, A. and Starkey, K. (eds) (1998) *Foucault, Management and Organization Theory*, London: Sage.

McNay, L. (1994) *Foucault: A Critical Introduction*, Cambridge: Polity Press.

Merquior, J. (1985) *Foucault*, London: Fontana.

Miller, J. (1993) *The Passion of Foucault*, London: HarperCollins.

Mills, S. (2003) *Michel Foucault*, London: Routledge.

Morgan, G. and Willmott, H. (1993) 'The "new" accounting research: On making accounting more visible', *Accounting, Audibility and Accountability Journal*, 6(4): 3–36.

Mowshowitz, A. (1996) 'Social control and the network market place', in D. Lyon and E. Zureik (eds), *Computers, Surveillance and Privacy*, Minneapolis, MN: University of Minnesota Press.

Munro, I. (2000) 'Non-disciplinary power and the network society', *Organization*, 7(4): 679–95.

Orlikowski, W. (1991) 'Integrated information environment or matrix of control? The contradictory implications of information technology', *Accounting, Management and Information Technologies*, 1(1): 9–42.

Orlikowski, W. and Baroudi, J. (1991) 'Studying information technology in organizations: Research approaches and assumptions', *Accounting, Management and Information Technologies*, 2(1): 1–29.

Poster, M. (1984) *Foucault, Marxism and History: Mode of Production versus Mode of Information*, Cambridge: Polity Press.

Poster, M. (1990) *The Mode of Information: Poststructuralism and Social Context*, Cambridge: Polity Press.

Poster, M. (1995) *The Second Media Age*, Cambridge: Polity Press.

Poster, M. (1996) 'Databases as discourse, or, Electronic interpellations', in D. Lyon and E. Zureik (eds), *Computers, Surveillance and Privacy*, Minneapolis, MN: University of Minnesota Press.

Poster, M. (2001) *What's the Matter with the Internet*, Minneapolis, MN: University of Minnesota Press.

Prado, C. (2000) *Starting with Foucault: An Introduction to Genealogy*, 2nd edn, Boulder, CO: Westview Press.

Probert, S. (1993) 'Interpretive analytics and critical information systems: A framework for analysis', in F. A. Stowell, D. West and J. G. Howell (eds), *Systems Science*, London: Plenum Press.

Quinby, L. (1999) *Millennial Seduction*, Ithaca, NY: Cornell University Press.

Rabinow, P. (ed.) (1984) *The Foucault Reader*, London: Penguin.

Reed, M. (1998) 'Organizational analysis as discourse analysis: A critique', in D. Grant, T. Keenoy and C. Oswick (eds), *Discourse and Organization*, London: Sage.

Robins, K. and Webster, F. (1999) *Times of the Technoculture: From the Information Society to the Virtual Life*, London: Routledge.

Sawicki, J. (1994) 'Foucault, feminism and questions of identity', In G. Gutting (ed.), *The Cambridge Companion to Foucault*, Cambridge: Cambridge University Press.

Scott Morton, M. (ed.) (1991) *The Corporation of the 1990s*, New York, NY: Oxford University Press.

Scranton, P. (1995) 'Determinism and indeterminacy in the history of technology', in M. Smith and L. Marx (eds), *Does Technology Drive History?* Cambridge, MA: MIT Press.

Sewell, G. and Wilkinson, B. (1992) ' "Someone to watch over me" surveillance: Discipline and the just-in-time labour process', *Sociology*, 26(2): 271–89.

Smart, B. (2002) *Michel Foucault*, revd edn, London: Routledge.

Sofoulis, Z. (2002) 'Cyberquake: Haraway's manifesto', in D. Tofts, A. Jonson and A. Cavallaro (eds), *Prefiguring Cyberculture: An Intellectual History*, Cambridge, MA: MIT Press.

Tallis, R. (1997) *Enemies of Hope: A Critique of Contemporary Pessimism*, Basingstoke: Macmillan.

Tinker, T. (1998) 'Hamlet without the prince: The ethnographic turn in information systems research', *Accounting, Auditing and Accountability Journal*, 11(1): 13–33.

Townley, B. (1993) 'Foucault, power/knowledge and its relevance for human resource management', *Academy of Management Review*, 18(3): 518–45.

Virilio, P. (2002) *Ground Zero*, London: Verso.

Walton, R. (1989) *Up and Running*, Boston, MA: Harvard Business School Press.

Webster, F. (1995) *Theories of the Information Society*, London: Routledge.

Webster, K. and Robins, K. (1993) ' "I'll be watching over you": Comment on Sewell and Wilkinson', *Sociology*, 27(2): 243–52.

Willcocks, L. (1989) 'Book Review of "In the Age of the Smart Machine" ', *Journal of Information Technology*, 4(2): 115–16.

Willcocks, L. and Mason, D. (1987) *Computerising Work: People, Systems Design and Workplace Relations*, London: Paradigm.

Winokur, M. (2003) 'The ambiguous panopticon: Foucault and the codes of cyberspace', *CTheory.Net*, March: 1–29.

Zuboff, S. (1988) *In the Age of the Smart Machine: The Future of Work and Power*, New York, NY: Basic Books.

8
Structuration Theory and Information Systems: A Critical Reappraisal

Matthew Jones, Wanda Orlikowski and Kamal Munir

This chapter discusses the contribution of Anthony Giddens' *structuration theory* in the context of information systems (IS) research. Giddens is one of the most widely cited contemporary social theorists (Bryant and Jary, 2001). His structuration theory, elaborated in four main books published between 1976 and 1984, has been notably influential. Structuration theory, however, is just one part of Giddens' prolific output. Since 1971 he has published more than 30 books and is reported to see all these works as elements of a single continuous project (Bryant and Jary, 2001). This chapter will therefore seek to consider structuration theory in the context of these other writings, rather than, as has generally been the case in the IS literature, treating it in isolation.

After briefly outlining the main themes of Giddens' major works and the way in which these have been used in the IS literature, we discuss his theoretical contributions in more detail, especially as these relate to IS research. A number of aspects of this contribution are then critically reviewed. We discuss the implications of structuration theory for IS research and of the possible future contribution of Giddens' work in the IS field. The chapter concludes with a discussion of how structuration theory is now moving beyond IS and beginning to be recognized as a powerful perspective within the larger technology management field.

A BRIEF OUTLINE OF GIDDENS' WRITINGS

Giddens' first books, *Capitalism and Modern Social Theory: An Analysis of the Works of Marx, Weber and Durkheim* (1971) and *The Class Structure of Advanced Societies* (1973), were, as their titles suggest, critical assessments of classic sociological writings. It was not until the publication of *New Rules of Sociological Method* (1976, 2nd edn 1993) that Giddens began to set out his own theoretical synthesis, structuration theory, subsequently elaborated in *Central Problems in Social Theory* (1979), *A Contemporary Critique of Historical Materialism* (1981, 2nd edn 1994) and *The Constitution of Society* (1984) (hereafter referred to as *NRSM, CPST, CCHM* and *CS*, respectively). Structuration is a general theory of social organization and has a primarily ontological focus. In other words, 'it tells us what sort of things are out there in the world, not what is happening to or between them' (Craib, 1992, p. 108). Urry (1982) identifies it as one of a number of similar theories, including those of Bourdieu (1977) and Bhaskar (1979), arising out of the social constructivism of Berger and Luckmann (1979).

The next major strand of Giddens' work was his analysis of the changing character of modernity, explored in *The Consequences of Modernity* (1990), *Modernity and Self-Identity* (1991) and *The Transformation of Intimacy* (1993) (hereafter referred to as *CM, MSI* and *TI*, respectively). Initially this sought to address changes at the societal level, in particular proposing that many of the trends being characterized as 'postmodern' could be seen as representing an intensification of modernity, and best understood as high or radical modernity. Later, the focus shifted more to the individual level, exploring the effects of these developments on personal identity. These ideas were subsequently developed—in response to Ulrich Beck's concept of the risk society (Beck, 1992)—in Giddens' contribution to *Reflexive Modernization* (Beck, Giddens and Lash, 1994) and in his 1999 Reith Lectures for the British Broadcasting Corporation, published as *Runaway World* (1999). The globalization theme explored in these lectures was further developed in *On the Edge: Living with Global Capitalism* (Hutton and Giddens, 2001) (hereafter referred to as *RM* and *RW* and *OE*, respectively).

Since the mid-1990s, Giddens has become increasingly engaged in practical politics, serving as an adviser to the British government from 1997 and emerging as a leading figure in the Third Way debate, which sought a new alternative for radical politics. These ideas have been discussed in his books *Beyond Left and Right* (1994),

The Third Way (1998) and *The Third Way and Its Critics* (2000) (hereafter referred to as *BLR*, *TW* and *TW&C*, respectively).

Giddens and IS Research

Giddens is one of the most widely cited social theorists in IS research (Jones, 2000). A recent survey (Jones and Karsten, 2003), for example, identified more than 350 articles in the IS field that had cited Giddens since 1986, of which more than 250 included significant discussion of his work. To put this in perspective, however, it should be recognized that this constitutes only a few percent of the articles published in leading IS journals and conferences over that period and Giddens' work therefore represents a rather specialized interest in the IS field.

The first references to Giddens in the IS field appeared in the late 1980s—somewhat after citations in organizational sociology (e.g. Manning, 1982) and organizational studies (e.g. Ranson, Hinings and Greenwood, 1981)—in the work of Poole and colleagues (e.g. Poole, Seibold and McPhee, 1985). This work was subsequently developed into a specifically IS-oriented version of structuration theory, called adaptive structuration theory (AST; Poole and DeSanctis, 1990, 1992). Two other prominent strands of IS research making early use of structuration theory were those of Walsham and colleagues (e.g. Walsham & Han, 1991; Walsham, 1993) and Orlikowski (e.g. Orlikowski & Robey, 1991; Orlikowski, 1992; Orlikowski & Yates, 1994).

Over the course of the 1990s, there emerged a growing body of IS research drawing on Giddens' work, especially structuration theory, about a third of which was AST research. Most work was published in the English language literature (although this included a significant contribution from Scandinavian researchers). Recently, however, structuration theory has also begun to attract attention in the Francophone IS literature (e.g. DeVaujany, 2000). Giddens' other writings, in contrast, have attracted only a small number of IS studies and his recent political writings, so far at least, do not appear to have been drawn on by IS researchers.

Thus, Giddens remains a relatively little-known force among IS researchers (social theory would appear to be a minority interest in the field as a whole). And when researchers do use his work, they usually draw on structuration theory, leaving aside the rest of his theoretical contributions. Moreover, much of the discussion of

Giddens within the IS field, while perhaps including one or two citations to his original work, is often concerned with debates based on secondary literature, such as AST or the positions taken by Walsham or Orlikowski. In order to appreciate the implications of this selective use of Giddens' ideas, it would first seem necessary to consider the full range of his theoretical contributions in more depth.

THEORETICAL CONTRIBUTIONS

Despite the fact that the interest of most IS researchers is focused on structuration theory, a familiarity with the various strands of Giddens' work is useful for a better understanding of his point of view. Accordingly, in this section we describe the different theoretical contributions made by Giddens, beginning with structuration theory but not being limited to it.

Structuration Theory

As Giddens describes in *NRSM*, structuration represents an attempt to develop a middle way between two competing traditions in sociology. On the one hand there is the tradition of 'naturalistic' sociology (*NRSM*(2), p. 1), sometimes referred to as positivism and exemplified by Parsonian functionalism (see Chapter 2). This tradition sees social phenomena as manifesting the operation of relatively enduring social laws by which objective, external social structures act on relatively passive human agents. On the other hand, there is the interpretive tradition of phenomenology, ethnomethodology and post-Wittgensteinian language philosophy that regards social structures as largely epiphenomenal, seeing society as primarily an effect of human agency.

For Giddens, naturalism is 'strong on structure, but weak on action' (*NRSM*(2), p. 4) and erroneously attributes purposes, reasons and needs to society rather than to individuals. Interpretive sociology, in contrast, is 'strong on action, but weak on structure' (*NRSM*(2), p. 4), having little to say on issues of 'constraint, power and large-scale social organisation' (*NRSM*(2), p. 4; see also Chapter 4). In structuration theory, therefore, Giddens sought to transcend the limitations of this unsatisfactory dualism by proposing that structure and human agency should rather be understood as a mutually constitutive duality. As he puts it:

While not made by any single person, society is created and recreated afresh, if not *ex nihilo*, by the participants in every social encounter. The production of society is a skilled performance sustained and 'made to happen' by human beings. (*NRSM*(2), p. 20)

Below we describe some key constructs underlying structuration theory.

Structure

In order to support this position Giddens adopts a characteristic, and often idiosyncratic, terminology, one of the key features of which is his treatment of structure (*CPST*, p. 66), as shown in Table 8.1.

Structure is 'both medium and outcome of the reproduction of practices' (*CPST*, p. 69), a continuous ongoing process rather than a static property of social systems. It is also 'a "virtual order" of transformative relations. . . that exists, as time–space presence, only in its instantiations in [reproduced social] practices and as memory traces orienting the conduct of knowledgeable human agents' (*CS*, p. 17). Social actors may not be fully aware of their knowledgeability, Giddens argues, as it may include 'unconscious sources of cognition' (*CPST*, p. 5) and practical consciousness, embodied in what actors know 'about how to "go on" in the multiplicity of contexts of social life' (Giddens, 1983) in addition to the partial explanations they may be able to offer from discursive consciousness (*CS*, p. 7).

Despite this knowledgeability, however, the unacknowledged conditions and unintended consequences of actions mean that social actors are never wholly in control. Thus 'the production or constitution of society is a skilled accomplishment of its members, but one that does not take place under conditions that are either wholly intended or wholly comprehended by them' (*NRSM*(2),

Table 8.1 *Giddens: some basic concepts*

Structure	Rules and resources, organized as properties of systems. Structure only exists as 'structural properties'.
System	Reproduced relations between actors or collectivities, organized as regular social practices.
Structuration	Conditions governing the continuity or transformation of structures, and therefore the reproduction of systems.

p. 108). In consequence, Giddens argues that universal laws in the social sciences are 'markedly implausible' (*CS*, p. 345) if not impossible. Social generalizations can therefore, at best, only be 'historical'; that is, temporally and spatially circumscribed.

Another implication of the ongoing production and reproduction of social structure is that human beings are necessarily in a constant state of reflexive monitoring of their situation rather than being the 'cultural' or 'structural dopes' (*CPST*, p. 52) implied by traditional views of structure. They may not always be aware of this, however, as their knowledge may be practical rather than discursive. Therefore, 'every member of society must know... a great deal about the workings of that society by virtue of his or her participation in it' (*CPST*, p. 250). Giddens argues that this awareness leads to a 'double hermeneutic' whereby the concepts observable in social settings are meaningful to the actors and can themselves become elements of the actors' understanding of their own condition. For example, an IS manager encountering the concept of 'communities of practice' in *Harvard Business Review* (Wenger and Snyder, 2000) may come to identify such communities in her or his organization and perhaps seek to encourage them.

For analytical purposes Giddens identifies three dimensions of structure, which he terms signification, domination and legitimation, drawing on the work of Durkheim, Marx and Weber respectively. These dimensions interact with human actions of communication, power and sanctions through *modalities* of, respectively, interpretive schemes, facilities and norms, as shown in Figure 8.1.

These concepts may be illustrated by considering the example of a university. While a university may have existed for centuries, how it

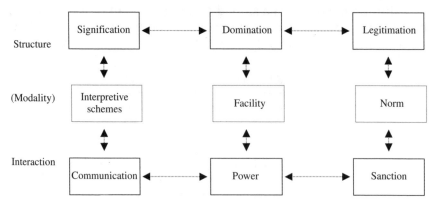

Figure 8.1   *The dimensions of the duality of structure (after Giddens, 1984, p. 29)*

operates today depends on the practices of its current members, who may continue or change its historical traditions, routines and conventions. The university may be conceived as involving structures of domination, for example it may have rights to confer degrees, perhaps backed by law, or rights to set terms for admission or student conduct based on established internal governance procedures. Viewed in terms of structures of legitimation, there may be particular modes of teaching and assessment that are seen as appropriate to university education, while structures of signification may include academic dress, seals, crests, modes of discourse, typical building forms, such as the quadrangle, that characterize the specific institution, and universities as a whole. These structures are sustained or can be altered by the day-to-day actions of those involved in contemporary university life. Thus new universities may be created; existing university bodies may approve new degrees and modify or abolish old ones; admissions or disciplinary procedures may be applied or amended in the light of changing circumstances; new means of teaching or assessment, for example to develop e-learning opportunities, may be introduced; new universities may adopt, or adapt, traditional symbols of academia.

The university thus exists through the actions of its members, but these actions are shaped by university life. The buildings or charters conferring rights to grant degrees therefore do not, of themselves, make the university; the buildings could be converted to other uses or the charters become documents of only historical interest. At the same time, being part of a university influences the sorts of activities in which people engage, such as admitting, teaching and assessing, although the particular form that these take may change over time as a result of the actions of those members.

Rules and resources

As the above definitions suggest, rules and resources play an important role in structuration theory. Giddens distinguishes (*CS*, pp. 17–23) between his concept of 'rules of social life [which are] techniques or generalisable procedures applied in the enactment/reproduction of social practices' and the more familiar types of 'formulated rules', such as those of a game or a bureaucracy, which are 'codified interpretations of rules rather than rules as such' (*CS*, p. 21). As an example of his view of rules Giddens proposes a mathematical formula such as $a_n = n^2 + n - 1$, not because 'social life can be reduced to a set of mathematical principles' (*CS*,

p. 20), but because the formula provides a rule for how to carry on in any given situation (n). An individual may also be able to state the formula without understanding its meaning or observe a sequence of numbers that obey it without being able to describe the principle involved.

With respect to resources, Giddens distinguishes between two types: allocative, which involve 'transformative capacity generating command over objects, goods or material phenomena', and authoritative, which involve 'transformative capacity generating command over persons or actors' (*CS*, p. 33). In keeping with Giddens' view of the virtual character of structure, even material allocative resources (such as land) which 'might seem to have a "real existence"... become resources only when incorporated within processes of structuration' (*CS*, p. 33).

Agency

Along with his virtual view of structure Giddens adopts a strongly voluntarist view of human agency, arguing that 'the seed of change is there in every act which contributes towards the reproduction of any "ordered" form of social life' (*NRSM*(2), p. 108). Unless they have been drugged and manhandled by others, human agents always 'have the possibility of doing otherwise' (Giddens, 1989, p. 258). This is combined with a relational model of power, based on a dialectic of control, whereby the operation of power relies on the compliance of others. Power is thus seen as being instantiated in action rather than being a type of act, or a resource to be drawn on, and all sanctions, no matter how oppressive and comprehensive, even the threat of death, carry no weight without the acquiescence of those threatened with them (*CS*, p. 175).

Time, Space and Routines

Structuration theory's view of society as being constantly produced or reproduced in every social encounter gives it a particular perspective on time, seeing the stability of social phenomena as being as much in need of explanation as change. This includes a focus on regularity, as routinization is 'vital both to the continuity of the personality of the agent... and to the institutions of society, which are such only through their continued reproduction' (*CS*, p. 60). Routines thus provide ontological security for the individual and sustain social structure.

For Giddens, temporality is therefore 'integral to social theory' (*CPST*, p. 198). Three 'planes' of temporality are identified as significant in understanding social phenomena: the *durée* of daily life, the finite life span of an individual and the *longue durée* of institutions (*CS*, p. 35). The first and last of these are described by Giddens as 'reversible', being characterized by routine and repetition, whereas the second has an inevitable and irreversible direction.

Space is also seen to be closely linked to time. Thus

> the 'problem of order' in the theory of structuration is the problem of how it comes about that social systems bind time and space, incorporating and integrating presence and absence. This, in turn, is closely related to the problematic of time–space distanciation: the 'stretching' of social systems across time–space. (*CS*, p. 181)

Two types of such integration are identified: social, defined as 'reciprocity between actors in conditions of co-presence', and system (in the sense defined above), that is 'reciprocity between actors or collectivities across extended time–space' (*CS*, p. 28). As time–space is zoned in routinized social practices it is regionalized, with certain spaces becoming associated with particular activities.

Radical Modernity

Giddens' subsequent work has received less attention in the IS or management (Whittington, 1992) literatures. An important strand of this work was initiated in *CM*, which sought to understand social developments at the start of the 1990s as a form of radicalized, reflexive or 'high' modernity, rather than then-fashionable postmodernity. In contrast to premodern societies, Giddens argues, time has becoming increasingly separated from space. For example, the daily routine once based on the apparent movement of the sun at a particular place has become oriented to a common, abstract and standardized world time. Space is also separated from place, as the shared settings of face-to-face, premodern interactions are replaced by interactions across large distances, often mediated by information and communication technologies. Social relations are thus disembedded, 'lifted out' of specific contexts and restructured 'across indefinite spans of time–space' (*CM*, p. 21), contributing to the globalizing character of modernity. Two particular disembedding mechanisms are discussed: 'abstract systems' of symbolic tokens, such as money; and 'expert systems', which have quite a different meaning from that familiar in the IS literature. These latter are 'systems of technical accomplishment or professional expertise' (*CM*, p. 27) such as those involved in building construction or in medical diagnosis. Giddens argues that individuals cannot hope to acquire the specialized expertise needed to understand how these 'expert systems' work, but must nevertheless trust in their enduring and generalized efficacy.

He further argues that another feature of modernity contributing to globalization is reflexivity. This is similar to the double hermeneutic discussed earlier, whereby theoretical knowledge about social practices comes to be drawn on in their reproduction. While the appropriation of this knowledge may be unevenly distributed within society, it does not necessarily have a fixed relationship to changes in values or outcomes. Unintended consequences mean that reflexivity is not always associated with more effective social action. Social knowledge also reenters and transforms its own subject. IS managers introduced to 'communities of practice' may identify informal work groups in their organizations of which they had not previously been aware and change their practice to support these.

While in *CM* Giddens discusses changes at the societal level (albeit with implications for the individual), in *MSI* he focuses more on how modernity promotes a 'reflexivity of the self' that is seen as contributing to existential anxiety about the nature of being, finitude and human life, the experience of others and the continuity of self-identity. Thus 'the self forms a trajectory of development from the past to the anticipated future' (*MSI*, p. 75) that provides a coherent and meaningful narrative of personal identity. Electronic media are seen to have a role in contributing to a 'collage effect', whereby news about the world becomes a patchwork of unconnected events not linked to any particular sense of place, and to the increasing intrusion of distant events into everyday life. They are also identified as contributing to the plurality of lifestyle choices that individuals face. Giddens further develops the personal dimension in *TI*, by discussing how modernity transforms the domain of sexuality, love and eroticism, giving rise to a decentred, 'plastic sexuality' that can be moulded as a trait of personality.

The Risk Society

The changing character of risk and trust explored in Beck's *Risk Society* (1992, but originally published in German in 1986) are a significant element of Giddens' writings on modernity, although these connections are more explicitly drawn in *RM*. Framed in the form of a debate with Ulrich Beck and Scott Lash about the contingency and reflexivity of the 'global society', Giddens argues that a major factor in creating these conditions has been the growth of human knowledge. This has given rise to 'institutional reflexivity', the routine incorporation of new knowledge into contexts of action that thereby reconstitutes them. In consequence there is a new agenda for social science concerning two, linked domains of transformation: the increasing temporal and spatial spread of modern institutions, universalized through processes of globalization, and the radicalization of modernity through the disinterring and problematizing of tradition.

An opportunity to develop these ideas for a popular audience arose when Giddens was invited by the British Broadcasting Corporation (BBC) to give the 1999 Reith Lectures. Conscious of the timing of these lectures at the end of the twentieth century, Giddens presented a broad analysis of global change under five headings: globalization, risk, tradition, family and democracy. These were later published as *RW*, subtitled 'how globalization is changing our lives'. The subject was also the focus of Giddens' most recent work, *OE*, a collection of essays on the transformations associated with global capitalism by, among others, Ulrich Beck, Manuel Castells and Arlie Hochschild.

The Third Way

In his remarks on reflexive modernization, Giddens pays particular attention to the changing character of politics and to the importance of democracy in different social contexts. These themes are further developed in *BLR*, in which he proposes a framework for radical politics linked to globalization, the emergence of a posttraditional social order and social reflexivity. Arguing that socialism is moribund and neoliberalism internally contradictory, he advocates a new politics for the late twentieth century. This project later became part of the so-called Third Way debate, championed by British Prime Minister Tony Blair and US President Bill Clinton, which sought to define a new future for social democracy in response to the twin revolutions of globalization and the knowledge economy. With his influential contributions (*TW* and *TW&C*), Giddens was seen as the one of the debate's leading figures. This identification was reinforced by his growing personal engagement with practical politics, acting as an adviser (or, as the cover of *TW&C* puts it, 'guru') to Blair.

A CRITICAL ASSESSMENT OF GIDDENS' WORK

As can be seen from the foregoing description of Giddens' contributions, his work provides an ambitious and wide-ranging analysis of contemporary society and social practices. While much of this may seem to address high-level theoretical matters that would appear to have little direct relevance to IS research, many of the issues addressed by Giddens touch on questions that are highly significant to the understanding of information systems as 'social systems which rely, to a greater and greater extent, on new technology for their operation' (Hirschheim and Boland, 1985, p. viii). In this section we provide a critical assessment of Giddens' conceptualization of the following issues, particularly as they relate to IS research:

- Materialism, concerning his consideration of material technologies in structuration theory.
- Voluntarism, concerning his treatment of the limits, or lack of them, on human agency.
- Time, concerning his concept of reversible time and time–space distanciation.
- Scope of application, concerning his predominant focus on social practices in western industrialized countries.
- Interest in IT, concerning his lack of specific attention to technology.
- Attitude to empirical research, concerning his primary interest in theory.

Materialism

Perhaps the most significant difficulty from an IS perspective is Giddens' anti-objectivist stance (Layder, 1987). His insistence that, from a structurational perspective, the 'real existence' of material 'allocative resources' is merely apparent, and that structure is 'a "virtual order" of transformative relations... that exists, as time–space presence, only in its instantiations in... practices and as memory traces... of knowledgeable human agents' (*CS*, p. 17), would seem a major stumbling block for a research field in which the study of social phenomena related to certain sorts of material artifacts, namely information technology, is a defining feature. For writers such as Berg (1998, p. 466), coming from an actor network theory perspective, therefore, structurational analysts unduly privilege human agency, causing 'technology to vanish from their accounts, appearing only as an occasion for structuring, without any activity or specificity of its own' (see also Chapter 9).

While Layder (1987) argues that Giddens' anti-objectivism is both problematic and theoretically unnecessary, from an IS perspective it does mean that any attempt to present structures as being 'embedded in', 'instantiated in' or otherwise existing in technology in some way is inconsistent with structuration theory. At least as Giddens presents it, this would be to objectify structure, to remove it from the minds and actions of social actors, and thereby to fix one half of an inseparable, dynamic and mutually constitutive duality.

A further implication of Giddens' position is that the effects of material artifacts on social practices are wholly dependent on the knowledgeability of social actors. While Giddens recognizes that this may involve unconscious sources of cognition and practical consciousness as well as actors' discursive explanations, material artifacts are only influential on social practices to the extent that actors' knowledgeability is instantiated in their practices. If actors are not knowledgeable about these effects, or their knowledge of these effects is mistaken, they have no independent influence on actors' practices. For example, lacking knowledge of the particular functionality provided by an application may mean that an individual may not use it for an activity for which it would be well suited.

The Layder critique is based on a critical realist position (see Chapter 10). This adopts a transformational model of social action that bears a number of similarities with structuration theory. Thus Bhaskar (1979) argues that social structures, unlike natural structures, do not exist independently of the activities they govern or of the agents' conceptions of what they are doing in the activity, and that social structures may be only relatively enduring (i.e. they may not be time–space invariant). Critical realism, however, argues that social structure necessarily precedes, and may be relatively autonomous of, action and that the two cannot therefore be mutually constitutive (Archer, 1995). This permits the possibility that structures may be influenced by material conditions in a more direct way than structuration theory allows and that these influences may not depend entirely on social actors' knowledge of them. These ideas are elaborated in the discussion of Bhaskar in Chapter 10 of this volume and will therefore not be pursued in detail here. What they indicate, however, is that analyses of the social influence of material artifacts may need to look to sources other than merely Giddens.

Voluntarism

A related issue with structuration theory is Giddens' treatment of agency. Viewing agency as the 'capacity to make a difference' and arguing that, apart from in quite exceptional circumstances, social actors always have the possibility to do otherwise, Giddens suggests that structure is never a binding constraint on action, but simply places 'limits upon the feasible range of options open to an actor in a given circumstance' (*CS*, p. 177). Structure is therefore always enabling as well as constraining.

Giddens' critics argue, however, that his equation of agency with action is problematic on at least two grounds. First, while defining agency as a capability for action may be necessary from a structurational perspective to explain its duality with structure, it does not mean that all agential effects are the products of activity. For example, Archer (1995) notes the effect of increasing numbers of students in a class on their educational experience—irrespective of their 'ability to do otherwise'—while Harré (1983) suggests that in well-ordered institutions, such as monasteries, social rules may dominate social reproduction and that individual structurational agency is thus insignificant or even absent (although by choosing to stay in class or in a monastery, the individuals can be said to exercise some agency).

Secondly, it is argued that structures may restrict agents' choices far more than Giddens suggests. Archer (1990), for example, proposes that individuals, such as a landless peasant at the start of the capitalist era, effectively had only one feasible option if they wished to survive, to sell their labour power. There may thus be a 'differentiated (and thus limited) topography for the exercise of agency rather than an endlessly recursive plain' (Storper, 1985, p. 419). Hence, as Layder (1985, p. 146) argues, structural power is 'not simply a negotiable outcome of routine and concrete interactions and relationships' in a specific context. Of particular relevance from an IS perspective, moreover, Barbalet (1987) proposes that material existents may be social structural resources in power relations, while Storper (1985) suggests that 'the *durée* of the material, although not imposing absolute constraints on system change, does mean that at any moment not everything is possible'. For example, the potential for video-on-demand services is likely to be significantly constrained by the available bandwidth.

Time

In *Time in Social Theory*, Adam (1990), while acknowledging the attention that Giddens pays to time, is critical of his claims for the reversibility of social time, either at the level of day-to-day existence or of institutions. Rather than the repetition of daily routine removing time, she argues—citing Heraclitus, who observed that we can never step in the same river twice—repetition always occurs in an evolving context. Similarly, to suggest that the role of institutions in the repetition of social practices makes these phenomena timeless is to misrepresent their emergent character. Bergmann (1992) and Nowotny (1992) have argued similarly that Giddens pays insufficient attention to the ongoing construction of temporality and is thus unable to see it as 'emerging from inter-subjective action' (Nowotny, 1992, p. 430).

Adam also criticizes Giddens' treatment of the linkage between power and time–space distanciation, arguing that his analysis is only meaningful for such societies as the contemporary industrial one, in which time is separated from the activities of social life and treated as an abstract, independent and quantifiable entity. For societies lacking such an objectified conceptualization, the idea of time–space distanciation as a measure of a society's 'stretching over time' makes no sense.

Scope of Application

Adams' comments reflect a broader criticism of the limited scope of application of Giddens' ideas. Strongly rooted in the traditions of European and American sociology, Giddens' theorizing is predominantly focused on the issues confronting these societies. While his more recent interest in globalization has broadened the scope of his analysis, this is still oriented towards the global spread of 'western' social practices, with other societies being treated as the 'traditional' setting on which these developments are encroaching. This is particularly evident in contrasting *Runaway World* with a work such as Manuel Castells' *Rise of the Networked Society* (Castells, 1996). While admittedly written for quite different purposes, Castells' study draws extensively, if not unproblematically, on empirical analysis of issues in a range of different global regions, often in cooperation with local experts. In comparison, Giddens' analyses of a few topics in a narrower range of settings appear limited. This contrast appears all the starker when set against the depth and subtlety of Giddens' analysis of contemporary industrial society.

Interest in Information Technology

Until he began discussing modernity in the early 1990s, Giddens had paid almost no attention to technology in his writings. Even then, in his discussion of time–space distanciation, disembedding, globalization and reflexive modernization—developments in which information technology might be seen as having had an important influence—it received few explicit references. Only in the most recent works, *TW&C* and *OE*, is there more than a single index entry to information technology, and then largely in the context of the knowledge economy.

Giddens' treatment of information technology in these recent works is surprisingly superficial and, as the introduction to *OE* puts it, very much on the side of the 'Gee-Whizzers'. The 'information revolution', he argues for example, is 'forcing the restructuring of the whole of the capitalist economy' (*OE*, p. 20),

> information and knowledge have now become the media of production, now displacing many forms of manual work... the trading of information and knowledge is the very essence of the global financial system... the dematerialised economy is also a world of images... products are defined according to the image they conjure in the mind of the consumer. (*OE*, p. 22)

Such arguments are unlikely to satisfy researchers in IS, many of whom have long argued against such technologically deterministic claims.

Attitude to Empirical Research

First and foremost, Giddens is a theorist. Where he draws on empirical evidence, it is usually in the form of secondary analysis of studies such as *Learning to Labour* (Willis, 1977). This has led some critics, such as Gregson (1989), to suggest that his ideas operate at too high a level of generality to inform research in specific empirical settings. Although Giddens does provide some guidelines on what

Table 8.2 Aspects of structuration theory that impinge most generally on problems of empirical research in the social sciences (adapted from Giddens, 1984, pp. 281–4)

1.	All human beings are knowledgeable agents.
2.	The knowledgeability of human agents is always bounded on the one hand by the unconscious and on the other by unacknowledged conditions/unintended consequences of action.
3.	The study of day-to-day life is integral to the analysis of the reproduction of institutionalized practices.
4.	Routine, psychologically linked to the minimizing of unconscious sources of anxiety, is the predominant form of day-to-day social activity.
5.	The study of context, or of the contextualities of interaction, is inherent in the investigation of social reproduction.
6.	Social identities, and the position–practice relations associated with them, are 'markers' in the virtual time–space of structure.
7.	No unitary meaning can be given to 'constraint' in social analysis.
8.	Among the structural properties of social systems, structural principles are particularly important, since they specify overall types of society.
9.	The study of power cannot be regarded as a second-order consideration in the social sciences.
10.	There is no mechanism of social organization or social reproduction identified by social analysts that lay actors cannot also get to know about and actively incorporate into what they do.

he sees as the implications of his work for empirical research (reproduced in Table 8.2), this might seem to confirm rather than refute the charges of his critics.

While arguing that social science is 'irretrievably hermeneutic' (*NRSM*(2), p. 13), Giddens does not preclude the use of 'technically-sophisticated, hard-edged' research (Giddens, 1991b, p. 219). Indeed, in *CS* he specifically states:

> I do not try to wield a methodological scalpel... there is [nothing] in the logic or the substance of structuration theory which would somehow prohibit the use of some specific research technique, such as survey methods, questionnaires or whatever.

Instead, he suggests that 'qualitative and quantitative methods should be seen as complementary rather than antagonistic aspects of social research' (*CS*, p. 334). He argues, however, that

> the intellectual claims of sociology do not rest distinctively upon [hard-edged research]. All social research... no matter how mathematical or quantitative, presumes ethnography. (Giddens, 1991b, p. 219)

Thus, while not ruling out the use of quantitative methods, the positivist theory-testing style of research with which they are traditionally associated is inconsistent with Giddens' hermeneutic epistemology. Indeed, it is one of the 'traditions' that he specifically sought to transcend with the development of structuration theory.

This does not mean, however, that IS researchers employing Giddens in their work cannot undertake comparative studies or explore causal explanations, but that their findings cannot constitute the law-like generalizations sought by positivist researchers, since interpretation and human agency are fundamental to his position. While not being methodologically prescriptive, Giddens' epistemological and ontological stance does carry with it some important implications for the conduct of research. However, in keeping with this position, it is recognized that these can never be binding on researchers' practices.

At the same time, Giddens has stated more than once that structuration is not intended as a concrete research programme (Giddens, 1983, p. 77; 1990b, p. 310) and that his principles 'are essentially procedural and do not supply concepts useful for the actual prosecution of research' (Giddens, 1990b, p. 311). He expresses reservations about studies that 'have attempted to import structuration theory *in toto* into their given area of study', commending, rather, those 'in which concepts, either from the logical framework of structuration theory, or other aspects of my writings, are used in a sparing and critical fashion' (Giddens, 1991b, p. 213) and proposing that the appropriate role of structuration in empirical research is the use of principles derived from it as 'sensitising devices' or to 'provide an explication of the logic of research into human social activities and cultural products' (Giddens, 1991b, p. 213).

APPLICATIONS AND EXTENSIONS OF GIDDENS' WORK IN IS RESEARCH

In a recent review of Giddens' work, Bryant and Jary (2001) analysed a large number of studies (about 175 in total) throughout the social sciences and humanities that have sought to use structuration theory. They suggest that their analysis disproves the claims of Gregson (1989) that Giddens' work is irrelevant to empirical research. Bryant and Jary (2001) categorize the 175 studies into five types: studies reconstituting a discipline; studies reconstituting a specialty; studies reconstituting an interdisciplinary field; studies facilitating empirical research; and studies analysing late modernity. While this typology is not necessarily particularly helpful for the analysis of applications and extensions in IS research—most of which would probably be characterized as facilitating empirical research with a small number reconstituting a specialty or analysing late modernity—it nevertheless gives some indication of the scope and ambition of the use of Giddens' ideas and sets the current discussion in context.

Application of Structuration Theory

The largest number of studies using Giddens' ideas in the IS field have probably been those 'applying' structuration theory. In general, these seek to use structuration theory in the analysis of empirical material to provide insights into IS phenomena. Examples include Orlikowski (1993, 1996), Jones and Nandhakumar (1993), Walsham (1993), DeSanctis and Poole (1994) and Karsten (1995). A substream of this research has sought to illustrate the application of certain elements of structuration theory such as duality of power (Elkjaer *et al.*, 1991), constraint (Nandhakumar and Jones, 1998) or time–space analysis (Sahay, 1997).

While most of these studies have attempted to remain generally faithful to the ontological and epistemological assumptions of structuration theory, this may be seen as both a strength and a weakness. On the one hand, they have been able to illustrate, with perhaps varying degrees of success, some of the subtle implications of structuration theory for the analysis of IS phenomena. On the other hand, however, they have not usually found, or necessarily sought, ways to overcome some of the limitations of structuration theory noted above. Equally, the attempt to provide examples of structurational concepts has required a detailed analysis of specific empirical settings, although often more focused at the level of individuals, groups and organizations than of institutions and societies. While this last criticism is perhaps not particularly exceptional in IS research as a whole, the broad social ontology of structuration theory should perhaps encourage attention to these broader levels too.

Moreover, given that the utility of these structurational concepts for IS phenomena has now been established (assuming this is accepted to be the case), it would seem desirable that future research should seek to take the analysis further rather than simply applying them in new empirical settings.

Extension of Structuration Theory

There have been two notable attempts in the IS field to, as Bryant and Jary (2001) put it, 'reconstitut[e the] speciality': DeSanctis and Poole's adaptive structuration theory (AST) and Orlikowski's duality of technology.

Adaptive structuration theory

AST was developed in response to the perceived weaknesses of previous structurational approaches, which were seen as giving only weak consideration to IT, being exclusively focused at the institutional level and relying on purely interpretive methods (DeSanctis and Poole, 1994). Among its key propositions are that 'social structures serve as templates for planning and accomplishing tasks' and that 'designers incorporate some of these structures into the technology', thereby reproducing or modifying them, thus 'creating new structures within the technology' (DeSanctis and Poole, 1994, p. 125).

DeSanctis and Poole argue that the 'social structures provided by an advanced information technology can be described in two ways: structural features of the technology and the spirit of this feature set' (1994, p. 126). Structural features, such as voting algorithms and anonymous recording of ideas in a group decision support system, provide meaning and control, equivalent to Giddens' signification and domination dimensions. The spirit of the feature set is described as the 'general intent with regard to values and goals underlying a given set of structural features' and equated to Giddens' legitimation dimension of structuration. This 'property of a technology as it is presented to users', it is argued, can be identified by 'reading' the philosophy of the technology based on an analysis of:

(a) the design metaphor underlying the system; (b) the features it incorporates and how they are named and presented; (c) the nature of the user interface; (d) training materials and on-line guidance materials; and (e) other training or help provided with the system.

DeSanctis and Poole (1994) argue that because IT is only one source of structure for groups, analysing the use of a particular technology requires consideration of other sources of structure such as work tasks and the organizational environment.

Another important concept in AST is that of 'appropriation', drawn from Ollman's (1971) discussion of Marx's writings. In AST, appropriations are the actions taken by individuals or groups that instantiate structures. Thus the structural features of a technology may be appropriated by groups through a variety of 'appropriation moves', for example by directly using technology structures or making judgements about them. The appropriation of technology may be 'faithful' or 'unfaithful', may occur for 'different instrumental uses or purposes' and display a variety of 'attitudes' such as 'comfort', 'respect' and 'challenge'.

The aim of AST for DeSanctis and Poole is to enable the development of propositions of the form:

> *Given* advanced information technology and other sources of social structure n_1 to n_k *and* ideal appropriation processes, *and* decision processes that fit the task at hand, *then* desired outcomes of advanced information technology will result. (DeSanctis and Poole, 1994, p. 131, emphasis in original)

If group interaction processes are inconsistent with technology's structural potential, however, then the outcomes will be less predictable and generally less favourable, illustrating the 'dialectic of control between the group and the technology'.

As an influential research programme in IS, AST has both strengths and weaknesses. Its strengths lie in its introduction of powerful social theoretic ideas to explain IS phenomena and its spawning of a large number of IS research papers, especially in the area of group decision support systems (Gopal, Bostrom and Chin, 1993; Chin, Gopal and Salisbury, 1997; Chudoba, 1999; Salisbury *et al.*, 2002). Its limitations lie in some inconsistencies with the agentic character of Giddens' theory, as evident in AST's view of structures as 'embedded within technology', its identification of other independent 'sources of structure' and its concept of a dialectic of control between 'the group and the technology'.

Duality of technology

In her various writings over the years, Orlikowski has attempted to use structurational concepts to offer 'a reconstruction of the concept of technology' that provides insights into the relationship between technology and organizations (Orlikowski, 1992, p. 398). In her 1992 paper, she proposes a structurational model of technology that emphasizes two key aspects of technology in organizations:

that technology is both shaped by and shapes human action (the duality of technology); and that the interaction between people and technology is ongoing and dynamic (the interpretive flexibility of technology). With respect to the duality of technology, Orlikowski argues that technology is physically and socially constructed by human action, while also becoming reified and institutionalized within processes of structuration. The notion of duality focuses attention on the creative aspects of technological development and use, as well as on the physical and historical boundedness of any technological innovation (that is, that technologies always reflect the knowledge, materials, interests and conditions at a given point in time). With respect to interpretive flexibility, Orlikowski draws on Pinch and Bijker's (1984) work in the social construction of technology (see also Chapter 9) to define it as 'an attribute of the relationship between humans and technology' and thus as influenced by three aspects:

> characteristics of the material artifact (e.g., the specific hardware and software comprising the technology), characteristics of the human agents (e.g., skills, experiences, motivation), and characteristics of the context (e.g., social relations, task assignment, resource allocations). (Orlikowski, 1992, p. 409)

Building on this structurational model of technology, Orlikowski and Robey (1991) propose a research agenda for IS research, focusing attention particularly on the following: the social processes through which technologies are developed, implemented, used and institutionalized within organizations; the intended and unintended consequences of developing, implementing and using specific technologies; the conditions under which human actors reinforce or change the features or use habits of specific technologies; and the conditions under which human actors use technology to reproduce or transform their organizations. Subsequent work by Orlikowski applied and extended her structurational model through a number of empirical studies into the organizational use of different kinds of technologies: computer-aided software development tools (Orlikowski, 1993), electronic media (Orlikowski and Yates, 1994; Yates, Orlikowski and Okamura, 1999), and collaborative tools (Orlikowski and Gash, 1994; Orlikowski, 1996).

Orlikowski's use of structurational concepts has helped to highlight the nature and influence of human agency in technological development and use, and has emphasized the critical role of humans in shaping (whether deliberately or inadvertently) the consequences of technology use in organizational life. However, this approach has also been limited in its attention to material and broader institutional influences. While acknowledging the importance of technology's material properties, Orlikowski's treatment of such materiality remains underdeveloped. Additionally, all of her studies have been conducted within organizations and her focus has been on the micro-level interactions of actors within specific institutional settings. This has largely ignored the broader institutional influences—industrial, economic, political, global—that shape IS phenomena.

Application of Other Concepts

There has been limited use in the IS field of Giddens' other writings. Among the few exceptions, Barrett and Walsham (1995) have taken up his work on identity, and Scott (2000) his treatment of risk. As the brief description of Giddens' ideas above has sought to indicate, however, their limited application may reflect a relative lack of exposure in the IS field rather than a lack of relevance to the understanding of IS phenomena. Indeed, not only may IS research benefit from greater familiarity with Giddens' ideas on reflexive modernity and globalization, but the analysis of reflexive modernity and globalization might also benefit from a stronger appreciation of the role of information technology in these developments.

OPPORTUNITIES FOR IS RESEARCH

As this last remark indicates, Giddens' writings appear to offer considerable opportunities for future IS research. Three avenues in particular would seem especially fruitful: further development of a structurationally informed theory of IS; application of concepts from his later work on reflexive modernization and globalization; and the extension of analysis to phenomena at the institutional and societal level.

Development of a Structurationally Informed Theory of IS

Recent contributions from Jones (1998) and Orlikowski (2000) have highlighted the strengths and weaknesses of structurational analysis in understanding IS phenomena. Seeking to develop a model of the relationship between IS and social practice that gives greater weight to the material properties of information technology than has traditionally been the case in structuration theory, Jones (1998) draws on Pickering (1995) to propose a temporally emergent model of the interaction of human and machine agency, whose character is worked out in practice. Thus while the material properties of technologies, such as the speed of processors, may influence how IS are used in ways that Giddens does not account for in structuration theory, this machine agency lacks the intentionality, reflexivity and social awareness characteristic of human agency. At the same time, however, the particular forms of practice that emerge from the interaction of human and machine agency cannot be fully foreseen.

Orlikowski (2000) adopts a practice lens to propose the notion of 'technologies-in-practice' to refer to the structures of technology use enacted by social actors as they interact with particular technological artifacts over time. She proposes this approach as a way of avoiding the erroneous tendency to see technology as embodying structures, which are then appropriated by users during their use of it. Seen through a practice lens, technology structures are emergent and enacted, not embodied and appropriated. Thus rather than starting with the technology and examining how actors appropriate its embodied structures, this view starts with human action and examines how it enacts emergent structures through recurrent interaction with the technology at hand. This lens includes consideration of the material properties of technology by viewing technologies-in-practice as both shaped by and shaping the use of material artifacts.

If it is the case that these approaches provide an analysis of IS that is more consistent with Giddens' own assumptions than earlier models such as AST or the duality of technology, it is also the case that they are then subject to the same criticisms of these assumptions discussed above. Thus realists' reservations about the anti-objectivism of structuration theory, or criticisms of its neglect of structural power, may apply equally to these approaches. An alternative route to a structurationally informed theory of IS may therefore require the selective revision (on the basis of clearly articulated theoretical principles) of certain elements of Giddens' ideas to deepen insights into how IS are implicated in organizational and institutional change.

Reflexive Modernization

The acknowledged importance of information systems in the development of radical modernity would seem to provide IS researchers with a significant opportunity to contribute to contemporary sociological thinking. Thus if the discussion of these developments is to advance beyond the current rather simplistic commentaries, then detailed analysis of evidence for the phenomena and of the processes through which information systems are implicated in them would seem necessary—a task that IS researchers are well placed to undertake. Such studies, however, require a considerable expansion of the theoretical repertoire of the IS field, both to engage with the original sociological debates and to develop a critical appreciation of such concepts as globalization, risk and identity.

While a few IS researchers have made some initial steps in this direction (as mentioned earlier), this would seem deserving of greater attention, especially if, as writers such as Baskerville and Myers (2002) have suggested, the IS field is to become a producer as well as a consumer of theory. Although by no means the only nor necessarily the most effective way of promoting the field's theoretical profile, critique and extension of Giddens' work on reflexive modernization would seem both timely, in terms of its relevance to contemporary sociological debates, and appropriate, in its scope for technologically informed analysis.

Extension of Analysis to the Institutional and Societal Level

The development of a structurationally informed model of IS linked to serious engagement with debates around reflexive modernization may be seen as part of a larger opportunity for IS research to extend the boundaries of analysis in the field. Traditionally IS research has focused on phenomena associated with computer-based information systems at the individual, group and organizational level, treating broader social developments as background and excluding other technologies, despite the increasing degree to which they rely on information technology. A structurationally informed model of IS, however, might be seen as a particular case of a more general approach to the understanding of other technologies, especially where these involve significant IT-based developments such as digital imaging (Munir, 2001). Informed by an analysis of reflexive modernization, such a model of technology could also contribute to broader analyses of institutional and social change.

The field of innovation and technology management, which examines a broad range of technologies including information and communication technologies, might be a particularly valuable arena for using and extending structurational concepts. To date, the use of structuration theory in the innovation and technology management literature is quite limited. Barley's (1986) study is among the few that have actively engaged a structurational framing. In this study, Barley argues that taking a structurational approach to the technology–organization relationship avoids three inconsistencies that have plagued research on technology. First, by viewing structure as a process, and hence acknowledging its temporal dimension, researchers are forced to adopt longitudinal as well as cross-sectional perspectives on technical change. Second, given the importance of the social context of actions and interpretations, it becomes unsound practice to lump together organizations with radically different institutional histories. Finally, since technologies are given meaning through action, one is forced to take into account how a technology is incorporated into the everyday life of an organization's members. All these issues pose challenges for current research in technology and innovation management, which tends to be mostly based on large cross-sectional samples, rather than longitudinal, in-depth studies of innovation or technology use. As Barley points out, in-depth studies of a single or few organizations allow us to see the different ways in which structures can be enacted, which would otherwise be completely missed in large cross-sectional samples, where such differences would tend to cancel each other out.

Dougherty *et al.* (1998) build on Orlikowski's work (Orlikowski, 1992; Orlikowski and Yates, 1994) to examine innovativeness in several large, complex firms. They find that greater interpretive flexibility enabled organization members to link technology design and use at multiple levels of action, enhancing their ability to build, deploy and transform their technologies in response to shifting opportunities. They suggest that the greater the interpretive flexibility in the relationship between human action and the organization's technology, the more readily organization members were able to develop new products in a sustained fashion. In other work, Garud and Rappa (1994) draw on Giddens' work to offer a coevolutionary account of the relationship between the cochlear implants technology and its environment. Their focus on how changing evaluation criteria for measuring the performance of the technology changed the industry's expectations resonates with the recursive process between structure and agency suggested by structuration theory.

The field of innovation and technology management thus appears to have some parallels with the IS field, in that both have drawn on structurational concepts but both have the potential to generate important insights about relationships between technology and human actors, groups, organizations, institutions and environments. We believe that these insights would be afforded by drawing more substantially on both structuration theory and Giddens' other work more generally.

CONCLUSION

As this chapter has sought to illustrate, Giddens' work provides a rich foundation for a whole range of IS research: from studies of individual, group and organizational usage of information systems to the institutionalization of new technologies; from explorations of the temporal organization of technology-supported work practices to analysis of the role of information systems in contemporary social change. The breadth of this potential may be seen as a reflection of the primarily ontological status of much of Giddens' theorizing, the implications of which play out in many domains.

While this makes Giddens' contribution broad, it does not mean that his work is without specific implications for the nature of IS research, if it is to be consistent with the approach he puts forward. These implications are ontological and epistemological, however, rather than methodological: suggesting what information systems are and the sorts of knowledge we can have about them, not prescribing the specific research techniques by which such knowledge might be gained. In setting out these ontological and epistemological assumptions in this chapter, our aim is not to prescribe or proscribe any particular form of research, not least because we would not claim any authority to do so, but to suggest ways in which work based on Giddens' ideas may be advanced.

Finally, if IS researchers wish to engage more widely with social researchers in other domains, then the work of Giddens, connecting as it does with many contemporary debates in social theory, might be a fruitful starting point. Moreover, in exploring the extent to which his ideas can accommodate the particular issues of IS research, such as the social influence of the material character of IT, there may be opportunities for IS researchers to make significant contributions to these debates.

A GUIDE TO THE LITERATURE

IS researchers interested in Giddens should probably read at least some of his original works to appreciate the character of his writing and judge his arguments for themselves. Of these, *The Constitution of Society* is perhaps the best overview of structuration theory, although the detail of the discussion may be rather daunting. Jones (1999) has attempted a review of structuration theory in the IS context that may be rather more accessible. Bryant and Jary (2001) and Giddens and Pierson (1998) also provide some accessible commentary on structuration, although framed in terms of sociological debates.

In terms of papers using structuration in an IS setting, Barley (1986) is one of the earliest, but provides a thoughtful analysis of relevant issues. Other early papers that set the tone of the debate around structurational IS research include Orlikowski and Robey (1991), Orlikowski (1992) and, for adaptive structuration theory, DeSanctis and Poole (1994). Orlikowski (2000) provides an interesting counterpoint to the somewhat mechanistic use of structuration in these studies.

REFERENCES

Adam, B. (1990) *Time and Social Theory*, Philadelphia, PA: Temple University Press.

Archer, M. (1990) 'Human agency and social structure: A critique of Giddens', in J. Clark, C. Modgil and J. Modgil (eds), *Anthony Giddens: Consensus and Controversy*, Brighton: Falmer Press, pp. 73–84.

Archer, M. S. (1995) *Realist Social Theory: The Morphogenetic Approach*, Cambridge: Cambridge University Press.

Barbalet, J. M. (1987) 'Power, structural resources and agency', *Current Perspectives in Social Theory*, 8: 1–24.

Barley, S. R. (1986) 'Technology as an occasion for structuring: Evidence from observation of CT scanners and the social order of radiology departments', *Administrative Science Quarterly*, 31: 78–108.

Barrett, M. and Walsham, G. (1995) 'Managing IT for business innovation: Issues of culture, learning and leadership in a Jamaican insurance company', *Journal of Global Information Management*, 3(3): 25–33.

Baskerville, R. L. and Myers, M. D. (2002) 'Information systems as a reference discipline', *MIS Quarterly*, 26(1): 1–15.

Beck, U. (1992) *The Risk Society: Towards a New Modernity*, Newbury Park, CA: Sage.

Beck, U., Giddens, A. and Lash, S. (1994) *Reflexive Modernization: Politics, Tradition and Aesthetics in the Modern Social Order*, Stanford, CA: Stanford University Press.

Berg, M. (1998) 'The politics of technology: On bringing social theory into technological design', *Science, Technology and Human Values*, 23(4): 456–90.

Berger, P. L. and Luckmann, T. (1979) *The Social Construction of Reality: A Treatise in the Sociology of Knowledge*, Harmondsworth: Penguin.

Bergmann, W. (1992) 'The problem of time in sociology: An overview of the literature on the state of theory and research on the "sociology of time", 1900–82', *Time & Society*, 1(1): 81–134.

Bhaskar, R. (1979) *The Possibility of Naturalism*, Brighton: Harvester.

Bourdieu, P. (1977) *Outline of a Theory of Practice*, Cambridge: Cambridge University Press.

Bryant, C. G. A. and Jary, D. (2001) *The Contemporary Giddens*, London: Routledge.

Castells, M. (1996) *The Rise of the Networked Society*, Oxford: Oxford University Press.

Chin, W. W., Gopal, A. and Salisbury, W. D. (1997) 'Advancing the theory of adaptive structuration: The development of a scale to measure faithfulness of appropriation', *Information Systems Research*, 8(4): 342–67.

Chudoba, K. M. (1999) 'Appropriations and patterns in the use of Group Support Systems', *DATA BASE*, 30(3&4): 131–48.

Craib, I. (1992) *Anthony Giddens*, London: Routledge.

DeSanctis, G. and Poole, M. S. (1994) 'Capturing the complexity in advanced technology use: Adaptive structuration theory', *Organization Science*, 5(2): 121–47.

De Vaujany, F. X. (2000) 'Usages de l'Intranet et processus de structuration de l'organisation', *Systèmes d'Information et Management*, 5(2): 79–100.

Dougherty, D., Borrelli, L., Munir, K. and O'Sullivan, A. (1998) 'The interpretive flexibility of technology and organizing for innovation', in J. Baum (ed.), *Advances in Strategic Management, Vol. 15*, Connecticut: JAI Press.

Elkjaer, B., Flensburg, P., Mouritsen, J. and Willmott, H. (1991) 'The commodification of expertise: The case of systems development consulting', *Accounting, Management and Information Technologies*, 1(2): 139–56.

Garud, R. and Rappa, M. (1994) 'A socio-cognitive model of technology evolution', *Organization Science*, 5(3): 344–62.

Giddens, A. (1976) *New Rules of Sociological Method*, London: Hutchinson. 2nd edn, 1993 Cambridge: Polity.

Giddens, A. (1979) *Central Problems in Social Theory*, Basingstoke: Macmillan.

Giddens, A. (1981) *A Contemporary Critique of Historical Materialism*, Basingstoke: Macmillan. 2nd edn, 1994.

Giddens, A. (1983) 'Comments on the theory of structuration', *Journal for the Theory of Social Behaviour*, 13: 75–80.

Giddens, A. (1984) *The Constitution of Society*, Cambridge: Polity.

Giddens, A. (1989) 'A reply to my critics', in D. Held and J. B. Thompson (eds), *Social Theory of Modern Societies: Anthony Giddens and his Critics*, Cambridge: Cambridge University Press, pp. 249–301.

Giddens, A. (1990a) *The Consequences of Modernity*, Cambridge: Polity Press.

Giddens, A. (1990b) 'Structuration theory and sociological analysis', in J. Clark, C. Modgil and J. Modgil (eds), *Anthony Giddens: Consensus and Controversy*, Brighton: Falmer Press, pp. 297–315.

Giddens, A. (1991a) *Modernity and Self-Identity*, Cambridge: Polity Press.

Giddens, A. (1991b) 'Structuration theory: Past, present and future', in C. G. A. Bryant and D. Jary (eds), *Giddens' Theory of Structuration: A Critical Appreciation*, London: Routledge, pp. 201–21.

Giddens, A. (1993) *The Transformation of Intimacy: Sexuality, Love and Eroticism in Modern Societies*, Stanford, CA: Stanford University Press.

Giddens, A. (1994) *Beyond Left and Right: The Future of Radical Politics*, Stanford, CA: Stanford University Press.

Giddens, A. (1998) *The Third Way: The Renewal of Social Democracy*, Cambridge: Polity Press.

Giddens, A. (1999) *Runaway World: How Globalization is Reshaping our Lives*, New York, NY: Routledge.

Giddens, A. (2000) *The Third Way and Its Critics*, Cambridge: Polity Press.

Giddens, A. and Pierson, C. (1998) *Conversations with Anthony Giddens*, Cambridge: Polity Press.

Gopal, A., Bostrom, R. P. and Chin, W. W. (1993) 'Applying adaptive structuration theory to investigate the process of Group Support Systems use', *Journal of Management Information Systems*, 9(3): 45–69.

Gregson, N. (1989) 'On the (ir)relevance of structuration theory to empirical research', in D. Held and J. B. Thompson (eds), *Social Theory of Modern Societies: Anthony Giddens and his Critics*, Cambridge: Cambridge University Press, pp. 235–48.

Harré, R. (1983) 'Commentary from an ethogenic standpoint', *Journal for the Theory of Social Behaviour*, 13: 69–73.

Hirschheim, R. and Boland, R. (1985) 'Series forward', in R. Hirschheim, *Office Automation: A Social and Organizational Perspective*, Chichester: John Wiley & Sons.

Hutton, W. and Giddens, A. (2001) *On the Edge: Living with Global Capitalism*, London: Random House.

Jones, M. R. (1998) 'Information systems and the double mangle: Steering a course between the Scylla of embedded structure and the Charybdis of material agency', in T. Larsen, L. Levine and J. I. DeGross (eds), *Information Systems: Current Issues and Future Challenges*, Laxenburg: International Federation for Information Processing, pp. 287–302.

Jones, M. R. (1999) 'Structuration theory', in W. J. Currie and R. D. Galliers (eds), *Re-thinking Management Information Systems*, Oxford: Oxford University Press, pp. 103–35.

Jones, M. R. (2000) 'The moving finger: The use of social theory in WG8.2 conference papers, 1975–1999', in R. Baskerville, J. Stage and J. I. DeGross (eds), *Organizational and Social Perspectives on Information Technology*, Dordrecht: Kluwer Academic Publishers, pp. 15–31.

Jones, M. R. and Karsten, H. (2003) 'Review: Structuration theory and information systems research', Cambridge: Judge Institute of Management working paper.

Jones, M. R. and Nandhakumar, J. (1993) 'Structured development? A structurational analysis of the development of an Executive Information System', in D. Avison, J. E. Kendall and J. I. DeGross (eds), *Human, Organizational and Social Dimensions of Information Systems Development*, Amsterdam: North-Holland, pp. 475–96.

Karsten, H. (1995) 'Converging paths to Notes: In search of computer-based information systems in a networked company', *Information Technology and People*, 8(1): 7–34.

Layder, D. (1985) 'Power, structure and agency', *Journal for the Theory of Social Behaviour*, 15: 131–49.

Layder, D. (1987) 'Key issues in structuration theory: Some critical remarks', *Current Perspectives in Social Theory*, 8: 25–46.

Manning, P. (1982) 'Organisational work: Structuration of environments', *British Journal of Sociology*, 33(1): 118–34.

Munir, K. (2001) 'The evolution and dominance of designs: Evidence from the photographic industry', unpublished doctoral dissertation, Montreal: McGill University.

Nandhakumar, J. and Jones, M. R. (1998) 'Designing in the dark: The changing user–developer relationship in information systems development', in K. Kumar and J. I. Gross (eds), *Proceedings of the 18th ICIS*, Atlanta, GA: Association for Information Systems, pp. 75–86.

Nandhakumar, J. and Jones, M. R. (2001) 'Accounting for time: Managing time in project-based networking', *Accounting, Organizations and Society*, 26: 193–214.

Nowotny, H. (1992) 'Time and social theory: Towards a social theory of time', *Time and Society*, 1(3): 421–54.

Ollman, B. (1971) *Alienation: Marx's Conception of Man in a Capitalist Society*, Cambridge: Cambridge University Press.

Orlikowski, W. J. (1992) 'The duality of technology: Rethinking the concept of technology in organizations', *Organization Science*, 3(3): 398–427.

Orlikowski, W. J. (1993) 'CASE tools as organizational change: Investigating incremental and radical changes in systems development', *MIS Quarterly*, 17(3): 309–40.

Orlikowski, W. J. (1996) 'Improvising organizational transformation over time: A situated change perspective', *Information Systems Research*, 7(1): 63–92.

Orlikowski, W. J. (2000) 'Using technology and constituting structures: A practice lens for studying technology in organizations', *Organization Science*, 11(4): 404–28.

Orlikowski, W. J. and Gash, D. C. (1994) 'Technological frames: Making sense of information technology in organizations', *ACM Transactions on Information Systems*, 2(2): 174–207.

Orlikowski, W. J. and Robey, D. (1991) 'Information technology and the structuring of organizations', *Information Systems Research*, 2(2): 143–69.

Orlikowski, W. J. and Yates, J. (1994) 'Genre repertoire: The structuring of communicative practices in organizations', *Administrative Science Quarterly*, 39(4): 541–74.

Pickering, A. (1995) *The Mangle of Practice: Time, Agency and Science*, Chicago, IL: University of Chicago Press.

Pinch, T. J. and Bijker, W. E. (1984) 'The social construction of facts and artefacts: Or how the sociology of science and the sociology of technology might benefit each other', *Social Studies of Science*, 14: 399–441.

Poole, M. S. and DeSanctis, G. (1990) 'Understanding the use of Group Decision Support Systems: The theory of adaptive structuration', in J. Fulk and C. Steinfeld (eds), *Organizations and Communication Technology*, Beverly Hills, CA: Sage, pp. 173–93.

Poole, M. S. and DeSanctis, G. (1992) 'Microlevel structuration in computer-supported group decision-making', *Human Communication Research*, 19: 5–49.

Poole, M. S., Seibold, D. and McPhee, R. (1985) 'Group decision-making as a structurational process', *Quarterly Journal of Speech*, 71: 74–102.

Ranson, S., Hinings, B. and Greenwood, R. (1981) 'The structuring of organizational structures', *Administrative Science Quarterly*, 25: 1–17.

Sahay, S. (1997) 'Implementation of information technology: A time–space perspective', *Organization Studies*, 18(2): 229–60.

Salisbury, W. D., Chin, W. W., Gopal, A. and Newsted, P. R. (2002) 'Better theory through measurement: Developing a scale to capture consensus on appropriation', *Information Systems Research*, 13(1): 91–103.

Scott, S. V. (2000) 'IT-enabled credit risk modernisation: A revolution under the cloak of normality', *Accounting, Management and Information Technologies*, 10: 221–55.

Storper, M. (1985) 'The spatial and temporal constitution of social action: A critical reading of Giddens', *Environment and Planning D: Society and Space*, 3: 407–24.

Urry, J. (1982) 'Duality of structure: Some critical issues', *Theory, Culture and Society*, 1(2): 100–106.

Walsham, G. (1993) *Interpreting Information Systems*, Chichester: John Wiley & Sons.

Walsham, G. and Han, C.-K. (1991) 'Structuration theory and information systems research', *Journal of Applied Systems Analysis*, 17: 77–85.

Wenger, E. C. and Snyder, W. M. (2000) 'Communities of practice: The organizational frontier', *Harvard Business Review*, 78(1): 139–46.

Whittington, R. (1992) 'Putting Giddens into action: Social systems and managerial agency', *Journal of Management Studies*, 29(6): 693–712.

Willis, P. E. (1977) *Learning to Labour: How Working Class Kids Get Working Class Jobs*, Farnborough: Saxon House.

Yates, J., Orlikowski, W. J. and Okamura, K. (1999) 'Explicit and implicit structuring of genres: Electronic communication in a Japanese R&D organization', *Organization Science*, 10(1): 83–103.

The preparation of this chapter was facilitated by the Cambridge MIT Institute under grant 074.

9
What We May Learn from the Social Shaping of Technology Approach

Debra Howcroft, Nathalie Mitev and Melanie Wilson

Research on information systems and organizations has recently moved away from managerialistic and 'technicist' interpretations and positivist and essentialist ontologies. IS researchers have begun to explore the use of interpretive sociological approaches to try to assess how current forms of sociological analysis—particularly of technology—can make better sense of IS phenomena than the common explanations found in the management and mainstream IS literature. In terms of social theory, technology is an 'off-stage phenomenon' that has not been seriously integrated (Sorensen, 2002) and the field of sociology has never steadfastly nurtured an interest in technology (Button, 1992). Given the nature of the IS field and our object of study, we need suitable ways of conceptualizing how we integrate the material (technology) into the analysis of human societies.

In this chapter we argue that much can be gained from the interplay of the social shaping of technology (SST) approach with IS research. SST both examines the content of technology and offers an exploration of the particular processes and context that frame the technological innovation. It achieves this with the provision of explanatory concepts that delve into a range of factors—organizational, political, social, economic and cultural—that pattern the design and use of technology. Although the SST approach has now become almost an orthodoxy in the treatment of technology in general, it is evident that, aside from a few notable exceptions, this is not the case in IS research. We establish the potential contribution of the SST approach to enlighten our study of IS phenomena in our discussion of a range of SST concepts. We believe that the application of SST concepts will enable a deeper appreciation of the process of IT development and use that goes beyond mainstream 'technicist' approaches, thereby potentially enabling researchers to broaden the research agenda.

The SST approach provides a range of conceptual tools that can be used to analyse the construction of sociotechnical entities (Williams and Edge, 1996). This approach rejects both technological and social determinism: it thus goes beyond traditional approaches that are concerned with assessing the 'impacts' of technology, to examine what shapes the technology that is having these 'impacts' and the way in which these impacts are achieved (Williams, 1997). Its advocates (Latour and Woolgar, 1979; Collins and Pinch, 1993) argue that there is no such thing as a social problem that does not have technological components; nor can there be a technological problem that does not have social components, and so any attempt to make such a division is bound to fail. They suggest that the development of technological devices should be interpreted within an analysis of the struggles and growth of 'systems' or 'networks'. This approach to the study of technology uses the 'seamless web' or 'actor-network' metaphors, which stress the importance of paying attention to the different but interlocking elements of physical artifacts, institutions and their environments, blurring different levels of analysis.

In this chapter we provide a somewhat minimalistic overview of key ideas and concepts within this broad area of study. It is neither a definitive nor exhaustive review of the area, which is vast; rather, our intentions are to provide some initial guidance on the core conceptual tools in the hope that the reader will pursue these ideas further and consider their application to the field of IS. Our goals are to provide a road map through this complex field; give a sense of order to some of the arguments; explain, compare and group the concepts; and suggest how they can be fruitfully applied to IS research. In the first instance, we outline the origins and basic premises of the social shaping perspective, noting the multitude of approaches with their differing ontological and epistemological positions, yet also pointing to areas of convergence and commonality. In the second instance, we illustrate the primary conceptual tools within social shaping, SCOT and ANT. A critique of these approaches then follows, before a discussion of implications for the IS field.

HISTORICAL CONTEXT

The 'social shaping of technology' has been described as a 'broad church' (Williams and Edge, 1996) encapsulating a wide range of perspectives and concepts that attempt to explain the relationship between technology and society. Its objects of study vary across differing types of technology, aspects of the innovation process or domains of application and use. Within this intellectual stream there has been the establishment of a dialogue between a range of scholars, many of whom are based in Europe and North America (Williams and Edge, 1996). Despite similarities in the nature of the research agendas, there are some fairly distinct 'national' styles in the way research is performed (Sorensen, 2002). These differences are shaped partly by national academic traditions and partly by the different political cultures within which the research is situated, which in turn translates into differing research problems and questions. This has resulted in the emergence of a number of analytical frameworks, which have drawn on different disciplinary roots, such as economics, politics, history and sociology. This cross-fertilization of ideas has provided a diversity of intellectual activity and research, with a vigorous programme of detailed empirical studies. There is now a substantial body of literature that focuses on the social study of technology. This includes journals such as *Science as Culture, Science, Technology and Human Values* and *Social Studies of Science* and the 'Inside Technology' book collection from MIT Press.

While this flourishing body of research is encouraging, it must be noted that the various authors with their differing perspectives (many of which are epistemological in nature) has given rise to areas of disputation. Consequently, the proliferation of such a range of concepts can be problematic for researchers intending to access these ideas. Aside from a couple of notable exceptions (such as Jasanoff *et al.*, 1995 and MacKenzie and Wajcman, 1985), there is little in the way of authoritative accounts. The problem is further compounded by the 'veritable mass of detail' associated with studies of this nature, which often result in book-length output (Walsham, 1997). Hence many SST researchers are often left floundering as they attempt to make sense of the plethora of seemingly overlapping concepts and tools.

The substantial growth and development of the SST perspective over the last decade have drawn on various traditions within social theory and technology studies. Given this variety of influences, coupled with the diversity of national characteristics, disciplinary backgrounds and research traditions, it is difficult to provide definitive accounts of this approach or even acknowledge the contributing strands. However, in order to make sense of this rich area of study that is devoted to furthering our understanding of sociotechnical change, we have identified key themes and trends within this perspective, noting their relevance to our particular domain of study. When considering the depth and width of application within the IS field, the provision of insightful and reflective accounts represents a considerable challenge. It is intended that the SST that utilizes different models and concepts can illuminate the numerous elements of sociotechnical change.

The phrase SST was launched with the reader (going by the same title) authored by Donald MacKenzie and Judy Wajcman (MacKenzie and Wajcman, 1985). This initiative coincided with other efforts to develop new approaches to technology studies and throughout the 1980s a range of different influences emerged. Yet within SST there are different strands or schools that reflect fundamental epistemological and ontological disagreements concerning the appropriateness of the various standpoints in dealing with technology (Williams and Edge, 1996). This included those who subscribe(d) in some way to the validity of meta-narratives that seek to provide general, even universal explanations of the nature of human society, such as Marxism and feminism (Noble, 1984; Schwartz Cowan, 1985; Wajcman, 1991; Webster, 1995b) and those who have rejected such universalizations as inappropriate for social scientists. This scepticism of so-called meta-narratives has induced SST researchers to look for more local-oriented approaches, such as the social construction of technology (SCOT; Pinch and Bijker, 1987) or actor-network theory (ANT; Callon, 1986a, 1986b; Latour, 1987). Before going on to outline the various influences, it is worth noting areas of common ground among these scholars.

First, social shaping researchers are united in their aim to critique the predominance of technological determinism. Technological determinism comprises two key ideas: technological development is seen as autonomous; and societal development is determined by the technology (Bijker, 1995). Whether depicting a utopian or dystopian vision, technological determinism portrays technology as an autonomous entity, with an 'inner logic' that develops in a direction of its own, which then coerces and determines social relationships and organizations (Williams and Edge, 1996). In effect, society is merely responsive, as technology moulds society according to its own needs. Technology is treated as given and assumed to provide an effective and reliable vehicle for social and organizational change. An example of this might include the 'promises' made on behalf of the implementation of computer-based information systems, which are assumed to offer greater accountability, efficiency and productivity.

The causal simplicity of technological determinism appears to provide great certainty and so provides immense appeal when discussing the social realities of technologies, such as computerization. However, the lack of realism that typifies such an approach is problematic on a number of levels. First, it assumes that technology is 'the *primum mobile* of change' (Webster, 1995a, p. 219), while simultaneously assuming that technology is beyond the realm of values and beliefs. This perception is misleading, since it separates technology from the social world within which it resides, while at the same time arguing that this autonomous force is *the* mechanism for bringing about social change. Secondly, quantitative increases in technology, as represented by certain indicators such as increases in computer networks, the development of Web browsers, the advances of e-commerce and so on, are seen to herald the emergence of a qualitatively different kind of society (Lyon, 1988; Webster, 1995a). In reality, the simplicity offered by such a perspective fails to acknowledge the difficulties in implementation and frequent failure to deliver predicted and desired outcomes (Peltu *et al.*, 1996).

Elements of technological determinism are clearly evident in relation to information technology and the predictions and speculations about its impact in organizations and society in general (see Grint and Woolgar, 1997 for an interesting analysis of the social processes of information technology). A large body of literature within IS has a prescriptive and predictive character, encompassing an implicit determinism with regard to information and communication technologies (Avgerou, 2002; Bloomfield *et al.*, 1997). Emerging through a critique of the technological determinist tradition, a range of arguments developed concerning its inadequacy as explanation and highlighting its ideological function in furthering the interests of those with a vested interest in technical change (Russell and Williams, 2002). SST researchers argued that the 'black box' of technology should be opened up for sociological analysis (Bijker and Law, 1992) by giving due attention to the process and content of the technology itself. This represents the second area of commonality among SST researchers, as we see a move 'upstream' from the traditional consideration of the 'impacts' of technology to consideration of how these technologies were constructed during the research, development and innovation phases.

Despite these areas of common ground, SST is not a single, well-defined theory and a number of approaches have been included under this umbrella. Coinciding with the initiative from MacKenzie and Wajcman (1985) were a number of efforts to develop new approaches to technology studies. This included the social construction of technology (SCOT), emphasizing interpretive flexibility and relevant actors; and actor-network theory (ANT), dealing with networks, inscription, translation and irreversibility. The three strands that we have selected to focus our attention on will be briefly reviewed in turn.

The SST reader published in 1985 carried radical connotations with definite neo-Marxist and feminist influences (Sorensen, 2002). The basic premise—that technology was shaped by particular social interests—was a radical one. The research was critical in the sense that it focused on macro-level, structural constraints and exposed how certain dominant groups were able to shape and use technology to promote their own interests. An SST approach advocated the querying of different options that present themselves during technology development by paying due consideration to political, economic and cultural interests and values. The collection raised questions such as 'how did the refrigerator get its hum?' (Schwartz Cowan, 1985) and provided an analysis that included consideration of issues relating to class and gender. Arguing from a position that technology was not neutral but in fact a carrier of particular social interests was a strong political statement and arguably a necessary step in achieving a better understanding of sociotechnical change. While the political message varied and was not well defined, nevertheless the level of analysis was strong. Studies included the fridge, the electric light bulb, domestic and military technologies.

The argument that technology is socially shaped represents only one wing within the sociological arena that argues that technology is socially constituted. Another wing has argued that technology is socially constructed. The social construction of technology (SCOT) approach was pioneered by Pinch and Bijker (1984) who argued that developments in the sociology of scientific knowledge (SSK) could be successfully translated to the study of technological artifacts. Their key argument was that artifacts are socially constructed by social groups and that the process of interaction among these groups enters into interpretations of 'success' and 'failure'. They suggested a number of mechanisms to map out the meanings given to technological artifacts by 'relevant social groups'. Key influential studies that illustrate the application of these concepts have been conducted of material technologies, notably of the bicycle, Bakelite and light bulbs (Bijker, 1997).

Actor-network theory (ANT) is an alternative approach to SCOT for studying the role of technology and adopts a different conceptual perspective, since it treats the social and the technical as inseparable and argues that people and devices should be analysed using the same conceptual apparatus (the principle of symmetry). Developed by Callon, Latour, Law and others, ANT is not a well-elaborated theory; rather, it adopts a useful theoretical position within the broader debates concerning the sociology of technology. The approach has been challenged and reviewed quite substantially (see Law and Hassard, 1999 for some of the debates). Indeed, Latour (1999a, p. 15) has recalled ANT, commenting 'there are four things that do not work with actor-network theory: the word actor, the word network, the word theory and the hyphen'.

ANT follows the strategies and actions of central actors who form elements of *heterogeneous networks* of aligned interests. A technology is conceived when a relatively stable network of aligned interests (both material and non-material) is created and maintained. The concept of an actor network is centred on the notion that the development of technology involves the building of alliances between various actors (or actants) and this includes individuals and groups, as well as 'natural' entities such as machines. As actors interact with each other to build and stabilize networks, they enrol a sufficient body of allies through a process of translation. As the network evolves, the nature of the project and the identities and interests of the actors are themselves transformed. The results of the translation process are subsequently inscribed into technologies. The technologies are said to embody the intentions of the actors and ANT has developed useful analyses of the ways in which actors inscribe their intentions into artifacts. The principles of ANT have been articulated through an elaborate vocabulary of conceptual tools that is aimed at describing the complexity of sociotechnical phenomena (Akrich, 1992; Callon, 1991; Latour, 1991, 1999b; Law, 1991).

Before moving on to outline the approaches, one aspect worth mentioning here is the issue of terminology. The 'constructivist approach' is often seen to include the actor-network approach, the social-constructivist approach, the social shaping approach and the systems approach to technology studies (Wajcman, 2002). Yet within these various strands debates have taken place regarding the range of interpretations concerning the relationship between society and technology. One issue that has been fiercely debated is that of 'strong' versus 'weak' constructivism (for instance, see McLoughlin, 1997 for an overview of the debate between Grint and Woolgar, 1997 on the one hand, and Kling, 1992 on the other). The debate centres on how technical capacities are perceived. 'Strong' constructivism believes that sociologists of technology should not adjudicate between different claims and constructs of technical capacity, since the process of technological change is seen as almost entirely locally constructed, negotiable and contingent. Technical capacities are not fixed but indeterminate and open to interpretive flexibility, not only during conception, design and development, but also when in use. By contrast, Kling (a 'weak' constructivist) adopts the position that the specific nature of the technology itself (computing and information systems specifically) has some bearing on its effects, whether that results in reskilling or deskilling. Woolgar and Grint view this position as 'technicist' and unacceptable, critiquing his 'quest for the reasonable middle way' between technological and social determinism. As Orlikowski (1992) has remarked, theory and research on the question of the relationship between technology and organizations remain at best 'ambiguous and conflicting' and arguments between the social/technical distinction will, no doubt, continue.

OUTLINE OF THE THEORETICAL APPROACHES

Given the above brief outline of the distinct schools of thought, we concur that 'There is no agreed definition of what constitutes or qualifies as an SST approach' (Russell and Williams, 2002, p. 39). This variety of models, conceptual frameworks and domains of study has led to the proliferation of terms. Consequently, there may be areas of overlap between the different terms, the same terms may have different meanings within different conceptual frameworks, or a new word may arise to describe established phenomena. In order to make sense of this intellectual arena, we take a fairly broad conception of its scope and of the contributing work. Yet at the same time we have opted to outline what we regard as the most important elements in an attempt to provide some guidance as to how they may be fruitfully applied in IS research. With this in mind, what follows is a discussion of the three perspectives, noting the key conceptual apparatus.

Social Shaping

The social shaping approach is a generic label for approaches that are committed to opening the 'black box' of technology for sociological analysis. These theorists suggest that technologies are socially shaped such that their resulting material form reflects the structural and political circumstances of their development. Therefore the social relations of production (the practices, assumptions, beliefs, language and other factors involved in its design and manufacture) are built into the technology, which has consequences for subsequent deployment. This model regards the innovation process as contradictory and uncertain, which contributes towards explaining why the excellence of a particular technological solution will not necessarily guarantee its success.

MacKenzie and Wajcman (1985) argue that through a number of mechanisms (which include science/existing technology, economics, social relations, the state and gender) the social is constitutive of technology and technology development. They include a wide range of studies to illustrate this point. For example, they cite Hughes' study (1985) of Edison's development of the light bulb to illustrate how technological reasoning and economic reasoning are often inseparable. In the case of Edison's invention, he was quite consciously the designer of a system. He intended to generate electricity, sell it to consumers, and also to sell them the apparatus they required to make use of it. To achieve this, he had to compete with the existing gas systems and supply electric light at a cost at least as low as the gaslight. These economic forces directly affected his design of light bulb and display the efficacy of the social.

Paradigmatic demonstrations of social shaping analysis were given in Winner's (1986) paper 'Do artefacts have politics?' He argued that technology can indeed have politics because the Moses Bridge (which connects Long Island to Jones Beach in New York State) was built in such a way as to preclude access via public transport (buses were too high to get under the bridge). Given that this form of transport was primarily used by black people and the poor, Jones Beach was left for the exclusive enjoyment of the rich whites. Artifacts are essentially politically shaped.

Further, MacKenzie and Wajcman call on Cockburn's study (1985) of compositors in the printing trade to show how the gender dimension has resulted in the perception that technology is the property of men through the exclusion of women in technological jobs. The gendered shaping of technology was later extended and developed by Judy Wajcman in her 1991 book *Feminism Confronts Technology*.

A revised edition of the SST reader was published in 1999 for a number of reasons. First, although SST had been well received in academic circles over the previous decade or so, it was still largely unheard of within wider popular culture; secondly, it could contribute to the teaching of engineering with its discussion of the intertwining of the social and the technical; and thirdly, there was a desire to strengthen the base of SST research and encourage further empirical research rather than sit at a high level of generality. Over time, the wider transfer of SST concepts has involved a set of translations in terms of aims, problems and concepts. Sorensen (2002) raises the question as to whether the original intentions have been betrayed or diluted in the process. In the revised edition the dominance of certain social interests is no longer at the forefront of the research interest. The notion of social interests is more diffuse, with less of a focus on fundamental differences in terms of the power bases of interests. Sorensen (2002) argues that what we see is not a loss of political argument in SST, but a loss of political innocence coinciding with the discovery of its potential political usefulness as a more pragmatic approach that can lead to social change that is both useful and relevant (for example, see Russell and Williams, 2002).

Social Construction of Technology

Both SCOT and ANT are social constructivist approaches. However, in contrast to ANT theorists who reject the society/technology dichotomy, Pinch and Bijker (1987) preserve the social environment. For them, the social environment shapes the technical characteristics of the artifact, and this is their primary focus of concern.

Pinch and Bijker (1987) argue that developments in the sociology of scientific knowledge (SSK) can be successfully applied to studies of technology[1] and utilize the three stages in the 'empirical programme of relativism' (a particular strain of SSK) for their analysis of the 'social construction of technology'. The first stage uses the concept of interpretive flexibility to demonstrate that technological artifacts are socially constructed. The second stage considers how the artifact achieves stabilization by having the 'relevant social groups' see that their 'problems' have been solved. Finally, the technological content of the artifact is related to the social via consideration of the meanings that are given to the artifacts by the relevant groups. These concepts will now be explained in greater detail.

Relevant social groups

Pinch and Bijker (1987) draw on the notion of different 'relevant social groups' (RSG) who will not only define a technological problem differently but also disagree over definitions of what constitute success and failure. They argue that if we are to understand the development of technology as a social process, it is crucial to take the artifacts as they are viewed by the relevant groups, since to do otherwise would imply that the technology has an autonomous life of its own. These groups are delineated according to similarities among their interpretations of technology, so that all members of a certain social group share the same set of meanings attached to a specific artifact. The term may be

> used to denote institutions and organizations (such as the military or some specific company), as well as organized and unorganized groups of individuals. (Pinch and Bijker, 1987, p. 30)

Having identified the relevant social groups for an artifact, the focus turns to the problems that each group has in relation to the artifact. Around each problem, a number of solutions can be identified. The social groups play a crucial role in defining and solving the problems that arise during the development of technology. In deciding which problems are relevant, the meanings that those social groups attribute to the artifact play a crucial role, since a problem is defined as such only when there is a social group for which it constitutes a 'problem'.

Stabilization and closure

Pinch and Bijker go on to explain that a technology can stabilize in circumstances where relevant social groups see their problems as having been solved by the technology in question. This is also more familiarly known as 'closure'. Various social groups not only define problems differently, they also have different opinions about achievement of closure and stabilization. Hence technological development is a multidirectional and non-linear process that involves constant negotiation and renegotiation among different groups. This type of model allows us to view the artifact and the range of possible variations, providing an understanding that the successful stages in the development are not the only ones.

Interpretive flexibility

Given that social groups define problems of technological development differently, there is no 'one best way' and instead there is flexibility in the way that things are designed. Interpretive flexibility is a useful concept for understanding how problems and solutions associated with a technology present themselves differently to different groups of people (Pinch and Bijker, 1987). Demonstrating the interpretive flexibility of an artifact amounts to showing that one seemingly unambiguous 'thing' (a technical process, or some material artifact such as a bike, computer or bridge) is better understood by tracing and identifying the meanings attributed by the relevant social groups. It sees the workings of technology as subject to radically different interpretations that are coextensive with various relevant groups (Kline and Pinch, 1999). Interpretive flexibility is a useful technique of deconstruction, since it 'shows that neither an artefact's identity nor its technical "working" or "nonworking" is an intrinsic property of the artefact but is subject to social variables' (Bijker, 1995, p. 252). The concept of differing groups with alternative readings of the technology has much resonance with IS researchers. The process of articulating information requirements, and the strategies needed to 'solve' the 'problems' of the various groups such as end-users or managers, are typified in many of the struggles that occur during the process of systems development.

Technological frames

To add context to the ways in which actors in relevant social groups interact with each other, Bijker (1997) added the concept of technological frames. A technological frame captures the diversity of interactions and structures the interactions among the actors of a group. The frames are located between actors and build up as interaction around an artifact also builds up. So if interactions move members of an emerging relevant social group towards the same direction, a frame will build up; if not, there will be no frame, no relevant social group and no future interaction. The technological frame itself comprises a multitude of *elements* that influence the interactions and lead to the attribution of meanings to technical artifacts. An example of the elements of a group of systems developers could typically comprise goals, key problems, problem-solving strategies, organizational constraints, attributes of the computer-based system, tacit knowledge, design methods and testing procedures. The list of elements is tentative and depends on the composition of each relevant social group and so the elements may vary, depending on the nature of the specific group.

Actor-Network Theory

In their rejection of technological determinism, SCOT and social shaping theorists are accused of a form of 'social determinism', since they over-stress social choice and environment at the expense of any technological considerations. By contrast, actor-network theory tries to avoid both forms of determinism, social and technological. It achieves this by its attempts to transcend the distinction between the so-called social and the so-called natural (i.e. technological) world (Callon, 1986a) and regards the technological process as a process of network building. One of the aspects of the actor-network approach is the systematic avoidance of what can be called 'methodological dualism': the making of *a priori* distinctions between what is 'technical' and what is not (Bloomfield and Vurdubakis, 1997, p. 85). As Latour (1991, p. 129) comments:

> Rather than assuming that we are dealing with two separate, but related, ontological domains—technology and organizations—we propose to regard them as but phases of the same essential action.

Elements of the social and technological world figure as actors enrolled into the network. Hence an actor network is configured through the enrolment of allies (both human and non-human) into a network by means of negotiations. This is known as the 'sociology of translation' and aims to describe, rather than explain, the many transitions taking place when networks are constructed. Callon (1986a, 1991) includes abstract notions such as science, technology, economics and politics in the category of actor. These 'human' and 'non-human' actors are the heterogeneous entities that constitute a network.

Translation

Translation is the effective persuasion of actors that it is in their interest to use the technology in the prescribed manner and that the technology is the answer to their 'problems'. This translation might involve issuing a polemic against alternative, competing translations, and/or establishing that a certain technological development is necessary or beneficial. Translation operates between actors: an actor gives a definition to another actor and imputes him/her/it/them with interests, projects, desires, strategies, reflexes and afterthoughts (Callon, 1991). An actor might be, for instance, the company that has conceived, produced and distributed a piece of software, and another actor its users. Taking into consideration conventions (Callon, 1991) that will regulate the translation process, the final shape and position of the innovation are unlikely to be those that were intended by the original developers. In each stage of its life, the project is taken and adapted by the actors that become involved in it. Only in the rare case when the future users can be persuaded to follow the initial goals does the innovation proceed as originally planned. All too often, however, the issue becomes sidetracked and unintended effects occur.

'Moments of translation' describe the means by which networks are constructed, whereby allies are recruited in such a way that the solution to their own problems only appears viable through the network. In one attempt to achieve a translation, the actor may suggest that it shares a 'common' problem with putative allies. This is known as *problematization* (Callon, 1991). If the actor can convince the allies that it has the necessary skills, knowledge or other resources to devise a solution to their 'common' problem, then it may come to be seen as indispensable. The original problem is renegotiated or translated, as the allies become actors within a network defined by their common ownership of the problem. *Interessement* involves a process of persuasion of other potential allies by those who profess a relevant solution to the problem. In order for an actor to secure or win the support of others it must in some way make itself indispensable (an *obligatory passage point*; Callon, 1986a) to them by translating their interests and *enrol* them so that they can only solve their problem via the technology. A successful negotiation/translation of an obligatory passage point is a condition of network stabilization (Latour, 1987). The *mobilization* of network members (i.e. those previously enrolled) occurs when social investment reaches a point where withdrawal would be unlikely (*irreversibility*).

Of particular interest for studying the success and failure of IS are the related concepts of stabilization, irreversibility and obligatory passage points. Network building is a search for stability that is enabled to the extent that changes set in train during network construction become irreversible (Callon, 1991), either because it would be too costly to reverse them or because to do so becomes unthinkable. A translation is irreversible in that it is impossible to return to a previous situation.

An example of translations in IS

As the reader is no doubt aware, one of the main problems with ANT is its inaccessibility and the highly abstract nature of some of the ideas and concepts. In order to provide further clarification, an illustration is provided. This concerns the problematic implementation of a computerized reservation system (CRS) at French Railways (SNCF). This study was investigated and analysed using ANT and one of its main tenets, the sociology of translation (Mitev, 2000). The Socrate project was an attempt to link different actors into a network: the French government and its transport policy agenda in a context of market deregulation pressures in Europe; SNCF management, its profitability objectives and organizational restructuring plans as well as politically sensitive public service obligations; different staff categories, their expertise and changing authority and legitimacy, in particular IT and marketing staff; new computerized ticketing, reservation, sales and price-optimization systems; sales employees, their changing roles, tasks and behaviours; passengers and their buying and travelling expectations. If the translation of the project is successful and accepted by the agencies, the actor network becomes indispensable. Particular agencies attempt to interest and enrol other agencies in their programmes. SNCF management translated transport deregulation, governmental pressures and expectations about technology into using the CRS to gain strategic advantage. The Socrate team translated this into techniques and strategies enacted by an information system to increase profitability and cater for public service obligations through yield management. Commercial expertise was inscribed in the form of new pricing rules and a new user–computer interface. Passengers were also expected to accept these new selling principles. However, sales staff and passengers in particular did not adhere to these translations.

Symmetry

Implementation failures can show that choices are neither obvious nor unproblematic. Compared to successes, failure studies often make it easier for the researcher to elicit more complex explanations from actors and to disentangle how technical and social issues are constructed and delineated (Akrich, 1993).

> To challenge the impression of obviousness which can be given by technical choices that lead to devices which 'perform well', there is no better strategy than concentrating on failure cases to show that it is impossible to distinguish between good and bad decisions. (Akrich, 1993, pp. 36–7).

Not only is the demise of IS failures highly implausible, as Sauer points out (Sauer, 1993), but the idea that failures can be eradicated reveals the underlying assumption, often found in the IS and management literature, that failures are atypical and irrational and that they can be corrected using managerial and/or technicist means. The dominant trend is to see the introduction, design and development of information systems as a rational decision-making process carried out on behalf of management. Designing an information system is equated to engineering, and it is believed that if the practices of the engineering professions are adopted there will be a decline in the number of failed projects in IS (Ewusi-Mensah and Przasnyski, 1995). As Knights and Murray (1994) comment,

> we note the utility of processual approaches emanating from within the functionalist tradition that begin to dissect the practical actions of managers, albeit from a perspective that usually ignores those larger contextual conditions that are a condition and consequence of such action.

Borrowing from SSK, which aims to be impartial to the truth or falsity of scientific beliefs so that they can be explained 'symmetrically', sociologists of technology have therefore argued that technology failures are of as much interest as success stories. You cannot, at the start of a project, tell if it is going to succeed. This implies that the same methods of analysis should be used to describe successful and unsuccessful projects and that hindsight should not be used to describe the problem. SSK also recommends that scholars interested in the development of science and technology choose controversy as one important site for research. The controversy is about the truth or falsity of scientific belief, or about the success or failure of a technology in solving problems.

Example of symmetry: Aramis and VAL

The notion of symmetry helps dismantle beliefs and assumptions of *obviousness* (Akrich, 1993). Latour's investigation (Latour, 1993, 1996) into the abandonment of a new revolutionary subway transportation system planned in the South of Paris, Aramis, is a good example of how to tackle symmetrically the failure story (Aramis) and the success story (VAL, a working automatic suburban train in the Northern city of Lille). It would be inadequate to say that VAL was more efficient, socially acceptable and better designed technically than Aramis, since 'all of the former's qualities and all of the latter's defects are *results* and not *causes*' (Latour, 1993, p. 382), of the success of VAL and the lack of success of Aramis. This would be 'asymmetric since it would look for social explanations only when something goes wrong—the straight path of happy technical development being, in contrast, self-evident and self-explanatory' (Latour, 1993, p. 383). Both projects tie together many interests, and in both cases these interests do not exist independently of the projects and (potential or eventual) artifacts. Latour claims that he does not practise two different interpretations, one about the nature of the artifact and the other about the meaning it has for social groups: 'it is the same task to define the artefact tying together the various groups or the groups tying together one artefact' (Latour, 1993, p. 381). Social actors are not considered as simply pressing their wills on inert passive things and, at the other extreme, artifacts are not autonomous technologies pressing their goals onto human actors. The notion of symmetry refuses to set the failure in the following dualistic terms: is it because Aramis failed that the interpretations diverged so, or because the interpretations are so divergent that the project never became an institution, a stabilized thing?

Actant: Human and non human actors

Another aspect of the symmetrical principle advocated by adopters of the ANT approach (and a consequence of the undertaking not to make *a priori* distinctions between what is 'technical' and what is not) is the use of the term and concept of 'actant' (Akrich, 1992). Their most contentious idea, actant is used for both human and non-human actors, thus enabling us to discuss in a non-deterministic manner the 'impacts' of sociotechnical networks. From the ANT perspective innovations are 'an attempt to build and stabilize a diffuse system of allies composed of both human and non-human entities' (Bloomfield and Vurdubakis, 1997). In this way, ANT brings to the fore materiality and technology, which are often absent from much social theory. Social relations are not independent of the technology; rather, the social is bound together by the technical. Society is coproduced with technologies and artifacts, which explains why Latour (1992) argues that we cannot ignore the 'missing masses' of mundane artifacts.

The notion of actant also fits with the metaphor of technologies as text (Latour, 1992; Woolgar, 1991) implied by the ANT approach. Hence technologies are compared to texts, which can be 'read' or interpreted flexibly. Akrich in particular has developed the notion of actant in relation to technology as text or a 'script'. There are significant implications of this extended metaphor of the script with the user as human actant, both for the way in which we view technology and for the focus of researchers' attention. First, within the metaphors of translation, texts and scripts, the actant/user is a reader who has the capacity to interpret flexibly the text/machine. The reader plays an *active* role in making sense of the machines. Secondly, Akrich (1992, p. 206) points to the constraints made on actants' actions and poses for analysis the extent to which the composition of a technical object constrains actants in the way they relate both to the object and to one another. Hence the script is an effective technique for analysing the construction of the user and the constraints placed on the free actions of the user. Thirdly, attention is drawn to the difference between the 'actual users' (those who confront the technology) and the 'presumed users' (those imagined by the designer), for designing technologies involves a process of predicting the future world in which the user will relate to and cohabit with the artifact (Woolgar, 1991). The notions of actant (actual user) and script (presumed user) encourage us to analyse the ways in which users resist the role ascribed to them (Akrich, 1992). As Lohan (2000) points out, we are dealing with issues of structure and agency here, stability and change. In ANT, the script highlights the potential obduracy of the technology, while opening the possibility of resistance through interpretive flexibility by human actants. The latter then allows for the reinscription by the user—or even rejection of both enforced technologies and user roles.

Inscription and standardization

The notion of script and presumed user leads us to another aspect of inscription. Bloomfield (1991) states that with its ability to change work practices, and the fact that it deals primarily with representations, IT brings with it the inscription of a moral order, privileging certain values and voices as well as hiding others (Bowker, Timmermans and Star, 1995). Scripting is both a useful and an accurate metaphor for the way in which a fixed configuration of the user is built into the design of machines. Thus the inscribed users are partly developed in relation to the roles and behaviour patterns that they are expected to perform, reciprocally to the machine: skills must be distributed appropriately in order for there to be close correspondence of the built-in users and the actual ones. According to Akrich, while designers are involved in scripting the world, the resultant innovations inscribe their prediction into the technical content of the object (the world made solid).

Scripting and inscription are related to the notion of standardization and 'making work visible' (Wilson, 2002). Frequently technology is used as a 'change agent' to bring about behaviour required by the implementers. Thus a connection can be made between scripting and the formalizing of standards, with IT constituting a rationalizing tool (Berg, 1997). This form of rationalization is examined by several authors in relation to healthcare information systems. For example, Bowker, Timmermans and Star (1995) have applied the notion to the Nursing International Classification (NIC) system they studied. They concluded that a view of what nursing is and should be is 'inscribed' into the technical content of the NIC.

Despite efforts to standardize through inscriptions, the script may not be played out: resistance is always possible. An important paradox is the dynamic relationship between global development and local appropriation where there is no evidence of cultural convergence (Sorensen, 2002). So we find that technological innovation is subject to two contradictory tendencies. On the one hand, suppliers provide standard products that are made available to the user and marketed as 'black-boxed' solutions with predictable and well-established attributes. At the other extreme, suppliers provide versions fitted to the unique requirements and characteristics of users, since they are highly diverse, even within one local area or application. As demonstrated in the classical work of Hughes (1983), national, regional and local structures each contribute to specific configurations of large sociotechnical systems. The technology is designed in such a way that it allows for configuration or modification by users, as they attempt to integrate it within the specifics of their local environment. In practice, we often see combinations of the two extremes, as suppliers choose which features

Table 9.1   *Summary of key concepts*

Term	Author/s	Description
SCOT		
Closure	Pinch, Bijker	Interpretations of an artifact by different groups are brought into agreement or one interpretation becomes dominant. Sees the emergence of a consensus.
Interpretive flexibility	Pinch, Bijker	The attribution of meanings to an artifact by different groups of actors. Interpretive flexibility is a useful concept for understanding how problems and solutions associated with a technology present themselves differently to different groups of people.
Relevant social groups	Pinch, Bijker	These groups are delineated according to similarities among their interpretations of technology so that all members of a certain social group share the same set of meanings attached to a specific artifact. The social groups play a crucial role in defining and solving the problems that arise during the development of technology.
Technological frame	Bijker	A technological frame refers to the structure of rules and practices that enable and constrain the interactions among the actors of a relevant social group. A technological frame is built up when interaction around an artifact builds up. It comprises heterogeneous elements (goals, problem-solving strategies, scientific theories, tacit knowledge, testing procedures, design methods) that influence the interactions within relevant social groups and lead to the attribution of meanings to technical artifacts—and thus to constituting technology.
ANT		
Actor	Latour, Callon	People are human actors and devices are non-human actors.
Actant	Akrich	Stands for both humans and non-humans enabling a non-deterministic discussion of sociotechnical networks.
Actor-network	Latour, Callon, Law	The technological innovation process is one of network building between actors leading to the formation of techno-economic actor networks. Also referred to as a seamless web that subsumes the distinctions between science, technology, economics, and politics.

Table 9.1 (*continued*)

Term	Author/s	Description
Heterogeneous engineering	Latour, Callon	Human and non-human actors form elements of heterogeneous networks of aligned interests that constitute an actor network.
Enrolment	Latour, Callon	Actors enrol a sufficient body of allies through a process of translation.
Translation	Latour, Callon	The innovation is translated or carried from one position to another by actors. A translation is an interpretive operation, according to actors' interests. The results of translations are inscribed into technological artifacts. The final shape and position of the innovation are unlikely to be those of the initial developers.
Inscription, scripts	Akrich	Technology as text of script. The script is a technique for analysing the construction of the user and the constraints placed on the free actions of the user.
Symmetry	Latour, Callon	1. Symmetry between the social and the technical. Treats the social and the technical as inseparable (distributed monism). The presumed separation between technology and organizations is a sense-making device and is socially constructed.
	Akrich	2. Symmetry between success and failure. The same explanatory resources must be used when reporting on successful and unsuccessful innovations.
Irreversibility	Callon	Network building is a search for stability that is enabled when changes set in train during network construction become irreversible (it would be too costly to reverse them, or to do so becomes unthinkable). Similarities with the concept of closure in SCOT.
Black box	Callon	A network that irreversibilizes itself is a network that has become heavy with immutable, durable devices, frozen elements or black boxes.
Obligatory passage point	Callon	In order for an actor to translate an innovation successfully, it must win the support of others and makes itself indispensable (an obligatory passage point—OPP) to them by translating their interests and enrolling them. A successful translation of an OPP is a condition of network stabilization.

should remain fixed and which should be left to local appropriation (McLoughlin, 1999).

As can be noted from the above, there is a wide range of conceptual tools available that may inform our approach to the study of IS. For simplicity, these are summarized in Table 9.1.

CRITIQUE

As noted earlier, the multiplicity of perspectives and concepts that form the constituent strands of the SST approach has resulted in a number of differences and controversies, some of which are possibly irreconcilable. Indeed, some of the difficulties with strong constructivist approaches have also been identified by IS researchers (Mitev, 2003; Nandhakumar and Vidgen, 2001; Stalder, 1997; Walsham, 1997). In this section, we will attempt the (somewhat hazardous) task of critical appraisal, summarizing the key points relating to areas of disputation.

Focus on Development

Let us begin with an area of contention that is of modest significance for SST researchers, but arguably of greater consequence to researchers concerned with information systems. Early SST work was criticized for giving undue attention to technology developers and prior technology design (Russell, 1986), thus downplaying the process of consumption of technology (Williams and Edge, 1996). As IS researchers are well aware, once the technology has materialized into an organization, a process of configuration or 'domestication' takes place as the users respond to the system. The way that users are represented and positioned—both in theory and in practice—may limit the development team in the process of technology development (often despite their best intentions). Consequently, the process of consumption usually results in a reconfiguration of the technical artifact, which itself may change significantly. This is especially the case with continually changing technologies such as information systems. The focus on development also has implications for the treatment of gender (see below).

Limited Analysis of Social Structures

A number of critiques have been powerfully articulated against both ANT and SCOT for their lack of consideration of wider social structures that operate at the macro level (Russell, 1986; Walsham, 1997; Winner, 1993). Both approaches tend to concentrate on micro-studies rather than concerning themselves with broader issues, such as the way in which social structures shape and influence interactions and outcomes at the local level. They may provide interesting accounts of local contingencies and material arrangements, but this neglects taking into account macro-social structures. Despite Latour's argument that it is possible to use ANT to move between micro and macro levels of analysis (Latour, 1991), many other theorists remain unconvinced by this.

While models of analysis that reject technological determinism and the notion of 'one best technology' are laudable, we contend that concepts such as variation and selection of technological options require some form of social analysis. In many contexts the process of research and development (and information systems development) is often controlled by certain interests, which implies that only a limited number of trajectories are accepted as 'progress', that some criteria for improvement are taken as given and others are ignored, that needs are interpreted, and thus that many options never surface for selection in any conscious sense (Russell, 1986). Social choices regarding technological outcomes are produced in a specific context of economic imperatives, government industrial policies, regulations, legal duties, political strategies, bureaucratic procedures and deeper cultural and intellectual traditions. These dynamics go beyond those that are revealed when studying immediate needs, problems and solutions. Indeed, these conditions influence actors and groups in various ways, since they are structurally biased in favour of some and against others. Again, this critique is also pertinent for those interested in studying gender (see below).

Macro–Micro Issues

An issue related to the problem of lack of consideration of social structures is the relationship between the macro–micro questions. The ongoing debate is concerned with different levels of analysis, usually referred to as the 'micro' (or 'local') and 'macro' (or 'global') approaches to sociology. Knorr-Cetina (1981) defines micro-sociology as the study of the micro-processes of social life; and they describe macro-sociology as the study of society, social institutions and sociocultural change. However, there are some signs of convergence here (Williams and Edge, 1996), despite strong epistemological differentiations. The last few years have witnessed an increasing rejection of macro-sociology and its perceived social determinism (the social whole determines matters for the individual) as many have been attracted by micro-sociology and its ability to account for local processes and influences (Knorr-Cetina, 1981). Conversely, micro-sociology has grown more concerned with the additional element of the context in which interaction is embedded and has 'scaled up' these processes to obtain broader understanding. For instance, MacKenzie (1988) states that, though traditional macro-sociology is more relevant politically than micro-sociology, 'the former is insufficiently puzzled by the phenomenon of structural power' (see below).

In their defence, ANT theorists are sceptical about the influence of macro-level influences such as social class and markets (Williams and Edge, 1996) and have been criticized for descriptive work that hands over too much power to individual actors, while ignoring structural interests and power issues. Interestingly, Callon and Latour (1981) argue against a micro–macro distinction. They do not think that we draw closer to social reality by descending to micro-negotiations or by rising towards the macro-actors. Macro-actors are not more complex than micro-actors and are just micro-actors 'seated on black boxes' (Callon and Latour, 1981, p. 299). They also, symmetrically, oppose the view that micro-negotiations are truer and more real than the abstract, distant structures of the macro-actors.

An Amoral/Apolitical Stance

A further criticism levelled at social constructivism concerns its stance on moral and political issues and its almost total lack of regard for the social consequences of technological choice. It has been argued that the lack of an evaluative stance can be equated to political indifference (Winner, 1993) and that sometimes we need to adopt a 'position' that passes judgement on the development of, for instance, chemical weapons or nuclear arms (see also similar criticisms made of Foucault in Chapter 7). Simply noticing a diversity of interpretations is insufficient and 'ultimately one has to decide what one is dealing with and why it matters' (Winner, 1993, p. 373).

The SCOT approach has been criticized for ignoring the political biases that can underlie the spectrum of choices for relevant actors (Winner, 1993). Considered social analysis requires more than mere identification and description and groups need to be located in a structured and historical context that takes into consideration the economic, political and ideological constraints and influences on them (Russell, 1986). Their structural positioning largely affects their relationship to the various technologies that confront them. This is related to issues of power and decisions as to which groups or actors to include/exclude in the analysis. What of the groups with no voice, who have been deliberately excluded or whose oppositions are never articulated or legitimated? Star (1991) refers to the 'networks of the powerful' and the way in which supposedly irreversible networks are only stable for some and discriminate against others. It is important to note not only how observable decisions are made but also which ones are excluded from the agenda (Bachrach and Baratz, 1963). A consideration of interpretive flexibility is inadequate, since an explanation of technological change must show not only what the different groups think about an artifact, but also their ability (resources of knowledge and power) to influence the outcome of its development and adoption (Russell, 1986).

Further, a growing critical and constructive exploration of ANT is also to be found in the science and technology policy literature (Howard, 2002; Radder, 1992; Woodhouse *et al.*, 2002). Questions raised relate to the theoretical attack on macro-contextual issues, seen as having political implications; how the 'descriptive turn' and its attendant 'value-free relativism' have been a turn towards or away from political agendas; how specific concerns of commercially driven innovation networks is not taken into account; how actors are representatives of organizational agendas and shift in and out of the network; and how the capture of innovation as networks and knowledge-generating activities can be (poststructurally) politicized.

The weaknesses outlined so far—the focus on development, the limited analysis of social structures and the amoral/apolitical stance—are all highlighted by feminist critiques of social constructivist failure to consider the gendered nature of technology, as described below.

ANT, SCOT and the Problem of Studying Gender

SST set out with a Marxist and feminist underpinning and actively encouraged more studies on the issue of gender and technology.

Indeed, one might argue that the *raison d'être* of feminism lies in seeking ways of transforming asymmetric relations between men and women (Lohan, 2000). However, this poses problems for the principle of symmetry proposed by other SST schools of thought (see below). So Judy Wajcman (2000) argues that despite the fact that the relationship between gender and technology has been theorized over the last 20 years or so, nevertheless a clear imbalance persists in the incorporation of gender analysis and innovation. In her feminist critique of SCOT and ANT she asks why, if social studies look at the social, they have largely ignored gender issues—leaving this task to feminists. SCOT and ANT's methodology focuses on observable conflicts among social groups and networks but largely ignores what Steven Lukes' (Lukes, 1974) radical analysis called the third dimension of power. This refers to the exercise of power beyond the observable but existent in the structural dimensions of power, where pre-exclusion and absence of parties are evidence of hidden manipulations of situations. Hence the need to look to structural arrangements to understand the systematic exclusion of women from areas of technological development. On this Susan Leigh Star comments:

> ANT does not always recognize that the stabilization and standard-ization of technological systems necessarily involve negating the experience of those who are not standard, 'a destruction of the world of the non-enrolled'. (Star, 1991, cited by Wajcman, 2000, p. 453)

On the positive side, a more constructivist approach suggests a consideration of the mutual shaping of gender and technology and how dualisms are coconstituted. Indeed, SST provides some useful tools that are particularly amenable to a feminist analy-sis of technology (Lohan, 2000). Yet social constructivism needs to attend to the relatively neglected issue of gender and technology. In attempting to further explain this neglect, Wajcman (2000) suggests that the absence of women from view is due in part to the con-centration by SST on technology at the design stage, where male 'heroes' dominate. The relative paucity of women in computing suggests that concentrating solely on the development of technolo-gies (where women are more likely to be excluded) could render women invisible. Yet employees and users play a role in shap-ing the development and application of technologies (Knights and Murray, 1994; Webster, 1995b). So one strategy to include women would imply 'widening the lens' to other areas of technology devel-opment and diffusion; that is, 'further downstream' where women are hidden. The point is that gender is an issue *even when women are absent*: gender should not just equate to women.

The Problem of Generalized Symmetry

ANT permits animate and inanimate phenomena to be associated in ways that are not traditionally provided for in sociological analysis as all entities within the actor network are given the same explanatory status. It may seem radical and problematic to confer the same status on artifacts as human actors (since it can be seen to reduce humans to mere objects), but proponents of ANT have argued that this is an analytical stance rather than an ethical one (Law, 1991), which enables researchers to increase the level of detail and precision. This position is unacceptable to some (e.g. Nandhakumar and Vidgen, 2001), who have argued that the symmetry between human and non-human actors goes too far in erasing distinctions and reducing people to the status of objects.[2] There are political implications of levelling human and non-human differences that cannot be ignored.

In relation to this point, Button (1992) argues that although ANT theorists are attempting to be comprehensive by introducing as many causes as possible and invoking the various actants involved, this is problematic since the technology vanishes in the quest to include all of its sources. As more and more actants are added to the actor network in the hope of better understanding what the artifact comprises, the details and the processes of 'association' are never addressed. Failure to account for the details of the associations, and the nature and process of the work practices, means that the technology 'vanishes in a puff of theoretical zeal' (Button, 1992, p. 24). As Walsham (1997) observes, identifying all of the heterogeneous associations within an actor network is difficult. Some problems are determining what 'all' the actors are; how to treat small and large actors and their power and political differences; knowing where one network starts and another stops; and understanding how they overlap. So what we are left with is the age-old problem of how to account for a particular state of affairs by combining various elements.

Description Rather Than Explanation

ANT has been commended for its ability as a method to describe, but criticized for its lack of ability to explain. The sociology of translation is useful as a descriptive language and for detailing relations between actors in networks, but may not be so effective in providing explanations (Collins and Yearley, 1992). Callon (1991) states that explanations are only offered by networks that increase their convergence and irreversibility (an agreement getting firmer) and that the descriptions delivered by intermediaries turn into explanations (and even predictions). But how can one explain the failure to converge in the case of a divergent, reversible and unstable network, which consequently cannot offer an explanation (but maybe a series of conflicting explanations?). If all explanations are the result of a stabilized network already in place, one could use explanations of other stable overlapping and neighbouring networks; but then the problem is transposed to 'where does one stop?'

The Content of Technology

It has been noted that despite the pronounced interest in the content of technology of SST theorists, it seems that this is far from visible or is strangely absent from their accounts of technology. Indeed, Button (1992, p. 16) argues that 'technology seems to vanish from view' in many narratives. In the SST reader (MacKenzie and Wajcman, 1985), he argues that the accounts are more likely to be centred around issues concerning, for example, gender relations or economics, and that technology is merely an arena in which these issues are played out. Likewise, within social constructionist examples, technology is also found to be subservient to sociological theories and categories of analysis. This is in keeping with comments from elsewhere concerning the use of ANT in IS studies, whereby some of this research either explains the technology at the expense of social interactions, or conversely portrays social interactions without giving detailed descriptions of the technological inscriptions (Walsham, 1997).

In accordance with the problems raised by the lack of focus on social structures and its attendant weaknesses (the micro and the macro, apolitical stance, gender), the next section includes an outline of strategies for compensating for some of these deficiencies focusing on the treatment of power. This is followed by comments on the particularity of information systems as innovations and the consequent limitations and possibilities for IS researchers adopting SST approaches, and then some suggestions for research agendas.

IMPLICATIONS FOR IS RESEARCH

Strategies for Dealing with Power and IS When Using SST

As stated above, some of the problems with ANT and SCOT's methodology are their flawed conceptualization of power (Wajcman, 2000). This evidently poses problems for IS research, which has an established record of publications in this area (Franz and Robey, 1984; Markus, 1983). Our first suggested strategy to deal with this is simply to draw on the earlier social shaping perspective, as outlined in the 1985 reader, which deals with macro-level issues, including power and gender, broadly applying a materialist method. Although the popularity of Marxist and feminist theory for informing innovation studies decreased in the intervening period, this does not mean that they are 'wrong' or any the less useful. As Hollis (1994) argues, we should not presume that what is unfashionable (especially in academic study) must be mistaken.

Alternatively, given that information systems often entail a treatment of organizations, another strategy for dealing with this weakness would be to supplement ANT and SCOT approaches with a critical management perspective. Critical management studies have been variously summarized (for example Alvesson and Willmott, 1996; Alvesson and Deetz, 2000; Burgoyne and Reynolds, 1997; Spencer, 2000) and entail a questioning of assumptions, being sensitive to power relations and a commitment to emancipation. A critical perspective can be used to question precisely those areas of organizational relationships left intact by a non-political approach (see, for example, Howcroft and Wilson, 2003; Mitev, 2003). Further, it acknowledges that some actors are disadvantaged in terms of power and skills in relation to others, and accepts that the level of commitment is likely to be uneven, as all members cannot be considered equal stakeholders.

In practice, various combinations have been adopted. Critical social theories have been used by IS researchers, for instance Foucault's concept of power/knowledge (Introna, 1997; see also Chapter 7); institutionalization (Silva and Backhouse, 1997); structuration theory (Orlikowski, 1992; see also Chapter 8; Walsham 1993); gender theories (Adam, Howcroft and Richardson, 2001); power and rationality (Drummond, 1996), Habermassian approaches (see Chapter 6) and critical realism (see Chapter 10). And in some cases, ANT has been combined with critical theories, for example technology drift theory (Holmstrom and Stalder, 2001), autopoiesis (Stalder, 1997), politics and power (Mitev, 2003; Silva, 1997). To illustrate more concretely the potential fruitfulness of combining ANT and a critical approach to power relations, we recap a worked analysis of a well-known IS failure case study, the London Ambulance Services (Beynon-Davies, 1995).

Power and politics: The example of the LAS information system

Silva and Backhouse (1997) concur that relying on the configuration of the actor networks for an explanation of IS phenomena is not enough. They suggest complementing ANT with organizational theorist Clegg's theory of power (Clegg, 1989) as a means of supplementing our understanding of the politics of organizations, especially the relationship between authority and power. Silva and Backhouse (1997, p. 397) realize this suggestion by developing the idea that if an information system is not fixed as an obligatory passage point, its institutionalization will not be achieved. They go on to analyse the failure of the LAS computer-aided despatch system, which collapsed shortly after launch in October 1992, as a consequence of which 20 people allegedly died. The system was abandoned and manual procedures were reintroduced. The chief executive officer resigned and the British government ordered a public inquiry. Managers had implemented the system to change the organizational culture and to improve the overall performance of the service. Silva and Backhouse use Clegg's theory of power in order to articulate an explanation covering all the possible political elements (Silva and Backhouse, 1997, pp. 402–7): the political 'exogenous contingencies' of the UK government introducing internal markets in the health system; the 'causal power' of agencies, for instance management's resources and control, staff discretion on operations and focus on jobs; the 'social power' of the IS, which was perceived by employees as a way of undermining participation and threatening their identity; the 'production power' dimension in that decisions about deploying ambulances were taken away from the controllers and programmed into the new system, bypassing local knowledge and experience. New tasks and rules failed to capture existing skills, staff perceived the system as disempowering and this caused disruption.

SST approaches are useful in examining relations between relevant groups of actors and exploring how exogenous contingencies are socially constructed and translated into techno-economic networks by actants. But a critical theory such as Clegg's can help systemize visible and invisible actors in terms of their weak or strong influence in organizational decision making in order to expose unequal power relations. These efforts to reawaken an SST critical sociological position should help infuse social analysis into IS research. The aim would be to investigate in what manner social order itself arises and to incorporate a richly informed, historically contextualized understanding of the social ordering of epistemological categories leading to patterns of inequity and hidden assumptions embedded in IS knowledge and practice.

In the next section, we develop further implications for IS researchers and practitioners. We outline the value of the SST approach for IS researchers and tentatively suggest rewarding research areas for those wishing to accept the invitation to apply SST concepts in their work.

Implications for IS Researchers and Practitioners

The strength of SST approaches is in their methodologies and as analytical devices, in that describing a techno-economic network in detail is a good contribution to building an empirical base, particularly for rich longitudinal in-depth case studies in their wider social and historical context. The notion of the 'seamless web' supports an open-ended and inclusive approach to actors in the largest possible sense, much more than is usually the case in IS research—even from an interpretivist perspective that does not theorize technology. The treatment of technology in a similar way to humans is intended to underline the fact that technology is not infinitely plastic, to be shaped in any way whatsoever by social forces, any more than technology is driven solely by its own internal logic, independently of society. SST conceptualizes the human–technology alloy as unstable and inherently contingent—it is constructed through the interpretive processes of actors and does not therefore embody any definitive capabilities or 'effects'. This approach, then, denies the 'technicist' viewpoints where technology is regarded as an independent variable on the grounds that no objective account of technical capabilities can be constructed. This does not mean that technology is unimportant; it does mean that what counts as technology and how various rhetorics adopt particular forms of explanation are social constructions, not concrete or objective 'facts'.

As an aid to the reader, we have included a summary in the form of insights that can be gleaned from the SST literature and potentially applied to the study of IS. Table 9.2 consists of references to

Table 9.2 Implications and insights

Conceptual tool	SST strand	Possible IT/IS themes	Key SST texts	Indicative IS texts employing concept
Technology shapes technology	Social shaping	• Legacy systems • Microsoft dominance • Standardized software	Armacost (1985)	Gillespie and Cornford (1996)
Economics shapes technology	Social shaping	• IT investment • Underfunding • Productivity paradox • Accounting systems	Hughes (1983, 1987)	Hanseth (2000) Thomas (1995)
Social relations shape technology	Social shaping	• IS and late capitalism? • Power—surveillance and control, security, privacy etc.	Schwartz Cowan (1985) Winner (1986)	Mackay (1995) Williams and Edge (1996) Raab et al. (1996)
The state shapes technology	Social shaping	• Military/defence systems • Hospital information systems • Public Sector IS development • Role of the government in Internet/e-commerce development and support	Roberts (1985)	Guice (1998)
Gender shapes technology	Social shaping	• Technological skills • Inequality • Levels of usage • IT professional hierarchy • End-user development	Schwartz Cowan (1985) Webster (1995b) Cockburn (1983, 1986)	Adam, Howcroft and Richardson (2002) Adam, Howcroft and Richardson (2001) Trauth (2002) Wilson (2001)

Concept	Approach	Themes	Reference 1	Reference 2
Interpretive flexibility	SCOT	• Resistance • Acceptance • Subjectivity of perception of problems and solutions	Pinch and Bijker (1987)	Sahay, Palit and Robey (1994), Sahay and Robey (1996)
Relevant social groups/technological frames	SCOT	• Stakeholders • Participants (users, project team, etc.)	Pinch and Bijker (1987)	Orlikowski and Gash (1994)
Closure	SCOT	• Success and failure • Project management and sign-off reports • (Re)definition of goals	Pinch and Bijker (1987), Bijker (1997)	Pozzebon (2001)
Obligatory point of passage	ANT	• Implementation strategy	Callon (1986a)	Silva (1997)
Stabilization/irreversibility	ANT	• Success and failure	Callon (1991)	Silva (1997) Mitev (2003) McLaughlin et al. (1999)
Translation	ANT	• Social policy at a distance • Problem/solution/resistance	Latour (1991)	Bloomfield and Best (1992)
Interessement/problematization/enrolment/mobilization	ANT	• Systems development • Participation • Empowerment (via information) • Evaluations • Exclusion of resistance	Callon (1991) Latour (1987)	Wilson and Howcroft (2000b) Bloomfield (1992)

(continued overleaf)

Table 9.2 (continued)

Conceptual tool	SST strand	Possible IT/IS themes	Key SST texts	Indicative IS texts employing concept
Actant/human–non-human symmetry	ANT	• (Active) users • Presumed user vs actual user • Resistance	Akrich (1992) Grint and Woolgar (1997)	Berg (1997) Nandhakumar and Vidgen (2001) Walsham and Sahay (1999) Wilson (2002) Wilson and Howcroft (2000a) McLaughlin *et al.* (1999)
Symmetry	ANT	• Success/failure	Akrich (1993) Latour (1996)	Mitev (2000) Wilson and Howcroft (2002) Silva, Dhillon and Backhouse (1997)
Standardization	ANT	• Standard software (ERP etc.) • Global systems • Deskilling • Standardization vs customization		Monteiro and Hanseth (1996) Berg and Timmermans (1997)
Script/inscription	ANT	• Moral order • Prescribed behaviour • Making activities 'visible' through reporting	Akrich (1992)	Bloomfield and Vurdubakis (1997) Walsham and Sahay (1999) Wilson (2002)

key SST texts that relate to the specifics of a given area; this is alongside some indicative readings from the IS literature. The table is neither definitive nor exhaustive, merely intended as an illustration of some of the ideas and their application to information systems.

CONCLUSION

A promising direction for IS research can be found within current SST debates. Some forms of SST focus on claims making and the rhetorics of claimants. Other forms of SST acknowledge assumptions about objective conditions and treat the evaluation of problems claims as an important part of the analysis; they study claims making within its context of culture and social structure (Best, 1993; Gergen, 2001; Gubrium, 1993). Like SST, critical social theories, for instance critical management studies, emphasize the fact that social reality is historically constituted; they object to 'managerialist accounts which assume or seek to justify existing social and organizational relationships as natural and/or unavoidable', and they aim instead to 'denaturalize' or 'unmask the power relations around which social and organizational life are woven' (Fournier and Grey, 2000, p. 19).

IS practice is particularly exposed to instrumentalist agendas and managerialist demands to deliver technical solutions. This type of rhetoric needs to be questioned in relation to the role of IS: from a practitioner's standpoint, SST clearly indicates that constructing technology as capable of solving socio-organizational problems seems to be overpowering and difficult to shift, in that it reflects a dominant 'technical orientation towards the world' (Feenberg, 2000). Still, we could for instance be 'more accommodating to localized practice that users deploy to make systems more usable', see organizations as containing many differently and often unequally placed actors, and perhaps attempt to strike 'some sort of accommodation. . . between new technology and these actors and interests' (McLaughlin *et al.*, 1999, p. 39).

Finally, in recommending SST and the hybrid approaches that we have discussed in this chapter, we should perhaps signpost to future investigators the fertile territory to be explored by additional reflection of the specificity of IS as technical and social innovations.

A GUIDE TO THE LITERATURE

Given the number of approaches that are included within this intellectual terrain, the key literature and representative authors pertaining to SST, SCOT and ANT will be briefly outlined. The originators of many of the key concepts that are used by the social shaping of technology approach can be found in Table 9.1 and numerous IS texts employing these concepts are suggested in Table 9.2. First, the SST reader (MacKenzie and Wajcman, 1985, 1999) offers an excellent introduction to the main concepts, with a number of examples illustrating the application of the approach. Within this collection, the chapter by Schwartz Cowan (1985) provides an especially interesting analysis of the social shaping of the refrigerator.

For the SCOT approach, the reader is referred to the original paper (Pinch and Bijker, 1984) that outlines how developments in the sociology of scientific knowledge can be usefully applied to our analysis of technology. The most influential study that uses these concepts is that of Bijker (1997) and his study of the bicycle, Bakelite and light bulbs. The key authors using ANT include Akrich, Callon, Latour and Law. Useful starting points include Akrich (1992); Callon (1986a, 1991); Latour (1987, 1991, 1992, 1999b) and Law (1991). In addition, two papers are highly recommended for the way in which they provide an overview of the area and summarize the links between these approaches: these are Williams and Edge (1996) and Wajcman (2002).

ENDNOTES

[1] A number of writers have serious doubts about the wholesale translation of SSK concerns to SCOT concerns. See Russell (1986); Button (1992); and Woolgar (1991) for more details.

[2] In this respect, some might argue that ANT is not immune from the accusation of anthropomorphism leveled at advocates of a 'hard' AI programme (Dreyfus and Dreyfus, 1986).

REFERENCES

Adam, A., Howcroft, D. and Richardson, H. (2001) 'Absent friends? The gender dimension in information systems research', in J. DeGross (ed.), *Realigning Research and Practice in Information Systems Development: The Social and Organizational Perspective*, Boston, MA: Kluwer, pp. 333–52.

Adam, A., Howcroft, D. and Richardson, H. (2002) 'Gender and IS, guest editorial', *Information Technology and People*, 15(2): 1.

Akrich, M. (1992) 'The de-scription of technical objects', in J. Law (ed.), *Shaping Technology/Building Society: Studies in Sociotechnical Change*, Cambridge, MA: MIT Press.

Akrich, M. (1993) 'Les objets techniques et leurs utilisateurs', *Raisons Pratiques (Les objets dans l'action)*, 4: 35–47.

Alvesson, M. and Deetz, S. (2000) *Doing Critical Management Research*, London: Sage.

Alvesson, M. and Willmott, H. (1996) *Making Sense of Management: A Critical Introduction*, London: Sage.

Armacost, M. H. (1985) 'The Thor-Jupiter controversy', in D. MacKenzie and J. Wajcman (eds), *The Social Shaping of Technology*, Milton Keynes: Open University Press.

Avgerou, C. (2002) *Information Systems and Global Diversity*, Oxford: Oxford University Press.

Bachrach, P. and Baratz, M. S. (1963) 'Decisions and nondecisions: An analytical framework', *American Political Science Review*, 57: 641–51.

Berg, M. (1997) 'The multiple bodies of the medical record: Towards a sociology of an artifact', *Sociological Quarterly*, 38(3): 513–37.

Berg, M. and Timmermans, S. (1997) 'Orders and their others: On the constitution of universalities in medical work', Actor Network Theory and After Workshop, Keele University.

Best, J. (1993) 'But seriously folks: The limitations of the strict constructionist interpretation of social problems', in G. Miller (ed.), *Reconsidering Social Constructionism. Debates in Social Problems Theory*, New York, NY: Aldine de Gruyter, pp. 129–50.

Beynon-Davies, P. (1995) 'Information systems "failure" and risk assessment: The case of the London Ambulance Services computer aided dispatch system', in G. Doukidis (ed.), *3rd European Conference on Information Systems*, Athens: University of Athens, pp. 1153–70.

Bijker, W. E. (1995) 'Sociohistorical technology studies', in T. Pinch (ed.), *Handbook of Science and Technology Studies*, Thousand Oaks, CA: Sage, pp. 229–56.

Bijker, W. E. (1997) *Of Bicycles, Bakelites, and Bulbs: Toward a Theory of Sociotechnical Change*, Cambridge, MA: MIT Press.

Bijker, W. E. and Law, J. (1992) *Shaping Technology/Building Society: Studies in Sociotechnical Change*, Cambridge, MA: MIT Press.

Bloomfield, B. P. (1991) 'The role of information systems in the UK National Health Service: Action at a distance and the fetish of calculation', *Social Studies of Science*, 21(4): 701–34.

Bloomfield, B. P. (1992) 'Understanding the social practices of systems developers', *Journal of Information Systems*, 2: 189–206.

Bloomfield, B. P. and Best, A. (1992) 'Management consultants, systems development, power and the translation of problems', *Sociological Review*, 40(3): 533–60.

Bloomfield, B. P. and Vurdubakis, T. (1997) 'Paper traces: Inscribing organisations and information technology', in D. Littler (ed.), *Information Technology and Organizations: Strategies, Networks and Integration*, Oxford: Oxford University Press, pp. 85–111.

Bloomfield, B. P., Coombs, R., Knights, D. and Littler, D. (1997) 'Introduction: The problematic of information technology and organization', in D. Littler (ed.), *Information Technology and Organizations*, Oxford: Oxford University Press, pp. 1–5.

Bowker, G. C., Timmermans, S. and Star, S. L. (1995) 'Infrastructure and organisational transformation: Classifying nurses' work', in J. I. DeGross (ed.), *Information Technology and Changes in Organizational Work*, London: Chapman and Hall.

Burgoyne, J. and Reynolds, M. (1997) *Managing Learning, Integrating Perspectives in Theory and Practice*, London: Sage.

Button, G. (1992) 'The curious case of the vanishing technology', in G. Button (ed.), *Technology in Working Order: Studies of Work, Interaction and Technology*, London: Routledge.

Callon, M. (1986a) 'The sociology of an actor network', in A. Rip (ed.), *Mapping the Dynamics of Science and Technology*, London: Macmillan.

Callon, M. (1986b) 'Some elements of a sociology of translation: Domestication of the scallops and the fisherman of St Brieuc Bay', in J. Law (ed.), *Power, Action and Belief*, London: Routledge, pp. 196–233.

Callon, M. (1991) 'Techno-economic networks and irreversibility', in J. Law (ed.), *A Sociology of Monsters: Essays on Power, Technology and Domination*, London: Routledge, pp. 132–64.

Callon, M. and Latour, B. (1981) 'Unscrewing the Big Leviathan: How actors macrostructure reality and how sociologists help them to do it', in A. V. Cicourel (ed.), *Advances in Social Theory and Methodology: Towards an Integration of Micro- and Macro-Sociologies*, London: Routledge & Kegan Paul, pp. 277–303.

Clegg, S. R. (1989) *Frameworks of Power*, London: Sage.

Cockburn, C. (1983) *Brothers, Male Dominance and Technological Change*, London: Pluto Press.

Cockburn, C. (1985) 'The material of male power', in D. MacKenzie and J. Wajcman (eds), *The Social Shaping of Technology*, Milton Keynes: Open University Press, pp. 125–46.

Cockburn, C. (1986) *Machinery of Dominance: Women, Men and Technical Knowledge*, London: Pluto Press.

Collins, H. and Pinch, T. (1993) *The Golem: What Everyone Should Know about Science*, Cambridge: Cambridge University Press.

Collins, H. and Yearley, S. (1992) 'Journey into space', in A. Pickering (ed.), *Science as Practice and Culture*, Chicago, IL: Chicago University Press, pp. 369–89.

Dreyfus, H. L. and Dreyfus, S. E. (1986) *Mind over Machine: The Power of Human Intuition and Expertise in the Era of the Computer*, New York, NY: Free Press/Macmillan.

Drummond, H. (1996) *Escalation in Decision-Making: The Tragedy of Taurus*, Oxford: Oxford University Press.

Ewusi-Mensah, K. and Przasnyski, Z. H. (1995) 'Learning from abandoned information systems development projects', *Journal of Information Technology*, 10: 3–14.

Feenberg, A. (2000) 'Constructivism and technology critique: Replies to critics', *Inquiry*, 43: 225–38.

Fournier, V. and Grey, C. (2000) 'At the critical moment: Conditions and prospects for critical management studies', *Human Relations*, 53(1): 7–32.

Franz, C. R. and Robey, D. (1984) 'An investigation of user-led systems design: Rational and political perspectives', *Communications of the ACM*, 27(12): 1202–9.

Gergen, K. J. (2001) *Social Construction in Context*, London: Sage.

Gillespie, A. and Cornford, J. (1996) 'Telecommunication infrastructure and regional development', in W. H. Dutton (ed.), *Information and Communication Technologies: Visions and Realities*, Oxford: Oxford University Press.

Grint, K. and Woolgar, S. (1997) *The Machine at Work: Technology, Work and Organization*, Cambridge: Polity Press.

Gubrium, J. F. (1993) 'For a cautious naturalism', in G. Miller (ed.), *Reconsidering Social Constructionism: Debates in Social Problems Theory*, New York, NY: Aldine de Gruyter, pp. 89–102.

Guice, J. (1998) 'Looking backward and forward at the internet', *The Information Society*, 14: 201–11.

Hanseth, O. (2000) 'The economics of standards', in C. Ciborra (ed.), *From Control to Drift*, Oxford: Oxford University Press, pp. 56–70.

Hollis, M. (1994) *The Philosophy of Social Science*, Cambridge: Cambridge University Press.

Holmstrom, J. and Stalder, F. (2001) 'Drifting technologies and multi-purpose networks: The case of the Swedish cashcard', *Information and Organization*, 11: 187–206.

Howard, J. (2002) *Towards a Reconstructivist Stance in Technology Studies*, New York, NY: Rensselaer Polytechnic Institute.

Howcroft, D. and Wilson, M. (2003) 'Paradoxes of participatory design: The end-user perspective', *Information and Organization*, 13(1): 1–24.

Hughes, T. P. (1983) *Networks of Power: Electrification in Western Society, 1880–1930*, Baltimore, MD: Johns Hopkins University Press.

Hughes, T. (1985) 'Edison and the electric light', in D. MacKenzie and J. Wajcman (eds), *The Social Shaping of Technology*, Milton Keynes: Open University Press.

Hughes, T. (1987) 'The evolution of large technological systems', in T. Pinch (ed.), *The Social Construction of Technological Systems. New Directions in the Sociology and History of Technology*, Cambridge, MA: MIT Press, pp. 51–82.

Introna, L. D. (1997) *Management, Information and Power*, Basingstoke: Macmillan Press.

Jasanoff, S., Markle, G. E., Petersen, J. C. and Pinch, T. (eds) (1995) *Handbook of Science and Technology Studies*, Thousand Oaks, CA: Sage.

Kline, R. and Pinch, T. (1999) 'The social construction of technology', in J. Wajcman (ed), *The Social Shaping of Technology*, Buckingham: Open University Press, pp. 113–15.

Kling, R. (1992) 'Audiences, narratives and human values in social studies of technology', *Science, Technology and Human Values*, 17(3): 349–65.

Knights, D. and Murray, F. (1994) *Managers Divided: Organisation Politics and Information Technology Management*, Chichester: John Wiley & Sons.

Knorr-Cetina, K. D. (1981) 'The micro-sociological challenge of macro-sociology: Towards a reconstruction of social theory and methodology', in A. V. Cicourel (ed.), *Advances in Social Theory and Methodology: Towards an Integration of Micro- and Macro-sociologies*, London: Routledge & Kegan Paul, pp. 1–47.

Latour, B. (1987) *Science in Action. How to Follow Scientists and Engineers through Society*, Cambridge, MA: Harvard University Press.

Latour, B. (1991) 'Technology is society made durable' in J. Law (ed.), *A Sociology of Monsters: Essays on Power, Technology and Domination*, London: Routledge, pp. 103–31.

Latour, B. (1992) 'Where are the missing masses? The sociology of a few mundane artefacts', in J. Law (ed.), *Shaping Technology/Building Society: Studies in Sociotechnical Change*, Cambridge, MA: MIT Press, pp. 225–58.

Latour, B. (1993) 'Ethnography of a 'high-tech' case: About Aramis', in P. Lemonnier (ed.), *Technological Choices: Transformations in Material Culture since the Neolithic*, London: Routledge & Kegan Paul, pp. 372–98.

Latour, B. (1996) *ARAMIS or the Love of Technology*, Cambridge, MA: Harvard University Press.

Latour, B. (1999a) 'On recalling ANT', in J. Law and J. Hassard (eds), *Actor Network Theory and After*, Oxford: Blackwell, pp. 15–25.

Latour, B. (1999b) *Pandora's Hope: Essays on the Reality of Science Studies*, Cambridge, MA: Harvard University Press.

Latour, B. and Woolgar, S. (1979) *Laboratory Life: The Construction of Scientific Facts*, Princeton, NJ: Princeton University Press.

Law, J. (ed.) (1991) *A Sociology of Monsters: Essays on Power, Technology and Domination*, London: Routledge.

Law, J. and Hassard, J. (eds) (1999) *Actor Network Theory and After*, Oxford: Blackwell.

Lohan, M. (2000) 'Constructive tensions in feminist technology studies', *Social Studies of Science*, 30(6): 895–916.

Lukes, S. (1974) *Power: A Radical View*, London: Macmillan.

Lyon, D. (1988) *The Information Society*, Cambridge: Polity Press.

Mackay, H. (1995) 'Theorising the IT/society relationship', in H. Mackay (ed.), *Information Technology and Society*, London: Sage.

MacKenzie, D. (1988) ''Micro'' versus ''macro'' sociologies of science and technology', ESRC PICT (Programme on Information and Communication Technologies) working paper no 2, Edinburgh University: Research Centre for Social Sciences.

MacKenzie, D. and Wajcman, J. (eds) (1985) *The Social Shaping of Technology*, Milton Keynes: Open University Press.

Markus, M. L. (1983) 'Power, politics, and MIS implementation', *Communications of the ACM*, 26(6): 430–44.

McLaughlin, J., Rosen, P., Skinner, D. and Webster, A. (1999) *Valuing Technology: Organisations, Culture and Change*, London: Routledge.

McLoughlin, I. (1997) 'Babies, bathwater, guns and roses', in I. McLoughlin and M. Harris (eds), *Innovation, Organizational Change and Technology*, London: International Thomson Business Press, pp. 207–21.

McLoughlin, I. (1999) *Creative Technological Change: The Shaping of Technology and Organisations*, London: Routledge.

Mitev, N. N. (2000) 'Toward social constructivist understanding of IS success and failure: Introducing a new computerized reservation system', in J. I. DeGross (ed.), *Proceedings of 21st ICIS*, Atlanta, GA: Association for Information Systems.

Mitev, N. N. (2003) 'Constructivist and critical approaches to an IS failure case study: Symmetry, translation and power', LSE working paper series no. 127, London: London School of Economics.

Monteiro, E. and Hanseth, O. (1996) 'Social shaping of information infrastructure: On being specific about the technology', W. J. Orlikowski, G. Walsham, M. R. Jones, and J. I. DeGross (eds), *Information Technology and Changes in Organizational Work*, London: Chapman & Hall.

Nandhakumar, J. and Vidgen, R. (2001) 'Due process and the introduction of new technology: The institution of video teleconferencing', *Proceedings of IFIP 8.2 Conference, Boise, Idaho, July 2001*, Boston, MA: Kluwer Academic Publishers.

Noble, D. (1984) *Forces of Production: A Social History of Industrial Automation*, New York, NY: Knopf.

Orlikowski, W. J. (1992) 'The duality of technology: Rethinking the concept of technology in organizations', *Organization Science*, 3(3): 398–427.

Orlikowski, W. J. and Gash, D. C. (1994) 'Technological frames: Making sense of information technology in organizations', *ACM Transactions on Information Systems*, 12(2): 174–207.

Peltu, M., MacKenzie, D., Shapiro, S. and Dutton, W. H. (1996) 'Computer power and human limits', in W. H. Dutton (ed.), *Information and Communication Technologies*, Oxford: Oxford University Press, pp. 177–96.

Pinch, T. F. and Bijker, W. E. (1984) 'The social construction of facts and artifacts: Or how the sociology of science and technology might benefit each other', *Social Studies of Science*, 14: 399–441.

Pinch, T. F. and Bijker, W. E. (1987) 'The social construction of facts and artifacts: Or how the sociology of science and technology might benefit each other', in T. Pinch (ed.), *The Social Construction of Technological Systems: New Directions in the Sociology and History of Technology*, Cambridge, MA: MIT Press, pp. 399–441.

Pozzebon, M. (2001) 'Demystifying the rhetorical closure of ERP packages', *Proceedings of the 22nd International Conference on Information Systems*, Atlanta, GA: Association for Information Systems.

Raab, C., Bellamy, C., Taylor, J., Dutton, W. H. and Peltu, M. (1996) 'The information polity: Electronic democracy, privacy, and surveillance', in W. H. Dutton (ed.), *Information and Communication Technologies: Visions and Realities*, Oxford: Oxford University Press.

Radder, H. (1992) 'Normative reflexions on constructivist approaches to science and technology', *Social Studies of Science*, 22: 141–73.

Roberts, A. (1985) 'Preparing to fight a nuclear war', in D. MacKenzie and J. Wajcman (eds), *The Social Shaping of Technology*, Milton Keynes: Open University Press.

Russell, S. (1986) 'The social construction of facts and artefacts: A response to Pinch and Bijker', *Social Studies of Science*, 16(2): 331–46.

Russell, S. and Williams, R. (2002) 'Social shaping of technology: Frameworks, findings and implications for policy with glossary of social shaping concepts', in R. Williams (ed.), *Shaping Technology, Guiding Policy: Concepts, Spaces and Tools*, Cheltenham: Edward Elgar, pp. 37–132.

Sahay, S. and Robey, D. (1996) 'Organizational context, social interpretation, and the implementation and consequences of geographic information systems', *Accounting, Management and Information Technologies*, 6(4): 255–82.

Sahay, S., Palit, M. and Robey, D. (1994) 'A relativist approach to studying the social construction of information technology', *European Journal of Information Systems*, 3(4): 248–58.

Sauer, C. (1993) *Why Information Systems Fail: A Case Study Approach*, Henley on Thames: Alfred Waller.

Schwartz Cowan, R. (1985) 'The industrial revolution in the home', in D. MacKenzie and J. Wajcman (eds), *The Social Shaping of Technology*, Milton Keynes: Open University Press.

Silva, L. (1997) 'Power and politics in the adoption of information systems in organisations: The case of a research centre in Latin America', PhD thesis, Department of Information Systems, London: London School of Economics.

Silva, L. and Backhouse, J. (1997) 'Becoming part of the furniture: The institutionalisation of information systems', in J. DeGross (ed.), *Information Systems and Qualitative Research: Proceedings IFIP 8.2 Conference, Philadelphia*, London: Chapman & Hall, pp. 389–416.

Silva, L., Dhillon, G. and Backhouse, J. (1997) 'Developing a networked authority: Nature and significance of power relationships', in R. O'Callaghan (ed.) *5th European Conference on Information Systems*, Cork: University of Cork.

Sorensen, K. (2002) 'Social shaping on the move? On the policy relevance of the social shaping of technology perspective', in R. Williams (ed.), *Shaping Technology, Guiding Policy: Concepts, Spaces and Tools*, Cheltenham: Edward Elgar, pp. 19–35.

Spencer, D. (2000) 'Braverman and the contribution of labour process analysis to the critique of capitalist production: Twenty-five years on', *Work, Employment and Society*, 14(2): 223–43.

Stalder, F. (1997) 'Actor-network theory and communication networks: Towards convergence', Toronto: Faculty of Information Studies, University of Toronto.

Star, S. L. (1991) 'Power, technologies and the phenomenology of conventions: On being allergic to onions', in J. Law (ed.), *A Sociology of Monsters: Essays on Power, Technology and Domination*, London: Routledge.

Thomas, R. (1995) 'Access and inequality', in H. Mackay (ed.), *Information Technology and Society*, London: Sage.

Trauth, E. (2002) 'Odd girl out: An individual differences perspective on women in the IT profession', *Information Technology and People*, 15(2): 98–118.

Wajcman, J. (1991) *Feminism Confronts Technology*, Cambridge: Polity Press.

Wajcman, J. (2000) 'Reflections on gender and technology studies: In what state is the art?', *Social Studies of Science*, 30(3): 447–64.

Wajcman, J. (2002) 'Addressing technological change: The challenge to social theory', *Current Sociology*, 50(3): 347–63.

Walsham, G. (1993) *Interpreting Information Systems in Organisations*, Chichester: John Wiley & Sons.

Walsham, G. (1997) 'Actor-network theory and IS research: Current status and future prospects', in J. DeGross (ed.), *Information Systems and Qualitative Research: Proceedings of the IFIP WG 8.2 International Conference on Information Systems and Qualitative Research*, London: Chapman & Hall, pp. 466–80.

Walsham, G. and Sahay, S. (1999) 'GIS for district-level administration in India: Problems and opportunities', *MIS Quarterly*, 23(1): 39–66.

Webster, F. (1995a) *Theories of the Information Society*, London: Routledge.

Webster, J. (1995b) *Shaping Women's Work*, Harlow: Longman Sociology Series.

Williams, R. (1997) 'The social shaping of information and communications technologies', in R. Williams (ed.), *The Social Shaping of Information Superhighways*, New York, NY: St Martin's Press, pp. 299–338.

Williams, R. and Edge, D. (1996) 'The social shaping of technology', *Research Policy*, 25: 865–99.

Wilson, M. (2001) 'A new paradigm for considering gender in information systems research', in J. DeGross (ed.), *New Directions in Information Systems Development*, Boston, MA: Kluwer Academic Publishers, pp. 353–65.

Wilson, M. (2002) 'Making nursing visible? Gender, technology and the care plan as script', *Information Technology and People*, 15(2): 139–58.

Wilson, M. and Howcroft, D. (2000a) 'The politics of IS evaluation: A social shaping perspective', in J. I. DeGross (ed.), *Proceedings of 21st ICIS*, Atlanta, GA: Association of Information Systems.

Wilson, M. and Howcroft, D. (2000b) 'The role of gender in user resistance and IS failure', in J. DeGross (ed.), *Organizational and Social Perspectives on Information Technology*, Boston, MA: Kluwer Academic Publishers.

Wilson, M. and Howcroft, D. (2002) 'Re-conceptualising failure: Social shaping meets IS research', *European Journal of Information Systems*, 11: 236–50.

Winner, L. (1986) 'Do artefacts have politics?', in L. Winner (ed.), *The Whale and the Reactor: A Search for Limits in an Age of High Technology*, Chicago, IL: University of Chicago Press, pp. 19–39.

Winner, L. (1993) 'Upon opening the black box and finding it empty: Social constructivism and the philosophy of technology', *Science, Technology and Human Values*, 18: 362–78.

Woodhouse, E., Hess, D., Breyman, S. and Martin, B. (2002) 'Science studies and activism: Possibilities and problems for reconstructivist agendas', *Social Studies of Science*, 32(2): 297–319.

Woolgar, S. (1991) 'Configuring the user: The case of usability trials', in J. Law (ed.), *A Sociology of Monsters: Essays on Power, Technology and Domination*, London: Routledge.

10
Re-establishing the Real: Critical Realism and Information Systems

John Mingers

Historically, most empirical information systems research and systems development, particularly in the United States, has been underpinned by a positivist (more generally in this chapter *empiricist*, see later) philosophy. This has been demonstrated in several surveys of the literature (Orlikowski and Baroudi, 1991; Walsham, 1995a; Nandhakumar and Jones, 1997; Mingers, 2003b) as well as in more theoretical contributions (Goles and Hirschheim, 2000; Iivari, Hirschheim and Klein, 1998; Hirschheim, Klein and Lyytinen, 1996; Benbasat and Weber, 1996; Banville and Landry, 1989). Broadly speaking, research in this tradition aims to remove any elements of subjectivity by focusing only on events that can be publicly recorded and measured, and then using statistical and mathematical models to capture the patterns that appear in the data (see also Chapters 1 and 2).

During the 1980/90s several streams of work based on different philosophies emerged. The main one was interpretivism (more generally in this chapter *conventionalism*; Lee, 1999; Lee, Liebenau and DeGross, 1997; Walsham, 1993, 1995a, 1995b), which emphasizes the inherent *meaningfulness* of the social world. Several different strands can be identified, for example ethnography (Harvey and Myers, 1995), hermeneutics (Olson and Carslisle, 2001; Myers, 1994; Boland, 1991), ethnomethodology (Bhattacharjee and Paul, 2001; Crabtree *et al.*, 2000) and phenomenology (Dreyfus, 1996; Mingers, 2001b; Coyne, 1995; Boland, 1985; Introna, 1997; see also Chapters 3 and 4). These approaches go in the opposite direction, focusing on individual and group subjectivity. They aim to generate a rich understanding and description of particular people's experiences of the social world.

There are other approaches to IS research based in distinctive philosophical traditions such as critical theory (Ngwenyama and Lee, 1997; Lyytinen and Klein, 1985; Ngwenyama, 1991; Janson, Cecez-Kecmanovic and Brown, 2001; Lyytinen, 1992; also Chapters 5 and 6 in this volume), postmodernism (Ciborra, 1998; Robinson *et al.*, 1998; Greenhill, 2001) and actor-network theory (Walsham, 1997; see also Chapter 9). Most of these approaches are covered in other chapters in this book. Each philosophical position tends to favour the particular research methods that fit its own assumptions.

There has been a range of reactions to this plurality of philosophical approaches. Imperialists argue for the dominance of one particular paradigm (usually positivism), either on epistemological grounds (that it is the correct way to generate knowledge) or in the belief that it is necessary to create a strong discipline (Pfeffer, 1993; Benbasat and Weber, 1996). Isolationists tend to accept the arguments of Burrell and Morgan (1979) that there are distinctively different paradigms within a discipline and that these are generally incommensurable; that is, they cannot be directly compared with each other because they are based on radically different assumptions. From this perspective, research should develop separately within each paradigm (Deetz, 1996; Parker and McHugh, 1991). Finally pluralists accept, and indeed welcome, a diversity of paradigms and research methods. Within this group we can distinguish between those who welcome diversity for its own sake (Van Maanen, 1995a, 1995b); those who see different methods as being more or less appropriate for particular research questions or situations (Robey, 1996; Landry and Banville, 1992); and those who argue that research should strive to be transparadigmatic, routinely combining philosophically distinct research methods (Mingers, 2001a; Goles and Hirschheim, 2000). The information systems discipline is not unique in respect of this diversity—most social sciences, for example organization theory, sociology, economics or geography, are equally split.

However, what is often not recognized is that there are significant problems within the underlying philosophies of science and social science themselves. Positivism has been extensively critiqued and the resulting consensus around a weak empiricist position (known as hypothetico-deductivism) leads to an impoverished view of (realist) ontology and causality. Within the social sciences extreme constructivist and postmodern positions have undermined even the most basic tenets of science and rationality.

This chapter considers a particular philosophy of science—*critical realism*—as a way of resolving or dissolving most of these issues, and providing a consistent and coherent underpinning philosophy for information systems. The first section discusses the problems with the philosophy of science, particularly as they inhibit a realist (although not 'naive' realist) approach. The second section develops critical realism and shows how it addresses these problems. The third section discusses criticisms and limitations of critical realism, and the final section makes this more concrete by considering IS research, in particular examining two important IS research methods—statistical analysis (positivist) and soft systems methodology (SSM) (interpretivist)—through the lens of critical realism.

CONTEXT

Problems in the Philosophy of Natural Science

In general, a *realist* understanding of science takes the view that certain types of entities—be they objects, forces, social structures or ideas—exist in the world, largely independent of human beings; and that we can gain reliable, although not perfect knowledge of them. However, from as long ago as the eighteenth century Hume (1967) and Berkeley (1995) undermined such a view by denying fundamental tenets like the existence of a physical world, causal necessity or unobservable entities. Berkeley argued that we only actually know objects through our ideas and perceptions of them and that, therefore, is all we can actually take to exist. Thus to be is to be perceived. Hume was highly sceptical of several basic notions such as causality, unobservable entities and induction. With regard to causality, he says that we often see one event regularly followed by another and we believe that event A (e.g. swing a bat) causes event B (a ball moving). However, all we can actually observe is the constant conjunction of the two events. Our belief that A *causes* B is simply that: a psychological belief. There is nothing more to causality than a regular succession of events. Hume is similarly sceptical about induction, the idea that witnessing an event occur many times (e.g. the sun rising) warrants us claiming it will always happen. These views, particularly that of Humean causality, underlie empiricism and have serious antirealist implications (for Hume see also Chapter 1).

During the twentieth century, 'naive realism' has continued to be under constant attack from empiricism (which restricts science to mathematical formulations of empirical regularities) on the one hand and the many different forms of conventionalism or constructivism (which deny the existence of a world independent of human thought and perception) on the other.

Empiricism

In very broad terms, empiricism refers to those philosophies that see science as explaining events that can be empirically observed. That which is not manifest and capable of observation must be non-scientific or even, in the extreme case of the Vienna Circle philosophers, literally meaningless. Events are expected to display regularities or patterns that can be explained as being particular instances of universal laws of the form 'given certain conditions, whenever event X occurs then event Y will occur'. Science is seen as the systematic observation of event regularities, the description of these regularities in the form of universal laws, and the prediction of particular outcomes from the laws.

Logical empiricism was developed during the 1920s by a group known as the Vienna Circle, for example Schlick (Schlick, Mulder and Velde-Schlick, 1979) and Neurath (Neurath and McGuinness, 1987), who aimed to specify a truly scientific conception of knowledge and the world. Their main tenets were:

- Scientific knowledge must rest ultimately on that which is empirically open to the senses. This meant that any scientific propositions must be able to be empirically verified, and that anything unable to be directly or indirectly observed must be non-scientific or even meaningless.
- Empirical observations must then be reformulated into some strict mathematical or logical language, following the work of Frege (Frege, Geach and Black, 1952) and Russell (Whitehead and Russell, 1925), generally expressed in terms of universal laws.
- There must be a unity of method across all sciences, thus social science and history must also be formulated in such a way.

These propositions rested on particular fundamental assumptions: i) the idea that observation and perception were unproblematic, simply providing a mirror on nature; ii) the Humean (1967) principle that the observation of one event following another (e.g. one ball hitting another) did not enable us to prove some underlying causal mechanism—all that we can claim are 'constant conjunctions of events'; iii) the principle of induction—that *universal* laws could be derived from a set of *particular* observations accompanied by the deduction of predictions from the laws.

This view of science was extensively critiqued. The idea of pure, objective perception and observation was exploded by psychologists (Piaget, 1969; Gregory, 1972), sociologists (Cicourel, 1973) and philosophers (Merleau-Ponty, 1962; Hansen, 1958; Popper, 1972). They showed, theoretically and experimentally, that the brain was not simply a blank slate on which the external world imposed itself, but rather that perception and conceptualization were an active construction of the nervous system. Hesse (1974), Popper (1972), Wittgenstein (1958) and Kuhn (1970) showed that observational terms—that is, the language we use to describe our observations—were not an atomistic picturing of reality but part of a pre-given linguistic structure—in short, that all observation was theory dependent. And Popper (1959, 1969), based on Hume, rejected the possibility of induction and verification, replacing it with deduction and falsification.

In response to these criticisms there developed the 'deductive-nomological (D-N)' or 'hypothetico-deductive' method centred around the work of Hempel (1965) and Popper. Science was still seen to be based fundamentally on empirical observations, although recognizing their theory dependence. From such observations theories were generated and expressed in terms of universal (nomological) laws ('covering laws'). Explanation, or prediction, then consisted of the logical deduction of particular events given some antecedent conditions and a set of laws. It was accepted that the laws might only be expressed in terms of statistical probabilities, and that they could not be *proved* to be true inductively. Some people maintained a confirmationist view that empirical evidence could provide support for a theory, while Popper developed the falsificationist approach that negative observations could definitely refute a theory. On this view, science should constantly aim to reject poor theories rather support or confirm good theories. Hume's view of causation was still largely accepted. There was still general scepticism about the ontological status of theoretical concepts that could not be observed fairly directly, leading to debates about the legitimacy of 'theoretical entities'. Perceptibility was the criterion for existence.

The D-N approach also suffers from a range of problems, some of which will be explained in the next section on conventionalist alternatives. But, to highlight a few:

- Falsificationism, certainly in simple form, does not stand up: does a failed experiment falsify an underlying theory, or simply the experiment itself and its supplementary theories? Theories often need to be developed despite initial failures, not just abandoned. Does not falsificationism implicitly rely on induction; that is, moving from particular instances (of failure) to the general statement that it will always fail?
- The covering law model, especially Humean causality, was very impoverished, simply providing a description of *what* happened in highly constrained experimental conditions, with no explanation of *why* it happened or sometimes did not; and with no mechanism for the generation of new theories or putatively real entities. This is particularly problematic from a realist point of view, as it restricts 'reality' to the domain of empirically observable events and prohibits underlying generative mechanisms.
- It did not correspond, in many ways, with the actual practices of scientists and could not therefore satisfactorily explain the *de facto* success of science.
- The proposal that the social world was in essence no different from the natural world simply could not be sustained.

Conventionalism

Problems with the empiricist view of science centre on the impossibility of pure, unmediated observation of empirical 'facts'. So the term conventionalism covers a wide range of philosophies that all emphasize the inevitable dependence of scientific theories on human perception, conceptualization and judgement.

The first position, *pragmatism*, derives from philosophers such as Dewey (1938) and Peirce (1878) and has been developed most radically (and perhaps somewhat illegitimately) by Rorty (1980, 1989). At a general level pragmatism is a view about the purpose of science—that it is essentially a practical activity aimed at producing useful knowledge rather than understanding the true nature of the world. Thus Peirce developed a pragmatist theory of meaning such that the meaning of a concept was specified purely in terms of the actual practical effects that it would have; and a consensus theory of truth as that which would come to be believed by a community of scientists in the long term, rather than as correspondence to reality (Habermas, 1978; see also Chapter 6). Dewey saw knowledge and truth as the outcome of processes that successfully resolved problematic situations.

The second position on the nature of science comes from those who study the actual practices of scientists and find that they do not correspond to the standard philosophical theories. This becomes more than mere description when it is used to critique the possibility of particular philosophical prescriptions. Kuhn's (1970, 1977) identification of major paradigms of thought throughout science is so well known as to need little exposition. The general idea is a development of the theory dependence of observation: at any one time there is a broad, underlying theoretical conceptualization (e.g. Einsteinian physics) that is unquestioned within 'normal' scientific activity. This paradigm informs all actual experimentation, which is simply puzzle solving within the paradigm. The failure of particular experiments does not refute, or even question, the basic paradigm. Only in periods of 'revolutionary' science, when there are many anomalies, do paradigms actually become questioned or compete.

This view leads to a much greater recognition of the social and psychological nature of scientific activity. A paradigm develops through consensus within a social community of scientists through many practical mechanisms such as learned societies, journals or funding bodies. Individual scientists come to accept the underlying assumptions concerning research practice, theoretical validity and core values as they become members of the community. Theoretical innovations that challenge the paradigm are generally rejected without serious consideration.

The basic idea of paradigms replacing each other over time has developed, particularly within social science, to the idea of there being competing paradigms existent at the same time (e.g. positivist, interpretive and critical). This is often combined with the claim that paradigms are incommensurable (although Kuhn himself did not agree with this; Kuhn, 1977). That is, each paradigm is so all inclusive in defining its ontological and epistemological presuppositions that it is literally not possible actually to compare them—each defines its own 'reality'. Clearly, the Kuhnian view has major relativistic implications for empiricism, since it points out the constructed, conventional nature of scientific theorizing and makes truth not correspondence to some external reality but that which is accepted by a scientific community at a particular point in time. The incommensurability thesis is even more undermining, since it makes it impossible to judge between paradigms or even assert that a later paradigm is actually superior to an earlier one.

The third viewpoint, the sociology of scientific knowledge (SSK), can be seen as an intensification of Kuhn's study of the actual practice of science. It investigates the way in which scientific and technological knowledge comes to be constructed and accepted within a scientific community (Bloor, 1976; Barnes, 1977; Latour, 1987; Bijker, Hughes and Pinch, 1987; Collins, 1985; Knorr-Cetina and Mulkay, 1983; Woolgar, 1988). The most radical theories from this perspective (e.g. Bloor) argue that in fact science is no different to other forms of purposeful social activity and actually has no greater claim to truth (see also Chapters 7 and 9).

The Relationship between Natural and Social Science

So far, the discussion has centred around the nature of natural science on the assumption that this was most relevant to information systems, but in recent years there have been persuasive arguments that since IS is conducted within social organizations, social science is also of relevance (Avison and Myers, 1995; Galliers, 1992; Myers, 1994; Boland, 1991; Orlikowski and Baroudi, 1991). This then brings into the picture major philosophical debates concerning the nature of social science in relation to natural science that can only be sketched here (for overviews see Outhwaite, 1987; Keat and Urry, 1981; Burrell and Morgan, 1979; Giddens, 1976).

Broadly, there are three possible positions:

- The naturalist view is that there is one general approach to science that applies to all domains. Within this category, positivists hold that for anything to be scientific it must follow the canons of positivism/empiricism and thus be based on universal generalizations from empirical observations (Giddens, 1974). This was in fact accepted by early sociologists such as Comte and, despite much criticism, continues in areas such as empirical and functionalist sociology and much IS research. Critical realists, on the other hand, maintain a modified naturalism that is non-positivist and that accepts there are some differences between the natural and social worlds.
- The antithesis is the view that the social world is intrinsically different to the natural world, being constituted through language and meaning, and thus involves entirely different hermeneutic (Bleicher, 1980), phenomenological (Schutz, 1972) or social constructivist (Gergen, 1999) approaches. The argument here would be the idealist one that ontologically social objects do not exist in the way physical ones do (i.e. as subject independent) and that epistemologically there is no possibility of facts or observations

that are independent of actors, cultures or social practices. Both Habermas (1978) and Giddens (1976) fall in this category (see Chapters 6 and 8).

- The most radical position denies the possibility of objective or scientific knowledge at all, in either domain. Arguments here come from the strong sociology of knowledge programme discussed above; poststructuralists such as Foucault (1980), who point out the extent to which even our most basic categories such as male/female are socially constructed, and the inevitable intertwining of knowledge and power (see Chapter 7); and more generally postmodernists (Best and Kellner, 1991), who attempt to undermine even the most basic categories of modernist rationality such as distinctions between truth and falsity, better or worse, or the existence of external reality.

AN INTRODUCTION TO CRITICAL REALISM

Critical realism has been developing for some years (Bhaskar, 1978, 1979, 1986, 1993; Keat and Urry, 1981) in response to the fundamental difficulty of maintaining a realist position in the face of the criticisms, outlined above, of an empirical and naturalist view of science. Its original aims (on which this chapter will concentrate) were:

- To re-establish a realist view of *being* in the ontological domain while accepting the relativism of knowledge as socially and historically conditioned in the epistemological domain (Bhaskar, 1978). In other words, to establish that there is an independently existing world of objects and structures that are causally active, giving rise to the actual events that do and do not occur. At the same time, to accept the criticisms of naive realism and recognize that our observations and knowledge can never be pure and unmediated, but are relative to our time period and culture.
- To argue for a critical naturalism in social science (Bhaskar, 1979). That is, to maintain that the same general process of science is applicable in both the natural and social domains, but to accept that the particular characteristics of the social world place inevitable limits on that process.

Originally Bhaskar referred to his work as either 'transcendental realism' or 'critical naturalism', reflecting these two aims, but these became contracted to 'critical realism'. In later work (Bhaskar, 1993,

1994) the use of the qualifier 'critical' related also to critical social theory (Habermas, 1974, 1978) and put forward the argument that no social theory can be purely descriptive, it must be evaluative, and thus there can be no split between facts and values. Following from this was the view that social theory is inevitably transformative, providing an explanatory critique that logically entails action (Archer *et al.*, 1998, Part III).

Critical realism is becoming influential in a range of disciplines: geography (Yeung, 1997; Pratt, 1995), economics (Fleetwood, 1999; Lawson, 1997), organization theory (Tsang and Kwan, 1999; Marsden, 1993; Ackroyd and Fleetwood, 2000; Reed, 1997, 2001), sociology (Archer, 1995; New, 1995; Sayer, 1997; Layder, 1994), international relations (Wright, 1999), Marxism (Brown, Fleetwood and Roberts, 2002) and research methods in general (Layder, 1993; Sayer, 1992).

Arguments Establishing an Independent Ontological Domain

The first step is to put forward arguments that establish the existence of an ontological domain separate from the activities and cognitions of human beings.

Bhaskar's (Archer *et al.*, 1998, p. 23) starting point is to argue, specifically against empiricism and positivism, that science is not merely a matter of recording constant conjunctions of observable events, but is about objects, entities and structures that exist (even though they are perhaps unobservable) and generate or give rise to the events that we do observe. The form of the argument is a *transcendental* (this follows a broadly Kantian interpretation of 'transcendental') one. That is, it begins with some accepted happening or occurrence and asks what the world must be like for this to occur or to be intelligible. In this case, what is accepted by both empiricism and many forms of idealism is that we do have perceptual experience of the world, and that science is carried out through experimental activity in which scientists bring about particular outcomes.

The argument is that neither empiricism nor idealism can successfully explain these occurrences, and that they necessitate some form of realist ontology. With regard to perception, we can note that as human beings we have to learn (as babies) to perceive things and events; that our perceptions can change or be mistaken (e.g. visual illusions); and that scientists, for example, have to be trained to make observations correctly. These all imply that there must be a domain of events that are independent of our perceptions of them—what Bhaskar calls an *intransitive* domain; and indeed, that these events would exist whether or not they were observed or whether or not there were even observers. Thus there is a domain of actual events, only a (small) subset of which are perceived and become empirical experiences. That which is not experienced is not known, but that does not mean to say that it does not exist. In other words, there is an infinity of events that do actually occur but are never empirically observed.

Moving on to experimental activity, this shows several things. We can note that the experimenter causes (i.e. brings about) the experimental conditions but does not cause the results; these depend on the underlying causal laws or mechanisms that are operative at the time. The regularities that are expected may or may not occur, which depends partly on how well the experiment is carried out rather than on whether the presumed laws are or are not working. In fact, the occurrence of empirical regularities (i.e. constant conjunctions of events) in general is fairly rare—that is why the experiment is necessary to try to bring them about in the first place. The world is not full of constant conjunctions. But despite this, experimental results do in fact hold outside the experiment, as is attested by the enormous success of our technology.

The implications of this are that causal laws (more precisely from a critical realist perspective causal mechanisms) must be different from and independent of the patterns of events they generate; and that the experimenter aims to produce a constant conjunction of events by *closing* what would otherwise be an open system. Thus the intelligibility and success of experimental activity demonstrate the existence of an intransitive domain of causal laws separate from the events they generate. And the corrigibility of perception demonstrates the separation of events from particular experiences of them. This leads to a conceptual separation between a domain of causally operative structures or systems; the events that they generate; and those events that are empirically observed. Thus empiricism is doubly wrong in identifying causal laws with empirical regularities. It reduces underlying laws or mechanisms to actual events, and then events in general to experiences.

The argument can be expressed in terms of the mistake that both empiricism and strong forms of idealism or conventionalism make; that is, the *epistemic fallacy*. The essential mistake is in reducing the ontological domain of existence to the epistemological domain of knowledge—statements about being (i.e. what exists) are translated into ones about *our (human) knowledge* or experience of being. For the empiricist, that which cannot be experienced cannot be. For the conventionalist, limitations of our *knowledge* of being are taken to be limitations on being itself. In contrast, the realist asserts the primacy of ontology—the world would exist whether or not humans did.

The argument so far establishes that, given the successful occurrence of science, there must be an intransitive world of events and causal laws, but what exactly are causal laws? Or rather, what is it that causes or generates events given both the regularities that can be established in experiments, and the common absence of regularity outside? Equally, how can we assure ourselves that event regularities are based on necessary connections rather than simply coincidence? The answer is that there must be enduring entities, physical (e.g. atoms or organisms), social (e.g. the market or the family) or conceptual (e.g. categories or ideas; Bhaskar, 1997), observable or not, that have *powers* or *tendencies* to act in particular ways. The continual operation and interaction of these entities generates (i.e. causes), but is independent of, the flux of events.

Entities are structures, consisting of particular components that have certain properties or powers as a result of their structure. Thus gunpowder has the power to cause an explosion, a plane has the power to fly, a person has the power to compose music, a market has the power to generate wealth, and an inequitable distribution system has the power to cause poverty. Entities may have powers without exercising them at a particular time (it may need an experiment or particular stimulus to trigger them), and powers may be exercised but not become manifest in events because of the countervailing operation of some other generative mechanism. The heart of this argument is that of a *causal* criterion for existence rather than a perceptual one. In other words, for an empiricist only that which can be perceived can exist, whereas for a realist having a causal effect on the world implies existence, regardless of perceptability.

Critical Realism and Natural Science

For Bhaskar, reality is both intransitive (existing independently of humans) and stratified; that is, hierarchically ordered (Archer *et al.*, 1998, p. 41). The first form of stratification is between structures or mechanisms; the events that they generate; and the subset of events that are actually experienced. These are known as the domains of the *real*, the *actual* and the *empirical* (see Figure 10.1). The real contains mechanisms, events and experiences—that is, the whole of reality;

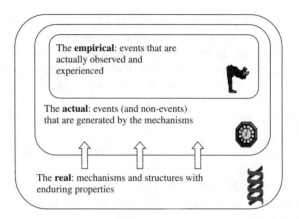

Figure 10.1   *Domains of the real, the actual and the empirical*

the actual consists of events that do (or do not) occur and includes the empirical, those events that are observed or experienced. These distinctions arise from the transcendental arguments above, namely that we should not reduce all events to only those that are observed, and we should not reduce enduring causal mechanisms to events.

A second form of stratification is within the realm of objects themselves (Archer *et al.*, 1998, p. 66) where causal powers at one level (e.g. chemical reactions) can be seen as generated by those of a lower level (atomic valency). One stratum is emergent from another (what Bhaskar terms 'emergent powers materialism'). The picture of the real is thus one of a complex interaction between dynamic, open, stratified systems, both material and non-material, where particular structures give rise to certain causal powers, tendencies or ways of acting, often called by Bhaskar 'generative mechanisms' (Bhaskar, 1979, p. 170). Although the term 'mechanism' sounds like a physical object, in fact Bhaskar uses it to refer to the powers or properties of an object. For example, a plane has the generative mechanism of the power to fly. The interaction of these generative mechanisms, where one often counterbalances another, causes the presence or absence of actual events.

Having established the intransitive *objects* of knowledge, we must recognize that the *production* of knowledge is very much the work of humans and occurs in what we could call the *transitive* dimension (Bhaskar, 1989, p. 18). Acknowledging the work of sociologists, the practice of science is a social process drawing on existing theories, results, anomalies and conjectures (the transitive objects of knowledge) to generate improved knowledge of science's intransitive objects. This distinction allows us to admit the *epistemic* relativity of science, the fact that knowledge is always historically and socially located, without losing the ontological dimension. We should also note that such epistemic relativity does not imply a corresponding *judgemental* relativity; that is, that all views are equally valid and that there are no rational grounds for choosing between them.

We can now characterize the realist method of science as one of *retroduction* (this is the same as 'abduction' as developed by Peirce—Habermas, 1978, p. 113—in contrast to induction and deduction). We take some unexplained phenomenon that has been observed and propose hypothetical mechanisms that, *if they existed*, would generate or cause that which is to be explained. So we move from experiences in the empirical domain to possible structures in the real domain. Such hypotheses do not of themselves prove that the mechanism exists, and we may have competing explanations in terms of other mechanisms, so the next step is to work towards eliminating some explanations and supporting others. Bhaskar summarizes this as description, retroduction, elimination and identification (DREI; Bhaskar, 1994, p. 24).

An obvious objection is how do we *know* that such hypothetical mechanisms actually do exist rather then being merely interesting ideas? At one level the answer is that we can never know for certain, since critical realism accepts that our knowledge is always ultimately fallible. More practically, however, the intransitivity of real structures means that they will always have the potential for effects that go beyond us—that is, are out of our control—and the methodology means that we should aim to eliminate alternative explanations by testing in some way for their potential effects.

So the main feature of a critical realist approach to science is a fundamental concern for *explanation* in terms of independent underlying causal or generative mechanisms, which may in principle be unobservable. This is in contrast to the empiricist approach, which limits itself to empirically measurable events and their abstraction into general laws; or the idealist approach, which has difficulty accepting a causally efficacious ontological domain.

Critical Realism and Social Science

We now move to the second major argument of critical realism, that social science is essentially similar to natural science in its realist character, albeit with modifications to reflect the particular nature of the social world. We can begin by asking what would rule out a realist approach to social science. The answer is that there are no intransitive objects for social science to investigate. Such an argument could come from the extreme constructivists (or superidealists, as Bhaskar calls them), who would also apply it to the natural world; or from those, such as Checkland (1989), who would argue for the distinctive nature of social phenomena as being intrinsically meaningful and not existing independently of social actors. Space precludes a full discussion of this complex issue (see Archer *et al.*, 1998, Part III; Bhaskar, 1979, 1994, 1997; Outhwaite, 1987; King, 1999a; New, 1995; Archer, 1995), but I will outline the argument for intransitive social structures; implications for the nature of societies; and the limits on naturalism that follow from the above two points.

The primary argument (Bhaskar, 1979, Chapter 2) is against methodological individualists, such as Popper (1962)—and Margaret Thatcher, who claimed that 'society' does not exist!—who argue that all explanations can be couched in terms of an individual person's beliefs and actions. The first refutation concerns emergent properties—there are attributes that can be applied to people that concern physical features such as height, weight; there are attributes that we share with other animals such as pain or hunger; but there are many attributes, essentially human ones, that are unavoidably social, for example 'bachelor', 'banker' or 'nun'. These are only intelligible within the context of a social institution or practice (Searle, 1996). The second argument is that many activities we undertake, most obviously perhaps language, must already exist and be available for people to learn and then use. As Wittgenstein (1958) argued, there can be no such thing as a private language—every time anyone has a conversation, uses a credit card or waits for a train they are assuming the existence of a structured, intransitive domain of resources, concepts, practices and relationships. The successful occurrence of social activities warrants the existence of causally efficacious, although unobservable, social structures.

Bhaskar (1979) does accept, however, that social phenomena are inherently different from material phenomena and that this does put limits on the nature of social science:

Ontological

- Social structures do not exist independently of the activities they govern or, put another way, they exist only in their effects or occurrences. Social structures enable social activities and through

that activity are themselves reproduced or transformed. Thus they are themselves the result of social activity. In contrast, the laws of the natural world are not affected by their own operation.
- Social structures do not exist independently of the agents' conceptions of what they are doing. Thus agency always requires some degree of interpretation and understanding of the meaning of the actions undertaken, although this does not imply that agents cannot be mistaken, and it does not require that they be fully aware of the consequences of their activity. In contrast, natural phenomena are independent of our conceptions of them.
- Social structures are localized in both space and time, unlike natural laws or tendencies, which are generally universal. They only hold in particular cultures or subcultures for finite periods of time.

Epistemological

- Social systems are inherently interactive and open. While the same is true for natural systems, it is the case that they can be artificially closed or controlled in the laboratory, and this indeed is the principal reason for experiments. This however is not (generally) possible in social systems. The main effect is that it is difficult to test theories, since predicted effects may or may not occur depending on a multitude of factors. It focuses attention on a theory's explanatory rather than predictive power.
- The possibilities of measurement are very limited since intrinsically the phenomena are meaningful, and meanings cannot properly be measured and compared, only understood and described.

Relational

- Social science is itself a social practice and is, therefore, inherently self-referential. This means both that social science knowledge can itself affect the social world and perhaps change it (e.g. the self-fulfilling prophecy); and that it is itself a social product and therefore will be shaped by the social conditions of its production. This does not make social science totally transitive—once an event has occurred or some theory been produced, it becomes intransitive relative to possible explanations of it.
- I would draw a second conclusion from this, that social theories must be self-consistent in not contradicting their own premises, since they are part of their own domain.

All of the above place limits or constraints on the practice of social science, but do not make it different in principle from natural science. It is still driven by the existence of an intransitive domain of generative mechanisms; recognition of the epistemic (but not judgemental) relativity of knowledge; and a retroductive methodology that explains events by hypothesizing underlying causal mechanisms.

CRITICISMS OF CRITICAL REALISM

It is interesting that little has been written as a direct critique of critical realism, especially within the philosophical literature. We may speculate that this is partly due to Bhaskar's disengagement from the philosophical establishment: he has never had a significant academic position, always remaining independent; he writes books but rarely papers and so is not well established in the mainstream journals; and he does not really engage in philosophical conferences and debates. His work has mainly been picked up in other disciplines, especially the social sciences, where the reception has usually been positive rather than critical. Indeed, even some of the critics discussed below (e.g. Chalmers and Callinicos) end up saying that despite their concern with particular arguments, they basically think that critical realism is true!

The first point is the status of one of the main planks of critical realism: the transcendental argument for an independent, stratified ontological domain. This form of argument is the reverse of the traditional syllogism—it goes from the agreed occurrence of some phenomena (in this case scientific experimental activity) backward to an inference about what, therefore, the world must necessarily be like (independent stratified ontology):

> The intelligibility of experimental activity presupposes then the intransitivity and structured character of the objects of scientific knowledge, at least in so far as these are causal laws. And this presupposes in turn the possibility of a non-human world... and in particular of a non-empirical world. (Archer *et al.*, 1998, p. 26)

Doubt can be cast on the strength of this argument in several ways. It seems to rest very much on what is meant by 'intelligible'. If it simply means understandable or explainable, then this seems quite a weak argument. Does it really imply the existence of an external world, or does it just imply that scientists have that belief, whether or not it is actually true? We could similarly argue that the intelligibility of religious activity implies the existence of God, but presumably we would only wish to argue that it implies a *belief* in God on the part of religious people. In fact, does the argument not rest on the *success* of science rather than its intelligibility (Chalmers, 1988)? In other words, it is not so much what scientists believe about what they are doing, but the fact that knowledge generated through experimental activity is found to hold outside the experimental situation, as testified by the enormous developments of successful technology.

We might also question whether the premises about experimental activity are actually shared by competing positions or, indeed, are an indubitable description of science anyway (Callinicos, 1995). How do we know that there are not competing theories about scientific practice and that these offer different accounts that still make the activity intelligible? Here Bhaskar would probably argue that his is an *immanent critique*. That is, his arguments are always contextual and directed against particular positions, in this case empiricism and some forms of idealism, rather than being totally general. There may well be other views on the nature of experiments, for example from a postmodern perspective, but then the nature of the argument would be different.

Finally, we could object that even if we accept the premises, the nature of the conclusions depends very much on the general scientific knowledge of the day. If a Greek or mediaeval philosopher attempted a similar argument they would come up with a very different picture of the nature of the world. I think this argument has to be accepted but is compatible with critical realism's wider acceptance of fallibility. Bhaskar accepts that knowledge is temporally relative and will change, and even accepts that critical realism itself is only 'the best explanation so far':

> the transcendental consideration is not deployed in a philosophical vacuum: it is designed to situate, or replace, an existing theory; and may of course come, in time, to suffer a similar fate. (Bhaskar, 1979, p. 6)

A second area of concern is the extent to which the theory of science is simply descriptive or actually normative, and the strength of its prescriptions. Many would agree that critical realism (Baert, 1996), with its acceptance of unobservable entities, the role of metaphor and analogy and the importance of explanation, is a much better description of the activities of actual (natural) scientists than is empiricism or even Popperianism. To what extent, however, does it provide powerful normative procedures for natural science; and to what extent does it apply to the activities of social scientists?

Methodologically, the description, retroduction, elimination and identification formulation has several weaknesses. Given the acceptance of the subjectivity of the transitive domain and the theory dependence of observations, it seems unlikely that one can begin with objective and agreed descriptions of particular phenomena. The description will already be imbued with underlying theoretical concepts and in the social sciences will also be highly value laden.[1] This will clearly condition the forms of generative mechanisms that are postulated to explain the phenomenon and make any sort of comparison or contrast very difficult.

Retroduction itself is clearly an intuitive and creative process, rather than a logical one,[2] and this is a necessary part of scientific endeavour, but it can result in a proliferation of possible explanations, some of which may well be untestable or at least unrefutable. This places a lot of weight on the latter stages of elimination and identification, but here critical realism runs into problems because of its critique of traditional empirical testing, verification and induction. How is the scientist, especially the social scientist, ever going to be able to undertake testing that unambiguously rules out or rules in particular hypothetical mechanisms, particularly when such mechanisms may be unobservable and their powers may be unactualized?

This is related to a third problem, the nature of truth within critical realism. While the basic orientation is towards a correspondence theory of truth—that is, that knowledge in the transitive domain in some sense corresponds to its objects in the intransitive domain—the acceptance of epistemic relativity means that we can never prove or be certain that this is the case. This potentially brings in elements of a consensus theory of truth. Bhaskar himself recognizes four dimensions of truth (Bhaskar, 1994): *normative-fiduciary*, truth as that which is believed by a trustworthy source; *adequating*, truth as based on evidence and justification rather than mere belief; *referential-expressive*, truth as corresponding to or at least being adequate to some intransitive object of knowledge; and *ontological/alethic*, the truth of things in themselves and their generative causes in the intransitive domain; that is, no longer tied to language although expressible in language. The fourth aspect is clearly controversial (Groff, 2000). We are thus left with a problem of precisely what criteria we can use to judge between competing explanations if not a clear view of truth.

A fourth area of criticism concerns naturalism; that is, the extent to which an approach developed largely in relation to natural science can be applied to social science. Clearly, Bhaskar recognizes the fundamentally different nature of the social world and the limitations that this places on science. But are not these limitations in fact so great that critical realism-type science is not possible? Giddens (1976) recognizes that even natural science involves a transitive, hermeneutic domain, but that social science involves a double hermeneutic in that the objects of knowledge are themselves intrinsically socially structured and human dependent. If social 'structures' are unobservable, and indeed only exist through people's activity; if social systems are open and not amenable to experiment; and social activities always rely to some extent on prior commonsense or theoretical conceptualization, then to what extent is it really possible to test competing explanations and identify 'true' ones?

Coming from the opposite direction, King (1999b) argues against the realist notion of a causally effective social structure over and above the knowledgeable actions of individual agents. He suggests that Bhaskar's concept of social structure involves two contradictions (or 'antinomies'). The first is that society is both dependent on individuals and is also independent of individuals. From Bhaskar's viewpoint this apparent contradiction is resolved through the idea of emergence. Society, as a separate ontological entity, emerges from but is separate to the activities of individuals. This allows for the development of a social theory with two separate types of entity—individuals and society—that interact with and mutually shape each other. King objects that such a view of society is a reification and that in fact

> The apparently structural and emergent aspects of society can be successfully accounted for by hermeneutic reference to individuals and their meaningful interactions with other individuals alone... Social reality is coextensive with the individuals involved and is neither more nor less than those individuals. (King, 1999b, pp. 271–2)

The second antinomy is that social action is said to be always intentional, yet is also said to be non-intentional and materially caused. The point at issue is related to the previous one: to what extent should individual action be explained in terms of external social and material structures as opposed to simply the intentions of the individual? This is clearly a major debate within social theory and I can only refer the interested reader to the literature.[3]

The fifth area of debate that I will discuss is the nature and extent of critical realism's claim to be 'critical', not so much in the epistemological sense but in the political sense of bringing about change in society. The idea is that social science is not value-neutral description but inevitably explanatory critique of the status quo.[4] Social science concepts must always be evaluative or moralized, never purely descriptive. For instance, it is more correct to say 'Two children were murdered' than 'Two young humans ceased functioning', since it is a more precise and accurate description requiring a more specific explanation. Social science will always reveal examples of false beliefs, unmet needs and unnecessary suffering, and will often be able to identify their structural causes. Other things being equal, it is then possible to condemn the causes and propose action to remove or absent them. We thus move from fact to values and from values to actions in support of a transformation of society.

Sayer (1997) accepts these arguments at a general level but points out the difficulty of enacting them in practice. In particular, it is not difficult to find many examples of false beliefs or suffering, but doing something about them requires both a correct identification of their causes and specific changes that are both desirable and feasible, and do not generate new problems elsewhere. The world is now highly complex and incredibly interdependent. Particular events or problems will often have multiple interlocking structural causes that are very difficult to untangle; possible changes will often have undesirable and unintended consequences and have to contend with an increasing diversity of values and cultures.

Baert (1996) maintains that Bhaskar's social theory is actually much better at explaining why societies remain the same rather than why they are transformed. Certainly it is true that Bhaskar's transformational model of social action (TMSA) emphasizes the way in which social actors necessarily draw on an already existing social structure and through their interactions reproduce it, and only potentially transform it.[5] Archer (1990, 1996, 1998) has addressed this point to some extent in her morphogenetic model, which emphasizes the independence of society from individual actors and therefore allows both reproduction and transformation through their mutual interaction. Baert also suggests that the TMSA model undervalues the extent to which social actors (not just social scientists) can develop their own discursive, theoretical knowledge of society and act on it to change rather than merely reproduce social structure.

Fine (2002) is particularly concerned with economics where there has been a significant attack on traditional theory, especially econometrics, from critical realism (Fleetwood, 1999, 2001, 2002; Lawson, 1996, 1997, 1999). Interestingly, rather than being a supporter of the status quo (in economics), Fine argues that critical realism is neither critical nor realist enough to have much effect. It is not critical enough because it has largely confined itself to critique at the level of methodology rather than substantive theory. Fine suggests that mainstream economists (and perhaps this can be extended to other disciplines) have no interest in methodology, or indeed realism or the real world. And critical realism is not realist enough in not having significant theoretical conceptions of core economic phenomena such as capital and capitalism. One could reply that Bhaskar has always maintained that the *philosophy* of critical realism is intended as a foundation for specific sciences, not as a replacement. So now perhaps is the time for critical realists within the disciplines to use it to generate more and better substantive theories and prove its worth in practice.

APPLYING CRITICAL REALISM TO INFORMATION SYSTEMS RESEARCH

Having discussed at some length the main problems in the philosophy of science and the ways in which critical realism can address them, it is now time to show more specifically why critical realism is highly appropriate as a philosophy for IS. So far little has been written within IS directly about critical realism, although its potential significance has been pointed out by Dobson (2001a, 2001b), Mutch (1999, 2002) and Mingers (2002).

In summary, I would argue that critical realism enables us to take a basically realist stance (which I am sure is intuitively held by the vast majority of IS colleagues) while accepting the major critiques of naive realism; it addresses both natural and social science and thus encompasses both hard and soft (and critical) approaches; and it does potentially fit well with the reality of IS as an applied discipline. The argument for the last point could be made either by considering the theory of IS, such as it is, or by looking empirically at its practice.

Given the limitations of space, I shall try to address both aspects by discussing two specific IS approaches. The two have been chosen for theoretical reasons—statistical modelling because it is arguably the dominant research analysis method within IS (Mingers, 2003b) and yet is apparently incompatible with critical realism, embodying an empiricist philosophy; and soft systems methodology (SSM), an important method for both research and intervention, which would seem to conflict with critical realism from the opposite direction, namely interpretivism (see Chapter 4). These two examples are important for my argument since it could be counter-argued that, because IS has paid little attention to critical realism and because many of its methods appear *prima facie* to be based on antagonistic foundations, critical realism cannot possibly fit IS. Against this, my analysis seeks to show that the fact that a research technique develops within a particular paradigm, and implicitly accepts the assumptions of that paradigm, does not prevent it from being reinterpreted or reconstructed in another way. Critical realism allows us both to see limitations of the prevailing approaches and to reconceptualize the technique in a more powerful way.

The Empiricist Approach: Statistical Modelling

In considering statistical modelling, including regression and other multivariate techniques such as ANOVA and factor analysis, we are moving to an approach that, in varying degrees, goes against critical realism in being essentially empiricist. In this section I shall show the weaknesses of the conventional interpretation of statistics, but also how it can be better employed within a realist framework (Mingers, 2003a). Consider first multiple regression, a technique used in a range of social sciences as well as in IS. It claims to be a causally oriented technique (in comparison with, say, ARIMA modelling) that aims to explain the variation in a dependent variable in terms of a set of supposedly causally related independent variables. A linear functional form is assumed and parameters are estimated from a sample of data. Inferences are drawn towards a wider population. In practice, where multiple regression has been used extensively, for example in econometrics, its predictive ability has been extremely poor (Lawson, 1997; Sherden, 1998). From a critical realism viewpoint this is hardly surprising, since there are severe limitations in this approach. In summary (for more detail see Mingers, 2003a) these are:

- The notion of causality embodied within statistics is extremely impoverished, being essentially the Humean one of a constant conjunction of events that underlies empiricism (Ron, 1999). The main problem with this is that it remains in the superficial world of the empirical, with little attempt to get at underlying mechanisms that may be responsible for the observed regularities.

- The procedure rests on an implicit assumption of closure (Olsen, 1999; Sayer, 1992), which, as we have already seen, cannot be expected to occur in social systems. By this I mean that the stability of the coefficients, and their statistical significance, rests on assuming that the factors that have not been included, usually because they are unknown or impossible to measure, have only a small and essentially random effect. In practice, the effect may well be large and there is no way of knowing what the influence will be outside of the sample data.
- The main assumptions of regression—multivariate normal distributions, independence of variables, one-way causality, linearity and so on—are highly implausible, to say the least.
- All of this makes it very difficult to choose between competing models for the same data. Elaborate methods have been devised—for example stepwise, best-subsets, fragility analysis—but in practice many different models are developed and choices made on essentially subjective grounds such as experience, usefulness or perhaps just intuition (Magnus and Morgan, 1999; King, 1991).

Given these problems, it might seem that critical realism would abandon statistical analysis altogether, especially since empirical verification is not a necessary feature of a realist scientific explanation (since causal tendencies may be possessed but not actualized). This is not the case, but it does require a rethinking of the purpose of such analysis, and also a differentiation between various techniques.

Critical realism proceeds by trying to discover underlying structures that generate particular patterns of events (or non-events). Statistical analysis can help in several areas:

- It can be very useful in the exploratory stage of research in detecting particular patterns within the data. Any non-randomness must imply some structure or set of constraints that is generating it; although, of course, this may be just as much a result of the mechanism of data production as any underlying generative mechanism. Nevertheless, detecting such patterns within large sets of multivariate data is very difficult and methods such as principal components, factor analysis, cluster analysis, correspondence analysis and regression are very valuable. The results, though, will merely be the starting point for more substantive investigations.

- Some techniques do lend themselves more towards identifying underlying structures, especially something like factor analysis, which aims to reveal common factors generating observed variables, or path analysis (Olsen, 1999), which involves a series of interrelated equations. Even here, however, the results are merely suggestive, not conclusive.
- Perhaps the main use might be in validating possible explanations by corroborating or falsifying them. This could be done either by testing the implications of a theory through collecting and analysing data (Porpora, 1998) or, more sophisticatedly, by regarding the analysis as a quasi-experiment, inducing artificial closure on a system by controlling for the influence of normally uncontrolled factors (Ron, 1999). Techniques such as multivariate analysis of variance and covariance are useful here.

The Interpretive Approach: Soft Systems Methodology

SSM could also be seen as being antithetical to critical realism. Checkland denies the ontological reality of 'systems', instead reserving this concept for *thinking about* the world (Checkland and Scholes, 1990, p. 277). He also distinguishes strongly between natural and social science, or rather positivist and interpretivist approaches within social science, and allies SSM clearly with the phenomenological tradition. I shall have to restrict myself to making a few observations on SSM from a critical realism perspective. The main problem is that Checkland takes positivism as the only alternative to interpretivism as a philosophy of (social) science. This inevitably means that he has to adopt a full-blown phenomenological position, denying ontological reality to social structures, which then generates all kinds of contradictions and problems in dealing with a 'real world' external to the observer that is, after all, what SSM aims to improve (Jackson, 1982; Mingers, 1984). The major advantage of a critical realist approach is that it maintains reality while still recognizing the inherent meaningfulness of social interaction.

It can be said that SSM is essentially idealist, only dealing with ideas or concepts (for example in root definitions or conceptual models) and that these are somehow less real than objects. Or that it is strongly relativist in accepting all viewpoints as being equally valid. Against this, critical realism demonstrates that ideas, concepts, meanings and categories are equally as real as physical objects

(Bhaskar, 1997). They are emergent from, but irreducible to, the physical world, and have causal effect both on the physical world (e.g. in the generation of technology) and the social and ideational world. They are also inevitably social products and participate in transformations of the social world, just the sort of transformations that SSM aims to bring about. With regard to relativism, critical realism makes a distinction between epistemic relativism and judgemental relativism: people may well hold different beliefs about processes in the world, but this does not mean that we are unable to rationally judge between them and prefer one to another given some particular purpose. Equally, ideas once expressed are no longer wholly subjective—they become intransitive and available for investigation, debate and judgement by others. This is an example of a more general idea—referential detachment (Bhaskar, 1994, p. 52)—that any communication must refer to something, that which it is about (even if it is self-referential), and this immediately establishes an intransitive dimension. Bhaskar goes further in arguing against the positivist distinction between facts and values (which would fit in well with both soft and critical OR/MS) and eventually to a moral realism; that is, the idea that there could be moral truths (Bhaskar, 1994, p. 108).

A final point is the weakness of SSM with regard to the origin of the *Weltanschauungen* that it explores, and an understanding of the difficulties of individual and organizational change. These both stem from the individualistic social theory that it embodies. With a critical realist interpretation both of these are avoided. On the one hand we can generate explanations of why particular actors may hold the beliefs they do in terms of their social and organizational position; their history of experiences, particularly as these relate to underlying social characteristics such as gender, race and age; and, of course, their individual personalities (Whittington, 1992). We are also in a position to understand the psychological and social structures that may impede or facilitate learning and change.

Critical Realist Research: Multimethodology

Critical realism does not have a commitment to a single form of research. Although it is sometimes seen as favouring interpretive rather than quantitative methods, this stems more from its critique of the superficiality of much empiricist research and its desire for in-depth explanation than antagonism towards quantification *per se*. Rather, critical realism involves particular attitudes towards the purpose and practice of research.

First, the critical realist is never content with mere description, whether it is qualitative or quantitative. No matter how complex a statistical analysis or rich an ethnographic interpretation, this is only the first step—critical realism wants to get beneath the surface to understand and explain *why* things are as they are, to hypothesize the structures and mechanisms that shape observable events.

Secondly, CR recognizes the existence of a variety of objects of knowledge—material, conceptual, social and psychological—each of which requires different research methods to come to understand them. And it emphasizes the holistic interaction of these different objects. Thus it is to be expected that understanding in any particular situation will require a variety of research methods (multimethodology; Mingers, 2001a), both extensive and intensive.

Thirdly, critical realism recognizes the inevitable fallibility of observation, especially in the social world, and therefore requires the researcher to be particularly aware of the assumptions and limitation of their research. A more detailed discussion about practical research methods within a critical realist framework can be found in Mingers (2003a), Sayer (1992), Layder (1993) and Pawson and Tilley (1997).

CONCLUSION

This chapter has made a case for the contribution of critical realism as an underlying philosophy for information systems research. It has approached this in two ways. The first was in terms of the unresolved problems within the philosophy of science, whether it be natural or social, that critical realism successfully addresses. These are in particular the impoverished view of explanatory theory within empiricism; the major critiques of observer and theory independence that empiricism assumes; the logical problems of induction and falsificationism; the dislocation between natural and social science; and the radical antirealist positions adopted by constructivists and postmodernists. Secondly, it has demonstrated across opposing research methods how critical realism's retroductive methodology can shape the practice of IS research.

A GUIDE TO THE LITERATURE

The single best book to serve as an introduction to critical realism is *Critical Realism: Essential Readings* by Archer *et al.* (1998). It splits the work up historically into four different stages and has quite detailed introductions to each stage, some written with Bhaskar. Within each section it then contains extended excerpts from Bhaskar's main works, together with essays written by others about the work.

In terms of Bhaskar's own writings, it must be said that many of them are hard work, with very condensed arguments and many new terms. One of the clearest overviews is a transcribed talk that Bhaskar gave, which is Chapter 1 of one of his more recent books, *From Science to Emancipation* (Bhaskar, 2002a). His principal works are as follows:

- *A Realist Theory of Science* (1978) sets out the basic philosophy of (natural) science known at the time as 'transcendental realism'.
- *The Possibility of Naturalism* (1979) develops this to cover the social sciences and was called 'critical naturalism'.
- *Scientific Realism and Human Emancipation* (1986) and *Reclaiming Reality* (1989) are books of essays that extend and elaborate on the basic ideas, for example developing the idea of the transformational model of social activity (TMSA). By now the concept was known as 'critical realism'.
- *Dialectic: The Pulse of Freedom* (1993) moves to a new phase that reformulates critical realism within a dialectical framework emphasizing the importance of absence as much as presence, and developing the four-stage model (1M ontology, 2E transformation, 3L holism, 4D agency). These ideas are also presented in a shorter, and supposedly introductory, work—*Plato Etc.* (1994)—which is extremely condensed. This phase is known as 'dialectical critical realism'.
- The most recent works, *From East to West* (2000) and *Meta-Reality* (2002b), mark yet another phase in which Bhaskar has brought in themes from eastern philosophy and spirituality. It is now known as 'transcendental dialectical critical realism'.

Critical realism is also being adopted within several other disciplines, for example sociology (Danermark *et al.*, 2002; Archer, 1995), management (Ackroyd and Fleetwood, 2000), economics (Fleetwood, 1999) and geography (Yeung, 1997).

ENDNOTES

[1] A point that Bhaskar clearly accepts.
[2] Indeed Peirce, who coined the term, called it basically guesswork.

[3]He includes in his critiques King (1999a, 2000); Giddens (1984); and Archer (1995, 2000).
[4]This is in direct opposition to positivism's insistence on a separation between fact and values.
[5]There are indeed many similarities with Giddens' theory of structuration, which is also criticized as being overly regulative.

REFERENCES

Ackroyd, S. and Fleetwood, S. (2000) *Realist Perspectives on Management and Organisations*, London: Routledge.
Archer, M. (1990) 'Human agency and social structure: A critique of Giddens', in J. Clark, C. Modgil and S. Modgil (eds), *Anthony Giddens: Consensus and Controversy*, Cambridge: Cambridge University Press, pp. 47–56.
Archer, M. (1995) *Realist Social Theory: The Morphogenetic Approach*, Cambridge: Cambridge University Press.
Archer, M. (1996) 'Social integration and system integration: Developing the distinction', *Sociology*, 30: 679–99.
Archer, M. (1998) 'Realism and morphogenesis', in M. Archer, R. Bhaskar, A. Collier, T. Lawson and A. Norrie (eds), *Critical Realism: Essential Readings*, London: Routledge, pp. 356–82.
Archer, M. (2000) 'For structure: Its properties and powers: A reply to Anthony King', *Sociological Review*, 48: 464–72.
Archer, M., Bhaskar, R., Collier, A., Lawson, T. and Norrie, A. (eds) (1998) *Critical Realism: Essential Readings*, London: Routledge.
Avison, D. and Myers, M. (1995) 'Information systems and anthropology: An anthropological perspective on IT and organizational culture', *Information Technology and People*, 8: 43–56.
Baert, P. (1996) 'Realist philosophy of the social sciences and economics: A critique', *Cambridge Journal of Economics*, 20: 513–22.
Banville, C. and Landry, M. (1989) 'Can the field of MIS be disciplined?' *Communications of the ACM*, 32: 48–60.
Barnes, S. (1977) *Interests and the Growth of Knowledge*, London: Routledge.
Benbasat, I. and Weber, R. (1996) 'Rethinking "diversity" in information systems research', *Information Systems Research*, 7: 389–99.
Berkeley, G. (1995) *A Treatise Concerning the Principles of Human Knowledge*, Indianapolis, IN: Hackett.
Best, S. and Kellner, D. (1991) *Postmodern Theory: Critical Interrogations*, New York, NY: Guilford Press.
Bhaskar, R. (1978) *A Realist Theory of Science*, Hemel Hempstead: Harvester.
Bhaskar, R. (1979) *The Possibility of Naturalism*, Hemel Hempstead: Harvester.
Bhaskar, R. (1986) *Scientific Realism and Human Emancipation*, London: Verso.
Bhaskar, R. (1989) *Reclaiming Reality*, London: Verso.
Bhaskar, R. (1993) *Dialectic: The Pulse of Freedom*, London: Verso.
Bhaskar, R. (1994) *Plato Etc.*, London: Verso.
Bhaskar, R. (1997) 'On ontological status of ideas', *Journal for the Theory of Social Behaviour*, 27: 139–47.

Bhaskar, R. (2000) *From East to West: Odyssey of a Soul*, London: Routledge.

Bhaskar, R. (2002a) *From Science to Emancipation*, London: Sage.

Bhaskar, R. (2002b) *Meta-Reality: The Philosophy of Meta-Reality: Creativity, Love and Freedom*, London: Sage.

Bhattacharjee, A. and Paul, R. (2001) 'System design and ethnomethodology', *Eighth Americas Conference on Information Systems*, Boston: Association for Information Systems, pp. 2207–11.

Bijker, W., Hughes, T. and Pinch, T. (eds) (1987) *The Social Construction of Technological Systems*, Cambridge, MA: MIT Press.

Bleicher, J. (1980) *Contemporary Hermeneutics*, London: Routledge.

Bloor, D. (1976) *Knowledge and Social Imagery*, London: Routledge.

Boland, R. (1985) 'Phenomenology: A preferred approach to research on information systems', in E. Mumford, R. Hirschheim, G. Fitzgerald and T. Wood-Harper (eds), *Research Methods in Information Systems*, Amsterdam: North-Holland, pp. 193–201.

Boland, R. (1991) 'Information system use as a hermeneutic process', in H.-E. Nissen, H. Klein and R. Hirschheim (eds), *Information Systems Research: Contemporary Approaches and Emergent Traditions*, Amsterdam: North-Holland, pp. 439–58.

Brown, A., Fleetwood, S. and Roberts, J. M. (eds) (2002) *Critical Realism and Marxism*, London: Routledge.

Burrell, G. and Morgan, G. (1979) *Sociological Paradigms and Organisational Analysis*, London: Heinemann.

Callinicos, A. (1995) 'Critical realism and beyond: Roy Bhaskar's dialectic', *Department of Politics working paper* 7, York: University of York.

Chalmers, A. (1988) 'Is Bhaskar's realism realistic?' *Radical Philosophy*, 49: 18–23.

Checkland, P. (1989) 'OR and social science: Fundamental thoughts', in M. Jackson, P. Keys and S. Cropper (eds), *Operational Research and the Social Sciences*, Cambridge: Plenum Press, pp. 35–41.

Checkland, P. and Scholes, J. (1990) *Soft Systems Methodology in Action*, Chichester: John Wiley & Sons.

Ciborra, C. (1998) 'Crisis and foundations: An inquiry into the nature and limits of models and methods in the information systems discipline', *Journal of Strategic Information Systems*, 7: 5–16.

Cicourel, A. (1973) *Cognitive Sociology: Language and Meaning in Social Interaction*, London: Penguin.

Collins, H. (1985) *Changing Order: Replication and Induction in Scientific Practice*, Beverly Hills, CA: Sage.

Coyne, R. (1995) *Designing Information Technology in the Postmodern Age*, Cambridge, MA: MIT Press.

Crabtree, A., Nichols, D., O'Brien, J., Rouncefield, M. and Twidale, M. (2000) 'Ethnomethodologically informed ethnography and information systems design', *Journal of the American Society for Information Science*, 51: 666–82.

Danermark, B., Ekstrom, M., Jakobsen, L. and Karlsson, J. (2002) *Explaining Society: Critical Realism in the Social Sciences*, London: Routledge.

Deetz, S. (1996) 'Describing differences in approach to organization science: Rethinking Burrell and Morgan and their legacy', *Organization Science*, 7: 191–207.

Dewey, J. (1938) *Logic: The Theory of Inquiry*, New York, NY: Holt.

Dobson, P. (2001a) 'Longitudinal case research: A critical realist perspective', *Systemic Practice and Action Research*, 14: 283–96.

Dobson, P. (2001b) 'The philosophy of critical realism: An opportunity for information systems research', *Information Systems Frontiers*, 3: 199–210.

Dreyfus, H. (1996) 'The current relevance of Merleau-Ponty's phenomenology of embodiment', *Electronic Journal of Analytic Philosophy*, 4.

Fine, B. (2002) 'Addressing the critical and the real in critical realism', *Dialogues in Economics: A Postautistic Economics Forum*, http://users.ox.ac.uk/~dialogue/documents/ben_fine_critreal.htm, accessed 14 April 2003.

Fleetwood, S. (ed.) (1999) *Critical Realism in Economics: Development and Debate*, London: Routledge.

Fleetwood, S. (2001) 'Causal laws, functional relations and tendencies', *Review of Political Economy*, 13: 201–20.

Fleetwood, S. (2002) 'Boylan and O'Gorman's causal holism: A critical realist evaluation', *Cambridge Journal of Economics*, 26: 27–45.

Foucault, M. (1980) *Power/Knowledge: Selected Interviews and Other Writings 1972–1977*, Brighton: Harvester.

Frege, G., Geach, P. and Black, M. (1952) *Translations from the Philosophical Writings of Gottlob Frege*, Oxford: Blackwell.

Galliers, R. (ed.) (1992) *Information Systems Research: Issues, Methods and Practical Guidelines*, Oxford: Blackwell.

Gergen, K. (1999) *An Invitation to Social Construction*, London: Sage.

Giddens, A. (ed.) (1974) *Positivism and Sociology*, London: Heinemann.

Giddens, A. (1976) *New Rules of Sociological Method*, London: Hutchinson.

Giddens, A. (1984) *The Constitution of Society*, Cambridge: Polity Press.

Goles, T. and Hirschheim, R. (2000) 'The paradigm is dead, the paradigm is dead... long live the paradigm: The legacy of Burrell and Morgan', *Omega*, 28: 249–68.

Greenhill, A. (2001) 'Managerial subjectivity and information systems: A discussion paper', *Eighth Americas Conference on Information Systems*, Boston, MA: Association for Information Systems, pp. 2154–60.

Gregory, R. (1972) *Eye and Brain*, London: Weidenfeld.

Groff, R. (2000) 'The truth of the matter: Roy Bhaskar's critical realism and the concept of alethic truth', *Philosophy of the Social Sciences*, 30: 407–35.

Habermas, J. (1974) *Theory and Practice*, London: Heinemann.

Habermas, J. (1978) *Knowledge and Human Interests*, London: Heinemann.

Hansen, N. (1958) *Patterns of Discovery*, New York, NY: Cambridge University Press.

Harvey, L. and Myers, M. (1995) 'Scholarship and practice: The contribution of ethnographic research methods to bridging the gap', *Information Technology and People*, 8: 13–27.

Hempel, C. (1965) *Aspects of Scientific Explanation*, New York, NY: Free Press.

Hesse, M. (1974) *The Structure of Scientific Inference*, Berkeley, CA: University of California Press.

Hirschheim, R., Klein, H. and Lyytinen, K. (1996) 'Exploring the intellectual foundations of information systems', *Accounting, Management and Information Technologies*, 2: 1–64.

Hume, D. (1967) *Enquiries Concerning Human Understanding and the Principles of Morals*, Oxford: Clarendon Press.

Iivari, J., Hirschheim, R. and Klein, H. (1998) 'A paradigmatic analysis contrasting information systems development approaches and methodologies', *Information Systems Research*, 9: 164–93.

Introna, L. (1997) *Management, Information and Power*, London: Macmillan.

Jackson, M. (1982) 'The nature of soft systems thinking: The work of Churchman, Ackoff, and Checkland', *Journal of Applied Systems Analysis*, 9: 17–27.

Janson, M., Cecez-Kecmanovic, D. and Brown, A. (2001) 'Information systems for the support of a participatory ethos: A study in communicative action', *Critical Information Systems*, Salford: University of Salford, pp. 73–87.

Keat, R. and Urry, J. (1981) *Social Theory as Science*, London: Routledge and Kegan Paul.

King, A. (1999a) 'Against structure: A critique of morphogenetic social theory', *Sociological Review*, 47: 199–227.

King, A. (1999b) 'The impossibility of naturalism: The antinomies of Bhaskar's realism', *Journal for the Theory of Social Behaviour*, 29: 267–90.

King, A. (2000) 'The accidental derogation of the lay actor: A critique of Giddens' concept of structure', *Philosophy of the Social Sciences*, 30: 362–83.

King, G. (1991) ' "Truth" is stranger than prediction, more questionable than causal inference', *American Journal of Political Science*, 35: 1047–53.

Knorr-Cetina, K. and Mulkay, M. (eds) (1983) *Science Observed*, London: Sage.

Kuhn, T. (1970) *The Structure of Scientific Revolutions*, Chicago, IL: Chicago University Press.

Kuhn, T. (1977) *The Essential Tension: Selected Studies in Scientific Tradition and Change*, Chicago, IL: University of Chicago Press.

Landry, M. and Banville, C. (1992) 'A disciplined methodological pluralism for MIS research', *Accounting, Management and Information Technology*, 2: 77–97.

Latour, B. (1987) *Science in Action*, Milton Keynes: Open University Press.

Lawson, T. (1996) 'Developments in economics as a realist social theory', *Review of Social Economy*, 54: 405–22.

Lawson, T. (1997) *Economics and Reality*, London: Routledge.

Lawson, T. (1999) 'Connections and distinctions: Post Keynesianism and critical realism', *Journal of Post Keynesian Economics*, 22: 3–14.

Layder, D. (1993) *New Strategies in Social Research*, Cambridge: Polity Press.

Layder, D. (1994) *Understanding Social Theory*, London: Sage.

Lee, A. (1999) 'Rigour and relevance in MIS research: Beyond the approach of positivism alone', *MIS Quarterly*, 23: 29–33.

Lee, A., Liebenau, J. and DeGross, J. (eds) (1997) *Information Systems and Qualitative Research*, London: Chapman and Hall.

Lyytinen, K. (1992) 'Information systems and critical theory', in M. Alvesson and H. Willmott (eds), *Critical Management Studies*, London: Sage, pp. 159–80.

Lyytinen, K. and Klein, H. (1985) 'The critical theory of Jurgen Habermas as a basis for a theory of information systems', in E. Mumford, R. Hirscheim, G. Fitzgerald and T. Wood-Harper (eds), *Research Methods in Information Systems*, Amsterdam: North-Holland, pp. 219–36.

Magnus, J. and Morgan, M. (eds) (1999) *Methodology and Tacit Knowledge: Two Experiments in Econometrics*, New York: John Wiley & Sons.

Marsden, R. (1993) 'The politics of organizational analysis', *Organization Studies*, 14: 93–124.

Merleau-Ponty, M. (1962) *Phenomenology of Perception*, London: Routledge.

Mingers, J. (1984) 'Subjectivism and soft systems methodology: A critique', *Journal of Applied Systems Analysis*, 11: 85–103.

Mingers, J. (2001a) 'Combining IS research methods: Towards a pluralist methodology', *Information Systems Research*, 12: 240–59.

Mingers, J. (2001b) 'Embodying information systems: The contribution of phenomenology', *Information and Organization (formerly Accounting, Management and Information Technology)*, 11: 103–28.

Mingers, J. (2002) 'Real-izing information systems: Critical realism as an underpinning philosophy for information systems', in J. DeGross (ed.), *International Conference on Information Systems*, Barcelona: Association of Information Systems, pp. 295–303.

Mingers, J. (2003a) 'Future directions in management science modeling: Critical realism and multimethodology', in S. Fleetwood and S. Ackroyd (eds), *Critical Realism in Action in Organizations and Management Studies*, London: Routledge.

Mingers, J. (2003b) 'The paucity of multimethod research: A survey of the IS literature', *Information Systems Journal*, 13: 233–49.

Mutch, A. (1999) 'Critical realism, managers and information', *British Journal of Management*, 10: 323–33.

Mutch, A. (2002) 'Actors and networks or agents and structures: Towards a realist view of information systems', *Organization*, 9: 513–32.

Myers, D. (1994) 'Dialectical hermeneutics: A theoretical framework for the implementation of information systems', *Information Systems Journal*, 5: 51–70.

Nandhakumar, J. and Jones, M. (1997) 'Too close for comfort? Distance and engagement in interpretive information systems research', *Information Systems Journal*, 7: 109–31.

Neurath, O. and McGuinness, B. (1987) *Unified Science: The Vienna Circle Monograph Series originally edited by Otto Neurath, now in an English edition*, Dordrecht: Kluwer Academic Publishers.

New, C. (1995) 'Sociology and the case for realism', *Sociological Review*, 43: 808–27.

Ngwenyama, O. (1991) 'The critical social theory approach to information systems: Problems and challenges', in H.-E. Nissen, H. Klein and R. Hirschheim (eds), *Information Systems Research: Contemporary Approaches and Emergent Traditions*, Amsterdam: North-Holland, pp. 267–80.

Ngwenyama, O. and Lee, A. (1997) 'Communication richness in electronic mail: Critical social theory and the contextuality of meaning', *MIS Quarterly*, 21: 145–67.

Olsen, W. (1999) 'Developing open-systems interpretations of path analysis: Fragility analysis using farm data from India', *Critical Realism: Implications for Practice*, Örebro: Centre for Critical Realism, Örebro University Sweden.

Olson, D. and Carslisle, J. (2001) 'Hermeneutics in information systems', *Eighth Americas Conference on Information Systems*, Boston, MA: Associations for Information Systems, pp. 2029–35.

Orlikowski, W. and Baroudi, J. (1991) 'Studying information technology in organizations: Research approaches and assumptions', *Information Systems Research*, 2: 1–28.

Outhwaite, W. (1987) *New Philosophies of Social Science: Realism, Hermeneutics and Critical Theory*, London: Macmillan.

Parker, M. and McHugh, G. (1991) 'Five texts in search of an author: A response to John Hassard's "Multiple Paradigms and Organizational Analysis" ', *Organization Studies*, 12: 451–6.

Pawson, R. and Tilley, N. (1997) *Realistic Evaluation*, London: Sage.

Peirce, C. (1878) 'How to make our ideas clear', *Popular Science Monthly*, 12: 286–302.

Pfeffer, J. (1993) 'Barriers to the advance of organizational science: Paradigm development as a dependent variable', *Academy of Management Review*, 18: 599–620.

Piaget, J. (1969) *The Mechanisms of Perception*, New York, NY: Basic Books.

Popper, K. (1959) *The Logic of Scientific Discovery*, London: Hutchinson.

Popper, K. (1962) *The Open Society and its Enemies*, London: Routledge and Kegan Paul.

Popper, K. (1969) *Conjectures and Refutations*, London: Routledge and Kegan Paul.

Popper, K. (1972) *Objective Knowledge: An Evolutionary Approach*, Oxford: Oxford University Press.

Porpora, D. (1998) 'Do realists run regressions?' *2nd International Centre for Critical Realism Conference*, University of Essex.

Pratt, A. (1995) 'Putting critical realism to work: The practical implications for geographical research', *Progress in Human Geography*, 19: 61–74.

Reed, M. (1997) 'In praise of duality and dualism: Rethinking agency and structure in organizational analysis', *Organization Studies*, 18: 21–42.

Reed, M. (2001) 'Organization, trust and control: A realist analysis', *Organization Studies*, 22: 201–28.

Robey, D. (1996) 'Diversity in information systems research: Threat, promise and responsibility', *Information Systems Research*, 7: 400–8.

Robinson, H., Hall, P., Hovenden, F. and Rachel, J. (1998) 'Postmodern software development', *The Computer Journal*, 41: 363–75.

Ron, A. (1999) 'Regression analysis and the philosophy of social sciences: A critical realist view', *Critical Realism: Implications for Practice*, Örebro: Centre for Critical Realism, Örebro University Sweden.

Rorty, R. (1980) *Philosophy and the Mirror of Nature*, Oxford: Blackwell.

Rorty, R. (1989) *Contingency, Irony and Solidarity*, Cambridge: Cambridge University Press.

Sayer, A. (1992) *Method in Social Science*, London: Routledge.

Sayer, A. (1997) 'Critical realism and the limits to critical social science', *Journal for the Theory of Social Behaviour*, 27: 473–88.

Schlick, M., Mulder, H. L. and Velde-Schlick, B. F. B. v. d. (1979) *Philosophical papers*, ed. H. L. Mulder and B. F. B. van de Velde-Schlick, trans. P. Heath, Dordrecht: D. Reidel.

Schutz, A. (1972) *The Phenomenology of the Social World*, London: Heinemann.

Searle, J. (1996) *The Construction of Social Reality*, London: Penguin.

Sherden, W. (1998) *The Fortune Sellers: The Big Business of Buying and Selling Predictions*, New York, NY: John Wiley & Sons.

Tsang, E. and Kwan, K. (1999) 'Replication and theory development in organizational science: A critical realist perspective', *Academy of Management Review*, 24: 759–80.

Van Maanen, J. (1995a) 'Fear and loathing in organization studies', *Organization Science*, 6: 687–92.

Van Maanen, J. (1995b) 'Style as theory', *Organization Science*, 6: 133–43.

Walsham, G. (1993) *Interpreting Information Systems in Organizations*, Chichester: John Wiley & Sons.

Walsham, G. (1995a) 'The emergence of interpretivism in IS research', *Information Systems Research*, 6: 376–94.

Walsham, G. (1995b) 'Interpretive case studies in IS research: Nature and method', *European Journal of Information Systems*, 4: 74–81.

Walsham, G. (1997) 'Actor-network theory and IS research: Current status and future prospects', in A. Lee, J. Liebenau and J. DeGross (eds), *Information Systems and Qualitative Research*, London: Chapman and Hall, pp. 466–80.

Whitehead, A. N. and Russell, B. (1925) *Principia Mathematica*, Cambridge: Cambridge University Press.

Whittington, R. (1992) 'Putting Giddens into action: Social systems and managerial agency', *Journal of Management Studies*, 29: 693–712.

Wittgenstein, L. (1958) *Philosophical Investigations*, Oxford: Blackwell.

Woolgar, S. (ed.) (1988) *Knowledge and Reflexivity: New Frontiers in the Sociology of Knowledge*, Beverly Hills, CA: Sage.

Wright, C. (1999) 'They shoot dead horses don't they? Locating agency in the agent-structure problematique', *European Journal of International Relations*, 5: 109–42.

Yeung, H. (1997) 'Critical realism and realist research in human geography', *Progress in Human Geography*, 21: 51–74.

11
Complexity and Information Systems

Yasmin Merali

It has been argued that the advent of the Internet and attendant emergent technologies has resulted in a step change in the level of complexity inherent in the effective world.[1] This is not to claim that the Internet *alone* has caused this change: many other socioeconomic and political factors are important in the advance of internationalisation and globalisation. However, the communication and information capabilities and processes enabled by the Internet and associated technologies are integral to the realisation of the network society and the network economy (Castells, 1996).

At the most fundamental level the technological developments have the potential to increase:

- Connectivity (between people, applications and devices).
- Capacity for distributed storage and processing of data.
- Reach and range of information transmission.
- Rate (speed and volume) of information transmission.

The exploitation of these capabilities has given rise to the emergence of network forms of organising as processes, information and expertise are shared across organisational and national boundaries.

Much of the recent managerial interest in complexity has been catalysed by the commercialisation of the Internet and the emergence of the network economy. Greater connectivity and access to an increased variety and volume of information constitute greater informational complexity (Chaitin, 1990). Increased global connectivity and speed of communication effectively contract the spatio-temporal separation of world events: informational changes in one locality can very quickly be transmitted globally, influencing social, political and economic decisions in geographically remote places. In the managerial discourse (Evans and Wurster, 2000; Axelrod and Cohen, 1999; Shapiro and Varian, 1999), these changes are seen as the harbingers of a 'new' economy (or 'information economy'), characterised by:

- The critical role of information and knowledge in competition.
- Increased dynamism, uncertainty and discontinuity in the competitive context.
- Pressures for fast decision making in the absence of complete information.
- The importance of flexibility and adaptability for survival.

The 'network' form of organising is a signature of the Internet-enabled transformation of economics and society (see also Chapter 7). We find that strategy and managerial discourse are shifting from focusing solely on the firm as a unit of organisation to networks of firms, from considerations of industry-specific value systems to considerations of networks of value systems, and from the concept of discrete industry structures to the concept of ecologies.

In the domain of information systems, the focus on discrete applications development has become imbued with issues of flexibility, connectivity and compatibility with other systems. Driven by the business need for intra- and inter-organisational integration of information processes, we have moved from concentrating on applications development to engaging with issues of information architectures.

The Internet is implicated as both an enabler and a driver of this interconnected world. At a more general level, there is an escalation of interest in the idea that information technology networks and social networks self-organise into a constellation of networks of networks (Watts, 1999, 2003; Barabasi, 2002). This is analogous to conceptualising the interconnected world as a kind of global distributed information system comprising networks of networks. The question is: do we need to change the way we conceive of information systems in order to participate effectively in a discourse about the networked world? Can the science of complexity provide concepts that are useful in articulating epistemological and ontological issues that are relevant to this discourse? Two issues that emerge as essential for us to deal with in the information systems discipline are:

- The need to engage with the network form of *organising*.
- The conceptualisation of an *information network-in-use*. It is important to note that the term 'information network' is used precisely to denote 'network of information' comprised of *informational* content and *informational* connectivity.[2]

In the wake of the realisation that the competitive context is becoming progressively more complex and less predictable as time goes on, it is being questioned whether the formalisations of decision making that have prevailed in the past are adequate for dealing with the contingencies of this new context. In recent managerial discourse there has been heightened interest in the 'science of complexity' or 'complexity theory' as a source of ideas, concepts and techniques in the quest for a new management paradigm (Stacey, 2001; Axelrod and Cohen, 1999; Eisenhardt and Galunic, 1999).

The concept of complexity is not new in the information systems domain. Successive developments in the epistemological domain have spawned methodologies for modelling and managing the complexity of systems. In this chapter I explore the notion of complexity and reflect on the possible contribution that concepts from the 'science of complexity' may make to the discourse on information systems paradigms for defining and representing complexity in the Internet-enabled world.

We begin by reviewing the way in which the 'classical' information systems paradigm addresses complexity before moving on to explore the potential contribution that concepts from the 'science of complexity' may make to this endeavour. The exploration in the next sections

- Identifies constructs for dealing with complexity in the 'classical' information systems paradigm.
- Outlines a connectionist information systems phenomenology of the Internet-enabled network.
- Identifies distinctive concepts from the 'science of complexity' that have the potential to contribute to a revised paradigm for information systems conceptualisation in the networked context.

- Considers the implications of a paradigm shift for information systems theory and practice.

COMPLEXITY IN THE 'CLASSICAL' INFORMATION SYSTEMS PARADIGM

Complexity is defined in the dictionary as 'the state or quality of consisting of interconnected or interwoven parts; composite; intricate or involved'. In this section we review the way in which the 'classical' information systems paradigm addresses the concept of complexity through its methodologies and constructs.

The earlier developments in the information systems discipline evolved from Bertalanffy's general systems theory (Bertalanffy, 1968), building on:

- The structural concept of the holistic system, having well-defined boundaries and comprising interconnected discrete components.
- The dynamic concept of open systems able to maintain themselves in a steady state far from equilibrium.

This systemic approach is embodied in the earlier structured methodologies for systems development and design to create informational representations of systems. Their focus is on the structural definition of systems in terms of data flows and dependencies. This family of methodologies is exemplified by the Yourdon Systems Analysis and Design Methodology SSADM, Jackson's Structured Systems Design and Programming, and James Martin's Information Engineering.

The cybernetic approaches (exemplified by Beer's viable systems methodology and Forrester's Systems Dynamics) that followed explicitly added the dynamic perspective to the characterisation of systems. The socially situated nature of information systems was the focus of the sociotechnical and soft systems methodologies (exemplified by Mumford's ETHICS and Checkland's Soft Systems Methodology).

These developments established the top-down paradigm for managing complexity that dominates information systems design and development to this day. For example, contemporary methods for object-oriented design continue to use classification constructs, modularisation and information hiding as mechanisms for handling complexity. Particularly important in this respect is the manner in which the holistic perspective, modular representation and the concept of the boundary are deployed in the informational representation of systems.

The Holistic Perspective and Reduction of Complexity

The system is perceived as a 'whole' that can be decomposed into a number of *interconnected* subsystems, each of which may in turn be decomposed into a number of interconnected subsystems and so on. The design and analysis of systems are predicated on *top-down* decomposition and modularisation. The system is represented as a set of *interconnected* but *non-overlapping* components (modules or subsystems).

This is an important way of managing complexity, as at any level of decomposition the subsystems can be effectively treated as black boxes, the internal complexity of which can be hidden and ignored until they are decomposed themselves.

Representation of the Boundary and Cleavage from the Environment

The concept of the boundary is essential in defining the modular system. The boundary is represented as a discrete structure defining the interface between the system (or subsystem) and its environment. At any given level of decomposition the internal complexity of each constituent component is 'hidden' behind its boundary definition. The concept of the boundary makes it possible to define the system discretely in terms of its inputs and outputs, and simplifies the representation of the system's relationship with its environment.

Dynamics

In the early structured methodologies, interconnections between systems components were defined in terms of data flows and dependencies. While the passage of time is implicit in the sequence of transactions represented in flow charts and entity life histories, the systems representations do not deal explicitly with the concept of time or with the definition of changing systems' states.

The subsequent adoption of the cybernetic approach redressed this omission by introducing the dimension of dynamics into systems representations, making it possible to represent stability and change in the states of systems in discrete time.

Feedback Loops as Representations of Causality and Control

In the cybernetic approach, interconnections and relationships between the system's components are defined in terms of their effectiveness as causal or control mechanisms in determining the system's states for different time frames.

The system's dynamics are modelled in terms of positive and negative feedback loops that respectively enhance or damp the activity of the component receiving the feedback. Changes in a system's state and behaviour can be explained (and predicted) as the summative effect of the feedback loops.

Thus in representational terms, the complexity of the system's behaviour can be reduced to the definition of requisite feedback loops. In pragmatic terms, the underlying assumption is:

- It is possible to identify and isolate a discrete and persistent set of feedback mechanisms and their effects, and to attribute causalities to the feedback mechanisms such that
- interventions can be designed to control systems behaviours by altering input or output parameters and inhibiting or enhancing the requisite feedback cycles.

To summarise, epistemologically the 'traditional' paradigm is concerned with mechanistic representations of complex systems in a manner that *reduces* the amount of complexity that can be confronted at any given level of decomposition of the whole. These methodological developments entail a top-down definition and representation of the system and its components, predicated on ontological assumptions of:

- a *persistent* hierarchy of organisation embodied in
- a fixed set of relationships between components and
- regulation of processes by feedback loops that
- implement the defined *causal* relationships leading to
- the achievement (or maintenance) of a desired steady state.

Regardless of whether the representation has been derived from an empiricist or constructivist account of 'reality', the system as defined in the representation is used as the basis for the construction of a valid model of reality.

It is interesting to note that this is the case even when the analytical process highlights the existence of multiple perspectives, the possibilities for social construction of information, meaning and the substance of 'reality', and the potential for diverse interpretation of actions, events, artifacts, symbols and signs (e.g. in Checkland's Soft Systems Methodology or Mumford's ETHICS). Although the potential diversity, relativity and reflexivity of socially situated information *systems-in-use* is recognised, ultimately information systems are defined in terms of the traditional paradigm and diversity is accommodated in, or negotiated out of, the final systems specification for action in the real world.

In the next section we review the nature of the complexity and dynamics of the Internet-enabled world, before moving on to examine the adequacy of the 'classical' paradigm for representing this phenomenology.

THE NETWORK PHENOMENOLOGY OF INFORMATION SYSTEMS

As outlined in the introduction, the potential of the Internet to enable ubiquitous connectivity will, if fully realised, result in an interconnected world that is comprised of networks of networks. We can conceive of this scenario as a kind of global distributed information system comprising:

- a complex multidimensional network that
- connects a diversity of entities (individuals, groups, institutions, nations) through
- diverse and multiple channels.

The fundamental technological network enables connectivity (between people, applications and devices) and distributed information capabilities (transmission, presentation, processing and storage). The socially defined and the socially defining nature of technology have long been the subject of debate in the information systems literature (Merali, 1997; Orlikowski, 1992; Hiltz and Johnson, 1990; Jarvanpaa, 1989; Davis, 1989; Zuboff, 1988; Markus, 1983; Leavitt and Whistler, 1958; see also Chapters 4 and 9). In our discourse we use the term *systems-in-use* to acknowledge the reflexive nature of socially situated information systems.

In the case of our Internet-enabled information network, the *system-in-use* embodies social, economic, political, informational and technological dimensions. In this chapter, we are concerned with understanding the aspects of complexity that arise when the technological network capability is deployed by human agents.

The network as a dynamic form of organisation has been analysed extensively in the study of complex systems. It is useful in our case to explore the connectionist concept of the network in order to appreciate features that give rise to the complex phenomena drawing us to the language and paradigms of the 'science of complexity' for their articulation.

The Connectionist Definition of Networks

Networks consist of interconnected nodes that are able to communicate with each other. Each node is connected by its interrelationship with other nodes and by its place in the network. Nodes send, receive, transform and transmit information throughout the network, and they can also be information repositories. The ways in which connections intersect create the distinctive traits and functions that differentiate nodes. Connections of each node have ramifications throughout the network.

Network Connectivity: Emergent Topology

In our case the network nodes are social entities. In the complexity literature the term 'agent' is often used to refer to the nodal entity, and I will adopt this terminology for the sake of consistency. Each agent may be connected to a number of different agents at any given time. Depending on the task at hand, attendant constraints and proclivities, individual agents activate particular connections in the network at particular times. A snapshot of the network reveals denser clusters of networks with looser connections to other clusters of networks (Watts, 1999, 2003; Barabasi, 2002; Buchanan, 2002).

The patterns of connectivity change over time: some connections may become stronger due to repeated transactions and the development of lasting relationships, new connections may appear as entities embark on innovative ventures, some connections may atrophy due to a lack of communication, while dying connections may be revived due to a renewed interest in collaboration. Over time we can expect to observe a dynamic network topology, with individual constellations in the network being activated selectively *as and when* needed for particular collaborative and transactional contingencies. If we were to plot the shape of the network in space over time, we would find changing patterns of connection that would redefine not only the intensity of existing connections between individual nodes in the network but also the edges of the network.

As noted earlier, in the case of the Internet-enabled world, the *system-in-use* embodies social, economic, political, informational and technological dimensions. While the technological infrastructure provides the *possibility* of communication between interconnected nodes, the *actual* form and content of the active *network-in-use* at any given time is defined by *interaction* of the agents with the technological network in order to communicate with other agents.

The contingent nature of the network dynamics highlights the emergent nature of the information *network-in-use*. Individual connections are established or activated in accordance with *here-and-now* local needs and the dispositions of individual agents. The global network form at any given moment is a manifestation of the collective pattern of interconnections.

Information Content: Emergent Diversity

This concept of the network-in-use is partially aligned with Luhmann's notion of social systems as self-producing networks of communication (Luhmann, 1990). Each agent both constitutes *and* utilises the network. The agents collectively give rise to both the *topology* (i.e. the network structure emerging from inter-agent connections) and the *information content* of the *network-in-use*. The information that is transmitted in the network is defined by the transmitting agents' selection and articulation of the informational content and the recipients' interpretation of the 'message' and its import. Hence each agent has the possibility of amplifying or attenuating the message. Different agents receiving the 'same' message may propagate a variety of interpreted versions.

We thus have a highly complex system of networks of networks of communication. The potential complexity of the networks arises both from the variable connectivity over time and from the multiple versions of information transmitted through the network.

Information and Action: Local Acts, Emergent Global Behaviour

Let us return briefly from the domain of information to the domain of action. The introduction of human agency, bounded rationality and free will adds to the complexity of the network. It is impossible for any one agent in the network to have complete knowledge of the state of the whole network at any given time. Agents must act on the basis of the limited information that they can glean from their network and immediate environment. The overall state of the network *emerges* from the local actions of the individual agents, none of whom has complete knowledge of the entire network, and all of whom are susceptible to conditioning by their diverse social and cultural environments and backgrounds, their personal experiences, and events and information about events from their immediate environment and their extended networks. The network thus embodies both a degree of path dependency (history matters) and a spontaneous departure from the past. Individual agents learn and they forget. Social groups have established rituals but also succumb to fads and fashions. Inventions may lead to sweeping innovations or they may die unnoticed. No overall design can predetermine exactly how the network will be at any future point in time.

To summarise, consistently with the 'classical' definition of systems the network is composed of a large number of interacting elements. However, the dynamics of interaction between elements gives rise to a number of features that are difficult to reconcile with some of the tenets of the 'classical' information systems paradigm. These are:

- The emergent, 'bottom-up' network dynamics challenges the classical 'top-down' paradigm for understanding systems structures and behaviours.
- The complex connectivity and evolving information content of the network make it impossible accurately to predict the exact state of the network for a specific future point in time.
- The network structure is difficult to represent with the classical method of structural modularisation.
- It becomes difficult to use the concept of the boundary to demarcate the cleavage of the system from its environment.
- The classical device of using discrete state changes for the *separation of 'becoming' from 'being'* does not capture the mutually defining relationship between dynamics and structure. In the case of the dynamic network, the global topology is defined by the collective dynamics and the global dynamics emerges from locally responsive actions, defined by structural coupling between local components.

It would appear, then, that the classical systems paradigm is limited in its capacity for representing and articulating the salient features of the structural dynamics and behaviour of the socially realised active information network.

Boundaries

Bertalanffy's general systems theory was powerful in articulating the existence of the system as a holistic unity, and systems are defined by their boundary. In conceptualising autopoietic systems, Maturana and Varela (1973) argue that the boundary is something that is *attributed to* the system. The unity, they maintain, is defined intrinsically by its form (a persistent pattern of relations between network components). An external observer perceives the system as a *unity* because there is a visible cleavage from the environment of the components that constitute the unity. They use the notion of *structural coupling* and *neighbourhood relations* to speak of the boundary relationship and the internal/external partitioning. Components of the unity have strong neighbourhood relationships with other components belonging to the same unity. Boundary components at the interface of the unity with the external environment have recurrent interactions with environmental elements, but these interactions do not display the same strength of sustained linkages as those that characterise internal neighbourhood relations.

Using the concept of the boundary to define the network as a holistic unity is problematic due to the following reasons:

- It is difficult to define the characteristics for describing the boundary. It is arguable that we could define the network by defining its edges at any given moment in time. However, in order to do so, we need to describe the significant difference that enables us to distinguish between agents that are at the network boundary and those that are not. We need to ask whether there are any characteristics or particular modes of interaction that distinguish boundary agents from other members of the network, or whether they are merely, coincidentally, juxtaposed to a space that is empty of other network members.
- If we plotted the shape of the network in space over time, we would find changing patterns of connections that would redefine not only the intensity of existing connections between individual nodes in the network, but also the edges of the network. Thus the network boundary is itself an emergent phenomenon.
- Discerning the boundary phenomenology is problematic. Because the boundary itself is an emergent phenomenon attributable to

the network dynamics, making the distinction between network and non-network agents is difficult, given that the relationship between 'the system' and 'the environment' is ambiguous, and network connectivity is dynamic.

- The permeability of the boundary becomes an important relational phenomenon. For example, agent networks may breach traditional boundaries of industries, institutions and social groups. Permeability of organisational boundaries increases as processes, information and expertise are shared across institutions through collaborative and sourcing relationships. This is exemplified by transdisciplinary, inter-organisational projects that can be conceptualised as transient structures for work organisation. In interfirm outsourcing relationships, the persistence of project-based work organisation may also be conceptualised as a virtual organisational form at the institutional level.

As we will see more clearly in the next section, this kind of network is actually a complex adaptive system, where the relationship between 'the system' and 'the environment' is ambiguous, so that the concept of a 'hard' boundary of the type assumed in the classical methodologies is not particularly useful in extending our understanding of this type of system.

CONCEPTS FROM THE 'SCIENCE OF COMPLEXITY'

In this section we outline the basic concepts and vocabulary that will be considered in the final discussion on the potential contribution that ideas from the science of complexity may make to the discourse on information systems paradigms for conceptualising and representing complexity in the Internet-enabled world.

The 'science of complexity' originates from investigations in the natural sciences of non-linear complex systems. These complex systems typically comprise a large number of simultaneously interacting constituents. The terms 'complexity theory' and 'complexity science' imply the existence of a clear-cut scientific paradigm, but in fact they refer to an emerging set of concepts and constructs that have surfaced during the quest for a scientific paradigm capable of addressing those aspects of complex systems behaviour and existence, which are not accommodated by the traditional deterministic and probabilistic conceptual frameworks of classical mechanics and thermodynamics.[3] Thus it is more realistic to see the developments in complexity science as an emergent paradigm shift[4] rather than as the birth of a new science. The discussion that follows is intended to be in the same tenor: it engages with the possibility of a paradigm shift from the 'classical' information systems paradigm to one that deals more effectively with the complexity of the Internet-enabled network context.

For the purpose of this discourse, the concept of 'complexity' is well articulated in the Santa Fe[5] definition:

> Complexity refers to the condition of the universe which is integrated and yet too rich and varied for us to understand it in simple common mechanistic or linear ways. We can understand many parts of the universe in these ways but the larger and more intricately related phenomena can only be understood by principles and patterns—not in detail. Complexity deals with the nature of emergence, innovation, learning and adaptation.

The 'science of complexity' is concerned with studying how collective behaviours of the focal system as a whole arise from the non-linear interactions of its constituents with each other and with the environment.[6] This is an interdisciplinary endeavour, transcending traditional boundaries of the disciplines of physical and social sciences. Its early roots can be traced back to the early history of mathematics, linguistics, economics and biology.

In classical science, it is possible to predict cause-and-effect relationships between system constituents and the environment and to institute requisite control and optimisation structures and processes. The 'classical' information systems paradigm reviewed in the introduction clearly originated from this *Weltanschauung*.

In the complexity paradigm we are concerned with systems that have:

- a large number of components with many interconnections and
- a reflexive relationship with the environment.

Such systems have simultaneously active positive and negative feedback loops, and it is difficult to predict with certainty exactly which of the loops will dominate at any given time and what the subsequent state of the system will be. Because of the non-uniform, dynamic interconnections between the constituents of a complex system, it is difficult to predict the extent to which the actions of one constituent will affect other constituents and the environment itself. A small change in one locality may be amplified and transmitted many times by intervening actors so that it has a very large and unexpected impact some distance away. On the other hand, it is also possible for the force of a large perturbation in the environment to be dissipated by the system.

The articulation of the concepts and language of complexity defined below derives from the results of mathematical modelling and computer simulations of complex systems. Many of these concepts were exposed in our earlier review of the Internet-enabled network phenomenology, and later in this chapter we will consider what their implications are for information systems paradigms and practice.

Describing Dynamics

The non-linear dynamics of complex systems rendered them intractable for the traditional analytical methods of mathematical modelling. This impasse was overcome with the advent of supercomputers in the last quarter of the twentieth century. The extraordinary increase in processing power in the 1970s gave rise to the development of computational techniques for exploring the dynamics of non-linear systems.

Most traditional approaches for dealing with systems dynamics have been concerned with the definition of discrete changes in the system's state at discrete time intervals. To capture the 'unfolding' of the emergent dynamics, we need to have methods that can provide a view of the dynamics of the *changing* state in continuous time. The complex systems approach to doing this is by describing state cycles using mathematical models or by running simulations (see below). Fundamental to the development of models to explore the relationship between order and chaos in complex systems was the development of the phase space technique for modelling complexity.

The phase space

The dynamics of a system is traced by plotting the value of each of its variables at different points in time. The variables of the system are displayed in abstract mathematical space, called the phase space. Each variable is allocated a dimension in phase space, and its value at any given time is represented by a coordinate in that dimension.

For example, if we wish to describe the dynamics of a pendulum, we would define its state in terms of two variables: its velocity and its angle of displacement. The dynamics of the system's state would thus be defined in a two-dimensional phase space. At any given point in time, its state would be identified by a point (defined by the values of the two coordinates) in the phase space.

Multidimensional phase space can be used to develop quite complex descriptions. So if we need to use 18 variables to define a system, it will be represented in an 18-dimensional phase. At any given point in time, the state of the system will be defined by the values of its 18 coordinates (one for each dimension of the phase space). At any given point in time the system's state will be described by a single point in the 18-dimensional phase space.

Attractors

As the system changes step by step from one state to the next, the succession of states traces a trajectory in the phase space. The concept of attractors is used to classify the trajectories of different sequences of state changes. There are three basic types of attractors:

- Point attractors describe the trajectories of systems reaching a stable equilibrium.
- Periodic attractors describe systems that are executing periodic oscillations (such as a friction-less pendulum).
- Strange attractors correspond to chaotic systems (see below). In these cases the system never repeats itself (i.e. it never covers the same trajectory in phase space more than once). However, the set of trajectories conform to a distinctive pattern. Although it is not possible to predict exactly which point in phase space will be traversed by the trajectory at any given point in time, it is possible to identify the pattern that it will trace out in phase space: all trajectories starting out in a given region of the phase space will eventually lead to the same attractor. The region is called the basin of attraction.

Chaos

The term chaos[7] has tended to dominate popular discourse on the relevance of complexity science in management. The concept of chaotic systems is often conflated with the concept of complex systems. However, it is important to recognise that in mathematical terms, chaotic systems have specific properties that are not universally shared by all complex systems.

The term 'chaos' has been popularised in the managerial literature on dynamism, innovation and creativity, and is often used to
refer to a state of disorder and randomness out of which arises a
new order. However, technically a chaotic system is a *deterministic*
system that is difficult to predict. As Bar-Yam (2000) points out,
in practice the concept of chaotic systems presents a paradox. By
definition, a deterministic system is one whose state at one time
completely determines its state for all future times, but in practice
a chaotic system is difficult to predict because of its sensitivity to
initial conditions[8]: what happens in its future is very sensitive to its
current state. In practice the degree of accuracy (of measurement of
start conditions) needed in order to predict an outcome is likely to
be impossible to obtain.

Chaotic systems share properties with complex systems, including their sensitivity to initial conditions. However, in the study of
chaotic systems, the systems' dynamics are generally described by
a small number of variables (i.e. they have a low dimensionality
in phase space). Consequently, models of chaos generally describe
the dynamics of a few variables, and the models reveal some
characteristic behaviours of these dynamics. However, generally
complex systems have many degrees of freedom, as illustrated
by our description of the information network: they are composed of many elements that are partially but not completely
independent, with ambiguous system–environment relationships.
Our discussion of the information network and the information
systems paradigms and practice is concerned with the wider class
of complex systems.

Emergence

Emergence refers to the phenomenon whereby the macroscopic
properties of a system arise from the microscopic properties (interactions, relationships, structures and behaviours) of its constituents.
The emergent macroscopic 'whole' displays a set of properties that
is distinct from those displayed by any subset of its individual constituents and their interactions. For example, the temperature and
pressure of a gas can be viewed as emerging from the large number
of gas molecules hitting each other: temperature and pressure are
properties that can be ascribed to the mass of gas, but they do
not exist as properties of isolated individual molecules. In other
words, the whole is more than (and certainly different to) the sum
of its parts.

At the microscopic level, the behaviour of an individual constituent at a given time and place is contingent on the current state of that constituent and on the here-and-now conditions prevalent in its local environment. For constituents that are active at the boundary of the system, the local environment will incorporate internal and external components. The collective behaviour of the individual constituents at the microscopic level will manifest itself as the behaviour of the 'whole system' visible at the macroscopic level.

The existence and persistence of the system are thus relational phenomena, predicated on the relationship of the constituents of the system to each other and to constituents of the environment in continuous time. Local, contingent, neighbourhood interactions and adjustments at the micro level are at the same time detectable as a coherent pattern of properties constituting the 'whole' system. This point is illustrated very clearly by Bar-Yam (2000) when he says:

> when we think about emergence we are, in our mind's eye, moving between different vantage points. We see the trees and the forest at the same time. We see the way the trees and the forest are related to each other. To see in both these views we have to be able to see details, but also ignore details. The trick is to know which of the many details we see in the trees are important to know when we see the forest.

This is consistent with our earlier observation that the classical separation of 'becoming' from 'being' does not advance our understanding of complex systems. In order to identify how emergent properties are produced, we need to be able to access descriptions of the system at multiple scales from the micro to the macro at the same time. This presents us with a problem of representation in the classical mode. Hence typically, complex systems representations are either developed as mathematical models or as computer simulations.

At the micro level, system and environment components interact in a contiguous space and, depending on the nature of particular relationships, can to a lesser or greater degree be considered to be mutually effective: the state and behaviour of the system constituents will affect the state and behaviour of the environmental constituents and vice versa. In other words, the dynamic definition of a system is contingent on the dynamic definition of its environment, and system constituents are an integral part of the landscape in which they exist. The concepts of systems adaptation and evolution are thus extended to the dynamics of the ecosystem within which systems are situated.

These characteristics also require us to revisit the concept of boundaries, possibly redefining the way in which boundaries are conceptualised. It may be useful, for example, to move from the classical view of boundaries as defining the bounds of a system, towards a more dynamic view of boundaries as relative and relational phenomena, linking system and environmental elements through differential coupling.

The emergence of the macro-level phenomenology from micro-level interactions and the mutually defining relationship between the system and its environment are defining characteristics of our information network dynamics. The question of how to deal with boundaries in this context remains a non-trivial one.

Complex Adaptive Systems, Co-adaptation and Co-evolution

Systems that adapt and evolve in the process of interacting with dynamic environments are referred to as complex adaptive systems. Adaptation at the macro level (the 'whole' system) is characterised by emergence and self-organisation (see below) based on the local adaptive behaviour of the system's constituents. Our information network, biological organisms and social organisations are thus all examples of complex adaptive systems.

As a consequence of the reflexive relationship between systems and the environment discussed earlier, changes in systems both shape, and are shaped by, changes in the environment. If a number of systems cohabit in a particular environment, the environment is itself an emergent manifestation of its multiple interactions with the systems it 'hosts'.

In classical representations of systems, the environment is viewed as the source of a discrete set of inputs and a sink for a discrete set of outputs. The paradigm of complex adaptive systems imposes the need to consider the dynamics and mutually defining consequences of the relationship between the system and its environment, taking us from issues of adaptation to issues of co-adaptation and co-evolution in dynamic contexts.

For example, consider an ecosystem cohabited by a diversity of species. The environment, each individual and each species will affect and be affected by the actions of the other individuals and species. The fitness or chances of survival for each species will be related to its ability to adapt to the environmental changes. Over time, selective pressures (resulting from the interaction of the habitat and surviving cohabiting species) will lead to the evolution of new traits in the various populations, changes in the habitat and the emergence of new species. Co-adaptation and co-evolution in dynamic environments can be viewed as important mechanisms for sustainability of the ecosystem. The capacity for adaptation is predicated on the capacity for self-organisation described below.

Fitness landscapes are often used to explore these dynamics. The fitness landscape is a simulation constructed from representations (in terms of the fitness function, which is a mathematical expression of the relative value of a population with reference to a particular criterion) of the relative fitness of all actors. The peaks and valleys in the landscape represent respectively the most and least fit. Each actor only has knowledge of the local environment and acts accordingly. The landscape undergoes distortions due to the actions of the actors and to changes in the environmental conditions. The concept of fitness landscapes has been used to develop simulations of competitive landscapes (see Kauffman, 1995b for examples).

Self-Organisation

Self-organisation is the ability of complex systems spontaneously to generate new internal structures and forms of behaviour. This *generative* aspect takes the complex systems concept of self-organisation beyond the early cybernetics concept of self-organisation, which focused on the self-regulatory and control aspects of organisation. The concept of ordered systems that are able to maintain themselves in states far from equilibrium underpins more profound ideas about the origins and evolution of life (Kauffman, 1995a; Maturana and Varela, 1973).

Spontaneous Creation of Order

Unlike the closed systems that were the subject of classical thermodynamics, complex adaptive systems do not evolve to maximum entropy. The generative process of self-organisation in complex systems highlights that they are open systems, with continuous flow of energy and resources passing through them, enabling them to maintain an existence far from equilibrium. In the self-organisation process, the components *spontaneously* reorient and restructure their relationships with neighbouring components, giving rise to the emergence of structures that embody an increased level of internal complexity.

Self-organisation is not the result of *a priori* design, it surfaces from the interaction of system and the environment and the local interactions between the systems components. This capacity for the spontaneous *creation* of order through *intrinsically* generated structures is captured in Stuart Kauffman's (1993) expression 'order for free', in the notion of Prigogine's dissipative structures[9] (Prigogine, 1967) and in Maturana and Varela's theory of autopoiesis[10] (Maturana and Varela, 1973).

Network connectivity and state changes

The emergence of self-organising structures is due not to the intrinsic properties of the components themselves, but to the complex patterns of interactions between components. The pattern of interactions is explained in terms of the network of interconnections. Network connectivity allows for the generation of self-regulating feedback loops. A diversity of feedback cycles may be interlinked in a variety of ways, with different consequences: the interlinked cycles may maintain a homeostatic condition or they may spontaneously generate new, more complex forms of organisation under certain critical conditions. The experimental foundations for this understanding come from artificial life simulations using cellular automata[11] (Langton, 1991; Berlekamp, Conway and Guy, 1982) and Boolean networks[12] (Kauffman, 1993).

In his experiments with cellular automata, Langton demonstrated that the patterns of behaviour of his emergent structures fell into a regular sequence (or cycle) of three distinctive states: an *ordered regime* (comprised of rigid structures that do not change or of periodic oscillations), a *chaotic regime* (which is too unstable for the emergence of order) and a *transition regime* (ordered enough to afford stability, but capable of transformation into new structures).

Kauffman (1993) also established the same pattern in his experiments with Boolean networks. He found that the degree of connectivity (that is, the number of connections that each component has with other components) is a critical factor in the emergence of self-organised structures: if the connections are too few, the network becomes 'frozen' into the same state cycle; if they are too many, the system becomes excessively unstable and highly disordered. At what Kauffman called combinatorial optimisation (i.e. between the frozen and the unstable states), there occurred the spontaneous emergence of self-sustaining webs. The critical transition takes place at the tipping point where quantitative change suddenly leads to qualitative change. The argument is that in the ordered regime, the connectivity is too low for changes to be propagated through the system, and in the chaotic region the system would be too sensitive to perturbations for persistent structures to develop.

Life at the Edge of Chaos

Kauffman proposes that living systems have a frozen core and separate islands of changing nodes. When he modelled the genome as a binary network, he found that such networks are stable in response to minor perturbations that cause slight displacements in the local behaviour cycles of particular nodes—the effects of the perturbation are localised, and the network as a whole quickly resumes its normal pattern of behaviour. In the face of more profound perturbations (e.g. structural changes in network connectivity), the network may remain stable or it may undergo a transformation and become reorganised into a new ordered state.

Concurring with Langton, Kauffman suggests that living systems exist 'at the edge of chaos', in the transition regime, as this offers the differential potential for homeostasis *as well as* for adaptation, evolution and transformation.

To summarise, the network form is integral to self-organisation: network connectivity is instrumental in both sustaining stability *and* in propagating transformational state changes. It is the capacity for self-organisation and adaptation that confers robustness on organisational forms in dynamic environments.

TOOLS FOR STUDYING COMPLEX SYSTEMS BEHAVIOUR

There are two main ways in which complexity concepts have been deployed to study complex systems and their dynamics. The first is through the direct use of complexity concepts and language as sense-making and explanatory devices for complex phenomena in diverse application domains. The second is through modelling to study the dynamics of complex systems interactions and to reveal emergent structures and patterns of behaviour.

The most popular simulation environments include cellular automata, Boolean networks and agent-based modelling (which can encompass the logic of Boolean networks and cellular automata). We have already encountered examples of the first two in Langton and Kauffman's experiments with self-organising structures. Cellular automata and Boolean networks can be used to produce quite sophisticated patterns of organisation (see Kauffman, 1993, 1995a; Sigmund, 1993; Farmer, Toffoli and Wolfram, 1984 for examples). However, the most significant enhancement to the power and versatility of models for studying emergent phenomena came from John Holland's conception of genetic algorithms (Holland, 1998) for agent-based models in general (see below).

The manner in which modelling is deployed in the 'classical' information systems paradigm is *fundamentally* different from the way in which it is used in the science of complexity. In the former, models are developed from definitions of the system. In the latter, models *are* arguably the specification of the system that emerges from the interactions of its specified components.

Take for example the problem that we highlighted in our earlier discussion of boundaries: in the 'classical' paradigm boundaries are used to define the system as a 'unity', but the conceptualisation of a boundary for a dynamic network is problematic. However, we can turn to simulation to reveal the pattern that constitutes the network as a dynamic unity in terms of state cycles: the execution of coordinated state cycles constitutes the unity, and this is an observable phenomenon when we run the models.

Agent-Based Modelling

An agent-based model comprises individual 'agents' commonly implemented as software objects (Holland, 1998; Casti, 1997). Agent objects have states and rules of behaviour. They can be endowed with requisite resources, traits, behaviours and rules for interacting with, and adapting to, each other. Running such a model is simply an exercise of instantiating an agent population, letting the agents interact and monitoring what happens. Typically these agent-based models deploy a diversity of agents to represent the constituents of the focal system and the modeller defines the environmental parameters that are of interest as the starting conditions for the particular study. Starting with some initial condition, the simulation consists of applying the rules through several iterations. Repeated runs of the model reveal collective states or patterns of behaviour as they emerge from the interactions of entities over time. On the whole, agent-based models are very well suited for revealing the dynamics of far-from-equilibrium complex systems, and have been widely used to study the dynamics of a diversity of social and economic systems.[13]

John Holland's conception of genetic algorithms (Holland, 1998) provided the means to explore adaptive behaviour and fitness in dynamic landscapes. The concept derives from the notion that biological fitness (i.e. survival and reproduction) is based on successful adaptation, and that adaptation is effected by genetic endowment subject to processes of mutation, variation and selection. These processes have been abstracted into the design of adaptive algorithms (called genetic algorithms). We can think of the string of instructions that each agent is endowed with as the 'genotype' of that agent. As agents interact with each other we have the opportunity of introducing variation and innovation into the available gene pool. The processes of mutation (random flipping of some part of the rule specification) and 'genetic' cross-over (when two different agents' rule sets exchange part of their complement of instructions, resulting in the birth of two new 'hybrid' gene complements) give rise to the generation of new 'gene' combinations. This injection of innovative combinations into the 'gene pool' of the population is associated with the possibility of the emergence of innovative behaviour traits in the agent population. If the new combinations are robust enough to survive the selective pressures exerted by the environment, we observe the emergence of new strategies and the phenomenon of adaptation or learning in agent populations over time.

Agent-based models are displacing the conventional mathematical theorising approaches in the study of complex social and economic systems. One reason for this is that it is often difficult (and sometimes impossible) to develop and solve adequate mathematical representations of the system to be studied. Moreover, there are several *advantages* of agent-based computational modelling that are particularly relevant when studying socially embedded systems such as the information network. The process of creating mathematical formalisations often entails making simplifying assumptions (such as the assumption of representative agents, information symmetry, symmetrical pay-off structures etc.) that are not realistic. Such assumptions compromise the validity of the model as a representation of the real world. This is a particularly significant issue, given the exploratory, sense-making nature of contemporaneous studies of the Internet-enabled society. However, as Axtell (2000) points out, in agent-based modelling it is typically easy to relax such 'heroic assumptions'—the rationality of agents can be limited, agents can be made diverse so that there is no need to appeal to representative agents, pay-offs may be noisy and information can be local. Finally, running the model furnishes us with an *entire* dynamical history of the process under study.

It is useful to relate this back to our discussion about the processes of emergence and self-organisation in complex adaptive systems. Complex systems have many degrees of freedom, with many elements that are partially but not completely independent, with ambiguous system–environment relationships. There is a greater diversity of local behaviours than there is of global outcomes. In order to achieve an effective representation of the dynamics of the processes connecting the local (micro-level) and global (macro-level) characteristics, we need to develop a multiscale description of complex systems. Agent-based modelling allows us to study the diversity of (local) behaviours at fine scales and to observe the emergence of the global characteristics at the large scale.

With regard to their utility, agent-based models have the potential to be deployed as decision support tools. For example, they provide a facility for:

- defining the phase space and state cycles of the system, and
- exploring the sensitivity of the system to perturbations

in order to gauge the system's resilience and the magnitude of impact to be expected from potential interventions.

Application of Agent-Based Modelling

Diversity and abstraction: Defining the phase space and recognising pattern

The diversity and heterogeneity of agents are important in the dynamics of emergence. This is very clearly set out in conceptual terms in the theory. However, it is a challenge to figure out how to deal with this aspect in practice: the computation of all possible consequences of all possible differences (due to diversity of agents, diversity of potential relationships, potential actions etc.) is not a viable option. Moreover, the problem is compounded by the importance of conditions in affecting system sensitivity (and consequent changes in state): in addition to dealing with the inherent diversity of the system, we need to engage with the perturbations in the environment. One way of dealing with diversity is through abstraction.

Abstraction can be achieved either by deploying a higher level of generalisation to describe system properties or by reducing the number of dimensions used to define the system. Efficient abstraction would entail defining the critical set of dimensions (or phase space) for characterising the dynamics of emergence.

How to define the right set of parameters for describing the system and its environment is a key issue.

As we noted earlier, what is important when dealing with emergent properties is to not get locked into the detailed definition of the micro-level features of individual agents, but rather to move between the appreciation of the micro-level diversity and the manifestation of the higher-level characteristics. In the science of complexity this is tackled by developing ways of recognising *patterns* of state cycles that emerge in the phase space defined for particular agents or types of agents, and by running agent-based models. Agent-based models can be employed as laboratories for experimentation—we could use repeated runs of the models with different parameters in order to 'discover' the appropriate phase space.

Agent-Based Models in the Exploration of the Network-in-Use

The *network-in-use* embodies social, informational and technological dimensions. The complexity of the networks, then, arises from the interaction of these three aspects, and is reflected in the following issues:

- Technological management of the information networks, with regard to performance, capacity, reliability, security, integrity, load and resource balancing etc.
- Patterns of technological innovation: the uptake of innovative technologies is subject to network effects. Dominant technologies emerge not necessarily because they are superior, but because there may be a number of social/economic/historical/political factors interacting with the technology trajectory to create a critical mass that tips the balance in favour of the winners. Much-quoted examples of this are VHS versus Betamax video recording systems (Arthur, 1996) and QWERTY versus Dvorjak keyboard arrangements (David, 1985).
- Patterns of interactions and exploitation of the networks: a diversity of complex patterns results from the entanglement of local network interactions and global strategies of communication and control.

- Informational and ideological evolution, with regard to the way in which language, information and misinformation can be propagated to create versions of 'reality'.

Agent-based modelling would appear to provide a promising epistemological device for information network dynamics. Modelling in the complexity science paradigm is very often about exploration and discovery. Models are used to *reveal* systems' state cycles and the consequences of interventions and changes in the system and environmental parameters. There are many examples of the deployment of agent-based modelling to solve problems in real-world networks, particularly when the problem is one of optimising network performance (Appleby and Steward, 1994). It has also been used effectively to provide insights into the dynamics of competitive contexts (for examples see Lomi and Larson, 2001).

However, as noted earlier, for social systems the specification of the components (agents) for the construction of agent-based models is itself often a challenging prospect. With the escalation of available computational power, it will be possible to build models with a million agents of reasonable complexity. The challenge of creating entire mini-economies in silicon is not one of processing power, but one of learning how to build sufficiently realistic agents: agents who trade in markets, who form firms, who procreate, who engage in political activity and write constitutions and bribe other agents for votes while trying to pass term limits (Axtell, 2000). The diversity of social relationships and the idiosyncrasy of individuals make it difficult to develop models that are both sophisticated enough to capture the essential features of the social interactions and characteristics, and simple enough to make visible the dynamics of the system. The difficulty lies in identifying what constitutes the requisite set of variables for defining social systems—and *this* is a matter that necessitates a discourse with the sciences of sociology, philosophy and psychology, among others.

Consequently, agent-based modelling is deployed as a sense-making device for the dynamics of complex social systems and their environment, rather than to solve specific problems. This is different from the usual low-dimensional chaos models, where typically the system is modelled in terms of a few variables and where often a single parameter is used to describe the entire behaviour of the system. Consequently, while mathematical modelling is still used extensively in the study of chaotic systems, agent-based models are more prevalent in the study of non-deterministic complex adaptive systems.

EVALUATION: APPLICABILITY OF COMPLEXITY CONCEPTS

In this section we reflect on the general useability of complexity concepts in the study of social systems. Implications for information systems paradigms and practice will be considered in the next section.

The science of complexity offers concepts that are compelling for those of us engaged in exploring the networked information society. The vocabulary of chaos, emergence and self-organisation allows us to articulate the aspects of adaptation, discontinuous change and dynamism that are attributed to life in the 'new' economy (Evans and Wurster, 2000; Axelrod and Cohen, 1999; Shapiro and Varian, 1999; Hamel and Prahalad, 1994). The concepts of chaotic and complex adaptive systems, of life at the edge of chaos and fitness landscapes, all offer themselves as metaphors for organisation. As such, they can be used to explore and develop new explanations for observed social phenomena and to inform designs for new forms of organisation.

The metaphors can also be both used and explored in models of complex systems (Holland, 1998; Merali, 2001). The utility of complexity models varies from the predictive through theory building to the loosely sense making and explorative. For certain classes of problems, such as optimisation of supply chains or airline baggage handling (Bonabeau and Meyer, 2001), the agent-based models yield directly useable results. These types of problems are relatively easy to articulate in terms of key variables, although the interaction between the variables may be complex. For others, such as forecasting of market dynamics and network effects (*Economist*, 2003), speculating on population dynamics for town planning or the depletion of fishery stocks (Allen and McGlade, 1987), the models provide valuable insights for decision makers.

With regard to understanding the dynamics of social systems, the science of complexity invites us to explore, as metaphors or as mechanisms, phenomena such as emergence, self-organisation and chaos. However, pursuing this invitation highlights a number of unresolved issues of pragmatics and philosophy.

Pragmatic Issues

The difficulty inherent in developing analytical mathematical models for the non-linear dynamics of complex systems severely diminished the accessibility of complexity concepts for the wider research community and the study of social systems. This problem was overcome to some extent by the advent of modelling techniques (such as agent-based modelling) to reveal complex dynamics. However, the development of agent-based models is itself still problematic on two fronts:

- The software environments (e.g. SWARM) for development of models require a measure of expertise for effective utilisation, although more 'user-friendly' environments are now becoming available.
- As discussed earlier, the definition of appropriate variables (i.e. the phase space definition) for modelling social systems is itself problematic.

The resolution of the first of these issues lies in current and future advances in the sciences of mathematics, computation and graphics (for visual representations of emergent patterns).

The second issue highlights a more fundamental problem. From a methodological perspective, we need ontological and epistemological frameworks to guide the utilisation of complexity concepts in studying and dealing with social systems. However, neither the science of complexity nor the social sciences offer the requisite frameworks. Turning to philosophy and the social sciences, we find that there are a number of existing philosophical perspectives which we may be able to draw on in order to explore the possibility of developing the requisite frameworks.

Philosophical Openings

A full discussion of the problem of developing the requisite frameworks for the application of complexity concepts to social systems is beyond the scope of this chapter. However, our exploration of complexity concepts brings us to some openings that invite a further investigation of several philosophical positions, and these are highlighted below for future speculation.

To assimilate and accommodate the phenomenology of chaos, emergence and complex adaptive systems, we need to identify a philosophical position that enables us to deal with:

- Inseparability of *being* from *becoming*.
- 'Fluidity' between system and context.

- *Potentiality* of the emergent system and its constituents, given that emergent phenomena are non-deterministic, path dependent and context sensitive.
- Assimilation of the present and persistent with the possible and transient.

Heidegger's *Being and Time* (Heidegger, 1962) offers us a number of enabling concepts for this endeavour.[14] His *Dasein* (*being-there* or *being-in-the-world*) gives us the articulation of individual and collective *being* and its relationship with past, present and future time (see also Chapter 3).

Dasein is the wholeness of being that includes the context and assimilates objects of the world into itself. This is an affirmation of *Dasein* in the present. However, *Dasein* in the present is in, and open to, a space of *possibilities* of the (collective) world (this is articulated in Heidegger's concept of *clearing*) and it is pressing *forward* into the possibilities (of the future). This pressing forward has a general direction (Heidegger's *towards-which* or *for-the-sake-of-which*), but no specific conscious goal. As Dreyfus (1987) puts it,

> *Dasein* is simply oriented toward the future, doing something now in order to be in a position to do something else later on, and all this makes sense as oriented towards something that the person is finally up to but need not have, probably cannot have, in mind.

So *Dasein* embodies the past, present and future: The 'pressing into the future' of *Dasein* in the *past* is the passage into *Dasein* in the *present*, which is already pressing into *Dasein* in the *future*.

In attempting to locate complexity concepts in relation to the map of established philosophical positions, Heidegger's existential phenomenology offers a promising starting point for our ontological framework: the notion of *Dasein* articulates the qualities of emergence (in the unfolding of *Dasein*), the contiguity of *being* with *becoming*, and the spontaneous organisation of *being* (incorporating the context, assimilating objects in the environment into the dynamics of *being*).

Turning to the social sciences, we find that critical realism[15] (Bhaskar, 1986) also articulates path dependency, emergence and transformation in social systems. As shown by Mingers in Chapter 10, it does so in terms of *causal mechanisms*, tracing the emergence of the experienced world from the existence of possibilities in the actual world, realised through generative mechanisms of the real world. In *Complexity Theory and the*

Social Sciences, David Byrne (1998) develops the proposition (Reed and Harvey, 1992, 1996) that critical realism constitutes the philosophical ontology complementing complexity as the scientific ontology.

With regard to the epistemological dimension, defining and studying the *being* of particular complex *systems-in-the-world* presents us with another problem. The moment we speak of *being,* it is interpreted (Eco, 1997). Interpretations are grounded in the system of interpretation or perspective of those who generate them. It is therefore possible to generate a diversity of interpretations from the observation or experience of any particular event or state of affairs. Similarly, the *possibilities* of *being* are transcendental, extending beyond the articulated experience, existence and imagination of any person. We are thus confronted with the problem of appreciating the potential (of *being*) beyond articulated accounts, representations or speculations about the past, present or future.

The problem of exposing that which lies behind and beyond language-based interpretations and descriptions of the world constitutes an opening for the exploration of Derrida's deconstructionist (Derrida, 1976, 1978) philosophy. This opening is explored in Paul Cilliers' *Complexity and Postmodernism.* Cilliers (1998) draws on Derrida to develop an excellent exposition of the parallels between the complexity of language systems (and the possibilities of meaning emerging from the relationship between language-based descriptions of the world and the world itself) and connectionist accounts of the complexity of social systems.

To summarise, while the science of complexity does not directly offer us ontological and epistemological frameworks for the application of complexity to social systems, complexity concepts resonate very strongly with several existing philosophical movements, highlighting a number of openings for future investigation.

IMPLICATIONS FOR INFORMATION SYSTEMS: PARADIGMS AND PRACTICE

In this section we take stock of the complexity concepts and the issues raised in this chapter, and reflect on the implications for information systems paradigms and practice.

The connectionist model of information systems suggests that in order to engage effectively in the discourse of the network society, there are two shifts necessary in the 'classical' conceptualisation of information systems[16]:

- A shift in the focus of 'systems thinking': from focusing on discrete bounded systems to focusing on networks; and from focusing on the structural properties of systems to engaging with the dynamics of systems.
- A shift in ontological assumptions about information: from focusing solely on discrete entities (individuals, organisations or applications) as loci for information creation and interpretation to incorporating the role of the network as a locus for these processes.

Below we consider the manner in which concepts from the science of complexity can be articulated in ontological and epistemological constructs for information systems in the network society.

Ontological Constructs from the Science of Complexity

With regard to the ontology of systems, the science of complexity offers us the following constructs.

Definition of information systems as complex adaptive systems

This definition of systems shifts the emphasis from the 'classical' characterisation of systems in terms of stability and structure to one that is engaged directly with the dynamic properties of systems' existence in relation to the environment. Implicit in this definition is the existence of networks of networks of interactions and emergence.

Origins and existence of information systems as emergent and contingent on a reflexive relationship with the environment

The concept of emergence transcends the classical separation of *being* from *becoming* (as in our earlier discussion of *Dasein*). The attribution of here-and-now dynamism and the open nature of systems results in a conceptual shift *away* from the 'classical' paradigm of top-down design to the bottom-up connectionist paradigm. It also imposes the need to deal with histories of systems dynamics in continuous time, instead of the tendency of the classical approach of working with 'snapshots' representing system states in a series of time frames.

Presence of information systems: informational (representational, perceived patterns) **and** *experiential (embodied in specific behaviours)*

This transcends the classical dichotomy between the socially constructed and the 'real', and resonates with the constructs of the philosophy of critical realism.

These constructs are attuned to the 'new' economy context of an interconnected, dynamic world. However, issues related to the complexity of the social pose questions about the transferability of complexity science concepts in their entirety to the domain of information systems. The concept of self-organisation is prominent in the natural science conceptualisation of complex adaptive systems. The identified mechanisms of self-organisation in the natural sciences do not translate directly to the social sciences. The sticking point is the question of teleology. Systems in the natural sciences are not attributed with a purpose beyond existence. In *being* and *becoming*, there is no design about making an impact on the external world. Kant (1790) articulates the phenomenology of self-organisation observed in natural systems as 'purposiveness without purpose'. Human beings, however, are endowed with free will, learn from experience, and speculate about the future and associated risks. Their position and role in the social system are defined (to a greater or lesser extent) by intent, purpose and utility. The mechanism of self-organisation that is expounded in the science of complexity must, in the study of socially situated information networks, be modified and annotated to acknowledge the existence of purpose. Doing so is in itself a complex undertaking and draws us to look to discourses in the social sciences for enlightenment. Particularly relevant to the domain of information systems are issues of ethics and power.[17]

Epistemological Constructs from the Science of Complexity

The corresponding epistemological constructs are primarily concerned with addressing the phenomenology and dynamics of complex adaptive systems, and they include:

- A focus on the system in its ecological setting.
- An articulation of emergence and emergent phenomena (bottom-up versus top-down).
- A means of identifying, representing and characterising network relationships.

- A means of dealing with dynamics in continuous time, as histories rather than snapshots.
- A means of dealing with multidimensional representations of system states.
- The utilisation of natural science metaphors (particularly those pertaining to organic and thermodynamic systems) for articulating concepts and making sense of observed behaviour patterns (Merali, 2001).

As discussed earlier, the issue of boundary definition for networks is problematic. One very practical problem associated with this is the difficulty of scoping the study of networks. While the 'classical' concept of the boundary is difficult to construct, the phase space technique and agent-based modelling provide a means of scoping the study in terms of the relevant phase space to be investigated.

However, as noted earlier, the definition of the requisite variables for defining social systems is problematic. In our connectionist phenomenology of the information network, we highlighted the existence of multiple networks concurrently giving rise to the emergence of multiple versions (informational representations) of the 'reality'. While the phase space technique allows us to build multidimensional representations of social systems, the issue of which of these versions is privileged in the construction of the phase space parameters raises questions about ethics, politics, power and social cohesion[18].

The problems flagged above remind us of the natural science origins of the science of complexity. The ontological problem that we identified is located at a point of incommensurability between the natural and social sciences: the existence in social systems of purpose and free will.

With regard to the epistemological issues, incompleteness of information necessitates a trial-and-error method, and patterns that emerge from running models may offer insights into problem situations and the possible solution space. For those used to a mechanistic approach, this may seem unsatisfactorily inconclusive.

CONCLUSION

The distinction between the 'classical' information systems paradigm and that of 'complexity science' is broadly articulated in Kant's (1790) distinction between the *mechanical* and the *organic*. The organic is characterised by emergence, self-organisation and networks of relationships, while the mechanical is organised according to an externally defined design for articulating structural components. The phenomenology of complex adaptive systems is an organic one.

As we have seen, while the classical information systems paradigm is quite adequate for dealing with the mechanical, it does not cater for the emergent nature of the organic. The complexity science paradigm, on the other hand, is primarily concerned with emergence and the dynamics of chaotic and complex adaptive systems, offering us:

- Language for describing complex phenomena.
- Concepts and modelling techniques for articulating the dynamics giving rise to those phenomena.

The inability of the classical paradigm to deal effectively with emergence limits its utility in conceptualising the information networks that characterise the 'new' economy. As shown earlier, the information *network-in-use* embodies the dynamic synthesis of technological and social evolution. Articulating the social, political, economic and technological dimensions of information networks within the complexity paradigm will be a trans-disciplinary endeavour drawing on the social and natural sciences.

The complexity science paradigm does not offer a ready-made theory of information systems for the 'new' economy. However in offering conceptual scaffolding for the articulation of information *networks-in-use* as complex adaptive systems, this paradigm opens up a vista of possible worlds for exploration in the information space. Such an exploration may well lead to the emergence of a new paradigm for information systems.

A GUIDE TO THE LITERATURE

Complexity

There are a number of good introductory texts on the origins and development of complexity theory. Waldrop's (1992) accessible account of the launching of the complexity enterprise at the Santa Fe Institute is of historical interest. However Capra (1996) and Coveney and Highfield (1991) provide a more comprehensive overview of the origins and development of complexity concepts.

Kauffman's (1993, 1995a) seminal works provide an excellent introduction to the field of complex adaptive systems and illustrate the power of simulation in providing insights into self-organisation.

For applications of complexity concepts in the social domain, two recent publications capture contemporaneous contexts. Johnson (2001) presents an excellent overview of the development of concepts of emergence and their significance in understanding the dynamics of an interconnected world. Axelrod and Cohen (1999) provide a good overview of the relevance of complexity concepts in the information economy.

In the more mainstream social sciences literature, two notable works are Byrne's (1998) compelling articulation of complexity theory, social systems and critical realism, and Cilliers' (1998) elegant discourse on complexity, postmodernism and the connectionist perspective of social systems.

Modelling

Holland (1998) gives us a lucid and accessible introduction to the development of agent-based models, while Casti (1997) affords a wider view of modelling concepts and their application. Lomi and Larson's (2001) compilation of papers on the deployment of agent-based models in the social sciences provides a good perspective on the range of interests that exists within the social sciences for the development of the agent-based technique.

Farmer, Toffoli and Wolfram (1984) provide a comprehensive introduction to the use of cellular automata, and Sigmund (1993) is a accessible and comprehensive overview of artificial life simulations with cellular automata.

ENDNOTES

[1] The term 'effective world' is used to connote the world as perceived/experienced/understood/believed to exist by players, which serves as the context within which decisions are made, actions taken and consequences realised.

[2] This is not to deny the relevance of technology and people in information processes, but to develop a concept of information networks that is not impaled on presumptions of information as either embodied or disembodied.

[3] See Fritjof Capra's *The Web of Life* (1996) and Coveney and Highfield's *Frontiers of Complexity: The Search for Order in a Chaotic World* (1991) for an excellent overview of this development.

[4] We use the term 'paradigm' in the Kuhnian sense to denote a set of concepts or systems of explanation shared by the members of a scientific community (Kuhn, 1962).

[5] The Santa Fe Institute (SFI) is widely referred to as the first home of complexity theory, and its purpose was to enable scholars from different disciplines to work

together towards developing a better, holistic understanding of the interconnected universe. See Mitchell Waldrop's *Complexity* (1992) for a very readable account of the origins and evolution of the SFI.

[6]The term 'focal system as a whole' is deployed for pragmatic convenience and refers to that part of the universe that we are interested in studying. As highlighted by the Santa Fe definition of complexity, and our subsequent discussion of emergence, the bounding of a system and the separation of the concept of 'the system' from 'the environment' is philosophically a non-trivial issue.

[7]See Gleick (1987) for a very accessible discussion of chaos theory.

[8]The 'butterfly effect' is a popular caricature of the sensitivity of chaotic systems: 'a butterfly flapping its wings over the Amazon leads to a hurricane on the other side of the world'. Technically the sensitivity is the phenomenon created by the divergence of trajectories of the system. Over time, a system starting from one state becomes less and less similar (further and further away in state space) to a system that starts out in a similar, but not exactly the same, state.

[9]Prigogine's explanation of the Bénard cell experiment furnishes us with a very elegant illustration of the non-linear dynamics of self-organisation in open systems that are far from equilibrium. The experiment is concerned with observing the changes in a very thin layer of liquid when it is heated from below. As the liquid is heated, when the temperature differential between the top and bottom surfaces of the liquid reaches a certain *critical value*, there emerges spontaneously, within the liquid mass, a honeycomb pattern of hexagonal cells (referred to as Bénard cells after Henri Bénard, who first recorded this observation). Heating the liquid further results in a loss of the ordered state. Prigogine explained this phenomenon in terms of non-linear equations to describe the dynamics in the mass of liquid as an open system receiving energy from outside. In this explanation, changes in the internal structure (observed as instabilities and the jump to the new structural form) are the result of local fluctuations in the interactions between molecules amplified by positive feedback loops. Prigogine called the emergent, ordered structures 'dissipative structures'. As Capra (1996) points out, in non-linear thermodynamics the 'runaway' positive feedback loops that had always been regarded as *destructive* in cybernetics appear as a source of new *order* and complexity in the theory of dissipative structures.

[10]Maturana and Varela (1973) identified *autopoiesis* (self-production) as the defining characteristic of all living systems. The term is sometimes used in a more general sense to refer to self-organising systems with non-equilibrium dynamics capable of maintaining stability over long periods of time.

[11]Cellular automata comprise a grid of rectangular squares or cells. The state of each cell is defined by the values that the cell takes, and there are rules defining how many of its neighbouring cells are allowed to influence its value. The state of the cell changes in discrete steps, which are determined by a set of transition rules that apply simultaneously to all cells. They are used extensively in experiments to identify the dynamics of self-organisation and provide an alternative to the use of differential equations (see Farmer, Toffoli and Wolfram, 1984 for an excellent exposition of this work). The complexity literature highlights the importance of cellular automata in revealing the emergence of complex behaviour from simple rules.

[12]Boolean networks are networks connecting sites that are only allowed to have one of two values (e.g. 'on' or 'off'). Using Boolean networks comprised of a number of interconnected light bulbs, Kauffman (1993) demonstrated that starting out with a random collection of connected sites, there developed over time a network of spontaneously organised cycles of interactions between sites. Varying the number of cells and the number of connections per cell in the network, he found that the level of connectivity (i.e. the number of cells sites with which a given site interacts) was a crucial parameter.

[13]Epstein and Axtell (1996) give a fairly comprehensive bibliography of agent-based models in the social sciences that were either in working paper form or published by 1996. Since then there has been a rapid expansion of agent-based modelling efforts, and anything like a complete listing of this work would reference several hundred papers. Lomi and Larson (2001) provide more contemporaneous examples of the use of agent-based models in social systems. Robert Axelrod's *The Evolution of Cooperation* (1984) demonstrates the potency of agent-based models for developing insights into the gamesmanship of social systems. Watts and Strogatz's (1998) work on small-world networks is particularly relevant to our current interest in Internet-enabled social networks. Anderson, Arrow and Pine's *The Economy as an Evolving Complex System* (1988) and Arthur, Lane and Durlaff's *The Economy as an Evolving Complex System II* (1997) provide an extensive treatment of complexity science-inspired models in economics. Axelrod and Cohen's *Harnessing Complexity* (1999) provides a very lucid overview of the use of models in addressing complexity in the competitive context. For more contemporary examples of the use of agent-based models in financial markets, supply chain management and e-business, see *Economist*, 2003, and Bonabeau, 2002; Bonabeau and Meyer, 2001. Steven Johnson's *emergence* (2001) provides an excellent overview of the development of concepts of emergence and their significance in understanding the dynamics of an interconnected world.

[14]Chapter 3 by Lucas Introna in this volume provides an extended exposition of Heidegger's concepts. Here we highlight the resonance of Heidegger's notion of *Dasein* with the phenomenology of complex systems.

[15]See Chapter 10 by John Mingers for an exposition of critical realism.

[16]Within the discipline of information systems apart from the 'classical' paradigm, there already exists an array of epistemological and ontological frameworks to deal with these aspects, as evidenced by the accompanying chapters in this book. However, the exploitation of these frameworks is arguably hampered by the tradition of 'classical' systems thinking that prevails in conventional approaches and resource allocations for systems development and implementation. The purpose of this discussion is to use the connectionist network phenomenology as the substrate for an exploration in which we use the lens of the 'science of complexity' to bring into focus essential issues of the discourse of information systems in the 'new world'. The resolution of many of these issues appeals to the application of the 'non-classical' frameworks introduced in the other chapters of this book.

[17]See Chapter 7 in this volume for a review of Foucault's discourse in relation to this issue.

[18] Actor-network theory and Foucauldian power dynamics (discussed in Chapters 9 and 7 respectively) provide significant insights into these issues.

REFERENCES

Allen, P. M. and McGlade, J. M. (1987) 'Modelling complex human systems: A fisheries example', *European Journal of Operations Research*, 30: 147–67.

Anderson, P., Arrow, K. and Pine, D. (eds) (1988) *The Economy as an Evolving Complex System*, Redwood, CA: Addison Wesley.

Appleby, S. and Steward, S. (1994) 'Mobile software agents for control in telecommunication networks', *British Telecom Technology Journal*, 12(2): 104–13.

Arthur, W. (1996) 'Increasing returns and the new world of business', *Harvard Business Review*, Jul–Aug: 100–9.

Arthur, W., Lane, D. and Durlaff, S. (eds) (1997) *The Economy as an Evolving Complex System II*, Reading, MA: Addison Wesley.

Axelrod, R. (1984) *The Evolution of Cooperation*, New York, NY: Basic Books.

Axelrod, R. and Cohen, M. (1999) *Harnessing Complexity: Organizational Implications of a Scientific Frontier*, New York, NY: Free Press.

Axtell, R, (2000) 'Why agents? On the varied motivations for agent computing in the social sciences', Center on Social and Economic Dynamics working paper no. 17, November, Washington, DC: The Brookings Institution.

Barabasi, A. (2002) *Linked: The New Science of Networks*, Cambridge, MA: Perseus Publishing.

Bar-Yam, Yaneer (2000) 'About complex systems', http://necsi.net/guide/.

Berlekamp, J., Conway, J. and Guy, R. (1982) *Winning Ways for Your Mathematical Plays*, New York, NY: Academic Press.

Bertalanffy, L. von (1968) *General Systems Theory*, New York, NY: Braziller.

Bhaskar, R. (1986) *Scientific Realism and Human Emancipation*, London: Verso.

Bonabeau, E. (2002) 'Predicting the unpredictable', *Harvard Business Review*, March: 5–11.

Bonabeau, E. and Meyer, C. (2001) 'Swarm intelligence', *Harvard Business Review*, May: 107–45.

Buchanan, M. (2002) *Nexus*, New York, NY: Norton.

Byrne, D. (1998) *Complexity Theory and the Social Sciences: An Introduction*, New York, NY: Routledge.

Capra, F. (1996) *The Web of Life*, London: HarperCollins.

Castells, M. (1996) *The Rise of the Network Society*, Oxford: Blackwell.

Casti, J. (1997) *Would-Be Worlds: How Simulation is Changing*, New York, NY: John Wiley & Sons.

Chaitin, G. (1990) *Information, Randomness, and Incompleteness*, Singapore: World Scientific.

Cilliers, P. (1998) *Complexity and Postmodernism: Understanding Complex Systems*, New York, NY: Routledge.

Coveney, P. and Highfield, R. (1991) *Frontiers of Complexity: The Search for Order in a Chaotic World*, London: Faber and Faber.

David, P. (1985) 'Clio and the economics of QWERTY', *American Economic Review*, 75(2): 332–7.

Davis, F. D. (1989) 'Perceived usefulness, perceived ease of use, and user acceptance of information technology', *MIS Quarterly*, 13(3): 319–40.

Derrida, J. (1976) *Of Grammatology*, Baltimore, MD: Johns Hopkins University Press.

Derrida, J. (1978) *Writing and Difference*, London: Routledge.

Dreyfus, R. (1987) 'Husserl, Heidegger and modern existentialism', in B. Magee (ed.), *The Great Philosophers*, Oxford: Oxford University Press, pp. 252–77.

Eco, U. (1997) 'On being', in U. Eco, *Kant and the Platipus*, London: Secker and Warburg, pp. 9–56.

Economist (2003) 'Agents of creation', 11 October, pp. 95–6.

Eisenhardt, K. and Galunic, C. (1999) 'Coevolving: At last, a way to make synergies work', *Harvard Business Review*, Jan–Feb: 91–9.

Epstein, J. M. and Axtell, R. (1996) *Growing Artificial Societies: Social Science from the Bottom Up*, Washington, DC/Cambridge, MA: Brookings Institution/MIT Press.

Evans, P. and Wurster, T. (2000) *Blown to Bits: How the New Economics of Information Transforms Strategy*, Cambridge, MA: Harvard Business School Press.

Farmer, D., Toffoli, T. and Wolfram, S. (eds) (1984) *Cellular Automata*, Amsterdam: North-Holland.

Gleick, J. (1987) *Chaos: Making a New Science*, New York, NY: Viking-Penguin.

Hamel, G. and Prahalad, C. (1994) *Competing for the Future*, Cambridge, MA: Harvard Business School Press.

Heidegger, M. (1962) *Being and Time*, trans. J. Macquarrie and E. Robinson, Oxford: Blackwell.

Hiltz, S. R. and Johnson, K. (1990) "User Satisfaction with Computer-mediated Systems". *Management Science* 36(6): 739–764.

Holland, J. (1998) *Emergence: From Chaos to Order*, Oxford: Oxford University Press.

Jarvanpaa, S. (1989) 'Effects of task demand and graphical format on information processing strategies', *Management Science*, 35(3): 285–303.

Johnson, S. (2001) *emergence*, London: Penguin.

Kant, I. (1790 [1973]) *Critique of Judgement*, trans. J. Meredith, New York, NY: Oxford University Press.

Kauffman, S. (1993) *The Origins of Order: Self-Organization and Selection in Evolution*, New York, NY: Oxford University Press.

Kauffman, S. (1995a) *At Home in the Universe: The Search for Laws of Self-Organisation and Complexity*, New York, NY: Oxford University Press.

Kauffman, S. (1995b) 'Escaping the Red Queen effect'. *McKinsey Quarterly*, 1: 119–29.

Kuhn, T. (1962) *The Structure of Scientific Revolutions*, Chicago, IL: Chicago University Press.

Langton, C. G. (1991) 'Computation at the edge of chaos: Phase-transitions and emergent computation', PhD dissertation, Ann Arbor, MI: University of Michigan.

Leavitt, H. and Whistler, T. (1958) 'Management in the 1980s', *Harvard Business Review*, 36: 41–8.

Lomi, A. and Larson, E. (eds) (2001) *Dynamics of Organizations: Computational Modeling and Organizational Theories*, Menlo Park, CA: MIT Press.

Luhmann, N. (1990) 'The autopoiesis of social systems' in N. Luhmann, *Essays on Self-Reference*, New York, NY: Columbia University Press.

Markus, L. M. (1983) 'Power, politics and MIS implementation', *Communications of the ACM*, 26: 430–40.

Maturana, H. and Varela, F. J. (1973) 'Autopoiesis: The *organization* of the living', in H. R. Maturana and F. J. Varela, *Autopoiesis and Cognition: The Realization of the Living*, Boston Studies in the Philosophy of Science 42, Dordecht: D. Reidel.

Merali, Y. (1997) 'Information, systems and *Dasein*', in F. Stolwell, I. McRobb, R. Landor, R. Ison and J. Holloway (eds), *Systems for Sustainability: People, Organisations and Environments*, New York, NY: Plenum, pp. 595–600.

Merali, Y. (2001) 'The organic metaphor in knowledge management', *Emergence*, special issue on organic knowledge management, 2(4): 14–22.

Orlikowski, W. (1992) 'The duality of technology: Rethinking the concept of technology in organizations', *Organisation Science*, 3(3): 398–427.

Prigogine, I. (1967) 'Dissipative structures in chemical systems', in S. Claessons (ed.), *Fast Reactions and Primary Processes in Chemical Kinetics*, New York, NY: Elsevier Interscience.

Reed, M. and Harvey, D. L. (1992) 'The new science and the old complexity and realism in the social sciences', *Journal for the Theory of Social Behaviour*, 22: 356–79.

Reed, M. and Harvey, D. (1996) 'Social science as the study of social systems', in L. D. Kiel and E. Elliott (eds), *Chaos Theory in the Social Sciences*, Ann Arbor, MI: University of Michigan Press, pp. 295–324.

Shapiro, C. and Varian, H. (1999) *Information Rules: A Strategic Guide to the Network Economy*, Cambridge, MA: Harvard Business School Press.

Sigmund, K. (1993) *Games of Life*, New York, NY: Oxford University Press.

Stacey, R. (2001) *Complex Responsive Processes in Organisations: Learning and Knowledge Creation*, London: Routledge.

Waldrop, M. (1992) *Complexity*, New York, NY: Simon and Schuster.

Watts, D. (2003) *Six Degrees: Small Worlds and the Groundbreaking Science of Networks*, New York, NY: Norton.

Watts, D. J. (1999) *Small Worlds: The Dynamics of Networks between Order and Randomness*, Princeton, NJ: Princeton University Press.

Watts, D. J. and Strogatz, S. H. (1998) 'Collective dynamics of "small world" networks', *Nature*, 395: 440–42.

Zuboff, S. (1988) *In the Age of the Smart Machine: The Future of Work and Power*, New York, NY: Basic Books.

Index